Praise for

The Devil's Gentleman

"Schechter has created satisfying, nuanced portraits of his main characters and set them in a late nineteenth-century New York that fairly throbs with exotic, specific life."
—*The New York Times*

"An intriguing read for true-life crime buffs."
—*San Antonio Express-News*

"An elegantly written true-crime story, rich in themes and vibrant details. Schechter is an addictive storyteller."
—*Bomb* magazine

"Harold Schechter breathes life into the strange and twisted saga of Roland Molineux . . . letting us taste the mood, lifestyle, customs and moral assumptions of a long gone era. . . . We can almost feel the chill in the courtroom. . . . A virtuoso performance."
—*New York Law Journal*

"[Schechter's] lurid tale of murder, jealousy and love also gives insight to the culture of the time period, blending history with vivid storytelling."
—*The Parkersburg News*

"Thrilling . . . a riveting tale of murder, seduction and tabloid journalism."
—*Publishers Weekly*

Also by Harold Schechter

NONFICTION

The A to Z Encyclopedia of Serial Killers (with David Everitt)

Bestial: The Savage Trail of a True American Monster

Depraved: The Shocking True Story of America's First Serial Killer

Deranged: The Shocking True Story of America's Most Fiendish Killer

Deviant: The Shocking True Story of Ed Gein, the Original "Psycho"

Fatal: The Poisonous Life of a Female Serial Killer

Fiend: The Shocking True Story of America's Youngest Serial Killer

Savage Pastimes: A Cultural History of Violent Entertainment

The Serial Killer Files: The Who, What, Where, How, and Why of the World's Most Terrifying Murderers

FICTION

Nevermore

Outcry

The Hum Bug

The Mask of Red Death

The Tell-Tale Corpse

The Devil's GENTLEMAN

The Devil's GENTLEMAN

PRIVILEGE, POISON,

AND THE TRIAL

THAT USHERED IN

THE TWENTIETH CENTURY

HAROLD SCHECHTER

BALLANTINE BOOKS NEW YORK

2008 Ballantine Books Trade Paperback Edition

Published in the United States by Ballantine Books, an imprint of The Random House Publishing Group, a division of Random House, Inc., New York.

BALLANTINE and colophon are registered trademarks of Random House, Inc.

Originally published in hardcover in the United States by Ballantine Books, an imprint of The Random House Publishing Group, a division of Random House, Inc., New York.

Photograph credits: Prisoners in stripes lined up © Bettmann/Corbis; electric chair at Sing Sing © Underwood & Underwood. Reprinted by permission of Corbis. Photographs of General Edward Leslie Molineux and Roland Molineux courtesy of William A. Molineux.

LIBRARY OF CONGRESS CATALOGING-IN-PUBLICATION DATA

Schechter, Harold.

The devil's gentleman: privilege, poison, and the trial that ushered in the twentieth century/Harold Schechter.

p. cm.

Includes bibliographical references and index.

ISBN 978-0-345-47680-7

1. Molineux, Roland Burnham. 2. Murder—New York (State)—New York.
3. United States—Social conditions—1865–1918. I. Title.
HV6534.N5S34 2007 364.152'3092—dc22 2007019705

Printed in the United States

www.ballantinebooks.com

9 8 7 6 5 4 3 2

Book design by Susan Turner

For Will and Mary Molineux

CONTENTS

Prologue

SING SING

FEBRUARY 1900

At the start of the twentieth century, death by electricity was a relatively recent form of capital punishment. It was only in June 1888 that New York became the first state to pass a law replacing hanging with electrocution. Two years later, on August 6, 1890, a thirty-year-old ax murderer named William Kemmler became the first man to die in the chair. After being hooked up to the apparatus, Kemmler was hit with a high-voltage charge lasting seventeen seconds. When the shock failed to kill him, the switch was thrown again. This time, the current was kept on for more than a minute. As Kemmler roasted, the room filled "with the stench of burning hair and flesh." Some witnesses vomited, while others fainted or fled in horror.[1]

Over the succeeding decade, more than three dozen criminals were put to death in New York by the new, presumably more humane, mode of execution. All were men. That particular gender barrier was broken in March 1899, when a hard-bitten housewife named Martha Place became the first female to be killed in the chair. In the weeks leading up to her electrocution, her case became a cause célèbre. Even while reveling in the lurid details of her crime (Mrs. Place had smothered her seventeen-year-old stepdaughter after flinging sulfuric acid in the girl's face), the *New York Journal*—William Randolph Hearst's wildly sensationalistic "yellow" paper—crusaded for clemency on the grounds of her sex. The effort proved unavailing. Governor Theodore Roosevelt refused to commute her sentence, declaring that, when it came to punishment, female criminals deserved equality with men. On the morning of March 20, 1899, clutching a psalm book and muttering "Lord, save me, Lord, save me," Mrs. Place was led to the death chair, becoming a pioneer of sorts in the women's rights movement.[2]

Eleven months later, during the second week of February 1900, the Sing Sing Death House received a convicted murderer whose notoriety outstripped even that of the infamous Mrs. Place. His name was Roland Burnham Molineux, and—largely thanks to the feverish attentions of Hearst and his fellow scandal-mongerer, Joseph Pulitzer—his case had riveted the country for more than a year.

At the time of his transfer to Sing Sing, he had already spent twelve months in the city prison, known as the Tombs. Since his arrest in early 1899, his clean-favored face had grown pasty and his athlete's physique had lost much of its muscular tone. Still, at thirty-four years old, he cut a striking figure. Even behind bars he was never less than immaculately dressed, grooming himself each morning as though preparing to visit his club. Unfailingly suave (if not supercilious) in manner, he bore himself at all times like a gentleman of the highest rank. Throughout his trial—the longest at that time in the history of New York State—he had barely been able to conceal his ennui. For a man convicted of what his accusers called "the greatest crime of the age," he struck observers as a marvel of nonchalance.

Once immured in the Death House—an environment so grim that, by comparison, the Tombs seemed like a Newport hotel—he managed to maintain his unflappable air. At least in the beginning. Within weeks of his arrival, however, something happened that shook even Roland Molineux's remarkable aplomb.

Among the other inmates on Death Row was a thirty-seven-year-old Italian immigrant named Antonio Ferraro. A year and a half earlier, in September 1898, Ferraro had bumped into a onetime friend, Lucciano Machio, on a Brooklyn street corner. Machio was overdue in repaying some cash he had borrowed from Ferraro, and before long, the two were hurling insults into each other's face. The words grew uglier. Knives were drawn. Within minutes, Machio lay dying on the sidewalk, a gaping wound in his throat.[3]

Convicted and sentenced to die, Ferraro pinned his last hopes on an appeal. Late on the afternoon of February 23, 1900, however, he received word that the effort had failed and his execution would take place within the week. Ferraro did not take the news well. As one paper reported, "he emitted a prolonged scream that broke in fearful violence on the silence of the Death House and terrified the other prisoners. For a half hour, the hopeless man shrieked hysterically and rushed around the cell, moaning and shouting curses."[4]

Though his priest, Father Orestes Allucci, eventually managed to calm him down a bit, Ferraro spent the next few days intermittently bursting into inhuman howls or spewing "fearful blasphemies." Even on the morning of his execution—Monday, February 26—Ferraro was still violently protesting his fate. The curtains had been drawn in front of the other condemned cells, so that Roland could see only shadows. But he could hear Father Allucci say, "Do you forgive your enemies?"

Ferraro answered with a bitter curse.

"But you must," Father Allucci pleaded as he walked beside the doomed man. "Say yes, for God's sake, say yes! You must, or God will not—" By then, the priest was weeping.

"No!" shrieked Ferraro. "No—no!"

That cry of maddened refusal was the last Roland heard of Ferraro. In another moment, the condemned man was led into the execution chamber. Later, Roland heard that it had taken five separate jolts of electricity to kill Ferraro. He had died, according to *The New York Times*, "harder than any man who has so far died in the electric chair."[5]

Roland was so badly rattled that, for days afterward, he found it hard to eat or sleep. Gradually, however, he recovered his composure. What, after all, did he have to fear? His father had vowed to win his freedom and bring him safely home. And if anyone could be counted on to keep his word, it was General Edward Leslie Molineux, who throughout his long and celebrated life had maintained a moral stance as upright as his posture; a man for whom the concepts of duty, honor, and justice were nothing less than sacred—however quaint and outmoded they might seem to his son.

Part One

THE SOLDIER AND THE CLUBMAN

1

On July 15, 1852, Edward Leslie Molineux—still three months shy of his nineteenth birthday—began what he called his "scrapbook." It was not a pasted-in collection of newspaper and magazine clippings (though in later years, when his own name began to appear regularly in the press, he would assemble several of those, too). Rather, this ledger-sized volume was a handwritten miscellany of striking facts, inspirational sayings, and practical information on everything from military tactics to medicinal recipes.

There is nothing remotely confessional to be found in this journal. His book has all the introspective quality of the official *Boy Scout Manual*, which it resembles in its single-minded emphasis on self-improvement and the cultivation of the higher civic virtues: industry, tolerance, charity, and a keen sense of duty to one's country. The very look of the pages—inscribed in a flawless hand, perfectly free of blots or corrections, and meticulously labeled with solemn headlines ("The Importance of Physical Exercise," "Useful Rules," "Maxims for the Wise")—speaks vividly of the young writer's capacity for self-discipline, concentrated effort, and high moral seriousness.

"Be virtuous in mind & body & let your thoughts be pure," he counsels himself in an early entry labeled "Rules for Living." This injunction is followed by a score of precepts designed to promote physical, mental, and moral soundness:

Use dumbbells twice a day.
Bathe every morning.
Always get up when you first awake, no matter what time it is. One hour in the morning is worth two at night!
Do everything in a cool, active, and energetic manner.
In times of danger or trouble, first think—then act coolly and decisively.
Never be idle—always have something to do.
Never shrink from an unpleasant duty.
Persevere—never give up a thing until you have tried it every possible way. Perseverance is the best school for every manly virtue.
Never be prejudiced nor allow yourself to be led by others.
If you are in the wrong, acknowledge it frankly.
Harden in every possible way your *body* but not your *conscience*.
Give up all bad habits.
Use no slang language.
Speak kindly.
Be truthful.
Be truly polite.
In studying, concentrate your thoughts solely upon the subject before you.
Be charitable in thought as well as action.
Love your God & read his doctrines & fail not to address him night & morning.[1]

Elsewhere in the journal, he transcribes the rules laid down by Benjamin Franklin as a prescription for happiness and success: "Eat not to dullness," "Avoid trifling conversation," "Waste nothing," "Let all things have their place," "Use no hurtful deceit," "Tolerate no uncleanness in body, clothes, or habitation," and so on.

Fascinated by every aspect of warfare, he fills his journal with extensive notes—often accompanied by his own diagrams and hand-drawn maps—on a sweeping array of military matters: the proper construction of field fortifications, the organization of the Hungarian army, the strategic deployment of troops in the battle of Waterloo.

At the same time, he had a lifelong love of poetry. He read Chaucer and Milton for pleasure and had a boundless admiration for the writings of Henry Wadsworth Longfellow.

He came honestly by his love of reading. His father, William, was a printer; his mother, Maria Leslie, a "remarkably intelligent woman [who] took great delight in reading French and German and was also a close student of English and American literature."[2]

Young Edward's enthusiasm for all things military was also a family legacy. His ancestors included soldiers who had taken part in the Norman invasion, fought alongside King Henry V at Agincourt, been slain on the battlefield during the War of the Roses, and received personal commendations for bravery from Henry VIII.

It was (and is) a proud and ancient line, whose origins can be traced to one Robert de Moulin—the son (according to family legend) of Abelard and Héloïse.[3] At the time of Edward's birth in October 1833, his father still retained the traditional spelling of his last name—Molyneux. It was only two years later—when William brought his wife and eight surviving children to the United States—that he adopted the somewhat less exotic-looking spelling.

Though the historical record is hazy, indications are that they settled in Manhattan, where William opened a print shop on the corner of Ann and Nassau streets, and where, two years later, the Molineuxs' youngest child, Arthur—just twenty-two months old—died and was laid to rest in the vault of the Methodist Church on First Street.

William himself died in 1857 at the age of sixty-eight. By then, he was no longer living with his wife and children. Exactly what caused this estrangement is a mystery, though given the stigma attached to broken marriages in those days, the reasons could not have been trivial. What is known is that by 1851 William was separated from his family and living on Staten Island. Maria and the children, in the meantime, had moved to the Fort Greene neighborhood of Brooklyn, where Edward Leslie Molineux would reside for the remainder of his long and eventful life.

At seventeen, Edward was a handsome youth—brown-haired, blue-eyed—whose erect, aristocratic carriage made him seem taller than his five feet three inches. He had been educated at the Mechanics School on Broadway and Park Place. (Despite its name, the Mechanics School was not a vocational institution. Run by the General Society of Mechanics and Tradesmen, it provided a tuition-free general education to the children of its members at a time before New York City had a municipal public school system. As the son of a printer, Edward was eligible for admission.)

That year, 1851, seventeen-year-old Edward found a job at the paint-manufacturing firm of Daniel F. Tiemann & Company, whose owner was active in New York City politics and would eventually serve a two-year term as mayor.[4] Within this bustling concern, young Edward—with his brains, ambition, and indefatigable energy—thrived. In the manner of a Horatio Alger hero, he quickly rose to a position of responsibility, handling all of the firm's voluminous correspondence and occupying the front office with several other clerks.

In 1854, even as Edward continued to establish himself in business and (partly through his association with Daniel F. Tiemann) involve himself in city politics, the twenty-year-old Molineux commenced what would be a long and illustrious military career.

On June 15 of that year, he enlisted in the New York State Militia as a member of the Brooklyn City Guard, a celebrated light-artillery company whose smartly executed drills and dress parades had inspired a popular parlor tune, "The Brooklyn City Guard Quick Step." The few extant records from this period in Edward's life show how quickly he advanced through the noncommissioned ranks—no surprise, given his ferocious drive and exceptional abilities.

In 1858, when the U.S. government needed a courier for an important diplomatic mission to Venezuela, the Department of State chose Edward, who discharged his duties with his usual professional grace. It was not long after his return in January 1859 that he was introduced to Hattie Davis Clark of East Hartford, Connecticut. Exactly where and under what circumstances they met is unknown, as are all details of their courtship. By the following December, however, they were betrothed. That Christmas, Edward gave her an illustrated volume of Schiller's poetry, inscribed "To Hattie from Ned." For the emotionally reserved, unremittingly proper Molineux, his use of his pet name—employed only by his family and closest friends—was a mark of the intimacy that had developed between them.

In the meantime, he continued to make himself indispensable to his employers—so much so that in 1860, he was made a partner in the firm. Business was bad for the Tiemanns, however. Most of their customers were Southern merchants, and sales fell off dramatically as tensions rose between the North and South following the election of Abraham Lincoln in November.

In late December of that year, Edward began a new journal, this one composed of his own philosophical musings. One of the earliest entries is dated January 1861. Titled "The First Day of the New-Year," it is written in Molineux's loftiest style, full of high-minded sentiments about the opportunities afforded by the coming year "to correct past errors, to cultivate new virtues, to accomplish greater things."

It is not until the end of the essay that the twenty-seven-year-old deals directly with the momentous events of the day and their immediate implications for his own happiness and well-being. Here, the tone becomes deeply affecting as he contemplates two radically different futures, and girds himself to face the worst with his usual courage, honor, and gallantry:

> And for myself, how far in this year of 1861 I may proceed, God alone knows; for who can tell what this eventful year may bring forth!
>
> If to happiness and peace, all thanks to the Almighty! But if plain visible duty points to the other path—where men's passions rage & where patriotism demands us to defend principles & secure future happiness at the bitter price of present suffering, danger & if needs be life itself—then let me rise superior to all considerations in defense of the right & let me recollect that "His Hand is above me" & let my foot be firm to do His Will.

It didn't take long for Edward Molineux to learn what the future held. On April 12, 1861—less than four months after he penned his New Year's essay—Confederate forces under General Pierre Gustave Toutant Beauregard opened fire on Fort Sumter.

The Civil War had begun.

On July 18, 1861, Edward Molineux and Hattie Davis Clark were married in her hometown of East Hartford. Three days later, Union forces were routed by the Confederate Army at Manassas, ending the fond hopes of Northerners that the war would be over in a matter of months. With his army shattered, Lincoln signed bills calling for the enlistment of 500,000 additional troops and extending the term of service from ninety days to three years.

By then, Edward Molineux himself was back in uniform, as a major of the Eleventh Brigade of the New York National Guard. A few months later, he was authorized to organize a regiment, designated as the 159th.[5] After several weeks of training at a camp on Staten Island, Edward and his men set out from New York City aboard the United States steamer *Northern Light.* On December 14, they joined a large fleet of transports at Ship Island, Mississippi, before proceeding up the river into enemy country.

During his three years of active duty, Edward would participate in campaigns from the Louisiana bayous to the Shenandoah Valley and take part in more than a dozen battles.[6] Following the fall of Savannah, he would be placed in charge of the city's fortifications and, after Lee's surrender, be appointed military commander of the District of Northern Georgia with his headquarters in Augusta.

All of these duties and more he performed with grace, valor, and an unswerving sense of decency that won him the gratitude of his government, the love of his men, and even the respect of his adversaries. His energies seemed inexhaustible. At the height of the war, it was nothing for him to spend nearly twenty-four hours in the saddle, return to his tent for three hours of sleep, then rise at dawn and conduct drills for another twelve hours before attending to regimental paperwork.

Stern as he could be when circumstances warranted it, Molineux was beloved by his troops for the fatherly care he demonstrated. His letters home are filled with requests for small gifts for his men—everything from candy and tobacco to stockings and sewing kits. At other times, he does what he can to relieve their anxieties about their loved ones back home. But it wasn't just Edward's concern for their welfare that endeared him to his men. It was his gallantry as a warrior. And nowhere was that courage—or the devotion it inspired—more dramatically in evidence than in the bloody engagement known as the Battle of Irish Bend.

On the morning of April 14, 1863, the 159th, along with several other regiments, was ordered to make a bayonet charge across a muddy sugar field to drive a force of Rebel soldiers from a dense strip of woods. Edward, on horseback, was in the lead. The field was so heavily plowed, however, that his horse kept stumbling in the furrows, and he quickly dismounted. Charging ahead on foot, Edward and his troops came under a ferocious crossfire from the Confederates, who were entirely concealed behind fences, canebrakes, and trees. As he turned to shout encouragement to his men, Edward saw that they were being cut down by the score.

Calling a halt, he ordered them to take cover in the ditchlike furrows and open fire. Under this fusillade, the enemy gunfire slackened a bit. Edward saw a chance to cover the remaining ground. Leaping to his feet, he called out, "Forward, New York!"

No sooner had he shouted the words than his face exploded in pain and he was hurled to the ground.

A rifle ball had torn through his mouth, blasting away the gums and teeth on the left side and exiting his cheek. Edward struggled to his feet and tried to urge his men forward, but—as he reported in a letter to his family—"I could not make myself understood and some stupid fool gave an order to retreat."

At that moment, the Rebels on their flank came charging upon them. Edward told his men to save themselves, but they would not leave him. "Such self-sacrificing fellows I never knew of," he declared. Four of them were struck by musket balls—one through the forehead—while carrying him to safety.

Within days, Edward hastened to assure his family that his wound was "nothing. It is ugly and painful, but not dangerous," he wrote.

For the rest of the war, Edward suffered from severe, at times incapacitating, headaches, which he attempted to treat with homeopathic remedies supplied by his mother. Despite these bouts of illness, he carried on as steadfastly as ever, sustained by his absolute belief in the righteousness of the Northern cause. His military service came to an end on July 29, 1865, when he tendered his resignation. When he departed for home three days later, he did so with the rank of major general by brevet "for gallant and meritorious service during the war."

After three grueling years, during which he had conducted himself with unwavering dignity and courage, Edward Leslie Molineux was returning to his family to enjoy a life of peace, prosperity, and enduring honor.

Or so he had every reason to expect.

General Edward Leslie Molineux was not a man to rest on his laurels. Possessed of "superabundant energies" (in the words of one awestruck observer),[7] he lost no time in throwing himself into a wide range of activities, from business and politics to military affairs and civic enterprises.

Shortly after his return to Brooklyn, he had a falling-out with his employer and patron, Daniel Tiemann, and left to join a rival firm, C. T. Raynolds, which he soon helped transform into the largest paint-making concern in the country. (It would later merge with another company, F. W. Devoe.) He commanded a division of the New York State National Guard, was a founding member of the National Rifle Association, embarked on a campaign to make military instruction a standard part of the public school curriculum, lectured and wrote papers on the suppression of riots, helped organize the Union Veteran's Patriotic League, served as a trustee of the Brooklyn Institute of Arts and Sciences, became the first president of the New York Paint and Coatings Association, and played an active role in local politics.

Then there were the numberless Civil War ceremonies: the regimental reunions, the anniversary receptions, the memorial services, the veterans dinners, the concerts and picnics and parades. For Edward, however, the most meaningful occasions were the reunions of survivors of the 159th. During one of these, he was presented with a specially made badge emblazoned with the image of a bear—the proud symbol of his beloved regiment. In a moving speech, his old friend and comrade-in-arms Frank Tiemann testified to the filial regard his soldiers felt toward the man who was "in every sense the Father of his regiment—a manly man, a gallant soldier and a true friend."[8] By the same token, for as long as he lived, Edward would always refer to the men of the 159th as "family."[9]

His actual family, especially his children, consistently expressed the same veneration for him. Given his repute as a "manly man," it seems fitting that Edward Leslie Molineux sired only boys.

There was the oldest son, Leslie Edward, born in 1862, who—mirroring his father—would prosper in business, serve as an officer in the army, and try his hand at politics, running (unsuccessfully) for governor of New Jersey as the Prohibition Party candidate in 1934.

There was the youngest son, Cecil Sefton, born in 1876, who—also like his father—would have a successful career in a paint company and involve himself in various patriotic organizations, most notably the Military Order of the Loyal Legion of the United States.

And then there was the middle son, Roland Burnham Molineux, born in 1866, whose notoriety would far outstrip his father's fame, and who—at a time when Edward should have been enjoying an honorable old age—would turn the family name into a byword for scandal, depravity, and cold-blooded murder.

2

Given their father's fervent belief in the importance of childhood exercise, it is hardly surprising that the Molineux boys were pushed to develop their bodies as well as their minds. All three grew into fine figures of young manhood. But Roland in particular matured into a superb physical specimen.

He seemed fashioned by nature for gymnastics, with a lithe, compact frame, exceptional coordination, and a ferociously competitive spirit that even in his adolescence burned beneath a carefully cultivated mask of upper-class hauteur. His specialty was the horizontal bar. With a tenacity inherited from his father, he spent countless hours at the gymnasium, perfecting acrobatic moves—somersaults, twists, and spectacular dismounts—that dazzled onlookers.

In 1882, shortly before his sixteenth birthday, Roland was pulled from the Brooklyn Polytechnic Institute—where, like his brothers, he was sent to study chemistry in preparation for a career in the paint business—and shipped out West. Little is known about this interlude in Roland Molineux's life, since the reasons for his sudden removal were kept secret from all but his closest relatives. According to some later accounts, he spent the time working on a ranch. In 1884, his father traveled West to fetch him home.[1]

His two years of rugged living had added muscle to Roland's already well-knit physique. Back home, he lost no time in returning to his former life, earning his high school equivalency while throwing himself into the city's flourishing athletic scene. One year later, in 1885, at a competition sponsored by the New York Athletic Club, he won the first of several national titles, becoming the amateur horizontal-bar champion.

To be an amateur sporting champion was no small distinction in 1885. In the decades since Edward Leslie Molineux published a widely reprinted essay deploring the "physical deterioration of the American race"[2] and calling for mandatory military and gymnastic exercises in the public schools, the country had been seized by what one contemporary observer called a "passion for athletic sports."[3] It was an era that witnessed a nationwide mania for bicycling, a craze for "physical culture," and the birth of modern sportswriting; when baseball became the national pastime; A. G. Spalding grew rich peddling sporting goods and guidebooks to the public; and heavyweight title bouts received the kind of frenzied, front-page coverage formerly reserved for Civil War battles and presidential elections.

There were, of course, sharp class distinctions in the realm of American sport. While gentlemen and shopkeeps, bankers and bricklayers might mingle at the ballpark or follow the Jeffries-Fitzsimmons rivalry with equally obsessive interest, the members of the upper crust tended to gather in elite athletic clubs. The first of these organizations in America was the New York Athletic Club, founded in 1868 by a small group of socially prominent sportsmen looking for like-minded young athletes to compete with. Created to foster the Victorian ideal of "pure" amateur sportsmanship, the NYAC rapidly evolved into a highly selective social club—a bastion of snobbery whose membership requirements (including steep initiation fees and annual dues) were designed to exclude lower-class applicants.[4]

By 1885, the NYAC—which had begun life in a rented flat equipped with Indian clubs, dumbbells, and a few other pieces of weight-lifting gear—had moved to an elegant building on Sixth Avenue and Fifty-fifth Street. In addition to its state-of-the-art athletic facilities—gymnasium, swimming pool, fencing and sparring room—it featured a luxurious dining hall, billiard parlor, and library. The unofficial credo of the club was articulated by one member, who told a *New York Times* reporter, "I have no aspersions to cast on men who work for their living with their hands, but they are not exactly desirable members for a club which wants to establish itself on the plane of social clubdom."[5]

It was a sentiment that Roland Molineux would have heartily endorsed.

Not that he himself was a member of the very upper reaches of society. He was, after all, the son of a tradesman. To be sure, the General had done very well in the paint business. But his success and social prestige merely placed his family in the ranks of Brooklyn's commercial aristocracy—a far cry from Mrs. Astor's 400.

Nevertheless, Roland, from an early age, put on the airs of a gentleman. Though certain of his acquaintances sneered at his pretensions, his own father looked upon them with tolerance, even a measure of pride. Why shouldn't his boy aspire to the very heights of gentlemanly refinement?

Despite his comparatively déclassé background, Roland developed a snobbishness worthy of Ward McAllister, tastemaker for the city's social elite, who famously sniffed that "a fortune of a million" was nothing more than "respectable poverty."[6] Punctilious in his dress, Roland would only deign to patronize the same tailors and haberdashers who catered to the "upperdom." Even when stripped for an athletic performance, he exuded an "air of aloof singularity and pride in station and form."[7] His most famous surviving photograph—taken during his reign as national horizontal-bar champion—shows him posing in his tight-fitting gymnast's uniform, chest outthrust, short sleeves rolled up to reveal his chiseled shoulder muscles, a look of patrician ennui on his finely molded countenance.

It was the image he would always project to the world: debonair, dashing, with a hint of aristocratic disdain. But his blue-blood persona masked a much darker reality.

Already, by adolescence, he was embroiled in trouble. Though years would pass before the world learned the truth, there was a shocking reason for his sudden withdrawal from high school and lengthy sojourn in the West. At just fifteen years of age, he had engaged in a dalliance with an older married woman—a neighbor named Mrs. Kindberg—and was named as a corespondent in the divorce suit brought by her husband when the affair came to light. Roland's father had hurried his boy out of town until the scandal was resolved.[8]

Given his own high moral standards—to say nothing of his admitted primness as regards "the *genus* female" (as he fondly referred to the opposite sex)—Edward Leslie Molineux could not have been pleased with his son's sexual misconduct. Perhaps he wrote it off to wild oats. Still, the General stood steadfastly by Roland, taking quick and decisive measures to save his son—and the family's good name—from public dishonor.

Following a brief course of study at Cooper Union, Roland, at the age of twenty-one, was put to work at his father's company, where he honed his skills as a chemist. He also continued to compete in gymnastic events, defending his title at the yearly competitions sponsored by the Amateur Athletic Union and making audiences "wild with enthusiasm" at the annual exhibitions held at the Adelphi Academy.[9] To all outward appearances, he seemed to have matured into a responsible young man—the prodigal son who, as the General hoped, had put his shameful ways behind him.

But Roland was nothing if not devious. Even at the C. T. Raynolds Company, under the watchful eye of his father, he could not keep from flirting with trouble and courting disgrace.

3

Edward Leslie Molineux's children left few accounts of their upbringing. He appears (as one would expect of so strictly disciplined a man) to have been a stern and exacting but affectionate father—the type who would insist on the precise performance of household chores before allowing his boys to dip into the candy jar; who might bestow a handsome new pocketknife on one of his sons, then dock him a dime if he failed to keep it clean; who saw to it that his children knew the correct way to fold an American flag, administer emergency first aid, and escape from a burning building. He was also a deeply pious man, whose faith had sustained him during many a dark hour in the Civil War and who raised his sons as devout Episcopalians.[1] Certainly, his loyalty as a father was unfaltering.

It is one of the great mysteries of parenthood that two children brought up in the identical way can grow up to be radically, if not diametrically, different human beings. And so it was in the Molineux household. The General's oldest son, Leslie Edward, turned out to be straitlaced to the point of priggishness. A staunch advocate of Prohibition, he never permitted a drop of alcohol to cross his lips. He stopped his car to bury roadkill and swept debris from the road with a special broom he kept in the trunk. Though obsessively punctual, he was once late for an important appointment because, just as he was about to leave the house, "The Star-Spangled Banner" began to play on the radio and Leslie felt obliged to remain standing at attention until the anthem stopped. He rarely missed Sunday service at St. Luke's Church, actively supported the American Red Cross, and enjoyed nothing better than spending an evening poring over the latest issue of *National Geographic* magazine.[2]

By contrast, Leslie's younger brother, Roland—born only four years later and raised in precisely the same way—grew up to be a libertine.

Her name was Mary Melando, though everyone called her Mamie. She grew up in Bayonne, New Jersey, a grim, smoky city of oil refineries, industrial plants, and railroad lines—a place, as one writer puts it, "short on greenery and long on fumes."[3] Before quitting to become a cop, her father worked for nearly twenty years at the Bayonne paint factory owned by the C. T. Raynolds Company, and in 1887, Mary went to work there, too.

It was shortly thereafter that she met Roland Molineux, the debonair son of the company's co-owner, who had just gone to work for his father. Within a few months of his arrival, Roland, twenty-one at the time, had seduced her.

With her small eyes, long nose, and heavy jaw, Mamie was not an especially attractive girl. She did, however, possess the vibrancy—and extreme vulnerability—of youth.

At the time their affair commenced, Mamie Melando had just turned thirteen.

Roland spent six years at the Raynolds factory in Bayonne, producing pigments for his father's company. Then, in March 1893, two New York City businessmen, Morris Herrmann and Leonard Levi, opened a paint factory in Newark and hired him as superintendent and chief chemist.[4]

Besides his salary, he was given a two-room apartment on the second floor of the big wooden factory building. Roland proceeded to furnish it in style, with Oriental rugs, a mahogany bed and matching bureau, a leather-upholstered settee and easy chair, and a handsome sideboard.

There was a large, well-equipped chemical lab in the factory, stocked with the various "dry colors" needed to concoct paint: kegs of Prussian blue, Paris green, chrome yellow, English vermilion, Tuscan red, and more, along with arsenic, mercury, and other poisonous substances. Roland also installed a big glass-paneled medicine chest in his apartment and filled it with an assortment of chemicals. He took his work seriously. He kept up with the major trade publications—*The Oil and Color Man's Journal*, *The Textile Colorist*, *The Paint, Oil and Drug Reporter*—and frequently stayed up late into the night, experimenting with various recipes.[5]

A number of Raynolds employees followed Roland to the new company. Among them was his lover Mamie Melando, by then all of eighteen. Roland made her a foreman, putting her in charge of a half dozen female workers. She also continued to perform other, more private, services for Roland. Under the euphemistic title of "housekeeper," she paid regular visits to his living quarters.

Neither Mr. Herrmann nor his partner Mr. Levi knew the slightest thing about paint pigments; they were strictly businessmen with offices on Pearl Street in Manhattan. In his capacity as chief chemist, Roland proved indispensable to the firm—so much so that there was talk of making him a full-fledged partner.

Roland bragged to his acquaintances about his importance to the firm. Still, he doubted that he would ever accept such an offer. After all, as a man who viewed himself as a member of the city's WASP aristocracy, he had certain standards to maintain.

Seducing a child was one thing; becoming the business partner of Jews was quite another.[6]

4

Five years after the dazzling debut of the New York Athletic Club's splendid Sixth Avenue quarters, another, even more spectacular clubhouse opened a few blocks away, on Forty-fourth Street and Madison. This one belonged to the NYAC's longtime rival, the Manhattan Athletic Club. Boasting sumptuous restaurants, a luxury hotel, a theater, bowling alley, and library, along with a magnificently appointed gym and the largest indoor swimming pool in the city, it quickly attracted more than two thousand members, including some of the country's best young athletes. Before long it was challenging the NYAC for supremacy in every field of amateur competition.

In just a few years, however, the MAC was in serious trouble, a victim of poor fiscal management, made worse by the Panic of 1893. By 1894, it had gone into bankruptcy.

One year later, it was resurrected by thirty-year-old J. Herbert Ballantine, scion of the famous brewery family, makers of New York's most popular beer. An ardent sportsman, Ballantine renamed his new acquisition the Knickerbocker Athletic Club and set about to restore it to its former glory.

To that end, he instructed his handpicked president, James E. Sullivan, to hire the finest athletic director in the country. The man Sullivan chose was Harry Seymour Cornish.

At the time Sullivan recruited him, Cornish—born on August 4, 1863—was not quite thirty-two. He had spent the first twenty years of his life in Hartford, Connecticut, leaving in 1883 to take courses at a business college in Pittsburgh. For the next five years, he made his living as a businessman before returning to Hartford to wed Adeline Barden (whose older sister, Celia, was married to Harry's big brother, William). Nine months and twenty-two days after the nuptials, Cornish and his wife became parents of a girl they named Edith.[1]

There was a swagger about Cornish, born partly of his proud heritage (he was a lifelong member of the Society of the Sons of the American Revolution), partly of his own physical attributes. He was a bullnecked, burly man with a jutting jaw, a handlebar mustache, and a prematurely balding dome that only enhanced his aura of extreme virility. A superb athlete, he was dedicated—in the fashion of that calisthenics-crazed age—to the pursuit of physical excellence. (Indeed, in later years, he would attend anatomy classes at Columbia College in order to learn as much as possible about the muscular system.)

Gruff in manner, he brooked no insults and was ready to "knock someone's block off" at the slightest provocation.[2] Aside from bodybuilding, bicycling, boxing, handball, and swimming, his most cherished pursuits were attending athletic events and hanging out with his chums at his favorite watering hole. He was also not averse to the occasional visit to a high-class brothel. Men admired him. Women found him deeply appealing.

His career as a sports professional began in Boston, where, after running the summer school for physical instruction at Harvard, he became athletic director of the Boston Athletic Club. His specialty was track and field. As a coach and trainer, he felt he had no equal. He boasted that he could tell precisely how fast a man was running simply by looking at him, without the aid of a stopwatch. After two years in Boston, he was hired away by the Chicago Athletic Club, where he continued to make a name for himself as one of the country's leading amateur sportsmen—a reputation reinforced when A. G. Spalding himself commissioned him to write a book on physical training, *All-Around Athletics*, for the popular Spalding's Athletic Library.[3]

It was during his years in Boston that Harry—by all accounts an inveterate philanderer—embarked on an affair with a widow named Mrs. Small. In 1893, when he and his family decamped for Chicago, his mistress moved there, too. Harry continued to see Mrs. Small on the sly until she died during an operation—reportedly, the abortion of Cornish's child. Cornish paid for her funeral expenses. Not long afterward, he became involved with another woman, Mabel Wallace.

When Harry left Chicago at the start of 1896 to take up his position at the newly formed Knickerbocker Athletic Club, his long-suffering wife remained in Chicago. The following year, she divorced him on the grounds of adultery and was given custody of their daughter, Edith, by then eight years old. Harry saw his child a few times a year, sometimes taking her to the Sportsmen's Show in Boston, where Addie and Edith moved following the divorce.

It seems possible that Harry's decision to leave Chicago was motivated at least partly by his desire to extricate himself from an exceptionally messy private life. Or perhaps Ballantine's offer was simply too attractive to turn down.

Whatever the case, his appointment was big news in Manhattan sporting circles. "Harry Cornish Coming Here," *The New York Times* trumpeted in a headline on December 18, 1895. "As a mentor and promoter of athletics," crowed the story, "Mr. Cornish is without a peer." After describing his accomplishments—which included staging the athletic games at the 1893 Chicago World's Fair—the paper predicted that, with Cornish at the helm, the club was sure "to be heard from in track and field sports in 1896. . . . If given good material, he will surely develop a team that will prove a worthy rival to any legitimate New York athletic club team."[4]

It was only the first of many times that Cornish would be extolled in the press as the leading light of the KAC—a situation that, in the heart of at least one club member, would rankle bitterly.

5

To ensure that his new athletic manager had what the *Times* called "good material" to work with, J. Herbert Ballantine set about recruiting the finest athletes he knew for membership in his club. Among these was the country's leading amateur horizontal-bar performer, the man typically referred to in the city press as "Champion Molineux."[1]

By the time Cornish arrived from Chicago, Roland was already ensconced at the club. Though he retained his private apartment in the Newark paint factory, he also rented a room on the second floor of the Manhattan clubhouse. With his highly developed sense of self-importance, he took it for granted that he would assume a position of authority in the club and managed—largely through his friendship with Ballantine—to get himself appointed as an officer on both the house and athletic committees.

Though admired as a gymnast, Roland, according to later accounts, was not an especially popular figure. Even in that citadel of snobbery, there was something about his highbred airs that set people's teeth on edge. His mouth seemed fixed in a patronizing smirk, and he held his head at a tilt that allowed him, quite literally, to look down his nose at the world. For all his prowess on the high bar, he struck more than one observer as a spoiled, slightly dandyish fellow—"a queer sort of person," in the words of one commentator.[2]

Queerest of all were his feelings toward Harry Cornish. From the moment he first set eyes on the new athletic director, Roland seemed to detest Cornish with a ferocity that left other club members baffled.

While the city's sportswriters spoke of Cornish in near-reverential tones, Molineux saw him as a mere employee and bristled whenever a story referred to the Knickerbocker athletes as "Cornish's men" or "Cornish's team." In an outraged letter to the Board of Governors, he demanded that all press announcements regarding club competitions refer to the participants as the Knickerbocker Team.

He was also relentless in his complaints about Cornish's performance as club supervisor. The evening exercise classes were not being conducted in the proper way. The restaurant was being mismanaged. Friends of Cornish were being allowed to use club facilities: foulmouthed "rowdies" whose "vile and obscene language" was deeply offensive to the delicate sensibilities of gentlemen like Roland. Cigar butts and expectorated tobacco juice had been left on the floor around the pool after a swimming competition.[3]

According to Roland, Cornish thwarted him at every turn. When Roland was put in charge of organizing the club's annual amateur circus in the spring of 1897, he asked Cornish to put together a list of the necessary props, costumes, and equipment. Cornish delayed until the last possible minute, then strode into Roland's bedroom, tossed the paper on his bed with a contemptuous flick of the hand, snarled, "There it is," and left.[4]

A short time later, after discovering that three of the gym's horizontal bars were broken, Roland ordered new ones from a manufacturer he knew and liked, a firm that "made bars for professionals." When the equipment arrived, however, Roland was shocked to discover that it had come not from his preferred supplier, but from the A. G. Spalding Company. Checking into the matter, he found that Cornish—who had a longtime association with Spalding—had altered the order form.[5]

The episode sent Roland into an even higher pitch of indignation. He had already lodged complaints about Cornish with various club officials, even writing to Herbert Ballantine himself that "Cornish could do more harm to the club in a minute than I could do it good in a year." Now he embarked on an active campaign to have Cornish demoted, if not dismissed entirely.

He demanded that the athletic director be stripped of various administrative responsibilities. He insisted that Cornish's desk be removed from the boardroom and placed in the gym, and that Cornish keep regular office hours. Most seriously, he asked that Cornish—who in addition to his $1,800 yearly salary had been given a room on the second floor of the clubhouse—be evicted.

Though Ballantine and other board members were quite satisfied with the performance of their new athletic manager, who had quickly made the KAC into a force to be reckoned with in the world of New York amateur athletics, they finally yielded to Roland's onslaught of complaints. Cornish was stripped of all his duties besides the training of teams and supervision of the athletic facilities. He was made to move his desk to the gymnasium. And in October 1897, he was forced to give up his room in the clubhouse and rent an apartment on West Eighty-fourth Street, just off Columbus Avenue.

At the time it was happening and for years to come, those who knew of the goings-on in the Knickerbocker Athletic Club were utterly baffled by Roland Molineux's relentless persecution of Harry Cornish, which seemed all out of proportion to any ostensible cause. What in the world was behind it?

Certainly, the two men couldn't have been more different in terms of their personal styles. Cornish was cut from much coarser cloth than the suave, supercilious Molineux. Interested in little beyond sports, whiskey, and women, the blunt-spoken Cornish was the type who would be found drinking with his pals at Jim Wakely's Sixth Avenue hangout or whoring at a brothel across the tracks on Forty-seventh Street, while Roland was attending the Metropolitan Opera or slumming with other swells in the titillating underworld of lower Manhattan.

Indeed, in Cornish's eyes, Roland, for all his athletic gifts, was nothing more than a spoiled little rich boy with absurdly prissy manners, and a hypocrite to boot, in view of certain stories Harry had heard regarding Roland's supposed involvement in various dubious activities.

Still, these differences can't account for the sheer inordinate intensity of Roland's instantaneous and abiding detestation of Cornish. How then to explain it?

Armchair Freudians would have little trouble in identifying several unconscious factors behind Roland's irrational hatred, beginning with his problems with authority. Here was a man who had grown up in the shadow of a strict, powerful, universally esteemed father. Roland himself never professed anything other than the deepest veneration for the General. At the same time, from his adolescence onward, he would contrive ways to inflict heartache, public ignominy, and financial ruin on the old man: a certain sign that, beneath his ostentatious avowals of love, there lurked far more destructive impulses toward his father. In the grip of such an acute Oedipal conflict (as a Freudian critic might say), it is little wonder that Roland projected his unconscious patricidal feelings onto the overbearing figure of the club's celebrated new athletic director.

And then there is the old standby of latent homosexuality. Just a few years before Roland Molineux and Harry Cornish had their first fateful encounter, Herman Melville, long forgotten by the public, died at home in Manhattan, leaving behind the unfinished manuscript of his final masterpiece, *Billy Budd.* The villain of that story, John Claggart, is possessed of such a bizarre, inexplicable malice toward the beautiful young hero that Melville can attribute it to nothing beyond "natural depravity." Some modern critics, in seeking to explain Claggart's motives, have found evidence of an unconscious homosexual attraction to Billy, feelings so profoundly threatening that Claggart must destroy the object who arouses them.

Could something similar have been operating in the case of Roland? Could his obsessive hatred of Cornish been the flip side of a feared homoerotic attraction? Certainly, as the case progressed, the newspapers would be filled with hints and innuendoes about Molineux's masculinity—his difficulties with women, his fondness for books on "sexual perversion," his friendship with men who lived in apartments "fashioned after the rooms occupied by Oscar Wilde."[6]

But all this, of course, is sheer and perhaps unwarranted speculation. All that can be said with certainty is that, from the moment Harry Cornish assumed his new job in January 1896, he became Roland Molineux's bête noir.

6

By 1897, telephones, invented twenty years earlier, were coming into common use. There were already more than fifteen thousand in New York City alone—and one of them could be found in the gymnasium of the Knickerbocker Athletic Club.[1] When it rang on an evening in April of that year, Harry Cornish answered. The caller was a Newark detective named Joseph Farrell, and his message, as it happened, was for Roland Molineux.

One of the workers at the paint factory had been caught in a raid at the Washington Hotel, a notorious brothel in Newark. This person had given the police Roland's name and told them where he could be contacted. Farrell, who was on friendly terms with Roland, wanted him "to come to the Newark police station as soon as possible" to resolve the matter.[2]

By this time, Cornish harbored a powerful antipathy toward Molineux, who had recently persuaded the Board of Governors to strip the athletic director of some of his privileges. Before long, Cornish was telling other club members that Roland made his money as a "rum seller" and that a building Molineux owned in Newark was used as a "disorderly house."

When Roland got wind of these rumors, he lodged yet another outraged complaint, demanding that Cornish be fired at once. Called before the House Committee, however, Harry denied having made such slanderous remarks and the matter was dropped.

Though Roland was left feeling deeply aggrieved, he had more serious things to worry about than his feud with the detested athletic director. A far more urgent matter was his relationship with the individual who had been arrested in the Jersey City brothel. This person hadn't been there as a customer but as an employee.

It was Roland's longtime lover, Mamie Melando.

Even before he learned that she was moonlighting in a whorehouse, Roland had begun to tire of Mamie. Now—by having the police phone him at his club to help get her out of trouble—she had exposed him to public ridicule. And there would soon be another reason why he wished to rid himself of the increasingly burdensome factory girl.

Roland—insofar as he was capable of feeling such an emotion—was about to fall in love.

Part Two

BLANCHE

7

Like Colonel Beriah Sellers—the lovably feckless hero of Mark Twain's *The Gilded Age*, who hatches one ridiculous get-rich-quick scheme after another—Blanche Chesebrough's father, James, had a brain that fairly crackled with supposedly surefire moneymaking ideas. Not all of them were completely worthless. He held a number of patents and sold the rights to one of his inventions—a hydraulic washing machine—for a decent sum. He even made some money from his device for curing diseases of the nose and throat. "He was either a crank or a genius," opined one New York City newspaper.[1]

Time would make it abundantly clear which of those two categories he fell into.

In pursuit of the pot of gold that always seemed to lie just beyond the horizon, he was constantly uprooting his family—his uncomplaining wife, Harriet, and six children. No sooner were they settled in a new home than James's wanderlust would seize him, and off they'd go to some distant place where his long-elusive fortune presumably awaited. At times, when one of his deals bore fruit, they enjoyed a fair degree of comfort. As the years progressed, however, their circumstances grew increasingly straitened, even desperate.

Blanche—the second-youngest child, born in 1874—spent her earliest years in Westerly, Rhode Island. It was there, according to later accounts, that she lost an eye when an unruly playmate threw a rock at her head. She was fitted with a glass eye and remained so sensitive about it that, for the rest of her life, she refused to be photographed except in profile—and only then at an angle that hid her left eye from the camera.[2]

Toward the end of her long life, Blanche—who would survive the other principals in the Molineux affair by many years—finally set down her memoirs. It is a work written in the sentimentalized style of the Victorian romances of her youth. ("In looking back, I see a girl—a young woman—who is now at a great distance. . . . She was in love with life—the life which her imagination painted in glowing colors. Naive, credulous, and filled with illusions, she did not recognize nor understand its verities until the enchanting rose color had turned to gray.") In her recollections of her childhood, she glosses over some of the most painful episodes. Beyond lamenting her father's lack of "sagacity in relation to money matters," for example, she does not dwell on the hardships that his family was made to endure as his behavior grew increasingly erratic.[3]

She was still a young girl when he dragged them from New England to the Midwest on another hopeless business venture. They were living in Minneapolis when Blanche experienced the "first stirrings" of the ambition that would dominate her life for many years to come. Her neighbors were a family named Beatty, whose youngest daughter, Louise, was Blanche's best friend. One day, while the two girls played jacks on the front stoop of the Beatty home, Blanche heard Louise's older sister practicing her singing lessons inside.

"It was then that an intense desire took possession of my childish fancy, some day to become a singer," Blanche would record in her memoirs.[4] The dream was not entirely unrealistic. Blanche was blessed with a lovely voice. Her little friend Louise—under her married name, Louise Homer—would herself grow up to be one of the great operatic contraltos of the early twentieth century.

Following his family's sojourn in the Midwest, the footloose James moved them to the South, where they lived for a time in Louisville, Kentucky. Then it was on to a rambling old house in North Carolina. Blanche would always remember the lush, tangled flower garden, "growing and blooming in riotous disorder, with a sun dial and purple and white wisteria climbing over an old porch and wall."[5] She formed a close friendship with the little girl down the road, the daughter of the former governor of the state, who lived in an "old and stately mansion" that had been used as a makeshift hospital in the waning days of the Civil War. Once, Blanche's little friend lifted a rug and showed her the bloodstains of the dying Confederate soldiers, still visible on the oaken floors.

Their stay in North Carolina lasted only six months. When summer came, James took them to a cottage on Long Island Sound, so remote from the nearest village that the only noises to be heard were "the night song of the inarticulate creatures of grass and trees, the bark of a dog, or the call of a bird to its mate."

By then, only Blanche and her younger sister, Lois, were still at home. Their brothers—Frank, John, and James, Jr.—were married and living in different parts of the country. The oldest of the three Chesebrough sisters, Izcennia ("Isia," as Blanche always called her), had also recently wed. And she had done quite well for herself, landing as a husband Waldo Harrison Stearns, scion of a wealthy lumber family.

Toward the end of Blanche's summer stay on rural Long Island, Izcennia came for a visit. A "proud and ambitious" woman (according to Blanche), Isia had already made up her mind to take her little sister under her wing. She would see to it that Blanche developed her talents, met the right people, and—most important—found a rich husband. Blanche was to come live with her in Boston, where Isia and Waldo would sponsor her musical studies.

In short order, Blanche was comfortably ensconced in Isia's lavish Longwood home, enjoying "an atmosphere of affluence which developed in me a rather lofty idea of living."[6] With Isia (or rather, Waldo) footing the bills, Blanche took private vocal lessons from the eminent George L. Osgood, director of the Emmanuel Church choir, the Boylston Club, and the Singers' Society of Boston; learned to read music from a young piano instructor; studied French and Latin diction; and attended concerts of the Boston Symphony Orchestra, along with other musical events. By the time the following spring came around, after months of practicing scales and doing endless breathing exercises, she was finally prepared to essay her first aria for the demanding Mr. Osgood—Gluck's "*Che farò senza Euridice.*" She would remember the thrill of that moment for the rest of her life.

She would also remember—even more intensely—another experience that happened to her a short time later. It was the last week in June, "the day before school closed for the summer." Even as an old woman, the moment would remain vivid in her mind:

> On the way home that afternoon, I cut across a little park where there were spots of dim shadowy shelter from the sun. A few benches were scattered here and there, and some ducks were floating around on a pool nearby. I was hot and tired and sat down on one of the benches to rest. I laid my books down beside me, took off my hat and fanned myself.
>
> Across from me in the shadow of the trees were a boy and girl. They were both much older than I. I remember them as being quite grown and I was envious of their added years. They must know so much more about things than I did!
>
> At first, I only glanced in their direction. Then I noticed they gave up their seats on the bench, and the boy pulled the girl down beside him on the cool shaded grass. They sat there for a few moments. Suddenly, the boy put his arms about the girl and pulled her into his embrace and down beside him on the ground. I watched—fascinated. He leaned over and kissed her. He drew her face and held it with both hands, close to his own. They lay there oblivious to everything, clasped in each others' arms.
>
> His gesture—when he drew her toward him and in a sort of masterful way held her—did something to me. My breath came in little gasps. Something stirred within me that made me feel first hot and then cold. I shivered and a little chill ran up and down and all over me.[7]

Blanche desperately "wanted to go home and tell Mother about having watched that boy making love to that girl." She wanted "to ask her why I felt so funny; why it affected me so." But she knew that she couldn't. Her mother—whose "outlook on life reflected the Puritan attitudes of her time"—would have been "horrified." Beyond cautioning her daughters that they must be "ever on their guard" against the coarse familiarities of men, Mrs. Chesebrough had never spoken a word about sex.

And so Blanche was left in confusion. She had no way of defining the erotic sensations that had been awakened in her. She knew, however, that something had changed forever. On that summer day in Boston, shivering with pleasure at the sight of the young couple embracing on the grass, "my childhood days ended."[8]

8

After staying with Isia for slightly more than a year, Blanche moved back in with her parents, who had taken a modest apartment in Boston. The cramped flat off Boylston Street—so small, Blanche later wrote, that "there was barely enough space for the piano and ourselves"[1]—took some getting used to after the luxury of her sister's Longwood mansion. Boston, however, like every place else she had ever lived, would prove to be only a way station.

Within months of his arrival, her father—bowing to what Blanche called his "irrepressible impulse to travel"—ordered his family to pack up their belongings yet again. This time they were going to New York City, where, so he assured them, he was absolutely certain to strike it rich with his latest invention. Though Isia offered to take Blanche back in and continue her musical studies, James wouldn't hear of it. A few weeks later, Blanche and her parents, along with her little sister, Lois, were settled in a small apartment on East Twenty-third Street, near Gramercy Park.

Despite the modesty of their living quarters, Blanche was delighted to find herself in "that great center of metropolitan life." In her memoirs, she describes, in a tone of breathless excitement, the thrill of those early days in New York City, as she wandered the surging streets, taking in the sights: "the splendid shops, the hotels, the restaurants and theatres."

Broadway offered a particularly dazzling spectacle with its endless procession of fashionable couples, the men with their "flawless top-coats, high-hats, and silver-headed walking sticks," walking arm in arm with their female companions, who were likewise arrayed in the "very best hats, shoes and gloves." Every block was a bazaar, lined with alluring shops—jewelers, florists, furriers, haberdashers, confectioners. "Pompous doormen in immense coats, shiny brass belts and buttons" posed in the doorways, while liveried coachmen in "tan boots, white tights, blue jackets, waited obsequiously for the mistresses of carriages who were shopping inside."[2]

At dusk, the electric "fire signs" of the "Great White Way" blazed to life. Hansom cabs drew up beneath the brilliant marquee lights, disgorging laughing, chattering patrons who streamed into the Olympia, the Casino, Daly's, and a dozen other theaters to watch Miss Julia Marlowe in *When Knighthood Was in Flower* or Miss Ada Rehan in *Sweet Nell of Old Drury* or young Ethel Barrymore in *Captain Jinks of the Horse Marines.*

And then there was Fifth Avenue, site of the city's most extravagant homes: the "magnificent abodes," as Blanche writes, "that gave the impression of royal palaces—the owners royal not because of birth but because of wealth!" Passing the Vanderbilt mansion on Fifty-second Street—a massive redbrick replica of a Renaissance chateau—Blanche wonders "what it must be like to possess such riches." She sounds (very aptly, as it would happen) like a character out of a Theodore Dreiser novel: a real-life Sister Carrie, a young girl from the provinces with her nose pressed to the glass, hungering for the glamorous life and glittering possessions just beyond her reach.

Blanche, of course, was hardly unique in her obsession with the social elite. It was an age when the doings of the city's moneyed aristocracy were followed with feverish interest by the public at large—when newspapers lavished coverage on everything from Chauncey DePew's departure for Palm Beach, to the gown worn by Mrs. Anson Phelps Stokes at the Easter cotillion at Sherry's, to the unforgivable lapse of Mr. and Mrs. Howard Gould's English butler, Tibbs, who—having surreptitiously sampled his master's wine—became tipsy at an "intimate dinner" for two dozen guests in honor of Senator and Mrs. John M. Thurston.[3] A particularly extravagant event such as the Bradley Martin ball of 1897—attended by seven hundred elaborately costumed guests and featuring a fifty-piece orchestra, floral decorations composed of six thousand orchids and twice as many roses, and a three-hour champagne dinner served by liveried waiters in knee breeches and powdered wigs—could monopolize the front pages for days.[4]

Most ordinary people, of course, could only view such excess with a mixture of tongue-clucking outrage and titillated envy. Blanche, however, had only to look at her older sister to see that, while the enchanted realm of the city's "upperdom" was closed to all but the fashionable few, a life of wealth and privilege was certainly available to a young woman who knew how to land the right husband.

Thanks to the generosity of her brother Frank, who was prospering as a businessman in Boston, Blanche was able to continue her singing lessons. She attended a studio near Union Square, where she joined a "little coterie of embryo artists"—among them Bessie Abott, who would become one of the leading sopranos of the day.[5] Later, Blanche studied with Frank Damrosch, a prominent figure in the New York City musical scene, who served as chorus master of the Metropolitan Opera House and founded the Musical Arts Society, an a cappella organization composed of experienced soloists who held concerts at Carnegie Hall.

Blanche displayed such talent that Damrosch invited her to join his group. A few weeks later, she was performing at Carnegie Hall in a gown of pale blue tulle, fashioned by her mother. Her future seemed limitless. "In that great whirling vortex of metropolitan life," she recalls in her memoirs, "my ambition soared."[6] Before long, she was auditioning for Jean de Reszke, the great Polish tenor, and singing for the world-famous diva Madame Melba, who seconded De Reszke's opinion that Blanche ought to study in Europe.[7]

It was a heady time for Blanche. Escorted by her musician friend Victor Harris, she was part of the first-night audience to see De Reszke and Emma Eames perform Verdi's *Otello* at the Metropolitan. She sang for the popular composer Robert Coverly at a private gathering and dined with Stanford White, the city's leading architect, designer of the Washington Square Arch, the New York Herald Building, and the Century Club, among other landmarks.[8] The meal—a typical Gilded Age blowout that began with oysters before proceeding to soup, sweetbreads, filet of beef, canvasback duck, celery salad, French peas, and string peas, with pistachio ice cream, fruit, and coffee to close—took place on the rooftop restaurant of Madison Square Garden, another building designed by White, who held forth during dinner with his usual bon vivant flair.

Nine years later, White would be shot to death on that very site by the millionaire madman Harry Thaw, whose showgirl wife, Evelyn Nesbit, had been White's onetime mistress. The killing of Stanford White in 1906 would become the city's second wildly sensational murder case of the new century.

The first, of course, was the one that Blanche herself would soon be embroiled in—a scandal that would consume her life and effectively put an end to her dreams of artistic glory.

9

Partly through the offices of her teacher, Frank Damrosch, Blanche became the contralto soloist at a church in Brooklyn Heights, whose choir included the wife of the famous American composer Harry Rowe Shelley. Her salary was ten dollars a week—a respectable sum for a part-time position at a time when the average yearly income for an American workingman was less than a thousand dollars.[1]

By then, her family was in desperate need of her earnings. Her father's improvident ways and successive failures had driven the little household perilously close to penury, and James was too proud to turn to his affluent offspring for help. As his material prospects grew grimmer by the day, he looked to religion for comfort, becoming increasingly caught up in a particularly zealous brand of evangelical Christianity.

Finally, in 1894, just before Blanche's twentieth birthday, James abandoned his worldly pursuits altogether. With his wife in tow, he returned to Rhode Island and consecrated himself entirely to church affairs, becoming, as newspapers later reported, "a constant attendant at revivals." In April 1895, Harriet died after a brief illness. Six months later, James himself fell ill. He refused medical attention, putting his faith in the Lord. He died shortly thereafter, in mid-October.[2]

By then, Blanche's younger sister, Lois, was living in high style on

West End Avenue and Seventy-second Street. Following a "whirlwind courtship," she had married Howard Oakie, a member of a socially prominent family with a big estate on Long Island.[3]

Alone and unwed, Blanche chose to remain in the Gramercy Park neighborhood, moving into a "diminutive" apartment at 51 East Twenty-third Street.[4] Her belongings were few: a console holding a silver-framed portrait of her parents alongside a slender flower vase; stacks of books and music cluttering the floors; a few nice sketches and drypoints adorning the walls; a bed and dresser, couch and easy chair. And, of course, her beloved piano.

Losing both parents within so short a time filled Blanche with a "terrible sense of desolation and sorrow." She distracted herself with her choir work, her vocal studies (now with the celebrated operatic teacher Emilio Agramonte), and her friendships with fellow students and other struggling young artists. She earned extra money by singing for socialites at "private musical evenings."

On one of these occasions she so impressed a wealthy female philanthropist that, as Blanche later wrote, the woman declared her "intention to help me realize my consuming ambition to study in Europe." Before this promise could be fulfilled, however, the woman took a transatlantic trip on the French liner *La Bourgogne*, which collided midocean with a merchant vessel and went down with more than seven hundred crew members and passengers, including Blanche's would-be patroness.[5]

Blanche was introduced to another potential patron through her wealthy new brother-in-law, Howard Oakie, whose family was on friendly terms with Gordon McKay, the millionaire industrialist who had earned his fortune in the shoemaking business. Hearing enthusiastic reports of Blanche's singing abilities from Howard's cousin, Corinne, the elderly McKay paid a visit to Blanche's modest apartment one early spring night in 1897. There—after serving him tea in one of the Sévres cups she had inherited from her mother—Blanche so impressed him with her rendition of Manuel Ponce's "Aimant la Rose" that he invited her to accompany Corinne on a visit to his Newport estate that summer.

It turned out to be a magical vacation for Blanche: her first direct experience of "what the possession of unlimited wealth really meant."

Nearly fifty years later, she could still conjure up in her imagination every detail of that enchanted scene:

> It was early June and we sailed through the Sound on the steamer *Puritan.* Upon our arrival, the beauty of the place was revealed in all its allure. With a background of blue waters, there were undulating grounds of velvety green, masses of foliage, blossoming shrubs and a rose terrace sloping away in the direction of the sea. There were also stables and a carriage house with the inevitable victoria and landaulet and phaeton of that day.
>
> The greenhouses were a marvel to me, with their forced growth of flowers and fruit. Ripening in the warm sun, which filtered through the ceiling of glass, were grapes that dropped in great clusters from the vines overhead. Beauty was everywhere! Hedges of Japanese roses ran along the edges of a portion of the grounds. A profusion of wild roses was growing and blooming in natural loveliness—pink and coral coloring against a purple and cobalt sky.
>
> In the distance was Rough Point. Some days the wind came out of the North, and from the cliffs we could gaze far off and watch the flying spray. We could glimpse the ocean, tearing and racing and curling in long lines over the white sand.
>
> There were drives each afternoon when all of fashionable Newport society would be abroad in glittering equipages. The Casino and the tennis matches were also open to us. There were luncheons aboard the yachts of McKay's friends, and for the first time in my life, I tasted champagne.[6]

It was not merely the beauty and grace of her surroundings, however, that made her stay in Newport so special for Blanche. Something else occurred during those long, bewitching days: her sudden awakening to the power and allure of what, in her memoirs, she consistently refers to as the "masculine element."

Though by no means conventionally beautiful, Blanche was, by all accounts, a captivating presence, even with her peculiar left eye. As one chronicler describes her, she was "possessed of a divine figure and a splendid carriage. She was tall, sinuous, yet graced by those happy and promising curves which were the splendor of the Gibson girl, the regnant beauty of her time. She wore clothes with astounding effect, and had the poise of a woman of the world."[7] In her memoirs, Blanche confirms that, from her adolescence on, men found her "vibrant" and "arresting."[8]

Up until her twenty-second year, however—at least according to her late-life recollections—she had never "given the slightest consideration to men. Music had been my one absorbing interest." All that changed, however, in the summer of 1897.

On several occasions during her stay in Newport, a group of "fledging Navy officers" from a nearby training station came to dinner at Gordon McKay's estate. Among them was a dashing lieutenant named Dillingham. In the company of these "smartly uniformed men," Blanche "suddenly discovered something—something that I really didn't understand. But whatever it might be, it was arresting! I decided that the masculine element . . . was rather disturbing and at the same time enormously interesting. I was suddenly infatuated with these gay young officers, with their poise and their *savoir faire*—their impressively good looks and sophisticated ways with women. I seemed to be treading on air. The flattery and attention was heady to a young girl experiencing it all for the first time."[9]

Though she "flirted outrageously" with the handsome Lieutenant Dillingham, Blanche rebuffed his physical advances. At the time, her sexual attitudes mirrored those of her mother: "Natural impulses and the sex-instinct must not be discussed or even thought about. Sex apparently was a thing to be ashamed of. The very word was tabu." She came home from Newport with her virtue intact.

From that point on, however, everything was different. She began to question her mother's "old-fashioned precepts" about sex:

> I couldn't understand why something that should be the most wonderful and beautiful of anything in existence must never be spoken of. It puzzled me a whole lot, and I began to study it out for myself. I decided it was all due to distorted vision. People were looking through lenses that were cracked; surely they saw only the doubtful and ugly reflections of their own minds! I wanted

> passion and love in my life; I wanted my existence to be fervid and glowing![10]

Because of her mother's puritanical teachings, Blanche had been kept "from a full realization of sex." Now, she "wanted to know it in its completeness, what it was all about." It wasn't mere curiosity that lay behind this desire, but the awakening of a long-suppressed hunger.

As Blanche, many years later, would say of her urgent new interest in erotic experience: "I was breathless for it."[11]

10

Mrs. Chesebrough's extreme reticence in relation to sex was, of course, perfectly in keeping with the mores of Victorian America. It was an age when marriage manuals advised young brides to avoid all "amorous thoughts or feelings"; when family physicians routinely recommended the cauterization of the clitoris as a cure for the ruinous habit of "self-pollution"; and when a woman with a healthy libido was likely to be branded as a hopeless "nymphomaniac." Adolescent girls from respectable families were kept in such complete ignorance of sexual matters that they commonly entered into marriage without the slightest conception of what coition entailed.[1]

In short, from a societal point of view, there was nothing at all wrong with Mrs. Chesebrough's prudery. On the contrary, it was Blanche, with her avid interest in sex, who would have been looked at askance. In her late-life memoirs, Blanche presents herself as an admirable free spirit, a precursor of the Jazz Age generation that would kick over the traces of their parents' Victorian values. To many of her contemporaries, however, Blanche would always be viewed in a very different light: as a frivolous young woman of limited means who was more than happy to sacrifice her chastity in order to achieve those material pleasures she so desperately craved—"good clothes, good dinners, good seats at the theatre." In short, as someone little better than a prostitute.[2]

Avid as she was for sexual experience, Blanche—so she says in her memoirs—was in no hurry to find a husband. "I was subtly conscious that I was shying away from marriage. It seemed a narrowing of horizons, a curtailment of freedom."[3]

It was precisely that sense of "freedom" that made some of her relatives nervous. To her sister-in-law Ellen—a prim Bostonian with traditional ideas about the proper role of women—Blanche's single life in New York City seemed dangerously "Bohemian."[4]

Blanche's own sisters were less alarmed by her "bachelorette" lifestyle. Even they, however, were eager to see her settled. Lois's marriage to the well-heeled Mr. Oakie had, to some extent, violated the natural order of things. By rights, Blanche should have been wed before her little sister.

Moreover, she wasn't getting any younger. To be sure, in the summer of 1897, she was still a few months shy of her twenty-third birthday. But she lived in an age when an unmarried woman of thirty was regarded as an old maid. In another few years, Blanche would rapidly be approaching the bounds of spinsterhood.

Izcennia in particular had made it her mission to see that her sister found a suitable husband. She had been playing Pygmalion for years, right down to the diction lessons she had provided for Blanche. Now, all that time, money, and effort were in danger of going to waste. If Blanche weren't careful, she would end up as the wife of one of the poor (if admittedly handsome) naval officers she had been dallying with all summer. The time had come to introduce her to some more financially desirable prospects.

In mid-August 1897, just a few weeks after Blanche returned from her idyll at Newport, a perfect opportunity presented itself.

She had been invited to stay with Isia and Waldo at their summer home, Craigsmere, on the Rhode Island coastline. Despite the beauty of the setting, life at the seaside estate, according to Blanche's testimony, was "uncommonly dull."[5] Waldo, though devoted to his wife, was something of a stick in the mud, a homebody with little interest in socializing. By contrast, Isia loved to go out and have fun. The long, placid, uneventful days at Craigsmere might have been a balm to Waldo; to his wife, they had grown unbearably tedious.

When Waldo announced in early August that he had business in Boston and would be gone for two weeks, Isia pounced. Over breakfast that morning, she asked his permission to take Blanche on a visit to Jamestown. It would—so Isia assured him—be an excellent chance to introduce Blanche to some eligible young men. Waldo, always indulgent of his wife and considerate of his sister-in-law, agreed. What Isia didn't emphasize, of course, was that the trip would be a treat for her, too—a holiday from her suffocating home life with the sweet but stodgy Waldo.

No sooner had he departed than Isia packed a bag with several of her nicest summer frocks and some accessories to augment Blanche's simple wardrobe. Then, leaving the servants in charge of Craigsmere, she and her sister took the ferry to Jamestown.

There they were invited by an old friend of Isia's—a socialite named Clark Miller—to accompany him and three male companions on a cruise to Portland, Maine, aboard his schooner-yacht, the *Monhegan*. The two women accepted without hesitation.

It was high noon when the *Monhegan*, flying the flag of the Larchmont yacht club, sailed into Portland harbor. "Bluest of skies were above, bluest of waters below," Blanche would recall many years later as she described that splendid midsummer day "so freighted with import for me":

> White sails and hulls gleamed in the light of a noonday sun. The brilliance caught and flashed back the shimmer of burning brass; rails and spars and polished surfaces of glistening decks reflected its rays. From one of the yachts, with its short, squatty funnels, fluttered the pennant of the New York Yacht Club, and below it the owner's flag lifted and fell again in the light wind from across the bay.
>
> The waters of the harbor were dotted with a fleet of these craft, the luxurious toys of their owners. They rode at anchor, swaying lazily with the motion of the tide. They were like great white birds, lightly and gracefully resting on the surface of limpid sun-drenched waters.[6]

The *Monhegan* slid into a berth beside an even more spectacular vessel, the *Viator*, skippered by Albert J. Morgan, a member of the fabulously wealthy family that manufactured the country's best-selling brand of soap, Sapolio. Before long, a luncheon invitation had been extended by Morgan, who sent his motorized launch to convey Blanche and the others across the sparkling water to his "great white pleasure craft."[7]

Climbing aboard the *Viator*, Blanche saw "deep-seated, gaily cushioned deck chairs drawn forward on the polished decks. Awnings softened the intense light of mid-day." After exchanging some pleasantries with his guests, Morgan disappeared belowdecks to issue orders to his steward, who emerged a short time later with a silver tray bearing pâté de foie gras sandwiches, small toasted squares piled with Russian caviar, and thin-stemmed flutes brimming with champagne.

"We drank the iced Moët & Chandon, its liquid amber like gold," Blanche rhapsodizes in her memoirs. "And the sun that day was gold, with the sea the color of sapphire. The wind was warm and sweet and came laden with the tang of salt—the flavor of the marshes. There was gaiety and lightheartedness and laughter, for happiness was abroad that brilliant midsummer's day."[8]

Later that afternoon, Blanche found herself on the afterdeck, making small talk with Morgan, who stood quite close to her, his arm resting behind her on the railing. The warm attention of the millionaire bachelor made Blanche—already light-headed from the champagne—feel positively giddy.

All at once, Morgan glanced over and noticed that a nearby deck chair—vacant only a few moments before—was now occupied by a young man with an open book on his lap. Morgan called to the fellow, who closed his book, dropped his feet from the low rail in front of him, tossed his cigarette into the water, then stood up and approached.

Blanche would always retain a particularly sharp image of that moment:

> One noticed that he was not very tall, but his body was slender, muscular and beautifully proportioned. He carried himself very erect and gave a nonchalant air of self-possession, poise and breeding. He had the most charming manners, greeting us with a quiet, infectious smile. Something flashed between us.[9]

Blanche, of course, had already been introduced to the handsome young man, though she had taken little notice of him, having been focused so intently on her host. Now, she felt her interest suddenly piqued by the debonair "Mollie," as Morgan fondly greeted him—though his actual name, as she now recalled, was Roland Molineux.

11

Describing that moment many years later, Blanche would strike a particularly portentous note: "On that day, how could I have guessed that Fate had already begun to spin her web? How casual that first meeting! Weighted—unknown to me—with such a significance! But the sun had shone and the wind was sweet, and lighthearted happiness was abroad that day. And now, even as it had been earlier at McKay's estate at Newport, the sea and all its allure was the background."[1]

Perceiving the spark of attraction that had instantly flashed between "Mollie" and the charming Miss Chesebrough, Morgan excused himself to attend to his other guests. No sooner had he gone than Roland led Blanche "to a couple of deck chairs in a snug corner, sheltered from the sun and wind." There, they "drank champagne and laughed over the most inconsequential things." Blanche could not fail to be captivated by the handsome and cultivated young man:

> He was clever and witty and amusing. . . . He had charm, grace of manner, and a bearing that was aristocratic. Normally rather fair, he was now tanned by exposure to wind and sun. He was debonair, and his poise and air were those of the cosmopolite. He possessed a decided gift for repartee, and about him there was

> a gay insouciance, an ease, a smiling indifference. For a time we both forgot the others in the party. I was absorbed in him as we talked together and he lounged there in his summer flannels.[2]

As their talk grew more intimate, Roland confessed that he had felt an immediate attraction to Blanche but had held back because he thought that she "had eyes only for Morgan." Blanche assured him that Morgan, though a delightful host, meant nothing to her.

By then, she had discovered something else about Roland that strengthened her belief that she and the handsome young man were, as she put it, *en rapport*: Roland was a music lover. "He had gone frequently to the Opera and numbered amongst his friends a few gifted people known in the musical life of New York."

When Blanche told Roland of her "own ambitions and work," he revealed that he held season tickets to the Metropolitan Opera.

"If you wish," he said with his engaging smile, "you shall have a surfeit of music this winter."

"To be surfeited would be impossible," she cried. "But to have a feast of music—how wonderful that would be!"[3]

Soon afterward, their tête-à-tête was interrupted by the appearance of Morgan and the others, who came over to join them. Blanche records in her memoirs that, for the rest of that day, "there was only a brief word or two exchanged between us; but I found myself frequently turning to glimpse him as we mingled with the others; and always his eyes followed me; and it was as though a silent and intriguing understanding had already begun to exist."[4]

According to Blanche, her first encounter with Roland Molineux ended around sunset, when she, Isia, Clark Miller, and his two male friends returned to the *Monhegan* aboard the launch that had carried them to the *Viator* earlier that day:

> We descended to the motor boat which had been bobbing alongside. Once more it noisily churned the waters and, leaving a long path of white foam in its wake, swung back to the other

> pleasure craft. The sails of Clark's racy schooner-yacht bellied out to the wind. Turning, she nosed into the channel and cruised slowly out through the sparkling blue waters of the bay. . . .
>
> The *Viator* with Morgan's guests aboard still lay anchored in Portland harbor. Those of us aboard the *Monhegan* were now heading in before a stiff breeze that swept the waters off Beaver Tail. The sky had faded from rose—that shade like the inner heart of a shell—to opal and mother-of-pearl. The pearl drifted into blue-gray against the horizon, and the sea and sky blended into one. The wind stiffened and ruffled the surface of the waters into wavering threads of white. The great sails also caught the force of it, and we were cutting through, clean as the blade of a knife. We keeled far over, and soon the decks were awash so that we were drenched with the flying spray. I sat huddled on the upper edge of the companionway. My hair was wet, my frock limp with the spindrift. . . .
>
> Clark came and wrapped a great coat about me. We laughed in high glee, like children. How tremendously exciting it was![5]

That, at any rate, was Blanche's official version of events. Other people privy to what transpired on board the *Viator* had a different tale to tell.

According to these sources, at the end of that intoxicating, champagne-soaked day, the men and women aboard Morgan's yacht—Blanche and Isia included—paired off, and a mock marriage ceremony was held for each couple. Then each set of make-believe newlyweds retired to a stateroom, intending to indulge in a very real consummation of their union.[6]

Which of these accounts is true has never been definitively established. In any case, the outcome—in one very crucial sense—was the same.

As events would show, Blanche, despite her earnest wish to divest herself of her virginity, returned from her trip aboard the pleasure-craft *Viator* still innocent of (as she put it) the "full realization of sex."

12

Roland returned from the yachting cruise determined to pursue the enchanting young woman he had met aboard the *Viator*. First, however, he had to sever his ties with Mamie Melando.

If Blanche, in her memoirs, often sounds as if she'd sprung from the pages of *Sister Carrie* ("Life's shop windows were filled with alluring things," she exclaims at one point. "I desired them with a great intensity!"),[1] Roland himself, in the fall of 1897, had come to resemble a character from a Theodore Dreiser novel: a young man caught between a coarse if devoted factory girl who had grown increasingly repellent in his eyes and the infinitely more refined, elegant, socially suitable woman he craved. Sometime in late October, in an effort to free himself of Mamie, he dismissed her from the Herrmann paint factory, giving her—as a reward for her many years of varying sorts of service—a new dress.[2]

Blanche, in the meantime, had moved to a different apartment. Wishing to be closer to her younger sister Lois, she had taken rooms at a fashionable boardinghouse on West Seventy-second Street, owned by a landlady named Mary Bell. An enormous bouquet of roses, sent by the ever-thoughtful Roland, was waiting to welcome her to her new living quarters.

It was only one of many gifts—baskets of fruits, boxes of sweets, the latest best-selling novels, such as Mr. Frederic's *The Damnation of Theron Ware*—that he would lavish on Blanche that fall, as he set about wooing her with the same singleness of purpose he applied to all his pursuits, from his amateur athletics to his persecution of Harry Cornish.

As promised, he provided Blanche with a surfeit of social activities. On a typical Saturday evening, they might take in a Broadway show or a comic operetta—Marie Dressler doing her star turn as Flo Honeydew in *The Lady Slavey* at the Casino Theater or Lillian Russell performing her piping high Cs in Gilbert and Sullivan's *Patience* at the Bijou.

Even more glorious were those nights when they attended the Metropolitan to hear the celebrated De Reszke perform the title role of Le Cid, or the great dramatic soprano Lillian Nordica sing *Siegfried.* Eyes fixed raptly on the stage, heart thrilling to the strains of Wagner or Verdi or Bizet, Blanche would, at certain moments, feel so overcome with emotion that she could not keep from reaching out and seizing Roland's hand. During intermission, they would stroll among the glittering crowd and excitedly discuss the performance. Their "mutual love of this enchanting art," writes Blanche in her memoir, "established a sympathetic bond between Roland and myself."[3]

Afterward, they would dine at the Waldorf or Delmonico's or Louis Martin's smart new establishment on Twenty-sixth Street, outfitted like a Parisian café with marble-topped tables and cushioned banquettes. Or perhaps Roland would take her to Louis Bustanoby's Café des Beaux Arts on Sixth Avenue and Fortieth Street, where a gypsy violinist would greet them at the door and serenade them with a polonaise as the headwaiter escorted them to their table.[4]

When they weren't together, they were in constant communication by letter, telegram, and the telephone in Mrs. Bell's parlor. As the winter approached, Roland's gifts became more expensive: an opal broach and a diamond butterfly pin, both from Tiffany's, where he had an account.

Then came the costliest—and most serious—gift of all.

It was a diamond ring, also from Tiffany's, inscribed with the Hebrew word *mizpah*, typically translated as "watchtower" or "lookout." Implicit in its meaning is the prayer: "May God watch over you when we are apart."

For Roland, the ring carried a solemn significance. By that time, he had not only resolved to marry Blanche but had made his intentions known to her.

Blanche, however, felt deeply divided about her suitor. She was happy to accept the diamond *mizpah* ring as a token of his friendship. But whenever the subject of marriage came up, she "would not be serious about it; always parried it; always laughingly told him I did not think I cared deeply enough for him."[5] Her teasing demurrals were partly a game, a way of playing hard-to-get. But she also had serious doubts about Roland.

With his physical beauty, charm, and money, he was certainly a good catch. And then there was their shared love of the opera.

At the same time, however, he seemed strangely deficient in that "masculine element" so prized by Blanche. She had certainly given him every opportunity to display it. Indeed, by November 1897, Roland had taken to spending so much time in Blanche's room—entire nights included—that Mrs. Bell's chambermaid, Rachel Greene, assumed the two were already husband and wife.[6]

And yet, despite Blanche's obvious willingness, their relationship remained unconsummated. Recalling that long-ago summer day in Boston, when she'd first been aroused by the sight of the teenaged boy pulling his girlfriend to the ground, she longed for a man who would take her in the same "masterful way." "When a woman senses an elusive intimation of mastery in a man, it is irresistible," she would declare in her memoirs. "There is a kind of brutality which is part of a great tenderness in the lovemaking of some men, and it is absolutely overwhelming."[7]

It was that "brute masculine force" that she dreamed of surrendering to. And Roland, she had come to conclude, "possessed none of it."[8]

13

Residing down the hall from Roland on the second floor of the Knickerbocker Athletic Club was a thirty-two-year-old bon vivant named Henry Crossman Barnet. Brown-haired, blue-eyed, with a small, neatly trimmed mustache and a decided paunch, he had joined the club, as one commentator put it, "with a pleasant hope of reducing his weight."[1] With his robust appetites and cheerful aversion to exercise, however, he had quickly abandoned that goal. Still, though he made little use of its impressive athletic facilities, the social life of the club perfectly suited his temperament. A thoroughly gregarious creature, he was well-liked by men and possessed an easy charm that made him—despite his fleshy cheeks and pudgy frame—highly attractive to women.

"Barney," as he was known around the club, had formed a warm friendship with Roland, based partly on their shared dislike of Harry Cornish. To be sure, Barnet wasn't weirdly fixated on the swaggering athletic director, the way Roland was. Still, he had his complaints. Cornish, he felt, was doing a poor job of managing the club facilities and was especially lax about supervising the janitorial staff. The pool area was always a mess after swim meets, and the hallway floors weren't kept clean enough—a particular problem for Barnet, who liked to walk barefoot between his apartment and the bathroom.[2]

One evening in early November 1897, Roland took Blanche to the

Metropolitan Opera to hear the Banda Rossa, a highly popular touring group that had only recently recorded their sprightly rendition of "Funiculi Funicula" for Mr. Edison's latest technological marvel, the phonograph.[3] During intermission, Roland spotted Barnet in the foyer, called him over, and introduced him to Blanche.

"From this encounter," Blanche would later write with atypical understatement, "a friendship developed that came to have great significance."[4]

Following the concert, the three of them proceeded to Delmonico's, where they were joined by the popular playwright Clyde Fitch, whose presence, as Blanche recalled, "gave the evening an additional bit of that glamor and brilliancy that so appealed to me." As the supper progressed, she found herself drawn to Barnet. Though he possessed none of Roland's cultivated wit, there was something about him—a "forcible, virile" quality—strangely absent from the infinitely more athletic Molineux.[5]

The following night, Barnet dined with the two of them again, this time at the club. By the time the coffee and liqueur were served, "a delightful camaraderie," in Blanche's words, had developed among them.

The subject of the forthcoming Club Carnival arose, and Roland—who was to perform on the horizontal bars as part of the festivities—asked Barney if he would mind serving as Blanche's escort until the show was concluded. Barnet was only too happy to oblige.[6]

Blanche, too, was secretly pleased. From her very "first meeting with Henry Barnet"—as she confessed many years later—she "was conscious that he possessed a little more than the average qualifications for holding one's interest. I sensed a hidden strength and a brute force in him, and it was as natural as breathing that I should capitulate to that!"[7]

On the night of the carnival, after thrilling to Roland's typically dazzling routine, the three of them repaired to his room to share a bottle of champagne. Though Blanche, who had never seen Roland perform before, gushed over his skill, her thoughts were really on Barnet. Indeed, by that time—less than a week after their first encounter—she was already entertaining highly charged fantasies about him. "Mentally, I had already yielded to him, and I was secretly thrilled at the thought of surrender."[8]

It didn't take long for Roland to sense the growing attraction between Blanche and Barnet, and he was quick to stake his claim. One evening shortly after the carnival, while the three of them dined at the club, Barney, in his jocular way, began telling Mollie how much he envied him.

"Congratulations, old man," he exclaimed, clapping him on the shoulder. "What a lucky fellow you are."

"Why, what does that mean?" said Blanche, feeling a sudden rush of irritation. "Roland and I are not going to be married."

"Oh, yes, we are," Roland coolly replied.

"But we are not even engaged!" said Blanche, laughing to soften her petulant tone.

"True, but we are going to be," said Roland, casting a pointed look first at Blanche, then at Barnet.

Blanche instantly understood what was going on. Roland had been observing her "growing infatuation for Barnet." He was "determined to leave no one in doubt concerning his feelings for me, and he would discourage any interest that might develop elsewhere."[9]

But Blanche was not about to be pressured into marriage. She was not in love with Roland. Nor, for that matter, with his friend. But she was determined to act on the powerful physical attraction she felt for Barnet.

She knew, of course, that she was playing with fire. But the element of danger only made the situation more "exciting and alluring." And why shouldn't she fling herself into an affair with the virile Barnet? After all, she told herself, "I was free, free as air and owed no allegiance to anyone."[10]

She made that position unmistakably clear on Thanksgiving Day, when Roland got down on one knee and formally proposed to her.

Blanche—trying to take the sting out of the rejection by assuring him that she might feel otherwise in the future—turned him down.

14

The holiday season of 1897 was an unhappy time for Roland Molineux. First came Blanche's rejection of his marriage proposal on Thanksgiving Day. Then, just before Christmas, his protracted feud with Harry Cornish reached a sudden and—from Roland's point of view—exceptionally bitter climax.

The unwitting catalyst was a gentleman named Bartow Sumter Weeks. The son of a Civil War colonel, Weeks had gotten his law degree from Columbia University before going to work in the Manhattan district attorney's office. In the fall of 1897, he had just entered into private practice with another former assistant DA, George Gordon Battle. Eventually, Weeks would become a New York State Supreme Court justice.

Besides the law, amateur athletics was the great passion of Weeks's life. A long-standing member of the New York Athletic Club, he had served as two-term president, chairman of the Athletic Committee, member of the Board of Governors, and captain of the club's athletic team.

He was also a close family friend of the Molineuxs and had known Roland for many years.

In October 1897, the pugnacious Harry Cornish had become embroiled in a dispute with Weeks, accusing him in print of an ethical violation. According to Cornish—who published his charge in *Harper's Weekly*—Weeks, in his eagerness to win an international meet, had paid a track star named Bernie Wefers, holder of the world record in the

100-yard dash, to switch membership from the Knickerbocker Athletic Club to the NYAC. Cornish was incensed over this payoff, a flagrant breach (so he argued) of the amateur code.

Cornish was after Weeks, not Bernie Wefers, whom he considered a friend. So when the Amateur Athletic Union suspended Wefers from competition until a hearing could be held, Cornish backpedaled and refused to testify. The hearing was canceled, Wefers was reinstated, Weeks was exonerated, and Cornish himself ended up receiving an official reprimand for bringing "false and malicious charges."

Afterward Cornish—seeking to mend fences with Bernie Wefers—sent him a letter on official KAC stationery. Though he apologized for the trouble he had caused the track star, he remained unrepentant in regard to Weeks. "I have got it in for Weeks," he wrote, "for I consider him to be as far beneath me as one man can be with another. He has been guilty of a dirty piece of business."[1]

Somehow, this letter ended up in Weeks's possession. And Weeks lost no time in showing it to Roland Molineux.

Whether Weeks had any sense of Roland's obsessive hatred of Cornish is unclear. In any case, the "Wefers letter" (as it came to be known) drove Roland to new heights of outrage.

Appearing before the Board of Governors, he demanded that Cornish be fired at once. After taking the matter under advisement, the board members—who were, on the whole, quite pleased with Cornish's performance as athletic director—opted for little more than a slap on the wrist. The Wefers letter, they concluded, was Cornish's private affair. He had every right to express his opinion of Weeks in however churlish a manner he wished—though not with the imprimatur of the Knickerbocker Athletic Club. Henceforth, he would be deprived of the use of club stationery for his personal correspondence.

As a gesture befitting the gentlemanly code of clubdom, the board also voted to throw a dinner for Weeks, at which they offered their formal apologies and expressed their admiration for the leadership of the NYAC. Weeks was placated, and the whole unfortunate incident appeared to be settled.[2]

Roland, however, would not let the matter rest. Not long after the conciliatory dinner, he issued an ultimatum to the board: either Cornish must go or he himself would quit the club. On the evening of December 20,

1897, the board met again. After deliberating for half an hour, they let Roland know that, while they valued his membership and sincerely hoped that he would reconsider his position, they had voted to retain Cornish. With a little bow, Roland promptly resigned.

Back in his room, he composed a letter to the club secretary, John Adams:

> My Dear Adams,
>
> Although I have resigned from the K.A.C., do not for one moment suppose that I wish it other than success. I entertain the highest personal regard for its officers, but I have been a disturbing element in its counsels because, with the very best intentions, I have opposed what I am confident is a wrong policy, that of allowing an employee to use the club for personal advertisement and to get even with gentlemen who displease him. This I am not in sympathy with. Believe me, it is best that I resign, which I do regretfully. I hope you will show this to Mr. Ballantine, that he may know how I stand on this matter. Wishing you all the compliments of this happy season, I am,
>
> Yours most cordially,
> *Roland Molineux*[3]

He sealed the letter in an envelope. Then, descending to the main floor, he strode across the empty lobby to Adams's office and slipped the envelope under the door.

As he returned to his room, he encountered Harry Cornish on the stairs.

"You son of a bitch," sneered Cornish, who had just learned of the board's decision. "You thought you'd get me out, and I got you out instead."

These were, as Cornish knew perfectly well, fighting words. If any man had dared utter them to *him*, Cornish would have promptly answered with his fists.

Roland, however, did not rise to the bait. Instead, he merely gave his strange, enigmatic smile, waved his hand blithely, and said, "You win."

Then he mounted the stairs to his room, where he proceeded to pack his belongings. By the following morning he was gone from the club, never to return.[4]

In the nineteenth century, the word *molly* (derived from the Latin *mollis*, meaning "soft") was derogatory slang for a male homosexual, the Victorian equivalent of the later slur *fairy*. It was also, as it happened, phonetically identical to Roland's nickname, "Mollie."

On the evening of his climactic encounter with Molineux, Cornish, as was his custom, visited Jim Wakeley's saloon. There, beneath the portraits of bare-chested pugilists and other athletic luminaries, he regaled his drinking chums with an account of his triumph over his longtime adversary.

As he repeated Roland's submissive parting words, Cornish snorted with contempt. It was just the sort of response, he and his cohorts agreed, that a man would expect from the aptly named Mollie.

15

Increasingly preoccupied with thoughts of Henry Barnet, Blanche was oblivious to Roland's troubles with Harry Cornish. Nor did Roland inform her of his resignation from the club. He had, after all, suffered a humiliating defeat in his final showdown with his nemesis and wasn't eager to reveal it to the woman he sought to impress.

The day after New Year's 1898, Blanche herself changed living quarters, moving in with a family friend named Alice Bellinger, a forty-year-old divorcée who quickly became her closest confidante. In the meantime, Roland retreated to his apartment in the Newark paint factory, where amid his books, laboratory equipment, and shelves of toxic chemicals, he passed much of his time brooding.

He had a good deal to brood about. His heart still rankling with hatred, he sent letters to various acquaintances, detailing Cornish's transgressions, which—so he insisted—were doing such harm to the KAC that Roland could no longer associate himself with the club.[1]

Blanche's relationship with Henry Barnet had also begun to eat at him. Roland had made it very clear that he desired to marry her, and he had no intention of putting up with her increasingly open flirtation with Barney.

In all of the public statements she was ever to make on the subject, Blanche would insist that her relationship with Harry Barnet had been purely platonic—nothing more than a warm friendship, conducted with the approval, even encouragement, of Roland Molineux. Only much later, when she set down her memoirs in old age, would she confess the truth.

Her description of the fateful evening when her flirtation with Barnet took a far more serious turn occupies an entire chapter of the manuscript. It reads—as does so much of her writing—like an overheated excerpt from a pulpy true romance magazine. Precisely because it *is* so clichéd, however, it serves as a revealing self-portrait of the author. More revealing, perhaps, than she intended, since it shows her in a not-very-flattering light: as a hopelessly histrionic woman who sees herself as the star of a glamorous grand opera even while coming across as a character in an embarrassingly cheesy bodice ripper.

It began on a wintry Monday evening in late January. Blanche had been asked to perform at a late-night soiree. Though Roland was to be her escort, her mind was focused entirely on Barnet. He, too, had been invited, and his presence was all she could think about.

It would be, she writes in her memoirs, "the first time Barney heard me sing."[2] Eager "to look particularly well" for him, she dressed in a "filmy tulle gown, together with black satin slippers, the high heels of which were studded with brilliants." Then, for the finishing touch, she added her diamond butterfly pin from Tiffany's.

It had, of course, been a gift from Roland. But she was wearing it for Barnet.

Descending from her bedroom to the parlor, she found her landlady and friend, Alice Bellinger, seated before the glowing fireplace.

"You look like a million," said Alice.

"Of course!" Blanche laughed. "And why not?"

"Your frock—it is quite too lovely," said Alice, surveying Blanche from head to foot. "It absolutely *breathes* Paris."

All at once, a shadow of concern crossed the older woman's face and her tone became solemn.

"I warn you," she said, as though reading Blanche's thoughts. "Stop your flirtation with Barnet or you are going to get into a lot of trouble. One can see in his eyes that Roland won't stand for it."

"Why, that is nonsense," said Blanche, with a dismissive wave of the hand. "That's perfectly silly."

At that moment, the doorbell rang. Grabbing her long white gloves and throwing on the chinchillas loaned to her by Alice, Blanche hurried to the door. There stood Roland in a "mood of lightheartedness" and "looking awfully well in his evening clothes."

After a quick ride downtown in a horse-drawn cab, they reached their destination, a handsome apartment in Washington Square filled with laughing, chattering partygoers, many of whom had just come from the Met. Blanche quickly realized that she was not going to be performing that evening. The crowd was so large and raucous that singing was out of the question. What disappointed her most, however, was that Barnet was nowhere to be seen.

When he *did* arrive, about twenty-five minutes later, he had an attractive young woman on his arm. Yet no sooner did his eyes fall on Blanche than he began to make his way toward her through the crowd. By the time he reached her side, he had managed to detach himself from his date.

"You look wonderful," he said. "Where's Mollie?"

"Over there," Blanche said, nodding toward the anteroom, where Roland was chatting with the host. "And where's your woman friend?"

"Lost in the crowd." Barnet laughed. "I'm sure she'll have a good time flirting." Then looking about, he said, "What a mob. Isn't there someplace we can escape to and talk?"

Before Blanche could reply he had taken her by one arm. "Come on," he urged. "Let's get out of this. I know where we can have a moment together. Shall we? Let's go—we'll get back before they miss us."

Still holding on to her arm, Barnet pushed through the crowd, then hurried outside while Blanche gathered up her wraps. By the time she emerged onto the street, he had secured a cab.

"Where are we bound?" she asked in an excited, slightly breathless voice as Barnet seated himself close beside her. "What sort of escapade have you planned, Barney?"

Even in the darkness of the cab she could see his rakish smile. "I have the keys to D——'s apartment," he said, naming a friend from the KAC.

"He's in Europe, you know. For six weeks. Said I could have it until his return."

Less than five minutes later, Barnet was unlocking the door to the uptown apartment, just off Fifth Avenue. The time was shortly before midnight.

The instant they entered, Blanche could tell from the decor that it was the residence of a well-to-do bachelor. She could tell something else, too: that arrangements had been made for a carefully orchestrated seduction.

> Barnet had prepared for this, I was sure. He must have planned our coming here, all in advance. The apartment was dimly lighted and a chaise longue was drawn up before an open fireplace. The logs were laid, and Barnet stooped to touch a lighted taper to them. The bits of paper underneath curled and blackened, and the flames raced to the driftwood, catching the heavy log which was upheld by massive old andirons of some early English period. The firelight played on the nearest objects and threw shadows on the opposite walls.

Reaching behind her, Barnet removed the furs from Blanche's bare shoulders and arms. He then disappeared into another room, returning a few moments later with a tray holding a bowl of ice, a flask of scotch, and a siphon bottle. Setting the tray down on a carved taboret, he mixed two highballs in tall crystal glasses and handed one to Blanche.

"To you," he said, touching the rim of her glass with his own. They drank. Then, rearranging the deep pile of damask-covered pillows on the chaise longue, Barnet said, "Lie there, where I can look at you."

She did as he asked while he seated himself close beside her.

"You certainly have set the stage for something, Barney," she said, sipping again from her glass.

"For you," he answered.

"We've done a perfectly wild thing," she said, "running away like this from the party. If they miss us, what then?"

"They won't," said Barnet. "I'll watch the time. No one will know we've escaped."

"Still," she said, "if Roland finds out that I came here with you . . ."

"Then why tell him?" asked Barnet.

"I shan't," said Blanche.

They spoke for a while about her feelings for Molineux. She confessed that, though she still entertained thoughts of marrying him one day, she was not really in love with him.

By then, she had finished her drink. "You know, Barney," she said with a smile, "it is terribly risqué, our being alone like this."

"Are you afraid of me?" asked Barnet.

"Somewhat," she said.

In truth, she felt no fear at all, but rather "an uncontrollable desire to touch him—to have him touch me."

Wanting him "to be conscious of the faint indefinable perfume of my hair, my flesh," Blanche bent forward. Barney's eyes shone as he stared at her, his gaze "like a caress as it rested on the little hollow between my white breasts, plainly discernible under the revealing outlines of my bodice."

All at once, "as though with an overwhelming impulse of desire, he caught me up in his arm, pulled me down against him, and buried his lips in mine."

> I don't know how many minutes I lay there with his arms about me. He kissed my hair, my neck, my shoulders and breast. My heart pounded against his heart, and my breath came in little gasps. It was like a torrent, his passion.
>
> "My God, what lips, what a body you have," he whispered. "You are like a flame. You have made me on fire for you!"
>
> He was drunk with the madness and passion of the moment, and I was trembling. He bruised my mouth, and afterwards there were little black and blue marks on my flesh. The brutality of it was an ecstasy!

They were still lying on the chaise when they heard the mantle clock strike one. Barnet rose, then reached out his hands and pulled Blanche to her feet.

"We have gone mad," said Blanche.

"Yes," said Barnet. "Isn't it wonderful?"

They kissed again. Then, throwing on their garments, they made their way to the street, found a cab, and drove off to rejoin the party.

16

When they met again a week later, Barnet showed none of his former ardor. Seated across the table from her at an uptown café, he extracted a cigarette from his engraved silver case and smoked it in silence, looking at her calmly—even coldly.

Blanche was fighting back tears. "What has happened?" she said in a tremulous voice. "What has Roland said to you?"[1]

"He knows I'm interested in you," said Barnet.

"Have you told him about us?" asked Blanche with a little gasp.

"No, but he knows it," Barnet said. "He says you are wearing his ring—that you are going to marry him. Is that so?"

Blanche took a moment to answer. "Perhaps," she said at last. "If I did, it would be through selfish motives. He has money—his father is very wealthy. You know how desperately I wish to study music abroad." She paused for a moment before adding: "But I am not in love with him."

"Then it is the promise of Europe?" he said, a trace of bitterness in his voice. "Nevertheless, he has made it perfectly plain to me that he wants you and means to marry you. He said I was to keep out of this."

"How did he come to tell you so much?" Blanche asked.

"Well, you know what good friends we are," said Barnet with only the slightest hint of irony. "I knew all about your affair from the beginning. He told me all about you, how gay and alive you were, how much in love with life."

Barnet took a long drag on his cigarette before expelling the smoke from his nostrils. "I know what happened on the yachting trip. He told me that you were a virgin."

A flush rose to Blanche's face—not of shame but of anger. Clearly, Roland had let it be known, either directly or by implication, that he had deflowered Blanche on board the *Monhegan*. It wasn't the dishonesty of the claim that upset her. She prided herself on being a free spirit, a woman who had overcome the benighted sexual attitudes of her puritanical mother. Had Roland proved capable of performing, she would happily have relinquished her virginity to him.

What sent the blood rushing to her cheeks was her sense of violation. To have been made the subject of such unseemly talk was, she felt, a terrible betrayal—not only by Roland but by Barnet as well.

"And what else did he tell you?" she said, making no attempt to hide her indignation.

"I'm sorry," he said. "I'm sorry this came up at all. I never intended that you should realize all I know."

"You must have thought I would be an easy mark," she said in the same scornful tone. "That's what men usually think, isn't it, if they know a woman has already capitulated once to a man?"

"Stop!" he cried. "Don't say that! You insult both yourself and me. I've told you I'm crazy about you."

A short time later, they drove back in silence to Alice Bellinger's brownstone. Barnet walked her into the dimly lighted vestibule. In her hands, she clutched the bouquet of gardenias he had brought her. She was still upset at Barnet. But as they stood facing each other in the faint light that filtered in through the delicate grillwork of the entrance doors, she felt the stirrings of that "ecstatic something" which existed between them.

She began to say good night, but before the words were out of her mouth he took her in his arms. "You are trembling," he said in a voice thick with emotion. "I won't let you go."

Then they were kissing madly.

That night, after Barnet had left, Blanche found herself unable to sleep. Her thoughts were not on her departed lover, but on the man who—even while claiming her as his future bride—had spoken so cavalierly about such intimate matters. “There smoldered within me,” she writes in her memoirs, “a wordless displeasure and the sense of an injury which I felt Roland had dealt to me.”

The next day, she telephoned Roland at the club and demanded that he come see her at once. He arrived within the hour.

“There followed a stormy interview,” Blanche writes. “A meeting between us full of bitterness and reproach.”

Pulling the *mizpah* ring from her finger, she tossed it onto a table. It bounced from the surface, rolled across the floor, and came to a rest in a far corner of the room.

“Why did you discuss with Barnet what you ought to have kept inviolate?” she cried. “There are things between us that ought to be deep and secret. But you talked of them—boasted to him!”

Roland stiffened, as if he had taken a blow. “That’s a damned lie. I’ve known Barnet for a long time,” he said coldly. “I know the sort of man he is. He will have a fling with you—then forget all about you.”

“You think that?” she said scornfully.

“Has he said anything about marrying you?” Roland asked. “I’ll wager he has not.”

“We’ve never discussed it,” Blanche said. “You yourself know I’m not interested in being married—not now. I want my music and a career.”

“I’ve offered you both,” said Roland. “But why prolong this? It’s getting us nowhere.”

He reached for his hat, which he had tossed onto a chair. “It is ended, you say? Very well, if that’s the way you wish it.” His voice was steady and cool. He bowed to Blanche, then crossed the room.

Just before he disappeared through the doorway, he paused, looked back at her, and with a hard, bitter laugh, said, “Tell Barnet the coast is clear—he wins.”

It was the same apparent admission of defeat he had made to Harry Cornish. And like Cornish, Blanche had no way of knowing just how ominous those words really were.

17

By 1898, Sigmund Freud had already embarked on his fearless exploration of the unconscious mind. Among his many discoveries was a phenomenon that seems particularly relevant to the case of Roland Molineux.

Freud describes it in an essay called "On the Universal Tendency to Debasement in the Sphere of Love," which deals with "psychical impotence"—that is, impotence rooted in psychological, as opposed to physiological, causes. Men who suffer from this disorder, according to Freud, are not totally impotent. They are able to sustain an erection—but only with prostitutes or partners they view as degraded. With their well-brought-up wives or other respectable women, they find themselves unable to perform. As Freud puts it: "Where they love they do not desire and where they desire they cannot love."[1]

Certainly Roland Molineux seems to fit this pattern. After all, he had engaged in sex with Mamie Melando—an uneducated factory girl and part-time prostitute—for nearly a decade. With the well-bred Blanche, however—a woman from his own social circle who shared his class biases and cultural pretensions—he apparently suffered from a disabling inhibition.

There is another, less psychoanalytic, explanation for Roland's behavior with Blanche. Evidence strongly suggests that he had contracted a venereal disease from Mamie, the symptoms of which had begun to manifest themselves by 1897.[2] Sexual debility, shame, or possibly the fear of infecting the woman he planned to marry might have kept him from consummating his relationship with Blanche.

Whatever the case, one thing seems clear: between his sexual problems with Blanche, her attraction to the more virile Henry Barnet, and Harry Cornish's gloating victory over him at the Knickerbocker Athletic Club, Roland Molineux, in the waning days of 1897, suffered a series of humiliations that could not fail to undermine his sense of manhood.

Little is known about Roland's life in the months following his falling-out with Blanche. Though he joined the New York Athletic Club at the invitation of his friend Bartow Weeks, he continued to live in his room in the paint factory, where despite their breakup, he received an occasional unbidden visit from Mamie Melando. It was during this period—so the evidence suggests—that he also began frequenting some of the city's less savory haunts.

Throughout the 1890s, "slumming" was a popular pastime among the smart young members of the better classes. Looking for cheap thrills in the seedy precincts of lower Manhattan, they visited the dance halls, dives, and other vice-ridden hangouts, where they mingled with showgirls, "dope fiends," and prostitutes of both sexes.

Their tour guide, more often than not, was a colorful character named George Washington "Chuck" Connors. A onetime bouncer who affected a gaudy costume of "bell-bottom trousers, a blue-striped shirt, a bright silk scarf, a pea jacket and big pearl buttons everywhere," Connors became the public face of the Bowery: a lowlife impresario who squired parties of upper-class slummers around the various "degenerate resorts," and even set up his own bogus opium den where his customers could gawk at "a white woman named Lulu and a half-Chinese man named Georgie Yee, who posed as addicts."[3]

There were, of course, a considerable number of actual opium dens in Chinatown: dark, squalid cellars where the noisome air was thick enough "to float wooden chips." There, for a fee of twenty-five cents, a person could lay on his side on a narrow shelf, his head pillowed on a wooden block, while the proprietor prepared the narcotic in a clay-bowled pipe, then extended the bamboo stem to the smoker.[4]

While a look inside an opium den was de rigueur for the serious slummer, few were moved to sample the product, let alone smoke it on repeated occasions. Only someone with a strong taste for the forbidden and a serious bent for disreputable behavior would be drawn to such an experience.

Someone like Roland Molineux.

Blanche and Barnet, in the meanwhile, continued their affair, conducted largely under the roof of Alice Bellinger's home, where Barnet had taken to spending the night.[5] Blanche rarely set foot inside the Knickerbocker Athletic Club anymore. A rare exception occurred in the spring of 1898, when she attended the yearly Amateur Circus as Barnet's guest—a delightful evening for Blanche, capped by an unchaperoned visit to her lover's second-floor bedroom.

For six months, neither one of them saw or heard from Roland. But Roland wasn't in hiding.

He was simply biding his time.

He reappeared suddenly, and as if by accident, on a summerlike evening in the second week of May. Barnet had promised to take Blanche to one of her favorite dining places—the restaurant of the Claremont Hotel, whose terrace offered a spectacular view of the Hudson and the Palisades.

She had dressed for the occasion in a flowing chiffon gown, a broad-brimmed spring hat tied with a matching chiffon scarf, and long white kid gloves.[6] A gardenia, presented to her by her unfailingly attentive lover, was pinned to her dress at the base of the V formed by her deep cut neckline.

As the two of them descended the stoop of Alice Bellinger's brownstone, they noticed a man standing at the curb, apparently about to step inside a waiting hansom cab. Drawing closer, they were startled to see that it was Roland Molineux. In the months since they had last set eyes on him, he had grown a large handlebar mustache.

Concealing his surprise with what Blanche described as "admirable savoir faire," Barnet greeted him warmly. "We were just on our way to the Claremont for dinner," he said after the two men shook hands. "Come along, won't you?"

Blanche hastened to second the invitation. "Won't you come? Please do," she urged. "It's such a heavenly evening. You will come, won't you?"

Roland, however, merely regarded them coolly. "It sounds delightful," he said with audible irony. "But thanks, no. I'm only in town for a short time tonight. I'm going over to Brooklyn."

"You're sure you won't join us?" asked Barnet.

"I think not," Roland said dryly. His eyes, Blanche noticed, "were suddenly hard." With a curt "good night," he turned and entered the cab.

For the rest of the evening, even as Blanche tried to focus on Barnet and the splendor of the riverside setting, her mind kept reverting to Roland. She thought of his "calm, cold indifference—that note of sarcasm in his voice—that tightening about his mouth, drawing it to that thin immobile line." It was clear that he still harbored a bitter resentment.

As for herself, she was aware that something powerful had been stirred in her by seeing him again, though she was "unable to interpret" her emotions. One thing, however, was certain: the brief, seemingly fortuitous encounter with Roland had left her with a "strange feeling of uneasiness."[7]

18

It's conceivable that Roland just happened to be standing outside Alice Bellinger's home when Blanche and Barnet walked out the front door. In view of subsequent events, however, it seems far more likely that he had come there with a specific purpose in mind—likely, to renew his relationship with Blanche. If that was indeed the case, he clearly hoped to have a private moment with her. It is hardly surprising that he reacted so badly when he found her heading out for a romantic evening with Barnet.

Seeing her on the arm of his rival might have been galling to Roland. But it did not deter him from his goal. On the contrary, it only seemed to strengthen his resolve. Despite his apparent capitulation to Barnet, Roland meant to have Blanche back.

First, though, there were certain problems that he had to take care of.

Nicholas Heckmann, forty years old, owned a small advertising agency located at 257 West Forty-second Street in Manhattan, not far from Jim Wakeley's saloon. To bring in extra income, Heckmann also rented out private letter boxes at the rate of fifty cents per month.

At approximately ten minutes past six on the evening of May 27, 1898—just a few days after Roland Molineux's encounter with Blanche and Barnet—the door to Heckmann's office opened and in strode a well-dressed gentleman who looked to be in his thirties. Though he did not know the gentleman's name, Heckmann recognized him right away, having passed him many times on the street. He was of medium height, with a slender, athletic build and the air of a man of breeding. He had strikingly handsome features and sported a large handlebar mustache.

Did Heckmann rent letter boxes? the gentleman inquired.

Heckmann confirmed that he did and quoted his rate.

"Very good," said the fellow, who explained that he wished to take a box for at least three months.

Heckmann got out his ledger, and seeing that box 217 was available, assigned it to his new customer.

"Name, please?" asked Heckmann, pen at the ready.

As Heckmann inscribed the information, the man looked down and, spotting a misspelling, pointed out that there was only one *t* at the end of his name. Heckmann made the correction.

Then, after paying for three months in advance, the gentleman—who had given his name as "Mr. H. C. Barnet"—turned and left the building.[1]

Dr. Vincent G. Hamill, a graduate of the University of Buffalo, was president of the Marston Remedy Company, headquartered at 19 Park Place in Manhattan. It was a thriving business, serving as many as twelve thousand customers each year, all of them male and all responding to the company's widely distributed advertising circulars:

PERFECT MANHOOD
AND HOW TO ATTAIN IT

A BOOK FOR MEN MARRIED AND SINGLE

A full explanation of a wonderful method for the quick restoration of

PERFECT MANHOOD, in all that term implies.

A method that overcomes EVERY EVIL CONDITION of the sexual system.

Gives to the weakest organs and parts their NATURAL VIGOR AND TONE.

And to those shrunken and stunted their NORMAL AND PROPER SIZE.

IT EXPLAINS how to build up all sexual vigor.

IT EXPLAINS how to avoid all the physical evils of married life.

IT EXPLAINS how to cure sexual weakness in any stage for all time.

IT EXPLAINS how to cure unnatural losses from dreams, in urine, etc.

IT EXPLAINS how to cure nervousness, trepidation, lack of self-confidence.

IT EXPLAINS how the entire sexual system of the male may be brought to that condition so essential to general good health and peace of mind.

IT EXPLAINS how to develop, strengthen, enlarge all weak, stunted, undeveloped, feeble organs and parts of the body which have lost or never attained a proper and natural condition, whether through early errors, ill-health, or other causes.

IT EXPLAINS how to be free from degrading thought, superior to debasing conditions, to feel

A VERY KING AMONG MEN!

The book, along with a one-month supply of an accompanying medicinal "remedy," cost five dollars. On May 31, 1898, Dr. Hamill received a letter, signed "H. C. Barnet." It contained the necessary amount of cash with a request that the manual and impotence remedy be mailed to box 217, 257 West Forty-second Street.

Dr. Hamill immediately sent back a "diagnosis blank," a four-page confidential questionnaire that potential patients were required to answer "as carefully as possible," so that—as the instructions explained—"a full and perfect understanding of each case may be had, and the proper remedies selected." There were sixty-three questions altogether, beginning with the applicant's age (given as thirty-one) and occupation ("clerk"), and continuing on to the most intimate matters of sexual functioning.

In answer to question thirty—"Have you had gonorrhea?"—the applicant answered yes. He went on to reveal that he had masturbated ("practiced self-abuse," in the idiom of the time) for ten years; that his erections were "very feeble"; and that "during connection" (sexual intercourse), his ejaculations were "very long delayed."

He was also asked for the size of his waist and chest, which he gave as thirty-two inches and thirty-seven inches, respectively.

On June 6, one day after Dr. Hamill received the completed form, the book and impotence medication were mailed out to the person who identified himself as H. C. Barnet but whose measurements, as he gave them, were those of a man with a far trimmer physique.[2]

Dr. Hamill was not the only peddler of impotence "remedies" in the latter years of the nineteenth century. Far from it. The 1890s were the golden age of patent medicines, a totally unregulated era when the American marketplace was flooded with snake oil. Generally compounded of little more than alcohol, opiates, and enough bitter-tasting ingredients to give them a suitably medicinal flavor, these high-sounding nostrums—Dr. Pierce's Golden Medical Discovery, Munyon's Miracle Phosphate, Horsford's Neuralgia Tonic, and thousands more—promised to cure every ailment known to man, from head colds to consumption, asthma to arthritis. Beyond inducing a mild state of intoxication, however, they had no effect at all.

Over a two-week period, beginning on June 4, 1898, packages addressed to Mr. H. C. Barnet arrived on an almost daily basis at his private letter box at Nicholas Heckmann's establishment. Virtually all of them contained marriage manuals, books of sexual advice, and guaranteed cures for impotence. Some of the latter came in liquid form, like Dr. Rudolphe's Specific Remedy for Impotence, sold by a physician named Fowler of Moodus, Connecticut. Others consisted of tablets or capsules, like a product called Calthos, touted in full-page newspaper ads as "the greatest sensation in the medical world today."

The purported invention of the "famous French specialist, Prof. Jules Laborde," Calthos had (so its maker claimed) restored the "vital forces" of countless satisfied customers, including several thousand male insane-asylum inmates, who had been reduced to their pitiable condition by youthful self-abuse. Anyone who suffered from "Lost Manhood or weakness of any nature in the Sexual Organs" could receive a free five-day trial treatment by sending a request to the manufacturer, the Von Mohl Company of Cincinnati, Ohio.[3]

On June 1, 1898—at precisely the same time that the man calling himself H. C. Barnet was sending out his requests for various remedies—an envelope of a distinctive blue color arrived at the Manhattan office of Dr.

James Burns. In addition to his private practice, Dr. Burns sold a mail-order nostrum called the "Marvelous Giant Indian Salve." Supposedly concocted from a secret Native American recipe—"buffalo tallow combined with healing herbs and barks"—Dr. Burns's ointment was, according to its ads, a "guaranteed, permanent" cure for male "atrophy." For twenty-five cents in cash, money order, or stamps, a sample box would be "mailed in a plain wrapper."[4]

The blue envelope was opened by Dr. Burns's bookkeeper, Agnes Evans, who was struck by the elegance of the enclosed sheet of stationery. It was the same robin's-egg hue as the envelope and embossed with a crest of three interlaced silver crescents. "Please find enclosed 25 cents, for which send remedy, and oblige," read the handwritten note.

The sender gave his return address as 6 Jersey Street, Newark, New Jersey—the location of the Morris Herrmann and Company paint factory. The letter was signed "Roland Molineux."

19

In the middle of June—after daily trips to his private letter box at Heckmann's—the man who called himself Mr. H. C. Barnet suddenly stopped picking up his mail. His disappearance coincided with the departure of Roland Molineux for a summer trip to Europe.

When Roland returned at the end of August—minus his mustache—he took a room at Travers Island, the New York Athletic Club's summer home on the Long Island Sound. He retained his living quarters at the Newark paint factory, though he rarely spent the night there anymore. He also made regular trips to Manhattan. Some of these were business-related.

Others had to do with matters of a more personal nature.

The offices of the Jersey City Packing Company—Henry Barnet's employer—were located in the Produce Exchange Building, a vast, imposing structure in lower Manhattan, long since demolished but once considered a landmark of architectural design.

On a morning in late August, not long after Roland Molineux's return from his European vacation, a small, slender package arrived in the mail, addressed to "H. C. Barnet, Room 342, Produce Exchange." Barnet was out of town, so his office-mate, a salesman named James J. Hudson, set the package aside.

When Barnet returned a few days later, Hudson handed him the package. Barnet tore off the light-colored wrapping and exclaimed in surprise.

Inside was a small white box containing a number of white, powder-filled capsules. The box, which had a sliding top, was labeled "Calthos, five days' treatment. The Von Mohl Company, Cincinnati, Ohio."

There was no accompanying message or note, nothing to indicate why the pills had been sent to Barnet. Certainly he had no need for them, never having suffered from the condition for which Calthos was purportedly a cure.

With a shrug, he stuck the little box in the side pocket of his jacket. Later, he put it in a drawer of his desk and forgot about it.[1]

20

Though Blanche was an old woman by the time she wrote her memoirs, she describes the key events of her earlier life in novelistic detail. She recalls precisely what gown she was wearing when she performed at Carnegie Hall with the Musical Arts Society, the way the sunlight sparkled on the water the day she met Roland aboard the yacht *Viator*; the furnishings of the room in which she and Henry Barnet first made love.

So it seems odd—and highly significant—that she is unable to say exactly what happened on that fateful afternoon in early September 1898, when, with startling suddenness, she renounced her relationship with Barnet and reconciled with Roland.

True, she remembers that it happened over lunch at the Waldorf-Astoria. She recalls the table by the "great windows that opened on Fifth Avenue" and the "throngs of passersby" visible through the panes. She even remembers that she and Roland dined on filet of sole and drank white wine.

But as for what brought about her sudden change of heart, she claims a complete loss of memory. "In some way—I hardly remember—Molineux and I bridged the separation between us" is all she writes of that moment.[1]

It is hard not to conclude that Blanche is being deliberately evasive here, that she simply prefers not to recall—or not to confess—the real reason for her surprising turnaround. Still, it is possible to speculate.

We know from her memoirs that Blanche's dearest dream was to visit Paris. It was a dream, as she had discovered by then, that she was unlikely to realize as the wife of Henry Barnet, whose financial circumstances were far less comfortable than Molineux's. Roland himself had just returned from a month-long vacation in Europe—proof positive that it was he, not Barnet, who was more likely to give her the kind of life she craved. Indeed, had Blanche accepted his earlier proposal, she would have been at his side on his trip. Her dream would already have come true.

While it is fair to assume that Blanche made some such calculation on that autumn afternoon, it is impossible to know exactly what was going through her mind. One thing is certain: by the time she left the restaurant, she had agreed to give up Barnet and marry Roland.

"Before the end of our luncheon," she writes in her memoir, "I had promised Roland I would again wear his ring—and this time with a pledge!"

However Roland managed to persuade Blanche to marry him—whatever inducements he offered—he couldn't change her feelings for Barnet. In the days following the luncheon at the Waldorf, she found herself "consumed" by thoughts of her lover. His "influence over" her—that power "which from the beginning had so swept me off of my feet"—had in no way diminished. Try as she might "not to think of him," she yearned "to see Barney."

She left messages at his club but received no reply. Finally, after a protracted silence that left her baffled and hurt, he telephoned her at Alice Bellinger's.

Yes, he knew about her engagement to Molineux, he said. He had "heard about it from someone at the Racquet Club." Despite the coldness in his voice, the mere sound of it brought a terrible longing to her heart. "I suddenly wanted him back more than anything in the world."

He agreed, somewhat reluctantly, to see her. They met in her apartment on an evening in late September. Barnet was understandably angry. What did Blanche expect of him? he demanded. She had erected an insuperable barrier between them by agreeing to wed Molineux.

"That is silly," she said. "There are no barriers. Can't we remain friends?"

He gave a harsh laugh. "That is ridiculous."

"But why?" she persisted.

"Good God!" he cried. "Molineux knows perfectly well that you and I have been seeing each other. You must know that. He hates me!"

"That is preposterous," Blanche said. "You two are old friends. He doesn't hate you."

"The enmity is veiled," said Barnet. "But if he ever knew I saw you again, it would be open hostility. You ought to know that. This is good-bye—it has to be."

Before Blanche could respond, Barnet took her in his arms and "kissed her with savage abandon." Then, pushing her away from him, he turned and strode from the room.

Blanche followed him into the hallway and "cried out to him" as he hurried down the stairs. But Barnet, turning a deaf ear to her pleas, "made no reply."

"I stood there on the lower landing of the stairway," Blanche writes in her memoir. "I believed he would return. But he went straight out the door."

She never saw Henry Barnet again.

21

In addition to his duties as night watchman of the Knickerbocker Athletic Club, Joseph Moore, a forty-year-old Englishman, performed valet services for various members, including Henry Barnet.

Early on the morning of Friday, October 28, 1898, Moore received an urgent summons to Barnet's room. He found the thirty-two-year-old clubman stretched out on his bed, ashen-faced and clutching his stomach. The normally dapper Barnet was wearing only an open-collared shirt and trousers, as though he'd been stricken while getting dressed for the day. His breakfast—which had been brought up to his room earlier—lay untouched on its tray.

"Moore," gasped Barnet. "Call Dr. Phillips."

Hardly had he spoken the words than Barnet let out a moan, leapt from the bed, and ran for the toilet. As Moore made for the staircase, he could hear the sound of violent retching through the closed door.[1]

The residence of Dr. Wendell C. Phillips, a surgeon at the Manhattan Eye and Ear Hospital and a longtime member of the KAC, was located on Madison Avenue, only a block away from the clubhouse. By 9:00 A.M.—less than fifteen minutes after Joseph Moore dispatched an errand boy to his home—Phillips was standing at Barnet's bedside.

"Hello, old man," he said. "What's the matter?"

Before Barnet could answer, he was seized with a spasm of sickness and had to dash for the bathroom, where he suffered another bout of simultaneous vomiting and diarrhea. Minutes later, he staggered back to bed, a ghastly pallor suffusing his face.

Phillips checked his pulse, which seemed normal. He also examined Barnet's throat. There was some inflammation of the membrane, though in Phillips's professional opinion, "no more than would be present when a person was vomiting."[2]

Phillips concluded that Barnet was suffering from "an irritant substance in the stomach" and asked if he had eaten anything unusual.

"It was that damned Kutnow's Powder," answered Barnet with a groan.

He explained that, after overindulging in food and drink the previous evening, he had awakened at around eight that morning feeling unwell. As it happened, he had received a sample tin of Kutnow's Improved Effervescent Powder in the mail two months earlier. Supposedly made of salts from the Carlsbad mineral springs, Kutnow's—a competitor of bromo-seltzer—was promoted as a surefire remedy for "biliousness, sick headache, loss of appetite, sour stomach, constipation, drowsiness, nervousness, gout, jaundice, and rheumatism." Potential customers could receive a free sample by sending in a letter with their name and address.[3]

Barnet wasn't sure *why* the little tin had been sent to him, since he hadn't requested it. Still, as he was in the habit of treating his hangovers with Kutnow's, he didn't think twice about taking a dose. Almost immediately, however, he had gotten dreadfully ill.

Phillips went downstairs to telephone a local pharmacy for some remedies. He then returned to sit with Barnet, who lay shivering beneath a heavy wool blanket when he wasn't in the bathroom throwing up and voiding uncontrollably.

After an hour or so, Phillips returned to his home, leaving Barnet in the care of Joseph Moore. Phillips checked on his patient two more times during the day. By 5:30 P.M., Barnet seemed greatly improved—so much so that, as Dr. Phillips would later testify, he saw "no reason to come again."[4]

Though the vomiting and diarrhea had abated by the following day, Barnet still couldn't eat. Swallowing food was too painful. His throat was agonizingly sore. Even his tongue hurt.

On Sunday, October 30, he went downstairs for the first time in two days and sought the advice of a friend, Colonel Austen, who suggested that Barnet get a second opinion from Henry Beaman Douglass, a fellow KAC member and prominent New York physician. A telephone call was promptly placed to Douglass's home.

A graduate of the College of Physicians and Surgeons, Douglass had interned for two years at Presbyterian Hospital, then studied overseas in Paris, London, and Berlin before returning to New York. In addition to his private practice, he served as adjunct professor of diseases of the throat at the Post-Graduate Medical College and assistant surgeon and pathologist at the Manhattan Eye and Ear Hospital.

Within a half hour of receiving the call, Douglass arrived at the Knickerbocker Athletic Club. He found Barnet in the café with Colonel Austen. Leading the doctor into the adjoining reading room, Barnet explained what had happened on Friday after he had swallowed the Kutnow's Powder.

"I was a damned fool to take something that came in the mail," he said. He then described his current symptoms—the burning throat and painful tongue.

"Well, I can't examine you here, old man," said Dr. Douglass.

Taking the elevator to the second floor, they proceeded to Barnet's room, where Douglass peered into Barnet's throat and saw (as he later testified) a "membrane on the right tonsil and uvula." He immediately concluded that Barnet had a case of diphtheria.

Leaving Barnet in his room, Douglass went out to a drugstore called Schoonmaker's, where he purchased two culture tubes. He then returned to the club, took samples from Barnet's tonsil, and departed again, this time for his lab in the Manhattan Eye and Ear Hospital.

When the cultures were analyzed, they revealed "streptococci in large numbers," though no evidence of "diphtheritic bacilli." Nevertheless, Douglass remained convinced that Barnet had a mild case of diphtheria and treated him accordingly, with injections of antitoxin.[5]

Over the next few days, Barnet—who was attended around the clock from that point on by two trained nurses, Addie Bates and Jane Callender—seemed to be in a convalescent state, though his tongue and gums continued to bother him.

By Friday, November 4, Barnet's mouth was still inflamed and his tongue ulcerated. Curious about the content of the Kutnow's Powder, Douglass brought the sample tin (which Barnet had saved) to a chemist named Guy P. Ellison for analysis.

No sooner had Ellison removed the cover of the tin than he detected the odor of bitter almonds, typical of "salt of cyanide." Taking a tiny amount on the tip of one finger, he tasted it and found that the Kutnow's had a "metallic, corrosive taste," also characteristic of cyanide.

Ellison then performed a series of tests on the powder—first adding hydrochloric acid, then iodide of potassium, and finally heating it slowly in a test tube. The results clearly showed that the Kutnow's Powder contained cyanide of mercury.[6]

When Douglass received the report, he decided that the sores on Barnet's tongue and gums were probably "mercurial stomatitis"—an inflammation of the mucous membranes of the mouth produced by the ingestion of mercury. But that conclusion set off no alarm bells in Douglass, who saw no reason to alter his original opinion.

It's natural to wonder why—when Dr. Douglass found evidence that Barnet had ingested mercury and pharmacist Ellison discovered cyanide in the Kutnow's Powder—neither of them suspected that the patient was the victim of foul play. The answer, bizarre as it seems, is that both mercury and cyanide, along with many other toxic substances, were standard medicinal ingredients in the late nineteenth century.

The soothing syrups and aromatic bitters and revitalizing tonics so popular in that elixir-crazed period might have been utterly worthless, giving great-grandma a mild high while allowing whatever disease was killing her to run rampant through her system. But the medications prescribed by legitimate physicians were often no better, and in many cases far worse. American medicine in the post–Civil War era had not yet emerged from the Dark Ages, as even a cursory glance at the 1899 edition of the venerable textbook the *Merck Manual* makes alarmingly clear.

It was a time when formaldehyde was routinely prescribed for the common cold, arsenic for asthma, strychnine for headaches, morphine for diarrhea—and mercury for everything from anemia to yellow fever. A woman with morning sickness might be treated with a heaping spoonful of belladonna, a constipated man with a cup of turpentine oil, and a colicky baby with a chloroform-soaked rag placed over its nostrils. Gargling with cyanide of mercury was a recommended cure for sore throats.[7]

It was clear to Dr. Douglass that Barnet had consumed mercury. But then, so had millions of other Americans who customarily took calomel, one of the most commonly prescribed remedies of the time. In addition to its supposedly salubrious effects, calomel (also known as mercurous chloride) frequently produced ulcerations of the tongue, gums, and throat, caused teeth to fall out, and occasionally destroyed entire jawbones.

In short, despite the absence of "diphtheritic bacilli" in the culture and the presence of cyanide of mercury in the Kutnow's Powder, Dr. Douglass was absolutely convinced that the symptoms displayed by Barnet pointed to only one diagnosis: a case of mild diphtheria.

22

There had been no communication between Blanche and Barnet since their stormy confrontation several weeks earlier. But her ex-lover—the man who had awakened her to a "full realization of sex"—was always on her mind.

During the first week of November, a dinner was to be held for General T. L. Watson, president of the New York Athletic Club. Roland was one of the organizers. Invitations had been issued to select members of rival clubs, including the Knickerbocker. Blanche, who always enjoyed these affairs, became even more excited when she learned that Barney was on the guest list.

She was keenly disappointed, therefore, when word reached her that Barnet was too ill to attend. She was also surprised. "I recalled how strong and vital he was, in what apparently perfect health," she would record in her memoir. "I was anxious for more detailed news and called the club to make inquiries. They repeated only what I already had learned, that he was suffering from a serious attack of diphtheria."[1]

When Roland arrived at Alice Bellinger's a short time later, Blanche rushed to meet him at the entranceway.

"Barney is ill," she cried. "Under the care of physicians at the club. Have you heard?"

"Yes," he calmly replied.

"I want to send him flowers," she said. "And a message."

Using Alice's telephone, Blanche called Thorley's Flower Shop and ordered a "huge box of shaggy chrysanthemums." "They seemed more appropriate for a man," she writes in her memoir. "They lacked cloying perfume and possessed a sort of rugged beauty."

She also wrote a letter to Barnet. Enclosing it in an envelope, she called a messenger, who conveyed it to Thorley's, where it was placed inside the flower box. The letter read:

> I am distressed to learn of your illness. I arrived home Saturday. I am so exceedingly sorry to know that you have been indisposed. Won't you let me know when you are able to be about? I want so much to see you. Is it that you do not believe me? If you would but let me prove to you my sincerity. Do not be cross any more and accept, I pray you, my very best wishes.
>
> YOURS, Blanche

Blanche waited to hear back from Barnet. But she never received a reply.[2]

The flowers were not delivered until early the following day, Monday, November 7.

Barnet was asleep when they arrived. When he awoke, his day nurse, Addie Bates, told him that he had received a big bunch of lovely chrysanthemums, along with a note.

Barnet asked her to read it to him. Addie proceeded to do so. When she was done, he closed his eyes and, in a voice barely above a whisper, said, "I wonder how she knew I was ill?"[3]

Two nights later—at around 4:00 A.M. on November 9—Barnet awoke from a troubled sleep and struggled out of bed.

He had been growing weaker by the day and seemed so unsteady on his feet that his night nurse, Jane Callender, urged him to lie back down at once.

Barnet refused. Despite the sponge baths he had been receiving, he felt unbearably filthy and was determined to give himself a thorough washing. Above the objections of Miss Callender, he made his way to the bathroom and shut himself inside.

When he emerged a half hour later, he barely had the strength to make it back to his bed.

Alarmed at his condition, Nurse Callender telephoned Dr. Douglass, who arrived at the Knickerbocker in short order. A brief examination of Barnet was all Douglass needed to see that his patient was in the throes of heart failure.

Barnet's brother, Edmund, was immediately summoned to his bedside. At Edmund's urging, two other physicians were called in for an emergency consultation. Each examined Barnet in turn. Each confirmed Douglass's grim diagnosis.

Barnet clung to life for another ten hours. His death, late in the afternoon of Thursday, November 10, 1898, was officially attributed to a weakened heart caused by diphtheria.[4]

A memorial service for Henry Crossman Barnet was held at the Church of the Ascension on Fifth Avenue and Tenth Street in Manhattan at 2:00 P.M. on Saturday, November 12. A tearful Blanche was among those in attendance.[5]

Exactly one week later, she took part in another ceremony. On Saturday, November 19, 1898, at the Church of Heavenly Rest on Fifth Avenue and Forty-fifth Street, Roland Burnham Molineux—as he had long vowed to do—took Blanche Chesebrough for his lawful wedded bride.[6]

The Knickerbocker Athletic Club

Part Three

DEGENERATE

23

When Joseph Pulitzer purchased the *New York World* in May 1883, a typical front page consisted of a half dozen columns of densely packed type, unrelieved by illustrations or eye-catching headlines. Viewed from a slight distance, the page resembled a solid block of gray print, so dreary in appearance that the layout was referred to as a "tombstone."[1]

The content was equally numbing. On May 10, 1883—its last day under the ownership of the financier Jay Gould—the *World* ran page-one stories on the recent nominations submitted to the Board of Aldermen, the forthcoming dedication of the Brooklyn Bridge, and the election of the executive committee of the American Cocker Spaniel Club. Little wonder that the paper had a daily circulation of fewer than twelve-thousand copies and was losing $40,000 a year.[2]

All that changed the moment Joseph Pulitzer got hold of it. An immigrant, Pulitzer saw himself as a champion of the weak and oppressed. The *World,* as he conceived it, would be a paper "dedicated to the cause of the people rather than to that of the purse potentates." In an early editorial, he laid out his goals, a ten-point program that included "punishing corrupt office holders," along with levying taxes on luxuries, inheritances, large incomes, monopolies, and "privileged corporations."[3]

His method of achieving these lofty aims was to appeal to his readers' lowest instincts. After all, he reasoned, the best a publisher could do was to "go for a million circulation, and when you have got it, turn the minds and the votes of your readers one way or the other at critical moments."[4] And the most effective way to reach that million circulation was by printing the kind of wildly sensationalistic stories that ordinary people have always gobbled up.

He lost no time in putting his plan into action. The very first issue of the *World* edited by Pulitzer featured front-page stories on a New Jersey fire that claimed the lives of a half dozen people; the last hours of a convicted killer who had beaten his wife to death in a drunken rage; the public execution of another murderer, a hard case named M'Conkey who went to his death cursing his jailers; a deadly lightning bolt that killed a man on Long Island; and a dynamite attack by Haitian rebels that left four hundred victims dead or wounded.[5]

The following days brought more of the same: headline stories about human sacrifices performed by religious fanatics; a little boy killed when his pony stumbled and fell on top of him; a smallpox scare in Hoboken; a killer tornado in Kansas; plus assorted homicides, suicides, holdups, beatings, and even a grave robbery.[6] By the following March, a typical week brought such attention-grabbing headlines as A CHILD FLAYED ALIVE; A BRUTAL NEGRO WHIPS HIS NEPHEW TO DEATH IN SOUTH CAROLINA; STRANGLED BY ROBBERS; DIED A DESPERADO'S DEATH; A LADY GAGGED IN A FLAT; and QUINTUPLE TRAGEDY—AN ENTIRE FAMILY ANNIHILATED BY ITS HEAD.[7]

The very look of the paper underwent a radical alteration. Headlines now stretched over several columns or were splashed across the entire top of the page. And there were cartoons, caricatures, lurid illustrations, and other voyeuristic visual aids. Not only were grisly murders reported in graphic detail; they were diagrammed so that readers could picture the horrors more clearly. When, for example, a New York City clergyman named Klemo slashed his wife to death in their fourth-floor apartment, then cut his own throat and hurled himself from the window, the story was accompanied by a drawing of the crime scene with a helpful alphabetical key:

> A—Door stained with blood; B—Window stained with blood from which Klemo leaped; C—Bed covered with blood; D—Table set and covered with blood; E—Chair in which Mrs. Klemo sat; F—Sink in which knife was found; G—Pool of blood.[8]

Soon, Pulitzer had added a Sunday supplement, providing readers with such uplifting Sabbath fare as "a long treatise on weapons used to commit murder in recent years, including a nail, a coffin lid, a red-hot horseshoe, an umbrella, a matchbox, a window brush, and a tea kettle"; "an account of the careers of two Vienna cutthroats who had specialized in courting lonely women and then murdering them"; "a description of life in the death house at Sing Sing"; a "thrilling narrative of cannibalism at sea"; and the supposedly true-life tale of an English explorer thrown into a pit of vipers by "fiendish" African tribesman.[9]

Pulitzer's sensationalistic strategy succeeded beyond all expectation. By March 1885, the *World* had a daily circulation of more than 150,000 copies—an astonishing tenfold increase in less than two years. That figure would double again before the end of the decade.

The age of yellow journalism had arrived.

Before his expulsion from Harvard in 1886, William Randolph Hearst—pampered heir to a mining fortune—had served as the business manager for the college humor magazine the *Lampoon.* The experience had awakened in the aimless young man a keen interest in journalism. Studying the various dailies from New York and Boston, he found himself enthralled by Pulitzer's newly reinvigorated *World.* Everything about it—from its crusading zeal to its shameless sensationalism—filled him with admiration. "If a man can be in love with a newspaper," declares his best-known biographer, "Hearst was downright passionate about the *World.*"[10]

As it happened, Hearst's father, George, owned a paper himself. In 1880, the elder Hearst—a shaggy-bearded ex-prospector who had struck it rich in gold, silver, and copper—had purchased the *San Francisco Examiner* as a propaganda tool to advance his political ambitions. Though George would eventually get elected to the United States Senate, the paper was a financial disaster, losing more than a quarter-million dollars during the years he controlled it.[11]

George's boy, Willie, thought he could do better. While still in college, he wrote a letter to his father, insisting that the *Examiner* could turn a profit by imitating publications like the *World*—"that class [of newspaper] which appeals to the people and which depends for its success upon enterprise, energy, and a certain startling originality." Illustrations were important, too, since they "attract the eye and stimulate the imagination of the lower classes."[12]

Twenty-four-year-old William got a chance to put his theories into practice in March 1887 when—after spending a year as a reporter for the *World*—he persuaded his father to give him the *Examiner*. Emulating Pulitzer, he set about creating a paper that, as one of his first employees put it, would fill readers with the "gee-whiz emotion."[13] Like Hearst's later publications, the *Examiner* was less a traditional newspaper than a "printed entertainment—the equivalent in newsprint of bombs exploding, bands blaring, firecrackers popping, victims screaming, flags waving, cannons roaring, houris dancing, and smoke rising from the singed flesh of executed criminals."[14]

Within a week of taking it over, Hearst was already trumpeting the *Examiner* in half-page advertisements such as THE MONARCH OF THE DAILIES! with THE MOST ELABORATE LOCAL NEWS, THE FRESHEST SOCIAL NEWS, THE LATEST AND MOST ORIGINAL SENSATIONS![15] Determined to "startle, amaze, or stupefy" readers on a daily basis, he served up the subjects that have always thrilled and titillated the public: scandal, sentimentality, sex, gossip, disaster, adventure.

And always, of course, crime, depravity, and murder—the more shocking the better.

24

With his genius for journalistic showmanship, Hearst quickly turned the *Examiner* into a phenomenon. Within a few years, it had gone from albatross to cash cow, becoming the second most profitable newspaper in the United States.[1]

In the meantime, Hearst had come into a fortune from his ever-indulgent mother, who sold her shares in the fabled Anaconda mine and gave the money to her son. Now a multimillionaire on his own, he set out to realize a long-cherished dream. In 1895, he laid out a pittance for a moribund paper, the *New York Journal*, bought an apartment in Manhattan, and proceeded to challenge his mentor, Joseph Pulitzer, for newsstand supremacy.

Over the next few years, the two men engaged in a furious competition for readers. With his bottomless pockets, Hearst launched a raid on his rival's workforce, at one point hiring away the entire staff of Pulitzer's Sunday edition in a single piratical swoop.[2] Determined not simply to entertain readers but to "convulse [them] with excitement,"[3] he took the sensationalistic tactics pioneered by Pulitzer and raised them to a frenzied new level. HAD FOUR WIVES; FIENDISH PARENTS; ALIVE IN A COFFIN; and TOTS BURNED TO DEATH were just a few of the front-page headlines in the weeks after Hearst took control of the *Journal*.[4]

His newly designed Sunday supplement offered even racier fare: lavishly illustrated features on sex, crime, and a dizzying array of oddities, all conveyed in a breathless, believe-it-or-not tone. Typical of these offerings was an article about the unspeakable rituals ostensibly performed by members of a Cuban serpent cult:

SNAKES ARE THEIR GODS
CUBAN DISCIPLES OF THE DEVIL HAVE HIDEOUS MIDNIGHT ORGIES

ALONE IN THE MOONLIGHT SAVANNAHS THEY DISPORT THEMSELVES LIKE FIENDS

BEAUTEOUS SINUOUS MULATTO GIRLS AT THE "DANCE OF THE ADDER" IN THE WITCH DOCTOR'S VILLAGE

EATING SNAKES TO WARD OFF EVIL[5]

Few things, of course, were better for circulation than a good, juicy homicide. Not content with merely describing murders in the most graphic possible detail, Hearst found ways to insert his paper into the investigations. He organized a "murder squad" of crime reporters to do their own detective work, ran regular articles taunting the police for their inefficiency, and enlisted the help of the public in solving crimes.

When a dismembered male torso and a portion of thigh washed up in the East River in June 1897, for example, Hearst turned the atrocity into a contest, trumpeting a "$1,000 Reward for Solution." He ran a page-one drawing of a man's body—resembling one of those butcher charts that indicate the different cuts of beef—so that readers could more easily visualize which limbs were still missing. And he assigned thirty crack reporters to the case, who managed to track down the killers while the police were still groping for clues.[6]

Mutilation-murder, however, wasn't the emblematic crime of the Gilded Age. Our own fascination with serial killers reflects the obsessive anxieties of our particular era: issues having to do with moral breakdown, the dangers of sex, and the profound vulnerability of our bodies.[7] In the age of Pulitzer and Hearst, the American public was afflicted with a different set of concerns. At a time when people could never be certain of what they were putting into their bodies—when medicines were made of strychnine and arsenic, bakers preserved their dough with sulfur of copper, babies consumed "swill milk" from cows fed on distillery waste, and soldiers received rations of "embalmed beef"—the knife-wielding psycho wasn't the boogeyman that haunted the imagination of the American public.

It was the poisoner.

25

Given the ubiquity of serial killers in our movies, TV shows, and paperback thrillers, a person might be forgiven for thinking that our country is crawling with homicidal psychopaths. In reality, the number of serial killers at large in the United States at any given time is, relative to the total population, infinitesimal: no more than fifty, according to the most reliable FBI estimates. The average citizen, in other words, is far less likely to be stabbed by a psycho while taking a shower than to slip in the bathtub and die.

The same sort of disparity existed in the nineteenth century in regard to poisoners. According to one crime historian, "poisoning accounted for less than one percent of murder cases that entered the criminal justice system" in the 1800s.[1] And yet, poison-murder was everywhere in the popular culture of the time. At least a hundred true-crime books were devoted to the subject, while writers of "sensation novels, detective stories, and other popular fiction turned frequently to poisoning as a plot device."[2]

Gilded age newspapers were quick to exploit the public's fascination with poisoners. During one month-long span in the late 1800s, the New York City dailies ran no fewer than five poison-related headlines: POISONED COLOGNE SENT TO BROOKLYN GIRL; ARSENIC IN JELLY; HIRED TO POISON A CHILD; GRANDMOTHER ACCUSED OF POISONING NEIGHBOR'S WELL; and POISON IN WINE PRETTY GIRL INDUCED HER LOVER TO DRINK. Even an instance of alleged pet murder—DOG DEAD BY POISON, SAYS MASTER—made the front pages.[3]

Several poisoning cases became bona fide media sensations. In 1891, for example, New York City was riveted by the story of Carlyle Harris, a medical student who murdered his young wife by putting a lethal dose of morphine in her sleeping pills. The following year, a Manhattan physician named Robert Buchanan used the same narcotic (mixed with some belladonna to conceal the symptoms of poisoning) to rid himself of his own wife, a former brothel keeper he had wed for her money. Shortly after Buchanan's trial came to an end, yet another physician, Dr. Henry Meyer, was convicted of murdering an acquaintance with arsenic and antimony as part of an insurance scam.

And then there was the irresistibly lurid case of the San Francisco femme fatale, Mrs. Cordelia Botkin.

The estranged wife of a fellow with the unlikely name of Welcome A. Botkin, Cordelia was thirty-eight years old in 1892—already past her prime in an era when a woman of forty was considered to be "in the cold and constricting clutch of middle age."[4] "Time had laid upon her the unkind stigmata of full-blown maturity," as one commentator puts it.[5]

Despite her advanced years, however, she possessed a powerfully seductive charm and, in September of that year, embarked on an affair with a young cad named John P. Dunning, a journalist ten years her junior with a wife and children of his own in Delaware. Their liaison lasted for nearly six years, until Dunning, tired of his "maturely alluring" lover, broke off the relationship and decamped for Cuba to cover the Spanish-American War as a correspondent for the Associated Press.

Not long afterward, on the afternoon of August 9, 1898, a package arrived at the Dover, Delaware, post office addressed to Dunning's wife, Elizabeth. Inside was a box of chocolate bonbons, along with a handwritten note reading: "With love to yourself and baby. Mrs. C."

That evening, after a dinner of trout and fritters, Mrs. Dunning sat on the porch and shared the treats with her older sister, her nephew and niece, and two young neighbors, Misses Bateman and Millington, who had stopped by for a visit. A few hours later, all six became violently ill. The children and the two young ladies eventually recovered, but Mrs. Dunning and her sister—who had devoured the lion's share of the candies—died painfully a few days later. Autopsies revealed the presence of lethal doses of arsenic in the viscera of both women, a finding confirmed when the leftover bonbons were analyzed by chemists.

John Dunning was immediately summoned home. He needed only a glance at the handwritten note to know who had sent the package. "Cordelia!" he gasped, then—"broken with grief and abased with shame"[6]—he proceeded to spill out the story of his affair with Mrs. Botkin.

The San Francisco papers quickly got wind of the investigation, and Hearst's *Examiner* turned the case into a full-fledged media circus. His "murder squad" located the confectionery store where the bonbons had been purchased, traced the arsenic to a local drugstore, and tracked down Cordelia Botkin herself, who had taken refuge at her sister's house in St. Helena. One of Hearst's ace women reporters, Lizzie Livernash, immediately sped to Mrs. Botkin's side and, ingratiating herself with the fugitive, wangled a series of interviews that were splashed across the *Examiner*'s front pages.

The frenzied coverage of Mrs. Botkin's trial, which began in early December 1898, boosted the already sky-high circulation of the *Examiner* to stratospheric new heights, proving that few stories could sell more papers in that era than a poisoning case with the right sensational ingredients. Hearst, then in the thick of his newspaper war with Joseph Pulitzer, could only hope that fate would supply him with an East Coast version of the Botkin affair, which he could exploit to equally dramatic effect in the *Journal.*

And then—even before Mrs. Botkin's inevitable conviction was handed down—fate obliged.

26

On Saturday, December 24, 1898—one year almost to the day since his gloating triumph over Roland Molineux—Harry Cornish arrived for work at his customary time, shortly after ten in the morning. As usual, he first checked his mailbox. Along with several letters, the box contained a surprise: a small package, wrapped in manila paper and tied with string. The wrapping bore several canceled postage stamps and a handwritten inscription:

MR. HARRY CORNISH
KNICKERBOCKER ATHLETIC CLUB
MADISON AVENUE AND FOURTY FIFTH STREET
NEW YORK CITY.

There was no return address.

Curious, he carried the package upstairs to the gymnasium and settled himself at his desk. When he tore off the wrapping, he discovered a pale blue gift box from Tiffany's. Removing the lid of the box, he found, at one end, a small receptacle resembling a silver candlestick, its lip and the rim of its base adorned with a beaded design.

At the other end of the box, separated by some crumpled tissue paper, was a small bottle labeled "Emerson's Bromo-Seltzer." With the manufacturer's wrapper removed, the bottle fit perfectly into the silver holder.

Cornish did not examine the bottle very carefully. Had he done so, he might have observed some odd features. The bottle appeared to be used, its label badly soiled as though from repeated handling. It was also smaller than the average bromo-seltzer bottle, and of a darker shade of blue.

Cornish's assistant, Patrick Fineran, and a club member named Harry A. King were standing beside the desk when Cornish opened the package. The three men chuckled. Clearly the gift was a practical joke—an amusing warning for Cornish not to overindulge during the upcoming holidays.

At Fineran's suggestion, Cornish—who had tossed the wrapping paper into his wastebasket—fetched it out and scissored off the address. Perhaps he might be able to identify the anonymous sender at some later time by the handwriting. Cornish stuck the scrap of paper into his desk drawer and turned his attention to other matters.

King, who was suffering from a mild headache, picked up the bromo-seltzer bottle in its sterling silver holder and carried it to the water cooler, just outside the gymnasium door. Somewhat to his annoyance, the cooler was empty. He returned the bottle, unopened, to Cornish's desk—unaware that he had just been the beneficiary of an extraordinary stroke of good luck.[1]

For the past two months, Cornish had been boarding with his distant cousins, Mrs. Katherine Adams—a sturdily built widow of sixty-two—and her grown daughter, Florence Rodgers, who was then separated from her husband.[2] When Cornish returned from work that evening and told the two women about his gift, they teased him about it, joking that it must have been sent by an unknown lady admirer.

Three days later, on Tuesday, December 27, Cornish brought the silver holder and the medicine bottle back to the apartment. As it happened, the design on the holder closely matched the pattern on Florence's toiletry items—her silver-handled brush, comb, and mirror. Cornish told her to keep the holder; he placed the bromo-seltzer bottle on the dresser in his bedroom.

That evening, Cornish and the two women attended the theater, then went for a late supper at the Colonial Cafe on Columbus Avenue and Eighty-second Street, where Mrs. Adams imbibed one too many glasses of wine.[3]

The next morning, December 28, Florence arose at her usual time, around 9:00 A.M. Emerging from her bedroom, she found her mother seated at the dining room table, looking very pale and pressing a moist compress to her forehead.

"Are you all right, Mother?" she asked.

Mrs. Adams replied that she had awakened with a bad headache. She had been up for an hour or so, puttering around the apartment in an effort to "work off" the pain. But the headache had only gotten worse. Was there anything in the house for her to take?

Florence was about to answer no when she remembered the bromo-seltzer her cousin had brought home the previous evening. Stepping to Harry's bedroom, she knocked on the door.

Cornish had been awake for the past half hour. He had washed up, dressed, and was now seated in his room, reading the newspaper, which was left outside the apartment door each morning by the building hallboy.

When Florence asked for the bromo-seltzer, explaining that her mother was feeling ill, he handed her the bottle and returned to the paper.

A few minutes later, he heard her call his name. Responding to her summons, he carried his paper into the dining room, where he found her seated beside her mother at the table.

"I can't get it open, Harry," she said. "Can you try?" She passed him the bottle and went off to use the bathroom.

Taking her seat, Cornish examined the mouth of the bottle. It was sealed with wax and tightly stoppered with a cork. With no corkscrew in the apartment, he was forced to make do with the tines of a dinner fork. After several minutes of concentrated struggle, he finally managed to work the bottle open.

"You'll need half a glass of water," he said, reading the directions on the label.

Mrs. Adams rose and repaired to the kitchen, returning a few moments later with two glasses, one empty, the other half full.

The directions specified a heaping teaspoonful of the bromo-seltzer. After banging on the bottle to dislodge some of the powder, Cornish poured it into the empty glass. Mrs. Adams then added the water from the other glass, stirred the mixture with a spoon, raised the glass to her lips, and sipped.

"Awful," she said with a grimace, setting the glass down on the table.

Indeed, the taste was so disagreeable that she'd been unable to finish the dose. A small amount remained at the bottom of the glass.

Cornish picked it up and took a swallow. "Tastes all right to me," he said. "It's supposed to be bitter—it's medicine." Then, he took up his paper and went back to his reading, while Mrs. Adams turned and left the room.

In view of our contemporary concerns about product tampering, it seems almost unbelievable that anyone would casually ingest medication received through the mail from an anonymous sender. That both Mrs. Adams and Harry Cornish (and others, too, as events would prove) did so without a second thought reveals something about their era, though exactly what is hard to say. Perhaps people were simply more trusting back then. Certainly, they paid little heed to the ingredients of the Kilmer's Acid Phosphate, Carlsbad Sprudel Salt, Cascarets Candy Cathartic, Peruna Catarrh Tablets, and countless other nostrums they routinely put into their bodies.

It was also true that the person who had mailed Cornish the bottle had taken care to make it appear unopened, sealing it with paraffin and enclosing it in its original manufacturer's wrapper.

Precisely how long it took for the potion to do its work is unclear—two minutes, three minutes, perhaps as many as five. Florence Rodgers was still in the bathroom when the door suddenly flew open and her mother burst inside, her face a sickly color. Staggering across the floor, she bent over the bowl and began to vomit loudly.

The window opened onto an air shaft, and Florence—embarrassed that the neighbors might hear her mother retching—asked her not to make so much noise. She then left the bathroom, assuming that her mother was having a bad reaction to the bromo-seltzer.

No sooner had Florence reached the dining room, however, than she heard her mother emit a "peculiar cry" (as she later described it). She immediately dashed back into the bathroom. Raising her head from the bowl, Mrs. Adams—whose complexion was now a ghastly blue—lifted her hands toward her daughter, then collapsed onto the tiled floor. Florence sprang to her mother's side and tried to raise her, but to no avail. "She was a dead weight," Florence later said, recalling the horror of the moment. Terrified, she shouted for Harry.[4]

Hearing his cousin's cry for help, Cornish rose from his chair. His legs felt oddly weak. By the time he made it into the bathroom, he was afraid he might throw up. Fighting back the nausea, he knelt beside Mrs. Adams's body and attempted to raise her. Though he normally could have carried her "as easily as a child," he found that he did not have the strength to lift her from the floor.[5]

With the assistance of a house guest, Fred Hovey—an old family friend who had spent the night at the Adams apartment—Florence and Harry managed to carry Mrs. Adams into the dining room and set her down on the sofa. Cornish then made for the front door and shouted for the hallboy.

"Get the doctor at once," he said. "Tell him that Mrs. Adams collapsed after taking some medication. Run!"

A few minutes later, at approximately 9:35 A.M., Dr. Edwin F. Hitchcock was seated in his office at 72 West Eighty-seventh Street when the hallboy burst in and conveyed the message. Quickly gathering up his emergency kit—which included a pair of hypodermic needles, a stomach siphon, and three tablet cases—he strode to 61 West Eighty-sixth Street and proceeded upstairs to the second floor. At the top of the landing, he saw a small group of people clustered outside the Adams apartment. They parted to make way for the doctor as he hurried inside.

Mrs. Adams lay unconscious on the sofa, drawing harsh, agonized breaths. Her complexion was blue, her features contorted with pain. At his first glance of the stricken woman, Dr. Hitchcock assumed that she had ingested some variety of irritant poison. Bending to the body, he made a quick examination. Her pulse was barely detectable, her forehead cold and clammy. He could see that she was near death.

Immediately, he went into action. He loosened her clothing, applied warm compresses to her chest, held ammonia to her nose, slapped her on the face, injected her with stimulants—whiskey and a small dose of sulphate of strychnine—and gave her artificial respiration.

While he worked, he put some questions to her daughter, who sat at one end of the sofa, cradling her mother's head in her lap. Florence explained what had happened—how her mother had gotten terribly ill after taking a dose of the bromo-seltzer that her cousin Harry had received in the mail a few days earlier. As Hitchcock kept up his hopeless efforts,

Florence clung to the desperate belief that her mother was simply "in a faint." Even when Mrs. Adams's jaw went slack and her bosom ceased its convulsive heaving, she wouldn't accept the truth. She continued to wave an open phial of ammonia beneath her mother's nose, trying to revive her.

From somewhere else in the apartment, Dr. Hitchcock could hear the sound of violent retching. "Who's that?" he asked Florence.

Explaining that it was Harry—who had taken the same medication that had sickened her mother—Florence urged Hitchcock to run in and help him. She would stay there with her mother.

Hitchcock found Cornish in the bathroom, bent nearly double over the toilet bowl, retching violently. Fred Hovey was holding Cornish's head. Hitchcock turned up the light from the gas jet and peered into the bowl to see if he could tell anything about the poison from the look of Cornish's ejecta. But the bowl was empty, Cornish having long since emptied the contents of his stomach.

When Cornish asked for something to quell the retching, Hitchcock refused. Though not an expert on poisons, he knew that copious vomiting was recommended for such cases.

Leaving Cornish with Hovey, Hitchcock returned to the dining room and resumed his efforts. He knew, of course, that they were futile. Mrs. Adams was already dead. But he wanted Florence to feel that everything humanly possible had been done for her mother.

Several minutes later, Cornish entered the dining room on wobbly legs, his normally ruddy complexion replaced by a blue-tinged pallor. Shakily, he lowered himself onto one of the chairs. The bottle labeled bromo-seltzer still sat on the table. Cornish picked it up and passed it to Hitchcock.

"Do you have any idea what this might be?" he asked hoarsely.

"Well, it's evidently not bromo-seltzer," said Hitchcock, examining the bottle.

Licking the tip of his pinky, he stuck his finger into the bottle and extracted a small quantity of the substance. He then brushed his fingertip lightly across the lapel of his jacket, knocking away all but a small particle, which he placed on the tip of his tongue.

Instantly, he tasted bitter almonds and knew that he had just ingested half a grain of one of the deadliest poisons in existence—cyanide.

Almost immediately, he began to feel sick. Taking a swig of whiskey to revive himself, he asked if Cornish felt strong enough to go for help.

Cornish rose to his feet and nodded.

Hitchcock asked him to go fetch Dr. E. Styles Potter, a colleague who lived two blocks away. In sending Cornish on this errand, Hitchcock had several motives. He wanted to keep Cornish moving and get him out in the open air. He also feared that he himself might soon be incapacitated (if not killed) by the poison he had just sampled.

While Cornish was gone, Hitchcock continued to work on Mrs. Adams's body, partly to keep himself active, partly to satisfy Florence Rodgers, who still begged him to help her mother. About ten minutes later, Cornish returned with Dr. Potter, who needed just a quick look at Mrs. Adams to see that she was (as Hitchcock later put it) "perfectly dead."[6]

Potter then turned his attention to the two poisoned men. After satisfying himself that they were in no danger of dying, he took a linen napkin from the dining room table and gently covered Mrs. Adams's face, while Florence Rodgers—unable to deny the truth any longer—buried her own face in her hands and wept.

27

By then, Cornish's nausea had subsided, though he'd begun to suffer from severe abdominal pain. A lesser man would have taken to his bed. Cornish, however, had no patience for any display of male weakness, particularly in a crisis.

Dr. Hitchcock had informed him that, in all likelihood, the coroner wouldn't arrive until nightfall—an intolerable delay as far as Cornish was concerned, since it meant that Mrs. Adams's corpse would remain in the apartment all day, in full view of her daughter. It was, as Cornish later put it, a most "unpleasant" prospect.[1]

Cornish had an acquaintance in the district attorney's office, a fellow named McIntyre, who might be able to expedite matters. Throwing on his overcoat, he left the apartment and made his way to the elevated train at Eighty-first Street.

No sooner had he boarded the car than he was seized by an intestinal spasm so acute that he was forced to hurry off at the next station and find the nearest bathroom. After relieving himself, he continued on his journey, though he had to leave the train four more times in frantic search of a toilet.

It was nearly 2:00 P.M. by the time Cornish made it to the DA's office. After a brief conversation with McIntyre, who agreed to telephone the coroner, Cornish took the trolley to the office of his closest friend, John Yocum, a chemist working for the United States Leather Company and a fellow KAC member. Yocum, who had boarded at the Adams residence before taking a room at the club, was shocked by the news and alarmed at Cornish's dreadful appearance. Perhaps a drink, he suggested, would help settle his friend's stomach. They repaired to a nearby saloon, where Cornish had a glass of whiskey and milk, which he immediately threw up. Giving Cornish his room key, Yocum urged him to go straight to the club and lie down.[2]

Ignoring this advice, Cornish first traveled to the Rose Street office of his cousin, Lewis, to deliver the unhappy news. Only then did he head for the club. Once again, the trip turned into an ordeal. He had just boarded the trolley when an explosion seemed to detonate deep in his bowels. Quickly disembarking, he made for the nearest saloon, where he shut himself in the bathroom for more than an hour. When he finally emerged, his legs were so wobbly he could barely walk. Eventually, he managed to make it to the club, where he dragged himself upstairs and collapsed onto Yocum's bed.

Cornish had never felt worse in his life. He summoned an errand boy, who ran to fetch Dr. Wendell Phillips, but Phillips wasn't home. Fortunately, another physician, Dr. Lewis Coffin, was visiting the club at the time. Hearing that Cornish was unwell, he proceeded to the room.[3]

He found Cornish shivering under the bedclothes, his face a ghastly gray and dark circles under his eyes. He looked as though he'd been sick for a month. Turning down the blankets and sheet, Coffin saw that the patient was tympanitic: his stomach was so grotesquely distended that he appeared to be pregnant, and he was belching intestinal gas. His pulse was weak and intermittent.

Concluding that Cornish was suffering from acute gastric enteritis, Coffin went downstairs to the telephone and ordered stomach and rectal tubes from a local pharmacy. They had just been delivered when Dr. Phillips—who had returned home to find an urgent message waiting—showed up at the club.

Working side by side, the two physicians threaded a tube down Cornish's throat and flushed his stomach with a solution. The "return matter" was (as Phillips later testified) "a thick, ropy mucus, so thick and ropy that when Dr. Coffin put his hand into the vessel and then lifted the matter up, it would string out all the way down."[4]

Another tube was then inserted into Cornish's rectum and his bowels were washed out. Like the previous procedure, this operation produced a "most inordinate amount of mucus, almost exactly the same as the return flow from the stomach, with the exception that it contained some blood."[5]

From the symptoms, Phillips was convinced that the patient was suffering from "irritant poisoning." Cornish's pulse was so weak that the doctors were afraid to let him get up to use the bathroom. Going home was out of the question. Coffin prescribed strychnine and caffeine to stimulate his heart, along with bismuth and salol to soothe the inflammation of his stomach and bowels.

The two doctors remained at Cornish's bedside for about an hour and a half. Before returning home, Phillips took Coffin aside. Something seemed to be troubling him.

It was odd, he said. This was the second time he'd been called to the club to treat a case like this. He mentioned no names, but Coffin—a frequent guest at the KAC—knew he was referring to Henry Barnet.[6]

28

The story broke in the papers on the very day of the murder, when the *Evening Journal* ran half a column on its second page. KILLED BY POISON SENT AS GIFT, read the headline. The article went on to relate the principal features of the case: Cornish's receipt of the Tiffany box containing a bottle labeled "bromo-seltzer" along with a small "silver stand"; Mrs. Adams's agonizing death upon "taking a dose from the phial"; Dr. Hitchcock's fruitless attempt to revive her "by the Silvester artificial respiration process"; Cornish's own terrible illness after sampling the remedy. Hitchcock was quoted as saying that, in his opinion, "the powder in the phial was cyanide of potassium." The article concluded by noting that "A peculiarity of the address on the package sent to Mr. Cornish was that the street name Forty-fifth Street was spelled 'Fourty fifth Street.'"[1]

Shocking as it was, there was little in this story to differentiate it from a dozen other recent poison-murders. Indeed, just the day before, the *Journal* had printed a page-one article about a still-unknown culprit who had poisoned the pancakes at a Paterson, New Jersey, rooming house, "putting the lives of the entire household in jeopardy" in order to kill his intended victim, a boarder named George Naef.[2] Certainly, the public had no reason to suspect that they were about to be treated to one of the most rabidly covered stories in the annals of American crime.

All of that changed on the following day, when, having sicced their newshounds on the story, the masters of the yellow press plastered their front pages with competing accounts of the crime. For William Randolph Hearst, the murder of Katherine Adams was a sensation-monger's dream come true: New York City's very own equivalent of the Cordelia Botkin case. The *Journal*'s headline on the morning of December 29 played up the similarity by comparing Mrs. Adams to Mrs. Botkin's intended target: MRS. KATE ADAMS KILLED LIKE MRS. DUNNING, BY POISON SENT THROUGH THE MAILS.[3]

Pulitzer's *World*, meanwhile, managed to best its bitter rival with a sensational scoop: DOUBLE MURDER MYSTERY IN A NEW YORK CLUB, screamed the headline. Crowing that it had "unearthed a chain of circumstances that may greatly assist the police in unraveling one of the most mysterious crimes of recent occurrence in New York City," the paper detailed the "strangely similar circumstances" surrounding the death of Henry Barnet, another member of the Knickerbocker Athletic Club who had recently "received a bottle containing what appeared to be a harmless remedy."[4]

There were significant discrepancies between the Hearst and Pulitzer accounts. According to the *Journal*, for example, Assistant DA John McIntyre believed that "the party suspected of sending the package to Mr. Cornish is at present out of . . . state." The *World*, on the other hand, quoted McIntyre as stating that "clues . . . point to certain persons who are not far away."[5] Both papers agreed, however, that there was only one "direct clue" that might lead to a break in the case: "the handwriting on the package that . . . was received by Mr. Cornish through the mail at the Knickerbocker Athletic Club."

Nowadays (at least if TV crime shows are to be believed), such a significant piece of evidence would be scanned with an electron microscope, studied with a fiber-optic fluorometer, tested for DNA, and checked against a national biometrics database, leading to the swift and sure identification of the culprit. In the late nineteenth century, however, forensic science was still in its infancy.

The world's first criminological lab had been established only fifteen years earlier by an employee of the Parisian police department named Alphonse Bertillon, who devised a way of keeping track of criminals by collecting detailed data about their distinctive physical traits, from the span of their arms to the length of their left middle fingers. Bertillon's "anthropometric" method, however, was good for only one purpose—identifying repeat offenders—and required little more in the way of equipment than a camera and tape measure.

Even a technique as basic today as fingerprinting (which would eventually render Bertillon's cumbersome system obsolete) had not yet been widely adopted in the late 1800s, though its essential principles had been discovered decades earlier. In 1858, a British civil servant in India named William Herschel began insisting that the native businessmen he dealt with "sign" their contracts with inked handprints. Over the next two decades, as he collected thousands of these "hand-mark" specimens, he realized to his amazement that the ridged patterns on the ends of the fingertips always differed from person to person and could therefore be used (as he wrote in a letter) as an "infallible method of identification."[6]

Simultaneously—and independently of Herschel—a Scottish physician and amateur archaeologist named Henry Faulds, while working in Tokyo, was struck by the distinctive "finger-tip impressions" left in pieces of ancient Japanese pottery. Taking up the study of the different "skin-furrows in human fingers," Faulds quickly concluded that these markings were not only unique to each individual but remained unchanged throughout a person's lifetime. In 1879, when a neighbor's home was burglarized, Faulds was able to identify the culprit by comparing the suspect's fingerprints to a sooty smudge left on a whitewashed wall at the crime scene. Recognizing the forensic importance of his discovery, Faulds published a letter in the British science journal *Nature* in which he declared that "bloody finger-marks or impressions on clay, glass etc., . . . may lead to the scientific identification of criminals."[7]

When Herschel learned of Faulds's piece, he wrote his own letter to *Nature*, asserting his claim to priority. In the meantime—while the two men launched a bitter dispute that would last for decades—the famed British anthropologist Sir Francis Galton turned his own attention to the subject and, in 1892, published a landmark book that set forth the first practical system for classifying fingerprints.

It was a police official in Argentina named Juan Vucetich, however, who first demonstrated the full potential of fingerprinting for solving serious crimes. The Croatian-born Vucetich (né Ivan Vucetic) immigrated to Buenos Aires in 1884 at the age of twenty-six. Within a year, he had gone to work for the La Plata police department and quickly rose through the ranks. Assigned the task of setting up a criminal identification bureau in 1891, he became intrigued by the technique of fingerprinting after reading an article about Galton's work in a French science magazine.

Armed with an ink pad and roller, Vucetich began collecting all the specimens he could, fingerprinting everyone from newly arrested prisoners to the mummies at the city museum. Before long, he had worked out a classification method that made small but significant improvements to Galton's system, affording police an efficient way of matching crime scene prints with archived identification records. He called his technique *dactyloscopy* (Latin for "finger description") and began to vigorously promote it in self-published pamphlets.

His superiors, however, remained skeptical—until fate supplied a startling vindication. In July 1892, a ghastly crime occurred in the coastal town of Necochea. A young boy and girl, the illegitimate children of a twenty-five-year-old woman named Francisca Rojas, were found murdered in their blood-drenched bed, their heads caved in. The hysterical mother blamed a man named Velazquez, a middle-aged, somewhat simple-minded laborer on a nearby ranch.

According to the story Rojas told the police, Velazquez was madly in love with her and had begged her to marry him. Rojas, however, was in love with someone else—a younger, far handsomer man. When she informed Velazquez of her feelings, he had flown into a rage and threatened to exact a terrible vengeance. A few days later, as she returned home from the marketplace, she saw to her surprise that her front door was open. As she drew closer, Velazquez burst from the house and fled. Inside, she found her two slaughtered babes.

Velazquez was immediately arrested and subjected to a merciless interrogation. When he refused to confess, he was bound with ropes, placed on the bed beside the mangled corpses of his presumed victims, and forced to remain there overnight. Even this torture, however, failed to produce an admission of guilt. Stymied, the Necochea police called in help from La Plata, and an inspector named Alvarez was dispatched to the village.

As it happened, Alvarez had taken a keen interest in the experiments that his colleague Vucetich had recently done with fingerprints. Examining the crime scene, the inspector discovered a bloody smudge on the children's bedroom door and recognized it at once as a thumbprint. Sawing off the blood-marked piece of wood, he carried it to the local police station. He then brought in Francisca Rojas, took impressions of her thumbs with an ink pad, and examined them with a magnifying glass. Even to his untrained eye, it was clear that the markings of her right thumb matched the bloodstained print from the door.

Confronted with this evidence, Rojas immediately broke down. Her handsome young lover—so she tearfully confessed—had agreed to marry her only if she "got rid of the brats." She had done the job with a large stone, then—after disposing of the murder weapon in a well—set about framing Velazquez.[8]

The 1892 trial of Francisca Rojas for the double murder of her children resulted in a legal landmark: the world's first criminal conviction obtained from fingerprint evidence. Four years later, Argentina adopted Vucetich's system as the country's sole method of criminal identification. Other South American nations soon did the same.

Largely for reasons of cultural chauvinism, however, police agencies in Europe and North America were slow to follow suit. Dactyloscopy would not be fully accepted in the United States until 1911.[9] This was unfortunate. In all likelihood, fingerprint evidence would have led to a speedy resolution of the Adams case. As it was, the New York City authorities would be forced to rely on what was, at that time, state-of-the-art forensic science in the United States: handwriting analysis.

Handwriting analysis had first played a prominent role in an American courtroom during the so-called Howland will case of 1867. Two years earlier, a fifty-nine-year-old spinster, Sylvia Ann Howland of New Bedford, Massachusetts, had died and left more than two million dollars to various beneficiaries. Hungry to get her hands on the entire fortune, her thirty-year-old niece, Hetty Robinson—a legendary miser, later nicknamed "the Witch of Wall Street"—contested the will. In support of her suit, she produced a document, supposedly signed by her aunt, which left the entire estate to Hetty.

The trial, one of the most dramatic of its time, hinged on the authenticity of that single signature. Among the many experts called to testify were engravers, bank tellers, penmanship teachers, and various eminent scientists, including Oliver Wendell Holmes, Sr., and—most critically—the

Harvard mathematician Benjamin Peirce, who used statistical methods to show that the disputed signature was, in fact, a forgery.[10] None of these men was a professional handwriting examiner, for the simple reason that such a profession did not yet exist in the United States. The next twenty years, however, witnessed the rise of handwriting analysis as a distinct, supposedly scientific, discipline with a growing number of practitioners offering their services as forensic specialists.

Within twenty-four hours of Mrs. Adams's death, William Randolph Hearst had already commissioned an opinion from one of these experts. Prominently featured on page one of the December 29 *Evening Journal* was a box containing the conclusions of a noted graphologist named David S. Carvalho, who deduced that the sender was a man "past the age of thirty years" who had failed in his efforts to disguise his usual handwriting. Carvalho expressed the utmost confidence that "no difficulty will be encountered in locating the identity of this writing when brought into juxtaposition with known writing."[11]

Carvalho's profile of the sender was, in fact, more accurate than those of other self-professed "experts" who had weighed in on the matter and who confidently declared that the writer was a woman.[12] Still, as Carvalho himself suggested, it was impossible to identify the sender from this sample alone, not without another piece of "known writing" to compare it to.

For that, Hearst enlisted the assistance of the public. Alongside Carvalho's analysis, and running down almost the entire length of the front page, he printed a facsimile of the handwritten address from the poison package. WHO KNOWS THIS WRITING? blared the headline.

As it happened, someone did.

29

Dr. Phillips had good reason to worry about his patient. Cornish spent half the night passing bloody mucus from his bowels. At one point, he stayed shut in the bathroom for three hours straight.[1] A less able-bodied man might not have survived. Cornish's years of athletic training, however, stood him in good stead. By the following morning—Thursday, December 29—he was sitting up in bed. That afternoon, he was strong enough to receive a visit from his friend Assistant DA John McIntyre, who showed up in the company of Captain George W. McCluskey, chief of detectives.

Apart from his imposing physique (he was nicknamed "Chesty" in tribute to his massive upper torso), McCluskey looked more like a Wall Street broker than a cop. A dapper dresser and bon vivant, he liked to mingle with the moneyed crowd and made Delmonico's his unofficial headquarters. Despite his slick appearance, smooth manners, and expensive tastes, however, he was a shrewd, tough-minded lawman who had come up through the ranks and was touted by his admirers as the greatest detective of his time—New York City's answer to Sherlock Holmes.[2]

McCluskey and McIntyre remained with Cornish for several hours, questioning him about possible suspects. Try as he might, however, Cornish could think of no one who might want him dead.[3]

That evening, McCluskey met with reporters in his office at police headquarters, where he displayed the small silver holder and medicine bottle received by Cornish. Despite its elegant packaging, the holder was not, McCluskey reported, "of Tiffany's manufacture. It is marked 'Sterling,' but I don't think it is real sterling. It looks like a dry goods store article."

His examination of the holder, moreover, had convinced him that "it has been in use some time; it is not new"—a conclusion that casts serious doubts on McCluskey's supposedly Holmes-like powers of observation, since it would prove to be utterly mistaken.

At a glance, the bottle itself—cobalt blue and labeled "Emerson's Bromo-Seltzer"—appeared to be no different from the ones sold in pharmacies. It would, McCluskey explained, be turned over to a state chemist for further analysis.

Though the case was only a day old, rumors were already circulating that the DA's office and the detective bureau were working at cross purposes. McCluskey, however, was vehement in his denials, insisting that there was "absolute harmony" between the police and the district attorney. "This will be a record case in criminal history," he told the reporters, "and we want to help make it memorable by capturing and then aiding in the conviction of the murderer."[4]

Coming just twenty-four hours after the story first broke, this is a remarkably prescient—and revealing—statement. Clearly, McCluskey already understood that the hunt for Mrs. Adams's killer was about to turn into the hottest show in town—a sensational real-life melodrama in which he would play a starring role.

John McIntyre also spoke to reporters that evening. Ignoring the opinion of graphologist David Carvalho—who was certain that a male hand had inscribed the address on the poison package—the assistant DA declared his belief that the person who had mailed the doctored bromo-seltzer to Harry Cornish was a woman.

Reporters also solicited the comments of the coroner's physician, Albert T. Weston. Weston had little to say, though he did make one important announcement. "I have seen the contents of the bottle, and am positive that it is cyanide of potassium," he said. "I know this from the odor and from the peculiar appearance of the poison."[5]

Weston's definite identification of the deadly ingredient as cyanide of potassium would be trumpeted in the next day's papers. And like McIntyre's remark about the sex of the killer and McCluskey's comment on the secondhand condition of the silver holder, it would turn out to be wrong.

McIntyre, of course, was not alone in his opinion that Mrs. Adams had been killed by a member of her own sex. Apart from the truism that poison was the murder weapon of choice for women, the public was still keenly aware of the case of Cordelia Botkin, whose trial was under way even at that moment. Mrs. Botkin had dispatched her deadly candies after being spurned by her lover. It seemed entirely plausible that a similarly scorned and vengeful female had sent the poisoned remedy to Harry Cornish.

Reporters digging into Cornish's life had already uncovered tales of his checkered past, details of which had emerged during his divorce trial. According to the *World*, Cornish had led a life "filled with exciting incidents" during his brief stint as athletic director of the Chicago Athletic Club.

The article cited a cabbie named P. J. Smith who had testified that, on one occasion, he had driven Cornish and an unnamed woman to the St. Bernard Hotel, when "the woman's husband appeared and there was a row." Not long afterward, Cornish and several other "convivial young men" were dining at the Schiller Café with "two or three women, one of them being the woman of the St. Bernard affair." When "the wronged husband again appeared and suggested to his wife the propriety of going home," Cornish and his chums "fell upon the husband and tossed him into the street."[6]

That Cornish had not abandoned his womanizing ways since coming to New York was confirmed, to some observers, by his unorthodox living arrangements. Rumors were already flying that he and Florence Rodgers Mrs. Adams's daughter—were more than mere housemates.

Florence Rodgers herself became the subject of dark suspicions when, on the afternoon of December 29, several detectives arrived at her home to whisk her off to police headquarters.

Like the sites of other sensational murders, the apartment building where Mrs. Adams was killed—the Elliott, as it was called—had quickly become a magnet for the morbidly curious. From morning until nightfall, the sidewalk on Eighty-sixth and Columbus was so thronged with onlookers that residents had trouble entering and leaving the building. The janitor, flanked by "two colored hall boys," stood guard throughout the day, admitting only tenants and various officials, like Coroner Edward H. Hart and Dr. Weston, who showed up around four o'clock to perform the autopsy on Mrs. Adams.

An undertaker named Brown arrived shortly thereafter. It was Brown who got the crowd buzzing with excitement when he announced to the assembled reporters that Mrs. Rodgers was about to be arrested for her mother's murder.[7]

The scene that ensued—remarkable at the time—would be familiar in the coming century, when celebrities, attempting to get from one place to another, would be forced to rely on elaborate dodges to elude their pursuers. Not long after Brown made his stunning announcement, a carriage pulled up to the building. Guessing (correctly) that it had come to take Florence Rodgers downtown, the crowd swarmed around the vehicle. Seeing that he was about to be surrounded, the driver managed to maneuver the carriage halfway down the block. "The crowd," one reporter wrote, "rushed wildly after him."

Just then, a hand emerged from a window of Florence Rodgers's third-floor apartment and waved frantically to the driver, who—following the signal—drove his carriage around the corner to 72 West Eighty-seventh Street, directly behind the Elliott. As the crowd ran to catch up with the vehicle, two women dressed in black—Florence Rodgers and her friend Edna Hovey—slipped through an alley connecting the two buildings, ran down some stairs, and hurried into the carriage, followed closely by a detective named Maher. Before the crowd could descend upon it, the carriage "sped rapidly away."[8]

A similar scene awaited them at police headquarters on Mulberry Street, where an even larger crowd had assembled. Spotting the mob, the driver pulled around to Mott Street. Surrounded by several officers, Mrs. Rodgers and Mrs. Hovey were then smuggled into the rear of the station house. No sooner had they pushed through the glass doors than "a large group of people waiting in the main corridor made a rush to see them." As the crowd bore down upon her, Mrs. Rodgers was hustled into Captain McCluskey's office and the door was slammed shut.[9]

MRS. RODGERS A PRISONER IN ADAMS POISON CASE, screamed the headline in the evening edition of Hearst's *Journal.* Even before the paper hit the streets, however, the sensational claim had been discredited.

Florence Rodgers, it turned out, had come to headquarters at McCluskey's request to give her own version of events. She had answered questions for an hour, then been sent home. "Published stories that Mrs. Rodgers had been arrested for poisoning her mother are absolutely false," McCluskey declared. There was "not a particle of truth" to reports that she was a suspect.[10]

If any woman had reason to feel betrayed by Cornish, it was his ex-wife, Addie—and reporters lost no time in tracking her down at her home in Boston. Any suspicions that she might have been the source of the fatal package, however, were quickly dispelled by her sheer graciousness and candor.

Despite having been bitterly wronged by her ex-husband, Mrs. Cornish retained only the kindliest feelings for him. He was, she continued to believe, a good and decent man who had "made a great mistake in taking a course that made it necessary for me to secure a divorce. I believe he will realize it someday."

"When was the divorce granted?" asked her interviewer.

"It was on my birthday, April 3, 1897, in Chicago," she replied, then added with a rueful smile: "Not a very nice birthday present, was it?"

"Not unless one was anxious to be free," said the reporter.

"Well, I wasn't," Mrs. Cornish said softly. "It was none of my doing. But sometimes, we can't have things just the way we would like them, you know."

Asked if she knew of anyone who might wish her ex-husband harm, Addie Cornish shook her head. "I did not know that he had any enemies. He is a very popular man."

"But the popular man might excite the jealousy of a woman," the reporter suggested.

"That is true," said Mrs. Cornish. "But I am sure I can't imagine who it could be. As I say, I have really known nothing about Mr. Cornish's life, companions, or associates for three years. I am greatly relieved to know he is unharmed. When I heard there was bad news for me, I thought at once of my child and her father. I am glad both are well."[11]

Over in Hartford, Connecticut, however, Addie's former in-laws, Mr. and Mrs. DeWitt C. Cornish—to whom she still paid an occasional visit—had suspicions of their own. On Thursday afternoon, they sent a telegram to the Manhattan DA's office, where John McIntyre and a colleague, Maurice Blumenthal, were now working full-time on the case. In their message, Cornish's parents revealed that, when Harry was just nineteen, he had been carrying on an affair with a married woman whose husband had been harboring a grudge against their son ever since. Perhaps, they suggested, the betrayed man was the source of the poison package.

This theory was, rightly, dismissed out of hand, since it seemed wildly improbable that a cuckolded husband would wait sixteen years before seeking revenge. Still, the telegram—whose contents were immediately trumpeted in the press—added weight to the growing belief that something in Cornish's rakish past had come back to haunt him.[12]

That the yellow papers had decided to turn the Adams case into a full-blown media sensation became unmistakably clear on the morning of Friday, December 30, when Hearst's *Journal* plastered a three-column headline across its front page:

THE GREAT MURDER MYSTERY
Investigated by
Julian Hawthorne

The son of the great American novelist, Julian Hawthorne possessed none of his father's genius, though he made up in sheer productivity what he lacked in ability. By the time of the Adams murder, he had already published nearly fifty volumes, along with countless book reviews, sketches, and short stories. He had a particular fascination with mystery, the occult, and crime (a subject he would come to know intimately in later years when he was convicted of mail fraud and sentenced to a brief stint in a federal penitentiary).

Despite the slipshod quality of his writings (some of his novels were dashed off in a matter of weeks), Hawthorne enjoyed a solid commercial success, and the popularity of his books—combined with the eminence of his family name—made him a figure in turn-of-the-century America. In employing him as a commentator on the Adams case, Hearst was pioneering a practice familiar in our own time, when no media circus is complete without at least one celebrity author to report on the proceedings.

Hawthorne's piece on the Adams murder proceeds in a leisurely, long-winded manner that suggests he was being paid by the word. In it, he considers the various theories then floating around—including the possibility Cornish himself was the murderer. Hawthorne pooh-poohs this notion. Apart from the fact that there was not a single shred of evidence to implicate Cornish, poisoning was hardly Harry's style. The famed athletic director, writes Hawthorne, was "a masculine, brawny fellow who was far more likely to knock an enemy down than to buy cyanide of potassium to do away with him."

On the other hand, Hawthorne acknowledges that—however innocent of murder—Cornish was no saint. He had evidently conducted "some affairs on the sly" while still married and had "not led a chaste life" since his divorce. In the end, Hawthorne concurs with the prevailing opinion that the culprit was probably "a woman scorned by her former lover," and that "all the police have to do is *chercher la femme*."[13]

Despite Hawthorne's reputation as a keen student of crime, his deductions would prove to be no more astute than those of any other armchair detective. In the course of his article, however, he does make one highly apt observation, though it appears as a casual aside. Noting that one disadvantage of employing poison as a murder weapon is the difficulty in obtaining it, he writes: "It is not always easy to get good poison; it has to be bought at a shop."

Then, almost as an afterthought, he adds: "Unless, indeed, the murderer also happens to be a chemist himself."

The possibility that the culprit might be a chemist—off-handedly mentioned by Hawthorne—was raised far more seriously in another news item that ran on Friday morning. Interviewed by a reporter from *The New York Times*, a physician named W. H. Birchmore—described as "a recognized expert on cyanides"—asserted that "the person who sent the poison to Harry Cornish and which caused the death of Mrs. Adams was one who possessed a thorough knowledge of chemistry."

The interview took place at Birchmore's home on Adelphi Street in the Fort Greene section of Brooklyn—not far, as it happened, from the residence of General Edward Leslie Molineux. According to Dr. Birchmore, "the instances in criminal annals wherein hydrocyanic acid has been used as poison" were so rare as to be virtually unknown. The reason for this was the "the great danger in handling the poison, except in a large way and with the most complete facilities for doing so, and even then only with the utmost caution." Producing it in small batches was such an "extremely risky piece of business," said Birchmore, that "there is hardly a drug clerk in New York who would undertake to prepare the stuff."

Because of the sheer difficulty in obtaining the poison and the "expert knowledge necessary" to concoct it, Birchmore was certain that the killer was no ordinary person.

"I am convinced," he declared, "that none but a physician of understanding, a pharmacist above the average of understanding of such in chemical knowledge, or a person not necessarily in either of those professions but well versed in chemistry can be the poisoner in this case."[14]

That same Friday morning, forty-eight hours after he sampled the lethal glass of bromo-seltzer, Harry Cornish finally felt strong enough to leave his bed and venture downstairs. He was seated at his desk in the gymnasium when the club secretary, John Adams, came hurrying toward him, a sheaf of papers clutched in one hand. From the look on Adams's face, Cornish could see that he had something urgent to convey.

A trim, handsome man nearing forty, Adams had become friends with Herbert Ballantine when the two were classmates at Cornell. After graduation, he had worked as a journalist for nearly twenty years, spending the last four of those as assistant editor of *Harper's Magazine*. In 1896, he had left publishing to become Ballantine's private secretary. When the brewer bought the Knickerbocker Athletic Club, he had made Adams the club secretary.

Though not a trained graphologist, Adams had read and answered so many letters over the years—first as an editor, then as Ballantine's assistant—that he had developed a certain expertise in handwriting recognition. And so, when Hearst's *Journal* had published a facsimile of the handwritten address from the poison package and asked for the public's assistance in identifying the sender, Adams had studied the item with great care. The longer he examined it, the more familiar it seemed, though at first he could not recall where, exactly, he had seen such script before.

All at once, he remembered.

Hurrying to his files, he quickly found what he was looking for: a sheet of stationery with a brief, carefully inscribed message. Comparing it with the facsimile, he became more convinced than ever that the handwriting was the same. He dug out other letters written by the same hand and spent more than two hours examining them before seeking out Cornish.

Explaining that he had made an important discovery, Adams placed the facsimile he had torn from the previous day's *Journal* on the desk before Cornish. Beside it, he laid the first of the papers he had removed from the club files. Even Cornish could see the similarities in the handwriting. He made a little noise—a kind of snort—as he stared down at the piece of stationery.

It was the resignation letter from a former member who also happened to be a professional chemist: Roland Burnham Molineux.[15]

30

By Saturday, December 31, the Adams murder had come to completely dominate the news. No other story drew a fraction of the coverage—not the conviction of Cordelia Botkin, who was found guilty on Friday afternoon and given a mandatory life sentence; not even the alarming case of Mrs. Mary Houley of Paterson, New Jersey, an inveterate gossip who cut off her own tongue with a butcher knife to cure herself of her vice.[1] For many months to come, "the Great Poison Mystery," as it had already been dubbed, would be the preoccupying topic of the New York City press—not only of the yellow papers but of their high-minded brethren such as the *Times* and the *Telegraph*, which regarded Hearst and Pulitzer's brand of raucous, no-holds-barred journalism with lofty contempt.

According to family lore, Arthur Carey was destined to be a lawman from the moment he was born. As he lay in his cradle, his father, Henry—himself a sergeant on the New York City force—looked down at the newborn and said, "He's a strapping youngster. Set up like a policeman. I think he'll make one."[2]

To prepare him for his preordained career, the elder Carey began bringing his son to work with him when the boy was only seven. While other children were out playing blindman's buff and ring-a-levio, Arthur was passing his time at the Chambers Street station house, watching the prisoners being processed at the sergeant's desk, listening to the patrolmen discuss their latest "collars," but mostly hanging around the basement office of the plainclothes detectives, who certified his status as their unofficial mascot by presenting him with a miniature billy club.

Within a short time, young Arthur had fallen utterly under the spell of these "tall, square-shouldered men in civilian clothes," who stood "aloof and apart" from their uniformed colleagues, spoke their own special lingo, and fearlessly penetrated the most notorious underworld hangouts, hellish dives "where a man was supposed to take his life in his hands whenever he entered": the Burnt Rag, Satan's Circus, the Slide, Cockran's Roost, McGuirk's Suicide Hall, and the Bucket of Blood.

The very names of their criminal adversaries—Shang Draper, Marm Mandelbaum, Funeral Wells, Deafy Hunt, Jersey Jimmy, Banjo Pete Emerson, Paper Collar Joe, Grand Central Pete—had a magical ring to young Arthur. In his eyes, the plainclothes detectives seemed possessed of a "magic power," a "glamour which uniformed men never had." By the time he was ten, he had resolved to become one of them, not merely a police officer but a plainclothes homicide inspector—a "murder man."[3]

Passing his civil-service exam at eighteen, Carey spent a few years walking a beat in lower Manhattan before being appointed to the detective bureau by its legendary chief, Thomas Byrnes (whose 1886 book, *Professional Criminals of America*, is still regarded as a classic text). Just a few months later, he played a key role in the city's most sensational poisoning case prior to the Adams affair: the killing of Mrs. Anna Buchanan, onetime madam of a Newark whorehouse, by her physician-husband, Robert. It was Carey, in fact, who arrested Dr. Buchanan after shadowing him for several days.[4]

In 1897, Byrnes was succeeded by Captain McCluskey, who immediately promoted Carey to detective sergeant. By then, Carey was an eight-year veteran, with dozens of murder cases under his belt. He had already built a reputation as the bureau's top homicide inspector. His father's prophecy—and his own boyhood dream—had been fulfilled.

And so it was only natural that when the Adams case exploded in the news, Arthur Carey was tapped by McCluskey to take a leading part in the investigation.

The most promising clue in the case was the small silver item now routinely described in the papers as a "vial holder." This was immediately turned over to Carey, who proceeded to study it with a magnifying glass. Under the lens, he clearly saw a small oval-shaped area where a gummed label—evidently a price tag—had been affixed to the underside of the base. Someone had scraped off the sticker with a knife, leaving the scratch marks that had led Captain McCluskey to assume, mistakenly, that the holder was not new.

It seemed clear that the sticker had been removed in an attempt to conceal the place of purchase. But there was another marking on the bottom of the holder that the buyer had made no effort to efface. Stamped into the silver was a tiny crescent with the letter *L* snuggled inside the curve. The word *Sterling* appeared above it; below it, the number 814.

Accompanied by a colleague, Detective John Herlihy, Carey made the rounds of local jewelers until he found one who could identify the mysterious insignia. It was, he learned, the manufacturer's hallmark of a silverware firm called Lebkuecher & Company, located on Ferry Street in Newark. Within the hour, Carey and his partner were on a train to New Jersey, the holder in Herlihy's coat pocket.

Proceeding directly to the silverware factory, they sought out the owner, Frank A. Lebkuecher, who after glancing at the holder confirmed that it had been made by his firm. Indeed, it was one of the first articles produced by his company, which had been founded only a few years earlier, in 1896. The crescent-flanked *L* was the company's trademark. The numeral below it—814—was the catalog number.

Contrary to reports in the press, said Lebkuecher, the item was not a vial or bottle holder but a receptacle for wooden matches. The cuplike base on which it stood was intended as an ashtray. It was, he explained, "a man's article, not a woman's. A woman would only purchase it as a gift."

What the detectives were most eager to find out, of course, was *where* it had been purchased. Consulting his records, Lebkuecher discovered that, of the thirty holders manufactured by his firm, seven were still in stock in the factory. The others had been sold to jewelers in cities across the country: Chicago; Baltimore; Philadelphia; Syracuse; San Francisco; St. Louis; Washington, D.C.; Jacksonville, Florida; Salem, Massachusetts;

and Middletown, Connecticut. More locally, three had been purchased by stores in Manhattan, Brooklyn, and Newark.

Copying down the names and addresses of the retailers, the detectives thanked Lebkuecher for his cooperation and returned to Manhattan.[5]

Though Carey and Herlihy were the lead inspectors on the case, they were not the only ones. Altogether, McCluskey had assigned sixteen detectives to the investigation. Added to these authorized representatives of the law were the newshounds of the yellow papers, who in their rabid pursuit of scoops were in competition not only with one another but with the police.

For his part, Captain McCluskey was happy to share certain information with the press when it suited his purposes. Within a day of Carey and Herlihy's trip to Newark, he had distributed a list of all twenty-three retailers that had purchased holders from the Lebkuecher company. Correspondents employed by the *Journal* and the *World* were immediately put on the case, following the trail of the silver match holders in cities across the country.

Unbeknownst to the newsmen, however, there was one key bit of information that the police had withheld from them. From examining the postal mark on the wrapping, authorities had determined that the poison package sent to Harry Cornish had been mailed from the general post office on Broadway.

And so, while Hearst and Pulitzer's men were running down leads from Baltimore to Jacksonville, San Francisco to St. Louis, Carey and his partner were focusing on the stores in the immediate vicinity: Black, Star & Frost on Fifth Avenue in Manhattan; M. Straus in Brooklyn; and C. J. Hartdegen, a jewelry shop located on Broad Street in Newark—just a short stroll from the Morris Herrmann company, where Roland Molineux was employed as head chemist.

The news that the silver holder had been traced to its source was trumpeted by the yellow papers, which did not scruple to take the lion's share of credit for the discovery. Declaring that its reporters were "working with indefatigable earnestness" to identify Mrs. Adams's killer, the *Journal* declared that, thanks to the sleuthing of its newsmen, "the great murder mystery seems to be approaching a solution. It is possible that, with the information the *Journal* is now able to present, the murderer will, within a few hours, or at the most a few days, be known."[6]

Despite this optimistic claim, the theories being promulgated at this point by Hearst and his competitors would prove to be wildly off-base. According to Saturday's *Journal*, the likeliest suspects were a couple who had acquired the holder from a jewelry store called J. R. Armitage & Co. in Baltimore. The *Herald*, meanwhile, proclaimed with equal confidence that the holder had been purchased by a woman in Hartford, then sent to Cornish by a male accomplice. In the pages of the *World*, a "medico-legal expert," Dr. William J. O'Sullivan, asserted that the culprit was a "criminal maniac" whose "mind was excited by reading of the Botkin affair"—what we would nowadays call a copycat. O'Sullivan felt sure that the killer was a man.[7]

Over at the DA's office, however, authorities remained convinced that the culprit was female. Meeting with reporters on Saturday night—New Year's Eve—District Attorney Asa Bird Gardiner issued a statement imbued with the casual misogyny of the time: "History shows that poisoning is essentially a woman's method of action. Women acted thus in ancient times, and following down through the ages, we find the same traits of character, the same outcroppings of human nature. It is easy to surmise the reason for this trait. Woman's nature is essentially subtle. From deeds of blood and violence she naturally shrinks because her nature steps in and prevents. What then follows? Her scheming brain begins to work. She turns to poison as the easiest and surest method, because if handled deftly and cleverly, it insures less suspicion and less possibility of detection."[8]

To the two main theories being bandied about—that Mrs. Adams had been murdered by either a woman acting alone or in concert with a male accomplice—Julian Hawthorne contributed a third. After noting, somewhat bizarrely, that the three digits stamped on the bottom of the silver holder—814—added up to thirteen (a "pregnant fact" that supposedly portended ill luck for the perpetrator), Hawthorne raised a possibility that had not been mentioned before, at least publicly: "that the sender of the poison, if not a woman, might have been an effeminate man."[9]

Hawthorne had little to say on this subject, which, he suggested, was too scandalous to be discussed openly in a family newspaper. But his speculation turned out to be prophetic, for the question of the killer's masculinity would, in fact, come to be a prominent feature of the case in the months ahead.

While his colleagues in the DA's office remained convinced that the killer was female, Captain McCluskey, who had also begun by suspecting a woman, had undergone a complete turnabout. And there was a good reason for this shift.

He had spoken to Harry Cornish.

After examining the handwriting samples provided by John Adams, Cornish had put in an immediate phone call to the chief of detectives, who arrived at the Knickerbocker Athletic Club late Saturday afternoon. McCluskey remained closeted with Cornish for several hours, comparing the newspaper facsimile with Roland Molineux's letters and listening to the athletic director describe his problems with his nemesis.

As McCluskey left the club that evening, he was accosted by reporters, who clamored for information. Though persuaded of Molineux's involvement in the crime, he was not prepared to divulge the news—not until he had a chance to confer with his colleagues. He would only say that Cornish "had finally remembered something" which might well provide "a promising clew."[10]

Inside the clubhouse, however, word had already spread. The whole place was abuzz with news of John Adams's discovery. Molineux's name seemed to be on every lip.[11]

Under the circumstances, it was only a matter of time before the press sniffed out the truth. Pulitzer's men were the first to get hold of the story. On the morning of January 1, 1899, the public awoke to find a sensational headline blaring from the front page of the *World*:

EVIDENCE GROWS THAT DEGENERATE WAS POISONER

THOUGHT CORNISH WAS HIS ENEMY

Had Been a Prominent Member of the Knickerbocker Club But Was Expelled for Serious Cause

Capt. McCluskey Asserts He Will Arrest the Poisoner by or Before 9 o'Clock This Morning, and That He Cannot Escape

The article that followed was wrong on a number of counts. It described the suspect as a man who worked in a "large Broadway mercantile concern," had married the "daughter of a well-known Wall Street operator," was "not fond of any other form of athletics than bicycling," and had been "ignominiously expelled" from the club because of his "immoral behavior."

For the most part, however, anyone privy to the goings-on inside the Knickerbocker would have had no trouble recognizing the person portrayed in the article: a former member who despite his "high social standing" was "unpopular" inside the club and who, following his departure, harbored "bitter resentment" toward certain other members, particularly Harry Cornish.[12]

The *World* also made another explosive announcement, drawing an explicit connection between the deadly Kutnow's Powder sent to Henry Barnet and the poisoned bromo-seltzer mailed to Harry Cornish: "Further investigation by *The World* has established that whereas this man had at one time been a warm friend of Henry C. Barnet, the relations between him and Mr. Barnet were so strained that Mr. Barnet did not speak to him. This was the more marked from the fact that both he and Mr. Barnet lived in the club house. . . . Thus two persons who were at enmity with this expelled club member received in the same manner poison which had fatal results."[13]

Most sensational of all, however, was the characterization of the suspect as a "degenerate." The term itself had been popularized in the late 1800s by Cesare Lombroso, the foremost criminologist of his time (though nowadays regarded as a hopeless crackpot). In his enormously influential 1876 book *L'Uomo delinquente* (*Criminal Man*), Lombroso argued that violent criminals were not merely barbaric in their behavior but were literal atavisms: savage, apelike beings born, by some hereditary glitch, into the modern world. With their jutting brows, big jaws, thick necks, and other supposedly telltale features, violent criminals were evolutionary throwbacks: specimens of humanity in its most degenerate state.[14]

It was not, however, this sort of being that the *World* had in mind when it ran its attention-grabbing headline. Citing an unnamed police official, the paper quickly made it clear that the suspect who had sent the poison to Cornish "was not a degenerate of the Lombroso type." Rather, he was a "moral degenerate"[15]—a man of "evil habits and evil associations," "immorality of character," with a taste for lavish decor that seemed highly suspicious. While at the club, he was rumored to have "luxuriously furnished" his room with "many fine bits of bric-a-brac, pictures, and all that sort of thing."[16]

In short, the *World* was employing the term "degenerate" in a way that would become increasingly common in the coming century: as a code word for homosexual.[17]

Though proclaiming that "the name of the suspected murderer is known to *The World*," the paper declared that—for the sake of civic duty—it was being "withheld from publication." Even at that moment, "the energies of the police are being devoted to completing the chain of evidence against the suspect." To release the suspect's name prematurely might jeopardize the case—"defeat the ends of justice."[18]

It was an uncharacteristic display of self-control on the part of Pulitzer. His rival, William Randolph Hearst, would show no such restraint.

31

In certain respects, Blanche's honeymoon had been everything she could have wished for. Roland had spared no expense, taking a suite in the Waldorf, squiring her to concerts and the theater, treating her to lavish gifts in the exclusive shops along Fifth Avenue. They dined at Delmonico's, attended a holiday party at the Opera Club, and traveled to Brooklyn for a celebratory meal with Roland's elderly aunts, Anne and Emma—the General's surviving sisters—who exuded a "highbred and aristocratic" air that Blanche, with her social pretensions, found deeply impressive.[1]

If she had hoped, however, that marriage would unleash the latent virility in Roland, she was gravely disappointed. On their wedding night, he had displayed none of that "brute masculine force" she so desperately craved. Though he had managed to consummate their union, Roland had proved to be a tentative, if not halfhearted, lover, and the entire experience left her baffled and dismayed.[2]

Under the circumstances, it was only natural that her thoughts kept returning to Henry Barnet, who unlike Roland had been so ardent, so *masterful.* It was still hard to believe that her former lover, with his irrepressible joie de vivre, was gone. The remembrance of Barney, Blanche would write in her memoirs, cast a deep pall over her honeymoon. Though she struggled to conceal her feelings, "secretly I grieved. . . . I thought of the times when we had laughed and been gay, had touched the rims of our champagne glasses, holding them high while he gave a little toast; and then our drinking to the now, and to the future days. There were persistent thoughts of him, sad and tender—full of grief."[3]

She did not, of course, expect Roland to share in these feelings. There had been too much "bad blood between the two men." Even so, she was taken aback by the ill will he continued to harbor.

"You are so strange and indifferent about Barney," she remarked at one point. "You knew him so well, and for so long a time. I think, when one dies, any little difference should be forgotten."

Roland gave a bitter laugh. "You think that? Well, let us talk about something else—anything else in the world."

It was clear to Blanche that "Roland's feelings were implacable. They had not changed, even though Barney had died."

As the days went by, Blanche's mood grew increasingly gloomy. "Married! But somehow, all glamour seemed gone." It was as though "something vivid, of splendid hue and intensity," had vanished from her life. Her new husband, so attentive during their courtship, now seemed distracted and remote. During the second week of December, he would disappear each afternoon on some unspecified errand, leaving her alone in the Waldorf, in the grip of a "feverish restlessness."

Her only consolation was that, "through this marriage, there would no longer be any monetary problems to face. All the anxieties relative to ways and means were in the past. Economic worries could be dismissed." Her dream of going abroad to study in Paris—"Paris! That fascinating city of the Seine with its charm and witchery and allurement!"—would finally come true.

And then, with the coming of Christmas, a change seemed to come over Roland, as if a great burden had been lifted from his mind:

> The Yuletide came and there were gifts and flowers galore. I was like a small child finding that Santa Claus was a reality beyond all imagining! In a spirit of merriment, Roland had added to the more beautiful things a pile of foolish and childish little gifts. These he had wrapped about in many folds of tissue, to give added zest and piquancy to my curiosity, as I delved for the hidden

contents. There was frolic, and merrymaking and fun! We jested and played, and Roland's gay wit flashed as it always did when, as now, the mood was upon him.

Two days later, their monthlong honeymoon at an end, Blanche and Roland moved back into her rooms in Alice Bellinger's home on West End Avenue. Within forty-eight hours, the Great Poison Mystery would burst into the headlines and Henry Barnet's name would be all over the papers.

In her memoirs, however, Blanche makes no mention of these early developments. Evidently, in the days immediately following the death of Katherine Adams, Blanche remained oblivious of the case. There is a perfectly plausible explanation for this. She lived, after all, in an era before 24/7 cable news—indeed, before the advent of television or even radio. To be sure, the "media," as it existed back then, had pounced on the Adams poisoning with all the prurient zeal of today's tabloid journalism. But in 1899, the media consisted entirely of newspapers, and it appears that—absorbed, as always, in the ever-fascinating drama of her own life—Blanche simply never bothered to glance at a paper during that time.

New Year's Day brought the predictable "restless round of gaieties." By then, Blanche—anticipating the time, not far off, when she would finally travel to Paris and immerse herself in the "life and atmosphere of the glamorous and enchanting Latin Quarter"—was feeling happier than at any point since her wedding day.

Her happiness, however, was to be exceptionally short-lived—"as ephemeral as mist before the sun, as the bubbles in a goblet of wine. How could I know," she writes in her most histrionic style, "that there would be drum-fire of another kind, when my dreams would end, and I would be driven like a dead leaf before the wind?"

On the second day of the New Year, 1899, Blanche was awakened by a commotion from below stairs. She opened her eyes and looked groggily about her. The room was so dark that she thought it must be midnight. Straining to hear, she could discern muffled voices speaking in an urgent tone. Then the tread of footsteps on the stairs, followed by a knock on the bedroom door.

Still only half awake, Blanche turned to her husband beside her. "What is it?" she mumbled.

"I'll see," he said. Rising from the bed, he crossed the room and threw open the door. The housemaid stood there, rubbing sleep from her eyes. Roland stepped into the hallway, shutting the door behind him.

Again, Blanche could only hear a low murmur of voices. An instant later, Roland came back inside, hastily donned his robe and slippers, and—without saying a word—left the room again.

By now, Blanche was fully awake. Lighting the lamp at her bedside, she looked at the clock on the night table and was startled to see that the hands pointed to the hour of six. Six in the morning! What in the world could have happened? Who could have come to their home at that ungodly hour, before daylight, to rouse her husband from their bed?

Throwing back the satin coverlet, she sat up, wrapped herself in her robe, and turned an ear to the door. She could make out several male voices talking rapidly. Suddenly, with a start, she recognized the voice of Roland's father, General Molineux.

Instantly, she was seized with alarm. Something dreadful must have happened. Perhaps Roland's mother had taken ill—or even died! Blanche sat on the edge of the bed, biting her lower lip nervously.

When, after what felt like forever, Roland finally reentered the room, Blanche sprang from the bed and cried, "Tell me, has anything—"

"Yes," he said before she could finish her sentence. "Something has happened." There was a tautness and anxiety in his voice that filled her with dread.

"Tell me, tell me quickly," she cried.

Roland's answer was so unexpected that, for a moment, Blanche could only stare at him in silence.

"You believe in me, don't you?" he said.

"That's a strange question—a strange thing to say," she stammered. "Why do you ask me that?"

Only then did she notice that he was clutching something in one hand—a newspaper. Now he held it up so that she could see the front page.

It was the *New York Journal*—Hearst's paper. Running across the top of the page was the headline POLICE WANT ROLAND BURNHAM MOLINEUX IN THE POISONING CASE.

Blanche stared at it, uncomprehending. She opened her mouth but was unable to speak—her throat had gone completely dry. She looked up again at Roland and saw that his forehead was beaded with sweat. He was saying something to her, but she could not understand the words.

"Tell me again, Roland," she finally managed to say. "What did you say?"

"My father and a reporter from the *World* are downstairs, waiting for me," he said. "We are going to see McCluskey."

"McCluskey?" she said. "Who's McCluskey?"

But Roland didn't answer. Handing her the newspaper, he quickly got dressed.

Blanche sank back onto the bed, scanning the paper, trying to make sense of it. It was something about a murder, a woman named Mrs. Adams who had taken poison sent to someone else—to Harry Cornish, Roland's old enemy at the Knickerbocker Club!

All at once, as she continued to read, Blanche's gaze fell upon a subhead, halfway down the page: MOLINEUX'S MARRIAGE TALKED OF.

She made a little whimpering sound. The story quoted unnamed members of the Knickerbocker Club who had been discussing the sudden death of Henry Barnet. "After Mr. Barnet died," read the article, "Molineux married a lady who had been exceedingly friendly with Barnet."[4] Blanche began to tremble violently. A nightmare had overtaken her. All at once, she became aware that Roland was standing over her, saying something. She willed herself to focus on his words.

"Everything will be all right," he was saying. "Don't worry. Go back to bed and try not to think about it."

In another moment, he turned and was gone.

Still frozen on the edge of the bed, Blanche tried to get hold of herself, but her thoughts were in chaos. Her husband of only one month—implicated in a poison murder!

Suddenly, the whole situation struck her as a hideous joke. She slid from the bed and began to laugh wildly.

When, a few moments later, Alice Bellinger burst into the room with the maid, they found Blanche on the floor, still in the grip of hysteria.

32

When Roland had first come downstairs after being roused by the maid, he had found his father in the company of William Inglis, an old friend and fellow member of the New York Athletic Club who worked as a reporter for Pulitzer's *World*.

In their unflagging efforts to outscoop their rivals, Hearst and Pulitzer's men kept constant tabs on each other's stories, and Inglis had managed to procure a copy of Monday's *Journal* while the ink was still damp on the page. Recognizing the storm that was about to engulf Roland, Inglis wanted to alert his friend but wasn't sure of his whereabouts. And so—despite the untimeliness of the hour—he had secured a cab and driven out to Brooklyn, where, shortly before 5:00 A.M., he awoke the General and showed him the headline naming Roland as the main suspect in the city's most notorious murder.[1]

At sixty-five years of age, Edward Leslie Molineux had lost none of the firm resolve or fighting spirit that had served him so well on the battlefields of Cedar Creek and Winchester. He still believed in the motto of his boyhood hero, Louis Kossuth: "It is the surmounting of difficulties that makes heroes." Less than a half hour after Inglis's arrival, the two men were in a carriage headed for Manhattan. Reaching 757 West End Avenue around six, they awoke the housemaid and had her fetch Roland from his bed.

When Roland saw the headline, the color drained from his face. "What a horrible accusation!" he cried. "What shall I do?"[2]

His father—coolly decisive as ever—immediately took charge. Though dawn was just breaking, they would proceed at once to the residence of Captain McCluskey and demand a retraction of the outrageous charge.

As it happened, McCluskey resided only a few blocks away, at 77 West Sixty-eighth Street. The sky was just showing the first inklings of daylight as Roland and the General, accompanied by Inglis, strode through the frigid streets, arriving at McCluskey's home just before seven.

Early as it was, McCluskey was already awake and on the job, conferring with a pair of detectives from the central bureau. After a curt introduction, the General thrust the newspaper at the captain, whose face assumed a look of marked displeasure as he read.

"This is newspaper work, not mine," he said when he was done, then turned to Roland and added: "I don't want you and never have." He advised Roland to go on about his business as usual. "Don't bother about this thing," he said. "Believe me, if we had wanted you, my men could have found you long ago."

Barely mollified, the General removed a card from his pocket and wrote out Roland's addresses both at home and at work, along with his own. "If you need us, you can find us at one of these places," he told McCluskey, handing him the card. "We are as anxious to get to the bottom of this matter as you, and wish to assist in every way in our power."[3]

With that, the General, Roland, and Inglis took their leave.

Their next stop was the residence of Roland's friend, Bartow S. Weeks, the prominent attorney and former president of the NYAC who had been the unwitting catalyst of Roland's resignation from the Knickerbocker. Weeks was immediately retained as Roland's counsel. Roland then returned home to Blanche, while the General traveled back to Brooklyn, where he paid an early-morning visit to his own lawyer, Hugo Hirsh, who was also put on the case.

By the time the General reached home, the *Journal* had hit the stands. The story set off the predictable furor, particularly in Brooklyn, where Edward Molineux was a revered and influential figure and Roland himself a renowned athlete. Within hours, a reporter for the *Brooklyn Eagle* had arrived at the Molineuxs' stately Fort Greene home, where he was granted an interview by the General.

With the loyalty and devotion that would never waver in the harrowing years to come, Edward scoffed at the notion that a bitter rivalry existed between his son and Harry Cornish. True, there had been a "difference of opinion" between them "in regard to the management" of the club. When the Board of Governors sided with Cornish, Roland had felt that "there was nothing to do but resign and make his residence the New York Athletic Club." It was, said the General, "the gentlemanly thing to do, and I supported him in the action." The whole matter was of an utterly "trivial character," and to suggest that it would lead Roland to plot Cornish's murder was more than preposterous—it was libelous.

> "He is a bold and fearless young man," said the General with undisguised pride. "From his childhood up there has never been anything in his life to indicate that he was the slightest bit ugly in disposition or quarrelsome, and certainly never held malice towards anyone. Everyone is interested in trying to find out who the villain is who would be guilty of so foul an act. But anyone who would accuse a man—a young and married man, especially—before the law has acted or the authorities have investigated the matter is guilty of malicious, vile conduct and deserves to be heavily punished.
>
> "They *shall* be punished," the General continued, sounding every bit the iron-willed commander who, in his army days, had made many a shirker quail. "They shall find out I am a fighting man when the occasion demands. I consider it my duty as a citizen and as a father to leave no stone unturned to clear him or any other unfortunate who is unjustly accused of such a fearful crime."[4]

The General's threats were echoed by the two lawyers he had immediately retained to deal with the crisis. Hugo Hirsh declared that he had every intention of instituting a libel case against Hearst, though he felt that "horse-whipping would be the proper course."[5] Bartow Weeks likewise announced that he would "proceed against the newspaper that printed this story." Almost sputtering with indignation, Weeks proclaimed his absolute faith in Roland's innocence. The idea that a man so "above reproach"—so "intelligent and refined"—might commit such a "dastardly" crime was too outrageous to contemplate. Why, it would make as much sense to accuse Weeks himself! "I also had trouble with Cornish over matters relating to the club. *I* might just as well be brought into the case as Mr. Molineux."[6]

Later that day, after meeting with McCluskey, Weeks arrived at Alice Bellinger's home to confer with Roland and Blanche. Though McCluskey had repeated the assurances he had given the General, it was clear to Weeks that the Molineux name was not going to disappear from the papers anytime soon. Not only Roland but his wife as well would be hounded mercilessly by "the reputation-destroying yellow wolves of the press."[7] The only sensible course was to flee Manhattan and seek refuge in the relative privacy of the General's home in Brooklyn.

Blanche reluctantly agreed. Within days, her apartment—where she had lived as a bride for less than a week—was "stripped and denuded. . . . My possessions were stored; my trunks packed. The doors of my honeymoon abode closed behind me."

Though she could not possibly have known it at the time, she would never go back there again. Her retreat to the Molineuxs' stately dwelling would turn into a seemingly endless imprisonment.

"The long siege," as she described it many years later, "had begun."[8]

33

In public, Captain McCluskey stuck to the story he had given the General. "The police weren't after Roland. "The amateur detectives of certain newspapers are not my detectives," he told reporters on Tuesday afternoon. "Their suspects are not my suspects. If they know who the culprit is, they know more than I do. If I knew who he was, I'd arrest him."

The situation was different behind the scenes. In point of fact, Roland was still very much a person of interest to the police. Without solid evidence in hand, however, they weren't about to make an arrest. Though the press had begun to complain about McCluskey's performance—POLICE MAKING POOR PROGRESS IN THE ADAMS MURDER CASE, chided a headline in the *New York Sun*[1]—his men had, in fact, made significant headway. Indeed, the detectives who had been conferring with McCluskey at the time of the General's early-morning visit—Arthur Carey and his partner, John Herlihy—were there to update him about a major discovery.

They had not only identified the store where the silver match holder had been purchased but had located the person who sold it.

It was the little oval smudge of mucilage—the vestige of the label glued onto the bottom of the holder—that proved to be the decisive clue. Checking the three jewelry shops in the metropolitan vicinity, the detectives had discovered that only one of the stores—C. J. Hartdegen of Newark—used stickers of that precise shape and dimension as price tags.

At first, no one at the store could recall when the holder had been sold. The owner himself, Charles Hartdegen, believed that someone had bought it months earlier. One of his clerks, however, seemed sure that he had seen it in the display window as recently as two weeks before.

Combing through the records, Carey came upon an entry for an item listed as a silver toothpick holder, priced at $5.75, which had been sold on December 21—a week before the death of Mrs. Adams and two days before the poison package was mailed at the general post office.[2] The sale had been made by Miss Emma Miller, a recently hired stenographer who in the rush before Christmas had helped out at the counter.[3]

Miss Miller having already left work for the day, Carey and Herlihy took the trolley to her home. She turned out to be a slender young woman, apparently in her early twenties, with sharp features and a correspondingly curt manner.

When Carey showed her the holder, she recognized it at once, clearly recalling the circumstances of its sale. It had been purchased by a well-dressed man, perhaps in his early thirties, of medium build and height, who arrived late in the afternoon when the store was crowded with holiday shoppers. Despite his gentlemanly appearance, he had elbowed aside several other customers in his haste to reach the sales counter.

He was looking, he said, for an item that would hold a bottle of bromo-seltzer. At first, she could think of nothing suitable. Then she remembered the silver holder in the display case. When she showed it to the gentleman and told him the price, he immediately said that he would take it.

Having sat on a shelf for nearly two years, the holder was visibly tarnished, but when Miss Miller offered to polish it, the gentleman waved off the suggestion and told her to wrap it up as it was. She did as requested, and the transaction was quickly completed. The fellow then turned on his heel and hurried away. Altogether, he had been in the store for only a few minutes.

"Can you remember anything else about this gentleman?" Detective Carey asked Miss Miller.

"I believe he had a beard," she replied. "A reddish beard."[4]

The news that the suspect in the poisoning case sported a reddish beard was quickly blazed across the front pages. Roland's attorney, Bartow Weeks, immediately pounced on it as further evidence of his client's innocence. "Mr. Molineux is clean shaven," he proclaimed to reporters, adding with a chortle: "I have a yellow beard—some might call it reddish. Perhaps the police should be looking for *me*."[5]

It was certainly true that Roland was clean shaven. But that hadn't been the case before Christmas, when he still wore the handlebar mustache he had grown the previous spring. The public got a good look at this impressive facial adornment when the *Journal* managed to obtain a series of photographic portraits of the mustachioed Molineux and plastered them across the top of page one.[6]

Though Emma Miller insisted that "she could not have mistaken a mustache for a beard," Detective Carey knew from long experience that "witnesses frequently transpose the two."[7] To test her reliability as an observer, he visited her again, this time at Hartdegen's.

There were several shoppers in the store when Carey arrived, and he waited until they were gone before speaking to Miss Miller. He began by asking her "about the other sales she had made on December 21." Not only was she "unable to recall the face of any other customer she had waited on," she could "not even give accurate descriptions of the people who were in the store" when Carey first entered.[8]

Even more doubtful now about Emma Miller's characterization of the purchaser of the silver holder as a red-bearded man, Carey began looking for other witnesses who might have seen the suspect enter or leave the store on December 21. He knew, of course, that "Christmas shopping was at its height on that day." Reasoning that the Newark Police Department might have assigned "extra men to the shopping district," Carey proceeded to headquarters. Asking around, he was pointed to a detective named Joseph Farrell.

As it turned out, Farrell had an interesting tale to tell.

On the afternoon of December 21, he had just come from a meeting with the mayor, who had asked him to perform a little errand in Irvington. Farrell was waiting for the trolley when Roland Molineux, dressed in a mackintosh and black derby hat, came striding up Market Street. Farrell—who had done some amateur boxing in his younger days—was an old acquaintance of Molineux's, a longtime fan of prizefighting. Though seemingly in a great hurry, Roland paused to exchange greetings with the detective.

"Did he have a beard?" Carey asked Farrell.

Farrell shook his head.

The two men had chatted only briefly. Roland, who was on his way back to the factory, made a point of telling Farrell that he had just come from a restaurant, where he'd dined with his boss, Morris Herrmann.

Farrell, of course, had no reason to doubt that story, though Herrmann himself would later testify that no such dinner took place on that date. The detective had noticed one thing, however.

When Carey asked if he recalled which direction Roland had been coming from, Farrell said, "Yes. He was walking up from the Hartdegen store."[9]

34

In the wake of the threats made by Roland's lawyers, the yellow papers were careful not to make direct accusations against him. Still, the blaring, lavishly illustrated stories that dominated the front pages day after day left little doubt in the public's mind that Molineux continued to be the prime, if not the only, suspect.

Even while piously declaring that it in no way intended to incriminate him, for example, Hearst's *Journal* ran a prominent item headlined THE MOLINEUX COINCIDENCE, listing a string of "strange facts" that made Roland "worthy of official attention":

1. YOUNG MR. MOLINEUX IS A MANUFACTURER WHOSE PLACE OF BUSINESS IS NEWARK, TO WHICH HE GOES DAILY. THE SILVER MATCH HOLDER, THE GIFT THAT ACCOMPANIED THE FATAL BOTTLE MARKED "BROMO-SELTZER," WAS BOUGHT IN NEWARK.

---

2. IT HAS BEEN EVIDENT FROM THE FIRST THAT THE POISONER MUST HAVE BEEN A CHEMIST. MR. MOLINEUX IS A CHEMIST.

---

3. THE DEADLY POISON SENT TO CORNISH WAS CYANIDE OF POTASSIUM. MR. MOLINEUX'S BUSINESS, THE MAKING AND MIXING OF DRY COLORS, NECESSITATED THE KEEPING ON HAND OF MANY CHEMICALS, AMONG THEM CYANIDE OF POTASSIUM.

---

4. Mr. Molineux had been a member of the Knickerbocker Athletic Club, of which Cornish was athletic director. Mr. Molineux admitted to a personal quarrel with Cornish, to whom the poison was sent.[1]

In a similar vein, Pulitzer's *World*, without invoking Molineux's name, described him to a tee in a page-one description of the "degenerate suspect" as a man who "worked as a chemist in a Newark factory"; resigned from the KAC as "an enemy of Mr. Cornish"; belonged to various "organizations devoted to the study of chemistry"; and had intimate "knowledge of the properties of many poisons."

To these familiar facts, the paper added two previously undisclosed details. First, that the suspect was a regular "customer of Tiffany's"—a significant point, since the silver holder and poison bottle had been enclosed in a robin's-egg-blue Tiffany's box. Second, that "among other evil habits tending to destroy all sense of moral responsibility, the suspected person is an opium smoker and has frequented low Mott Street dives."[2]

To the tongue-clucking critics of the yellow press, the latter revelation was simply another deplorable example of cheap "reputation-destroying" sensationalism. But it was a mark of the extraordinary detective work performed by Hearst and Pulitzer's men—who were generally several steps ahead of the police—that it turned out to be true.

That the socialite son of the unimpeachable General Molineux was a habitué of Chinatown opium dens seemed easier to believe after the *Herald* ran an item headlined KNOWS 'CHUCK' CONNORS, which revealed that Roland was an intimate of the colorful Bowery character. Interviewed on Tuesday, January 3, Connors—employing the swaggering street dialect that his role demanded—leapt to Roland's defense and violently denounced the person who had stirred up such trouble for his chum. "Say, the man that mixed that muss for Roland ought to be killed," he growled. "I haven't got a better friend in the world than Roland."[3]

Well-meant as it may have been, this was not the sort of endorsement likely to create a flattering impression of Roland in the minds of the public. Under pressure from the General—not a man to take slurs against the

Molineux name lying down—Bartow Weeks began an aggressive campaign to counter the insinuations of the yellow press.

A key part of Weeks's strategy was to demonstrate that his client had nothing to hide and was eager to assist the investigation in any way possible. To that end, on the morning of January 3, the two men traveled to Newark, where—after a brief stop at police headquarters for a consultation with Chief Hopper—they proceeded to Hartdegen's jewelry shop.

Introducing himself and his client to the owner, Weeks asked to see Miss Miller, who was at her desk in the rear office. Leaving Roland in the front of the store, the attorney entered the little back room, where he found the young stenographer working at her books. Apologizing for the intrusion, Weeks questioned her about the man who had purchased the silver holder.

"Would you know him if you saw him again?" asked Weeks when Miss Miller had finished describing the fellow.

Miss Miller thought she would.

"Let me bring a gentleman to you and see if you remember him," said Weeks, stepping from the office.

Moments later, he returned with Roland, who was swaddled in a long woolen overcoat and wearing a tall hat. He had shaved only hours before and his handsome face was perfectly smooth.

"Is this the gentleman to whom you sold the holder?" asked Weeks.

After studying Roland intently for a moment, Miss Miller shook her head. "No. I have never seen him before."

"You are positive?" asked Weeks.

"Yes," she said.

"So this is not the man who bought the holder?"

"No. It was a man of entirely different appearance. He had a red beard and was not like this gentleman at all."

Thanking her for her help, Weeks and Roland left the store, "well gratified," as one paper reported, "by this result."[4]

To a casual observer, Roland was certainly not behaving like a guilty man. He had not gone into hiding or attempted to flee. He announced his willingness to cooperate with the authorities and did not shy away from facing witnesses, as his meeting with Emma Miller showed.

The police, however, were unimpressed by this behavior. Detective Carey, for example, acknowledged that "flight was the surest sign of guilt." But he knew from experience that some criminals took a different tack. Instead of running away from the situation, they brazened it out. They stuck "close by the scene of their crime, trusting themselves to the enfolding embrace of their lawyers," who did all the talking for their clients.[5]

That was certainly true of Roland. He continued to "appear much in public, unconcerned and gay," comporting himself with the proud bearing expected of a son of General Edward Leslie Molineux.[6] But he was rarely seen anymore without his legal mouthpiece, Bartow Weeks, at his side.

Indeed, the police had little doubt that Roland was their man. Rumors began to abound that an arrest was imminent. Emma Miller's testimony, however, represented a serious stumbling block. Before he could proceed with a case against Roland, McCluskey felt he had to "reconcile Miss Miller's description of the purchaser as a red-bearded man with the known fact that Molineux never in his life wore a beard."[7]

There were several ways of explaining this disparity. The first, espoused by Detective Carey, was that the stenographer was simply an unreliable witness. Another—the one toward which McCluskey inclined—was that Roland had been wearing a disguise.

Proceeding on the latter assumption, McCluskey immediately dispatched several of his men to Newark with orders to canvas the city's wig makers. Only a few blocks from Hartdegen's jewelry shop, they located a store called Zimmerman's Hair Emporium, whose owner—as *The New York Times* put it—"related a circumstance of great interest."[8]

About ten days before Christmas, according to Mr. Zimmerman, a gentleman had come in and asked for a red beard. Zimmerman gave him a few to try on, but none seemed to fit. The wig dealer offered to order a larger one from Manhattan, but when the customer heard how long it would take to arrive, he thanked the proprietor and left.[9]

While the police were focusing on Oscar Zimmerman, the sleuth reporters of Hearst's special "murder squad" were conducting an investigation of their own.[10] Before long, they had turned up another, equally intriguing lead in the person of a "hair-goods man" named William A. Fisher. According to the *Journal*'s page-one account—published with great fanfare under the headline RED BEARD MYSTERY SOLVED!—Fisher owned an establishment, located "within three little blocks of Hartdegen's," whose "business was to provide hairpieces and beards to actors, both amateur and professional, along with people who are embarrassed at their capillary deficiencies."

On the afternoon of December 2, a stranger sporting a well-groomed mustache appeared at Fisher's store, looking for a wig and fake beard. Fisher showed him various items but the man was "exceptionally hard to please." He "tried on outfit after outfit and found fault with them all. Some were too burly, others were too close cut. But the thing which condemned them all was that they were not of the color he wanted. He needed hair and beard light enough to conceal his natural darkness of hair and hue, and yet not light enough to attract notice to him."

Eventually, after several visits, he purchased a wig and matching beard "of natural hair, and so fine in workmanship that, when he donned them in the store, they transformed him entirely, and his own barber would not have known him." So pleased was the man that, though the price for both pieces came to nearly ten dollars, he declared that he "didn't mind the cost of it," since "it made him look perfectly natural."

Asked by the *Journal* reporter about the precise color of the beard, Fisher described it as "grayish brown," though "under the light it took on a tinge bordering upon auburn." What made his account particularly compelling, however, was the description he gave of the stranger, which matched Roland Molineux's appearance in every important detail, right down to his cleft chin and upturned nose.

The purchaser of the beard, said Fisher, was a "medium built man," perhaps five feet seven inches tall and 150 pounds, who "stood erect." His complexion was fair, his nose "well-shaped, the end slightly tilted," and "there was a dimple or dent in his chin." He wore a dark mustache "of medium size," the ends "straight and drawn down nicely." His "forehead was high and the hair dark and thin on top as if he was beginning to lose it."

It was clear that, unlike so many of Fisher's customers, the stranger was "not a theatrical man. Invariably an actor announces his profession in making a purchase and always knows exactly what he wants," Fisher explained. This man "made no reference to the purpose for which he intended the disguise." Though not the easiest customer to satisfy, he was never less than a perfect gentleman. Everything about him, from his courteous manners to his "custom-made clothes," bespoke good breeding.

"Do you think you can identify the stranger?" the reporter asked Fisher. "Could you pick him out from any considerable number of men?"

"Yes," Fisher answered without hesitation. "I could pick him out among a hundred."

With that, the reporter reached into his coat pocket and removed one of the photographs of Roland with his handlebar mustache that had been printed that week in the *Journal.* "What do you say about his resemblance to this?" he asked, showing it to Fisher.

Fisher looked at the picture for only a moment before saying, "There's a remarkable resemblance." His wife, who worked beside him at the store and claimed to have a clear memory of the stranger, was even more emphatic.

"That is the dead image of the man," she declared.[11]

With the discovery of the two Newark wig sellers, the yellow papers lost no time in declaring that—thanks largely to the detective work of their own enterprising reporters—the "last and greatest obstacle which has prevented the police from arresting" the suspect had finally "been removed."[12] The "fake-beard theory" in which McCluskey had placed such faith appeared to have been confirmed. According to the papers, it was only a matter of days—perhaps even hours—before the poisoner was in custody.

It wasn't long, however, before McCluskey's optimism had turned into "grave disappointment and even sorrow."[13]

For reasons he never explained—even when offered "good compensation" by representatives for Pulitzer and Hearst—William Fisher steadfastly refused to go to Manhattan to identify Molineux. With the cooperation of Roland's attorney, the police therefore made alternate arrangements to have the two men come face-to-face.

On Friday, January 6, Roland and Weeks traveled to Newark, where they met with a detective named Christie. The three spent about twenty minutes working out final details of the plan, which called for Molineux to be on the eastbound platform of the Newark railroad station at 2:00 P.M. Christie then proceeded to Fisher's shop and persuaded the wig dealer to accompany him to the station.

When the two men arrived, there were about twenty people waiting for the train to New York, including Roland and Weeks. Christie asked Fisher if any of the travelers resembled the man who had purchased the wig and beard from him. Fisher walked from one end of the platform to the other, studying the faces. Then he returned to Christie.

"I don't recognize anyone here," he said.

"Try again," said Christie. Fisher made another round of the platform with equally fruitless results.

Christie then led Fisher over to Molineux. "Ever see this gentleman before?"

"No," Fisher promptly replied.

"Sure?"

"Quite sure," said Fisher.

"He wasn't the gentleman who came into your shop for a red beard and wig?" asked Christie.

"No more than you are," said Fisher, much to the delight of Roland and Weeks, who exchanged broad smiles.

Fisher was then introduced to Molineux, and the two men spent several minutes chatting away before Roland and his lawyer boarded the 2:07 train back to the city.[14]

Later that afternoon, Fisher was visited in his shop by a reporter from the *Herald.* Why, asked the newsman, was Fisher so confident that Molineux was not the man who had purchased the red beard and wig? After all, when Fisher had been shown the photograph of Molineux, he had "detected strong points of resemblance to the customer."

"I would never attempt to identify a man from a photograph," Fisher insisted. "Especially not from a newspaper reproduction. Defects are inevitable. But I am certain that the man introduced to me today as Roland Molineux was not the fellow who visited my shop."

"What did you and Mr. Molineux talk about?" asked the reporter.

"Oh, about the case," Fisher said vaguely. "I tell you, that man is incapable of such a crime. My business makes me a student of faces and I should be able to judge," he added—insisting, in effect, that he could tell if a person was guilty simply by looking at him.

"But when you saw the photograph," the reporter persisted, "you were not quite so positive. Could the fact that Mr. Molineux has since shaved off his mustache deceive even a person like you, who has made such a careful study of facial characteristics?"

"Absolutely not," said Fisher.[15]

McCluskey's hopes of proving that Molineux had worn a disguise to purchase the silver match holder now rested with the wig dealer, Oscar Zimmerman. But when Zimmerman was brought to New York to meet Molineux, he, too, failed to make a positive identification.[16]

The hunt for the phony red beard having led nowhere, the papers began floating another theory. Perhaps the beard wasn't fake at all, just as Emma Miller claimed. Perhaps the man who had bought the holder from her wasn't Molineux in disguise but a red-bearded accomplice.

Conducting a "vigilant search" of the barbershops of Newark, reporters for the *World* quickly turned up a barber named Valentine Kuhn who recalled having removed the "full reddish" beard from the face of a stranger just a few days before Christmas. Kuhn remembered the customer partly because he seemed "very nervous" and partly because it was highly unusual for a man to want his "beard shaved off in the middle of winter."[17]

Within twenty-four hours, sketches of the supposed red-bearded accomplice were plastered all over the papers. But no one came forth to identify him.

The red-bearded man would remain forever a phantom.

35

Less than a week after his men traced the silver match holder to Hartdegen's, it was clear to Chief Detective McCluskey that he would need a different way to link Roland Molineux to the crime. Fortunately, the police were in possession of other key pieces of physical evidence. The holder had been only half of the diabolical "gift" sent to Harry Cornish. The other was the cobalt blue bottle labeled "Emerson's Bromo-Seltzer" and the deadly powder it contained.

By the first of January, the bottle was already in the hands of the renowned toxicologist Dr. Rudolph A. Witthaus.[1] A professor of chemistry at both the University of Vermont and Cornell, Witthaus was a pioneering figure in American medical jurisprudence, whose four-volume text, *Forensic Medicine and Toxicology*, would become a classic in the field. He had long experience with criminal cases, having helped convict both Carlyle Harris and Dr. Robert Buchanan, the perpetrators of the two most sensational New York City poison-murders prior to the death of Katherine Adams.

In early 1898, Witthaus himself was at the center of a highly publicized scandal, when, during a bitter dispute over alimony payments, his former wife accused him of attempted murder. According to the affidavit, Witthaus—who had been carrying on an affair with another woman prior to his divorce—tried to rid himself of his wife in 1896 by giving her poisoned quinine after she came down with a case of malaria. The charges were withdrawn when Witthaus sought an indictment against his ex-wife for criminal libel.[2] By the time he was enlisted to work on the Adams poisoning case, his good name had been restored and he was universally recognized as America's foremost expert in the nascent field of forensic toxicology.

Within days of Mrs. Adams's death, Detective Carey had delivered to Witthaus's private lab on East Forty-second Street the blue bromo-seltzer bottle, still about half full of the lethal powder. Carey also brought along the empty glass from which Mrs. Adams had drunk the potion and the teaspoon with which she had measured out and mixed the fatal dose.

It would be nearly two weeks before Witthaus completed his work on this evidence and submitted his formal report. But as early as Wednesday, January 4—just a few days after he began his analysis—word had already leaked to the press that he had made two significant discoveries.[3]

First, the substance that killed Katherine Adams wasn't, as initially reported, cyanide of potassium but cyanide of mercury. Though the two produced equally nasty effects on the human body—excessive salivation, constriction of the throat, nausea, uncontrollable vomiting and diarrhea, violent convulsions, and death—cyanide of potassium was much easier to obtain. It was used, among other things, as a fixative by professional photographers and was available in most drugstores.

Once upon a time, cyanide of mercury could also be purchased in almost any pharmacy. Up until the Civil War, it was commonly used as an antiseptic and gargle. Since then, however—though it continued to show up as an ingredient in certain patent medicines—few responsible physicians prescribed it. Even in an age when family doctors routinely dispensed strychnine and arsenic to infants, the American medical establishment had concluded that cyanide of mercury was more dangerous than the ailments it purportedly cured.

As a result, it was no longer stocked by most druggists. Even killers shunned it. Witthaus, who possessed an encyclopedic knowledge of poison-murders, knew of only five recorded cases involving cyanide of mercury, none more recent than the mid-1870s.[4]

To Chief Detective McCluskey and his colleagues, Witthaus's discovery was a heartening development. Clearly, there were very few places where the killer could have acquired cyanide of mercury. It should be a relatively simple matter—so the detectives believed—to locate the seller, who could then supply them with a solid description of the man who had purchased the poison.

Once again, however, McCluskey's hopes were quickly deflated. His men spent several days going from one Manhattan apothecary to the next with fruitless results. The demand for cyanide of mercury was so negligible that most pharmacists didn't bother to carry it. Of the few who did, two couldn't remember the last time they had sold any. Only one Fifth Avenue druggist recalled selling an ounce of the poison—and that had been twenty-five years before.[5] Investigators had no better luck in Newark, where they canvassed 120 pharmacies. Just two druggists, Arthur B. Crooks and a man named Guenther, had sold any cyanide of mercury in recent years—Crooks to his son Harry, also a druggist, and Guenther to another retail pharmacist who still had the poison in stock.[6]

Having come up empty in their attempt to locate the source of the poison, the police turned their attention to the second of Witthaus's findings. In examining the little blue bottle that had been mailed to Cornish, Witthaus had discovered that—despite its label—it wasn't a bromo-seltzer bottle at all. For one thing, genuine bottles of Emerson's Bromo-Seltzer had the manufacturer's name embossed prominently in the glass. The one sent to Cornish bore no such marking.

A real bottle of Emerson's Bromo-Seltzer, moreover, wouldn't fit into the silver holder. It was slightly too large. Evidently, the killer had steamed off an Emerson's label, then reglued it to a different chemical bottle of roughly the same appearance but small enough to slip inside the holder.

There was clear evidence of tampering. With the help of a magnifying lens, Witthaus could see that the bottle had been opened, then resealed with paraffin, thickly applied and pressed into shape by hand.

Turning the bottle over, he also noticed four small, hyphen-shaped protrusions, spaced at regular intervals around the periphery of the base.

These markings, blown into the glass, turned out to be a vital clue. Within a few days of receiving Witthaus's preliminary report, investigators had determined that the four little dashes were the private stamp of a chemical manufacturing firm called Powers & Weightman, located in Newark.[7]

In short order, Carey and Detective Sergeant William McCafferty were on their way back to Newark, where they interviewed the manager of Powers & Weightman. A check of the ledgers revealed that the little blue bottle disguised as bromo-seltzer was, in reality, one of ten bottles of cyanide of mercury that had been sold to a Newark pharmaceutical supplier, C. B. Smith & Co, in early July.[8]

Proceeding directly to Smith & Co, Carey and his partner spoke to the owner, Charles Smith, who informed them that six of the ten bottles were still in stock. Of the four that had been sold, two had gone to Professor George C. Sonn of the Newark High School for experimental use in his chemistry lab. Offhand, Smith couldn't account for the other two. There was only one way to find out who had bought them: by checking the sales slips for the past six months.

This, however, was no simple matter. For one thing, the firm averaged about eight thousand orders per month, meaning that there were nearly fifty thousand sales slips to go through, some listing as many as a hundred items. Even if the detectives were willing to undertake the job themselves, they would have had an impossible time of it, since the orders were full of Latin medical terms and abbreviations. Only people with pharmaceutical training could accomplish the task.

Smith had clerks who were qualified for the job, but he couldn't afford to loan them out for an indefinite period of time. At that point, however, the yellow papers, with their genius for self-promotion, insinuated themselves into the proceedings. The *World*—which never wearied of trumpeting its own invaluable contributions to the case—offered to reimburse Smith for his clerks' time.

Four of Smith's men were immediately installed in a large second-story room in the warehouse, specially equipped with electric lights to make their job easier. Working round the clock, they pored over thousands of sales slips—without success. By the third day, Smith declared that the task was hopeless. "It's like looking for a needle in a haystack," he declared, helpfully adding: "We know that the needle is there, but there is so much hay that we can't find the needle."[9]

Then, shortly after 6:00 P.M. on Tuesday, January 17, one of the bleary-eyed clerks came running into Smith's office, waving a little sheet of paper. Dated October 5, 1898, it was a sales receipt for two one-ounce bottles of cyanide of mercury, purchased for thirty cents each by an employee of a firm called Balbach & Co. Balbach, Smith explained to Detective Carey, was the country's largest smelter of silver and gold.

As it happened, it was also located only a few blocks from the Morris Herrmann factory, Roland Molineux's workplace and part-time living quarters.

The next morning, readers of the *World* found a front-page reproduction of the sales receipt beside a headline announcing: WORLD FINDS THE PURCHASER OF THE POISON BOTTLE. The first line of the article declared, with typical immodesty, that "The *World* made a most important discovery yesterday which should solve the poison mystery and enable the police to arrest the murderer."[10]

The self-congratulations, however, turned out to be premature. Indeed, by the time the newspaper appeared on the stand, Detective Carey and his partner had already visited the smelting concern and spoken to the person who had bought the cyanide of mercury, a chemist named Morton M. Liebschultz. Questioned closely by the detectives, Liebschultz explained that he had accidentally blown up one ounce of the cyanide while attempting to purify it with prussic acid. He had used the remainder in an experiment involving platinum. The two empty bottles had been disposed of in the trash.[11]

As for Roland Molineux, Liebschultz had never met the man. Nor had he ever dealt with Molineux's employer.

It was another frustrating turn for the police. As Carey left the office of the smelting firm, he couldn't fail to be galled at this latest setback. He was so close to his quarry that, standing on the street outside Balbach's, he could see the hulking form of the Morris Herrmann factory over the rooftops of the intervening buildings.

And yet, for all that, he was no nearer to getting his man.

36

Though cloaking themselves in the guise of selfless crusaders for justice, Pulitzer and Hearst were, of course, primarily interested in whipping up public excitement and selling as many newspapers as possible. Nevertheless, however self-serving their motives, their reporters were, in fact, in the forefront of the investigation. Even Captain McCluskey was forced to acknowledge the contributions of the yellow papers. Early in the investigation he publicly praised the *World* for the "remarkable collection of evidence" it had assembled and conceded that he and his men were unaware of certain facts "until we saw them in the *World*."[1]

The *World*, of course, had been the first to reveal the fact that another member of Roland Molineux's club—Henry C. Barnet—had died under mysterious circumstances. Now, having learned that Professor Witthaus had found cyanide of mercury in the powder that killed Katherine Adams, Pulitzer's men took the lead again, uncovering an even more direct link between the two cases.

HENRY C. BARNET *DID* RECEIVE POISON BY MAIL AND *DID* TAKE IT, proclaimed the headline on Wednesday, January 4. ANALYSIS SHOWS THE BOTTLE SENT HIM HELD CYANIDE OF MERCURY. Crowing that it had once again outscooped its archrival with an "exclusive" revelation, the *World* presented "conclusive" proof that "the person who sent the deadly dose to

Mr. Barnet" was "identical with the person who sent the vial of poison to Harry Cornish at the same club."

The "proof" offered by the *World* was the formal statement made to the police by Dr. Henry Beaman Douglass, the man who had attended Barnet during the latter's final days. Dr. Douglass's testimony was printed in its entirety under the blaring headline BARNET POISONED, DECLARES HIS PHYSICIAN.

Anyone who bothered to read the accompanying text from start to finish would have discovered something interesting. Far from believing that his patient was poisoned, Dr. Douglass continued to cling stubbornly to his original diagnosis. "I believe that Mr. Barnet died of heart failure following diphtheria, which heart failure was brought on by undue exertion," he declared. "I do not believe that any mercurial poisoning contributed in the least to cause his death."[2]

That Pulitzer's paper would so completely distort the facts was, of course, consistent with the journalistic ethics of the yellow papers, which never let anything as trivial as mere accuracy get in the way of a good story. In this case, however, the *World* could be forgiven. Guy Ellison—the Park Avenue chemist who, at Douglass's request, analyzed the Kutnow's Powder sent to Barnet—*had* found cyanide of mercury in the medicine. Douglass's refusal to admit that Barnet had been murdered, even in the teeth of this evidence, was a matter of sheer self-interest: a desperate attempt to preserve his professional reputation and avoid any charges of incompetence.

Having learned of Ellison's findings—and thwarted in his efforts to trace the items sent to Cornish—Captain McCluskey now shifted his focus to the death of Henry Barnet. "I'm convinced," he announced a day after the *World* ran its story, "that the same mind sent the two poisons."[3]

McCluskey began by speaking to the people who had spent time with Barnet at the end of his life. Dr. Douglass, who bridled at any suggestion that he might have misdiagnosed his patient, had nothing helpful to say.[4] On the other hand, Joseph Moore—the night watchman of the Knickerbocker who doubled as a valet—offered a vivid, often poignant account of Barnet's dying days.

According to Moore, who had been summoned to the sick man's room soon after Barnet was first stricken, the clubman suspected from the first that he had been poisoned.

"Why, what have you taken?" Moore had asked, alarmed at Barnet's condition.

"There's the damned stuff in the wastebasket," said the ashen-faced man between groans.

Moore dug through the trash but could find nothing. Heaving himself from the bed, Barnet staggered over to the basket and fished out a small tin of Kutnow's Powder, which he handed to Moore before being overcome with a spasm of nausea.

As Barnet made for the bathroom, Moore undid the lid, dipped the end of his first finger into the powder, then touched it to his tongue. It had, he told McCluskey, "a bitter, metallic taste, not like any medicine I've ever tasted. It was as though I had a mouthful of copper pennies."

Even after he was diagnosed with diphtheria, Barnet continued to believe that, as he told Moore, he had "taken enough poison to kill fifty men." He seemed to know, despite his doctors' reassurances, that he would never recover. At one point, Moore found him sitting up in bed, gazing out the nearby window with a look of infinite sadness.

"Moore," said Barnet, coming out of his reverie, "I owe a tailor some money." He then instructed the valet to telephone his banker and have fifty dollars sent up to the room. Moore obeyed, and a short while later, a messenger arrived with the cash. Barnet then instructed Moore to take eight dollars to the tailor.

Even at the time, Moore had been struck by this seemingly minor request. It was as though Barnet were settling up his debts before his final leave-taking.

"And what happened then?" McCluskey inquired.

"I paid the tailor," Moore replied, "and kept the receipt and a few days afterward gave it to Mr. Barnet's brother." By then, Barnet was dead.

McCluskey was curious about the timing of certain incidents in Moore's account. Exactly when, he asked, had Barnet remarked that he had taken enough poison to kill fifty men?

"I think it was three days before he died," said Moore. "I could fix the time more accurately if Miss Bates was here. She overheard the conversation."[5]

"And who is Miss Bates?" asked McCluskey, scribbling the name in his notepad.

She was one of the two private nurses hired to be with Barnet around the clock, explained Moore. Her first name was Addie. She lived at a rooming house at 12 West Twenty-second Street.

Detective Arthur Carey was sent in a coupe to pick up Miss Bates and bring her back to police headquarters for questioning. Her testimony, when reported by the yellow press, would add a sensational new element to the case, and help throw a circumstantial net around Roland Molineux that he would have an increasingly hard time wriggling out of.

On the first of November, as Miss Bates explained to her interrogators, Dr. Douglass had summoned her to his home, where he told her of a man named Barnet, a member of the Knickerbocker Athletic Club, who was suffering from a case of diphtheria. Agreeing to accept the case, she proceeded to the club, where she found the patient suffering from a "very sore throat."

Later that same afternoon, Dr. Douglass arrived and gave her instructions. For the next nine days, until Barnet's death, she remained at his side for twelve-hour stretches, administering his medicine, spraying his throat, and feeding him whatever small amounts of nourishment he was capable of taking.

It was clear to the nurse that Barnet was a very popular man. "Many messages of sympathy came for him over the telephone." Miss Bates spoke to each of the well-wishers, explaining that the patient was too weak to take the call. Several of Barnet's club members also came to his door, hoping to be let in to see him, though at Douglass's orders none was admitted. One gentleman who lived down the hall made daily inquiries about Barnet's health and had flowers sent to the room on several occasions.

Barnet, in his failing condition, seemed utterly indifferent to these gestures. Only once did he display a spark of interest. It happened a few days before his death, when he awoke from a troubled sleep to find that a big bouquet of chrysanthemums had been delivered to his room. It was accompanied by a note, which, at Barnet's request, Miss Bates read aloud to the stricken man. The "affectionate nature" of the message left little doubt in her mind that the writer, a woman, "had a deep regard" for Barnet.

"I wonder how she knew I was ill?" was all Barnet said when Miss Bates finished reading the note.

And who, exactly, sent this affectionate message? McCluskey now asked.

The nurse could not say. The writer had not used her full name. Miss Bates did, however, clearly recall the signature on the note: "Yours, Blanche."[6]

37

For a free spirit like Blanche with her bottomless appetite for "gaiety and glamor," the circumstances in which she now found herself were almost unbearably grim. Instead of the life she had envisioned when she finally accepted Roland's proposal—the dinners at Delmonico's, the evenings at the opera, the parties with "people of brilliance and clever ability"—she was trapped within the confines of her in-laws' "staid and dull" Brooklyn home, whose heavy mid-Victorian furnishings and somber atmosphere made it feel less like a refuge than a mausoleum.[1]

To keep the family safe from the prying eyes of reporters and curiosity seekers, the General saw to it that the draperies were drawn at all times. The wintry daylight never penetrated the house. The only illumination came from the elaborate, old-fashioned ceiling fixtures and the glowing coals in the black onyx fireplaces.[2]

Intensifying the gloom of her surroundings was the dark mood of the people she shared them with. To be sure, the General did his best to maintain a cheerful demeanor. But at times, Blanche would see him sitting alone, looking heartsore and haggard—an old, careworn man. As for Roland—who now spent much of his time huddling with his attorneys—his assurances that the whole absurd affair would soon be resolved struck her as increasingly forced and brittle.[3]

Newspapers claimed that, after reading accounts of the investigation,

Blanche had suffered a complete nervous collapse and was in such dire condition that her family feared for a "fatal termination of her illness."[4] But like so much of what passed for truth in the yellow press, this report was wildly exaggerated. In point of fact, Blanche had only the sketchiest idea of what was happening beyond Fort Greene Place, since at the General's orders, newspapers were forbidden in the house. She had no way of knowing that, thanks to the ballyhoo whipped up by Pulitzer and Hearst, the Molineux case had already become the biggest crime story in years. Or that she herself had become the focus of intense—and decidedly prurient—fascination.

That the yellow papers intended to exploit the Molineux case for every last bit of entertainment value was made vividly clear in their splashy Sunday supplements, which—in addition to their usual mix of lurid adventure tales (WHITE WOMAN AMONG THE CANNIBALS!), pseudoscientific essays (ARE SEA SERPENTS REAL?), believe-it-or-not oddities (HE HICCOUGHED FOR FIVE DAYS!), mildly risqué features (PRETTY ANNETTE'S GAUZY SILK BATHING SUITS), and full-color comics—began running regular articles related to the Great Poison Mystery.[5]

In early January, for example, the *World*'s Sunday supplement featured a lengthy piece titled HISTORICAL POISONERS AND HOW THEY HAVE SLAIN THE VICTIMS OF THEIR HATE AND PASSION. In graphic and gruesome detail, the article recounted the "horrible crimes" of illustrious Old World poisoners, from Caligula to Louis XIV. The main focus of the piece, however, was Lucrezia Borgia, whose seductively posed portrait—reproduced from a painting by German artist Wilhelm von Kaulbach—occupied the center of the page. So great was her notoriety, the article noted, that her very name had become a byword for female treachery. "Thus," said the writer, "we hear that 'Mrs. Botkin is a Borgia,' or that 'there may be a Lucrezia Borgia in the Adams-Cornish mystery.'"[6]

Hearst's *Journal*, meanwhile, countered with a remarkable Sunday feature titled OLD SLEUTH'S DAUGHTER UNRAVELS THE MYSTERY OF NEW YORK'S GREAT POISON SECRET. A thinly fictionalized account of the Adams-Barnet affair, this story was written by one Rena I. Halsey, daughter of a popular dime novelist named Harlan P. Halsey, whose most famous creation was a detective known as "Old Sleuth." The elder Halsey having died the previous year, Hearst had hired the daughter to "take up the facts as known to the public and work out a solution to the mystery."

In the resulting story, "Old Sleuth" encounters barely disguised versions of Roland B. Molineux, Blanche Chesebrough, Henry Barnet, Harry Cornish, and Katherine Adams (here renamed Reginald B. Martineau, Bertha Chesney, Robert Bennett, Harold Cornell, and Mrs. Albro). Inevitably, the ace detective cracks the case, though readers expecting anything like a plausible solution to the actual crime were in for a disappointment, since the killer in Miss Halsey's tale turns out to be a wholly fictitious creation named Florence Applegate—an aging beauty with "strange, weird" eyes who murders out of jealousy.[7]

Hearst's recasting of the Adams-Barnet case as a cheesy whodunit was a pioneering instance of a phenomenon that would define the coming century, when the boundary between news and entertainment became increasingly blurred. On another day, the *Journal* ran a feature on the death of Henry Barnet in the form of a "graphic story": an eight-panel comic strip illustrating the fate of the "first victim of the poisoner" from his drinking of the Kutnow Powder to his final illness.[8]

Not to be outdone, Pulitzer's paper presented a summary of the case in the form of a stage play, complete with a "Cast of Characters"; a synopsis of the "Great Double Poisoning Drama" divided into acts and scenes ("ACT I—Death of Barnet. SCENE I—Barnet's apartment in the Knickerbocker Athletic Club. Barnet and Dr. Beaman Douglass in consultation"); and the kind of cliff-hanging conclusion that, a few decades later, would become a staple of Saturday matinee movie serials ("ACT IV—The Audience Waits for the Arrest. But of whom? And when, if ever? What dramatist's imagination has set the stage for such a play as this?")[9]

•

In keeping with the increasingly melodramatic coverage of the story, Blanche was first introduced to the public in the stock role of the Dark Lady, a mysterious seductress whose entrance was heralded with teasing hints and (quite literal) foreshadowings.

ENTER THE INEVITABLE WOMAN, announced the *Journal* on January 6, reporting the discovery of a "mysterious letter, signed with a woman's first name" that had been "sent to Henry Barnet during the illness that preceded his death."[10]

WHO IS BLANCHE? blared the paper on the following day, publicly identifying for the first time the signature on the "affectionate" missive that Barnet had supposedly "read and reread . . . up to the very time of his death."[11]

On that same day, the *World* featured a lurid, attention-grabbing drawing on its front page. The illustration shows a gloved hand labeled "Police" pulling back a dark curtain to expose a bottle of cyanide of mercury. In the glaring light, the bottle casts the shadow of a young woman's profile. The caption reads: "A Qualitative Analysis."

For anyone following the Adams-Barnet case—which, by that point, would have been much of the city's population—the meaning of this cartoon was unmistakable. As the police investigation brought more facts to light, it was increasingly clear that behind the death of Henry Barnet loomed a beautiful woman.

The face of that shadowy figure was first revealed to the public a few days later. FIRST PUBLISHED PORTRAIT OF MRS. ROLAND B. MOLINEUX, trumpeted a headline in the *World*. The accompanying picture—a handsome pen-and-ink sketch apparently copied from a group photograph of a choral society Blanche once belonged to—showed a smiling young woman with the radiant all-American charm of one of Charles Dana Gibson's idealized beauties.

By then, reporters had not only identified the mysterious sender of the Barnet letter as Roland Molineux's wife but had dug up a wealth of information on the former Blanche Chesebrough. LIFE OF MRS. MOLINEUX READS LIKE A ROMANCE, proclaimed a lengthy article in the *World*, which offered a surprisingly detailed—if not wholly accurate—account of her life, from her peripatetic childhood through her early musical studies to her marriage to Roland Molineux. The picture that emerged in the paper was of a young woman whose beauty, grace, and exceptional singing talent made her irresistibly alluring to both Roland and Henry Barnet, turning the two men into bitter rivals for her affection. "Molineux is said by his friends to be of a very jealous disposition," the paper reported, "and it was not long before he and Barnet became engaged in a quarrel about the handsome girl. Their mutual dislike grew into hatred and it soon became known among their friends that they were avowed enemies on account of Miss Chesebrough."[12]

Immured in the Molineuxs' fortress-like home, where (as she writes in her memoirs) "the news sheets were not even unfolded in my presence,"[13] Blanche was unaware of her new notoriety. Up until that point, the Adams-Barnet case already had the makings of a major media sensation: scandalous doings in the upper-crust world of Manhattan's elite athletic clubs; the scapegrace son of a Civil War hero; deadly poisons sent through the mail; dark hints of drugs and strange disguises and unspecified "degeneracy."

Now, with the introduction of a romantic triangle involving a beautiful young woman and her two vying lovers, the last lip-smacking ingredient was added to the mix: a generous dollop of sexual titillation.

38

In commissioning Harlan P. Halsey's daughter to produce a mystery story based on the Adams-Barnet case, Hearst's paper was not simply offering its readers a bit of weekend diversion but taking a swipe at the New York City police. "The detectives of real life have studied, guessed, and theorized and arrived at no solution of the mysterious poisoning of Henry C. Barnet and Mrs. Kate Adams," the editors explained in a prefatory note. "The letters from 'Blanche,' the relations of Roland Burnham Molineux and his wife with Barnet, the bottles of poison, the addresses on the wrappers, and a dozen other interesting discoveries have apparently led to nothing. The *Journal* has therefore asked 'Old Sleuth,' the famous detective of fiction, to take the facts as known to the public and work out a solution to the mystery."[1] The message couldn't have been clearer: even a make-believe detective could do a better job than the city's so-called professionals.

As the days passed without an arrest, the yellow papers became increasingly harsh in their criticism of the detective bureau. The *Journal* was especially nasty. In one jeering cartoon, a fox labeled "Poisoner" runs circles around a big lumbering dog with a police helmet and the face of Captain McCluskey. In another, a hapless police bloodhound sniffs the air for clues, completely oblivious of the big wooden sign directly above his head that points to the solution of the poisoning case.

In its relentless persecution of McCluskey, the paper described a half dozen murder mysteries that his bureau had failed to "unravel," from the strangling of a young woman named Margaret Clarkson Crowley in March 1898 to the Christmas Eve stabbing of an "old florist" named Jean Baptiste Colin in his West Twenty-eighth Street tenement. MUST THE ADAMS CASE GO ON THIS FAILURE LIST? the headline demanded.[2]

The paper was even more scathing on its editorial page, accusing the police not merely of incompetence but of corruption. "It will be time to credit the police having an honest intention in this matter when they have accomplished something," one editorial thundered. "So far, they have only muddled the case, and have added to their customary stupidity the criminal offense of premeditated indifference."[3]

A few days later, Hearst leveled even more damning charges against McCluskey and his men:

> The same old farce is being played in the poisoning case. No arrests and no possibility of any. The police keep up a semblance of activity but they are very careful not to take any positive step.
>
> In the handling of this important case they have failed to demonstrate the slightest ability. No clew of value has been discovered by them. They have blundered at every point.
>
> With a stupidity that must have behind it the incentive of an authoritative suggestion, the police have avoided confirming suspicions that might reveal the identity of the murderer. They have applied neither energy nor skill to the work, leaving to others the task of bringing the offense to justice.
>
> The public cannot be deceived by a pretense of eagerness. The promises of the police are valueless. They are only part of the carefully planned scheme to conceal the most brazen exhibition of official negligence that even the Police Department of New York has been guilty of.[4]

To incite his readers to an even higher pitch of outrage, Hearst argued that the failure of the police to bring the poisoner to justice was worse than reprehensible; it was an active threat to the well-being of the public. POLICE TIE-UP IN THE ADAMS MYSTERY BREEDS NEW POISONINGS, blared one of the *Journal*'s more inflammatory headlines.[5] According to the article, the poisoner's success in eluding capture had emboldened other killers to emulate him, setting off a rash of copycat crimes.

In Paducah, Kentucky, Mr. and Mrs. Edward Raab were poisoned "with a deadly drug in their breakfast." William Bauer, a little boy from Sandusky, Ohio, "ate some candy which was given to him and died." Poisoned tea was the culprit in the case of C. A. Glesner, a farmer from Carlinville, Illinois, who found a package of pekoe in his buggy, took it home, and drank a fatal cup with dinner. Pearl Holmes, "a little colored girl" from Annapolis, Maryland, perished after eating oatmeal spiked with arsenic, though "who would want to poison the little one is a mystery." And in New York City, a young hairdresser named Marie Appell fell violently ill after eating an arsenic-laced "chocolate drop" from a box ostensibly sent to her by an unknown admirer.

All of these cases and more—so many as to amount to a veritable "poison epidemic"—were directly inspired by the Adams-Barnet case, at least according to the yellow papers. The situation had grown so dire that, as a public service, Hearst's *Evening Journal* began running a graphic front-page warning: a drawing of a box of bonbons with a death's head superimposed on it and a caption reading: "Don't Accept Presents of Candy Unless You Know Who Sent Them!"[6]

Hearst's attack on the police was, of course, perfectly in keeping with his self-appointed role as fearless defender of the common man. If the murderer of Katherine Adams and Henry Barnet had been a common criminal, the *Journal* maintained, he would have been arrested long ago. The man believed guilty of the crimes, however, had extraordinary advantages. Thanks to his family's "financial resources," he had the finest "legal and expert assistance" available. He was also being shielded by friends of his father, who were exerting "powerful influence of a political character" to keep the authorities from doing their job. "The Police Will Have to Be Unraveled Before They Can Unravel the Poison Mystery," read the caption of one editorial cartoon, which showed a uniformed officer being trussed up and gagged by a pair of powerful hands labeled "Politician."[7]

That influential friends of General Edward Leslie Molineux had intervened in the case was not beyond the realm of possibility. A politician described as a "power in Tammany Hall" had reportedly paid a visit to police headquarters, where he "delivered an ultimatum from his superiors which has effectively tied the hands of the police."[8] And the district attorney, Colonel Asa Bird Gardiner, was known to be an old friend and battlefield comrade of the General's who had socialized with him many times at the city's innumerable veterans' functions.[9]

Confronted with such charges, Gardiner vehemently denied that the suspect was being shielded by powerful friends. The police, he asserted, were conducting their investigation in precisely "the right way." "This will take time," he stressed. "It is only proper that the police should proceed carefully and have matters in shape before any definite action is taken. There are still missing links in the chain of evidence that make it impossible to take a decisive step at this time."[10] McCluskey, too, scoffed at the notion that his men were "being held back by some potent influence." "It is ridiculous, utterly ridiculous," he replied when confronted by a group of reporters. "Since I have had charge of this office I've been permitted to investigate every case without the slightest interference. The statement that my hands are tied and that I'm being prevented from making an arrest is absolutely without foundation. It's almost funny."[11]

And indeed, even as the yellow papers were accusing the detectives of deliberately dragging their feet, McCluskey's men were pursuing a significant new clue—one that would cause Hearst himself to revise his low opinion of their efforts and lead to what his paper would call "a startling new chapter in the Great Poisoning Mystery."[12]

39

It had been a difficult two weeks for Herman and Gustav Kutnow. Ever since the story of Henry Barnet's death broke, their business had fallen off dramatically. To stem the damage, they had issued a string of reassuring statements, declaring that no toxic chemicals were used in the making of their product, an all-natural "pleasant-tasting effervescent salt" derived from the Carlsbad mineral springs. But their efforts had made little impression on a public exposed to daily graphic descriptions of a healthy thirty-two-year-old clubman who had suffered a miserable death after taking a dose of their medicine.

"The fact that the murderer employed a bottle of our powder as an instrument in his design against Barnet has given our preparation the most undesirable kind of advertising," Herman Kutnow told one reporter in mid-January. By then, sales of the once-popular patent medicine were essentially "at a standstill."[1]

Desperate to see the case resolved, the Kutnows posted a $500 reward "for the conviction of the poisoner." "We make the offer," Herman explained, "to stimulate the detectives to exercise their greatest efforts."[2] They also let it be known that they were eager to assist the investigation in any way possible. And so, when Arthur Carey showed up at the Kutnows' Astor Place office, the brothers were ready to give the detective whatever help he needed.

Carey had brought along the little tin from which Barnet had taken the fatal dose. Examining it, Gustav Kutnow confirmed that it was one of the company's free samples. Stuck to the bottom was a label that warned: "Any person selling or exposing for sale this sample at any time will be liable to all the punishments and penalties of the law."[3] The company had only begun attaching this notice to its samples in July 1898, six months earlier.

How, Carey wanted to know, were the samples distributed?

There were three ways, explained Kutnow. During the previous summer, he had spent a week in Asbury Park, New Jersey, handing them out from a booth on the boardwalk. People could also receive a sample by coming to the Kutnow brothers' office and asking for one.

The vast majority of the little tins, however, were distributed through the mail as the result of the company's newspaper ads. Anyone sending in a letter with his name and address would receive a free sample by return mail.[4]

Carey asked if the Kutnows kept records of the people who wrote in for samples.

Indeed they did, said Gustav. In fact, they carefully preserved the actual letters in order to compile a mailing list of potential customers.

This was good news to Carey, who was eager to find any piece of physical evidence that would link the suspect to the Barnet murder.

The bad news was that, during the six-month period in question, the Kutnows had received approximately 100,000 of these letters.[5]

Beginning that day, Carey—seated in his shirtsleeves at a desk in the Kutnow brothers' office—methodically went through stack after stack of the letters. In this task he was assisted by two of his colleagues, Detectives Herlihy and McCafferty, along with the Kutnows' bookkeeper, a young woman named Elsie Gray. To help her identify the letter he was looking for, Carey gave her a facsimile of the handwriting on the poison package received by Harry Cornish.

Exactly one week after the search began, as the four of them were huddled at the desk, Miss Gray let out a little gasp. "I think I've found it," she said. Feeling a jolt of excitement, Carey reached out and took the sheet of paper from her hands. Even at a glance, he could see that the penmanship bore a striking resemblance to the writing on the poison package. But as he read the letter, his excitement gave way to confusion.

The one-line request for "a sample of salt" was written on a sheet of what was obviously expensive stationery. The paper was eggshell blue in color and embossed with a distinctive silver crest, consisting of three small interlinked crescents. Only a man of hopelessly snobbish habits, thought Carey, would use such fancy stationery for his everyday communications. A man like Roland Molineux.

Like most of his colleagues on the force, Carey felt sure that Molineux was the poisoner. He'd been hoping that, once it turned up, the request for the Kutnow's Powder would confirm that belief—that it would be signed with Molineux's name, or have, as a return address, the Morris Herrmann factory or the New York Athletic Club or perhaps even the imposing house on Fort Greene Place.

But the return address supplied by the sender was none of those places. It was 1620 Broadway in Manhattan. And the letter wasn't signed "Roland Molineux."

It was signed "H. Cornish."[6]

40

The Kutnow brothers were sticklers for record keeping. Whenever a sample tin was sent out, a clerk stamped the mailing date on the letter of request. The date on the letter Elsie Gray had found was "Dec. 23, 1898."

Carey was puzzled by this. He was sure that the letter he now held in his hands had come from the poisoner; there was no mistaking the handwriting. And yet, Henry Barnet had died on November 10—six full weeks before the date rubber-stamped on the robin's-egg-blue stationery.

Carey could think of only one explanation: the killer had sent in a request for *another* sample tin of Kutnow's Powder more than a month after murdering Barnet. And he had done so under the name of Harry Cornish.

Carey and his partners proceeded directly from the Kutnow brothers' office to the address on the letter: 1620 Broadway. It turned out to be a small-time operation with the grandiose name of the Commercial Advertising Company. The proprietor was a man named Joseph Koch, who derived much of his income from renting private letter boxes—little pigeonholes built into a wall behind a wooden counter—for fifty cents a month or five dollars a year.

Shown the letter from Kutnow's, Koch checked his ledger and confirmed that, on December 21, he had rented box Number 10 to a man calling himself Harry Cornish. Though "Cornish" had taken the box for two months, neither Koch nor his clerk had ever seen him again.

Carey, who was hoping to collect as much physical evidence as possible, asked Koch to check box Number 10. To the detective's disappointment, the box was empty.[1]

Two days later, on January 14, Koch made a surprising discovery.

While distributing the morning mail, he noticed that two small packages addressed to "H. Cornish" had inadvertently been placed in the wrong letter box—Number 9. One was a manila clasp envelope, the other a small cardboard box. Koch put the packages aside, intending to bring them down to police headquarters later that afternoon, though he didn't make the trip until the following day, when he turned them over to Captain McCluskey.[2]

Seated at his desk, McCluskey opened each package in turn. The first, from Von Mohl & Company of Cincinnati, Ohio, contained a small box labeled "Calthos." Inside were five conical gelatin capsules, along with directions for their use. Studying these instructions, McCluskey saw that the pills were intended as a remedy for "male debility"—impotence. He immediately sent a telegram to the Cincinnati Police Department, asking them to check the records of the Von Mohl Company for any communication from "H. Cornish."

The second package, postmarked December 23, contained a tin of Kutnow's Powder—obviously the sample mailed out in response to the request turned up by Elsie Gray.

At McCluskey's orders, Detective Carey sought out Harry Cornish and brought him down to Koch's office. Though admittedly nearsighted, Koch had no trouble confirming what the detectives already believed: that Cornish was *not* the man who had rented letter box Number 10.[3]

Like Carey, McCluskey wondered why the poisoner had sent for another tin of Kutnow's Powder more than a month after killing Henry Barnet—and why he had written the request and rented the letter box under Cornish's name. Perhaps, McCluskey thought, it was all part of a diabolical plot to frame Cornish for Barnet's murder if the attempt on Cornish's own life failed. According to McCluskey's theory, the poisoner "probably thought that, if Cornish didn't take the deadly bromo-seltzer, the letter-box scheme would eventually become public and show that Cornish had written for the samples sent to Barnet. That would connect Cornish to Barnet's death. And the next best thing to killing an enemy is to have him accused of murder."[4]

Upon receipt of McCluskey's telegram, Superintendent Detsch of the Cincinnati Police Department dispatched a detective named Herman Witte to the offices of Von Mohl Company at 506 Lincoln's Inn Place. Witte spoke to the manager, Joseph Brewster, who referred him to a clerk named C. B. Pugh.

Within the hour, Pugh, searching through the company files, turned up a letter from "H. Cornish" requesting the free "5 day trial" offered in the company's newspaper ads. Witte took the letter with him and, that afternoon, mailed it special delivery to Captain McCluskey.[5]

It arrived late the following afternoon, Tuesday, January 17. Seated at his desk, the "boss-sleuth" examined the letter. McCluskey was no graphologist, but to his eyes, the letter had clearly been inscribed by the same hand that had addressed the lethal package to the real Harry Cornish. And like the request that Elsie Gray had found among the files of the Kutnows' firm, it was written on a robin's-egg-blue sheet embossed with a little crest of three interlinked silver crescents—the kind of ostentatiously elegant stationery that was meant to proclaim the writer's superior taste and that, to a man like "Chesty" McCluskey, seemed positively effeminate.[6]

41

Early in the investigation, the police had retained the services of a pair of well-known handwriting experts: William J. Kinsley, editor of the venerable *Penman's Art Journal*, and David Carvalho, who had been much in the news before Christmas for his role in a sensational blackmail trial involving robber baron Jay Gould.[1] All penmanship samples relevant to the Adams-Barnet murders, beginning with the address scissored from the infamous poison package, were immediately turned over to these specialists. By Tuesday, January 17, they had already received the fake Cornish request found by Elsie Gray.

Now, having completed his own examination of the latest "Cornish" letter sent to Von Mohl Company, McCluskey planned to forward it to Kinsley and Carvalho. Even as he prepared to do so, another startling discovery was taking place in Cincinnati.

Up until that point, the newshounds in the pay of Pulitzer and Hearst had played a leading role in the investigation, not only goading the police into action but often beating them to important clues. This time, though, it was another paper—the *New York Herald*—that was ahead of the pack.

No sooner had its editors learned about the letter found among the files of Von Mohl Company than a telegram went out to the *Herald*'s Cincinnati stringer. Quickly repairing to the offices of the patent medicine firm, the reporter spoke to the manager, Joseph Brewster. Was it possible, he asked, that other correspondence signed with Cornish's name might exist in the company's records?

With the newsman looking on, Brewster began searching through the files. It wasn't long before he came upon a piece of mail—still in its original envelope—whose handwriting bore a marked resemblance to that on the earlier "Cornish" letter. It, too, was a request for a five-day trial sample of the company's widely advertised impotence cure, Calthos. Only this time, the sender had supplied a different address: 257 West Forty-second Street. And the signature on the letter—much to the astonishment of both the reporter and Brewster—wasn't "H. Cornish." It was "H. C. Barnet."[2]

Though less given to blowing its own horn than its more shameless rivals, the *Herald* couldn't keep from trumpeting the news of its "important and sensational discovery" in its morning edition. By the time its readers were learning of this stunning new development, a reporter for the *Herald* was already at the address given on the fake Barnet letter.

Number 257 West Forty-second Street turned out to be a shabby little "advertising agency" run by one Nicholas Heckmann, whose office, like Joseph Koch's, was furnished with a rack of wooden pigeonholes that were rented out as private letter boxes. Questioned by the reporter, Heckmann recalled that the previous May, a well-dressed gentleman had come into his office, inquiring about a letter box. Heckmann knew the man by sight, having seen him around the neighborhood for years. When Heckmann quoted his fees, the man opted for the quarterly rate—$1.50. He then paid the money in advance and gave his name as Mr. H. C. Barnet, correcting Heckmann's spelling when the latter added an extra *t* to the end of the name.

For the next few weeks, the gentleman picked up his mail every other day, generally in the late afternoon or early evening. Most of what he received appeared to come from various patent medicine concerns, including Von Mohl of Cincinnati, a firm that had stuck in Heckmann's mind because the return address—Lincoln's Inn Place—sounded so unusual.

Then, a month after renting the letter box, "Mr. Barnet" had abruptly ceased to show up. Heckmann had never seem him again, though various small packages and letters continued to arrive in his name. Heckmann—who generally held on to his customers' uncollected mail for several months—still had a number of items addressed to "Barnet" in his possession and let the reporter examine them. There were letters from patent medicine firms in New York City, Detroit, and Ohio. Checking the postmarks, the reporter noticed that the most recent was dated November 29, 1898.

Or so he initially thought. Heckmann, however, drew his attention to an item that, by a strange coincidence, had arrived for "Barnet" just the previous morning—an advertising circular for a concoction called Dr. Rudolphe's Specific Remedy, sold by a Professor F. C. Fowler of Moodus, Connecticut.

The *Herald*'s man had just finished studying this advertisement when the office door banged open and in strode two plainclothes detectives, Arthur Carey and his partner, William McCafferty. They had been dispatched to Heckmann's place by Captain McCluskey, who had learned of the discovery of the fake Barnet letter only a short time earlier, when he'd seen that morning's *Herald.* Taking Heckmann aside, the detectives began to question him in hushed, urgent tones. About twenty minutes later, after taking possession of all the Barnet material, they left.

By then, the reporter from the *Herald* was already on his way to the train station.[3]

He rode the New York, New Haven, and Hartford Railroad to Connecticut, changing cars once at Valley Branch, then hiring a buggy to drive him five miles from Goodspeed Station to the little village of Moodus in the far eastern part of the state. When he arrived at the offices of Professor Fowler's patent medicine operation, he spoke to the manager, George Hill, who began to look through the company's files for any communication signed H. C. Barnet. Hill was still searching when Fowler himself showed up and took over the task. He combed his records for nearly two hours before he found what he was looking for.

It was a printed order sheet for the company's ostensible impotency cure, Dr. Rudolphe's Specific Remedy. The sender had enclosed the requisite fee—$3.12—and supplied some basic information, though he appeared to have filled in the blanks rather hastily. (In response to the question "Married or single?" for example, he had written "Yes.") He indicated that he had been afflicted for ten years and that he suffered from an advanced stage of his condition. The name was given as H. C. Barnet and the return address as "Box #217, 257 West 42nd Street, NY City."

In the judgment of the reporter—who had brought along a newspaper facsimile of the address from the poison package mailed to Harry Cornish—the handwriting was "exactly the same."[4] He was also struck by the postmark on the envelope: May 31, 1898.

Captain McCluskey, in the meanwhile, had started his own man for Moodus—a detective named Tinker. Unfortunately, Detective Tinker had missed a connection and found himself stranded in central Connecticut overnight. When McCluskey received a message from Tinker, the chief immediately wired Fowler, directing him to "send without delay any document in his possession signed by H. C. Barnet."

By then, however, it was too late. Fowler (for an undisclosed monetary consideration) had turned over the "Barnet" order form to the reporter, who was already on his way back to New York City.[5]

The following day, the *Herald* ran a crowing headline, POLICE FOLLOWING THE HERALD'S CLEWS. The story described the "new and important clews" discovered by its intrepid reporter at Nicholas Heckmann's letter box agency and Professor Fowler's lab in Moodus, Connecticut. Noting that the order form sent to Fowler had been postmarked May 31, 1898, the newspaper concluded that the plot to murder Henry Barnet and Harry Cornish had been hatched as far back as the previous spring, then carried out with "fiendish deliberation."

Fearing a libel suit, the paper refrained from naming a suspect. It did, however, mention a "strange coincidence." Describing the uncollected letters that had arrived for "Barnet" at Heckmann's place, the story noted that one of these had been postmarked November 19, 1898—"the very day that Blanche Chesebrough, who was said to be a close friend of H. C. Barnet, was married to Roland B. Molineux, who was known to be jealous of Miss Chesebrough because of Barnet's admiration for her."[6]

There was another odd coincidence that the *Herald* failed to note, though it would not escape the attention of later commentators. Of all the letters requesting impotence cures and marriage manuals mailed out under the names H. C. Barnet and H. Cornish (and there would turn out to be many of them), all were postmarked either in the spring or fall of

1898. None had been mailed out in July or August—the months when Roland Molineux was out of the country on his summer trip to Europe.

While the *Herald* was claiming bragging rights for the latest discoveries in the case, Detective Carey was quietly pursuing another lead.

Among the uncollected "Barnet" mail that he and McCafferty had confiscated at Heckmann's was a letter from the Marston Remedy Company of 19 Park Place, Manhattan. Proceeding to that address, Carey spoke to the owner, Dr. Vincent G. Hamill, who, in searching through his records, came upon the four-page "diagnosis blank" filled out by the man who signed himself H. C. Barnet.

Though the questionnaire required little more than one- or two-word answers, it was a revealing document. From it, Carey learned that the sender suffered from recurrent bouts of impotence, had contracted a case of gonorrhea three years earlier, and was "contemplating marriage." Carey also discovered that there was at least one case of consumption—tuberculosis—in the man's family. In the space marked "Age," the applicant had written "31."

Carey was particularly struck by the chest and waist measurements given by the sender—thirty-seven and thirty-two inches respectively. Carey had never met Henry Barnet, but from what he had read and heard, he knew that the murdered clubman had been stout. He also knew that Barnet had been thirty-two years old at the time of his death.

Carey took possession of the questionnaire and left. Within twenty-fours hours—by asking around at the Knickerbocker Athletic Club—he had found out the name of Roland Molineux's tailor. A trip to the shop confirmed what Carey already surmised. Molineux's chest and waist measurements corresponded exactly to those given on the "diagnosis blank."

A few days later, Carey was able to ascertain that Molineux's maternal grandmother had died of consumption several years earlier in East Hartford, Connecticut. He also obtained a copy of Molineux's birth certificate from the Board of Health. It showed that, at the time the questionnaire was submitted, Roland Molineux was thirty-one.[7]

42

January 28 was a grim anniversary—one month to the day since Katherine Adams had swallowed the cyanide-laced bromo-seltzer and, in the vivid phrase of Harry Cornish, dropped to the floor "like six foot of chain."[1] In the intervening weeks, McCluskey and his men had come under increasingly furious fire for their failure to make an arrest. Now, with the discovery of the letters mailed to the various patent-medicine concerns, a breakthrough appeared to be imminent. As C. B. Pugh—the clerk for Von Mohl Company—remarked to a reporter, "If the New York officials will but locate the man who rented the letter boxes at No. 1620 Broadway under the name of Cornish and at No. 257 West Forty-second Street under Barnet's name, they will have no trouble in clearing up the mystery."[2]

Captain McCluskey, of course—along with Arthur Carey and every other member of the detective bureau—had no doubt who that man was. But they required confirmation. Their hopes were now pinned on the two letter box men, Koch and Heckmann. Both had viewed the suspect up close and could presumably identify him with little trouble. Indeed, Heckmann had assured a reporter that he could pick the fake Mr. Barnet "out of a million."[3]

Once again, however, the police were in for a painful disappointment. After being publicly identified as a key witness in the case, Koch became afraid that the murderer might try to eliminate him and began to carry a revolver. Soon afterward—pleading poor eyesight—he told McCluskey that he would be unable to identify the mysterious "Mr. Barnet."[4]

As for Heckmann, he proved to be a highly problematic witness. Taken to a midtown hotel where Roland and his lawyers had gone for a meeting, Heckmann failed to make a positive identification, claiming that he had not been able to get a good enough look at Molineux. A few days later, a reporter for the *World* named Buchignani brought Heckmann to Roland's workplace in Newark and contrived a face-to-face confrontation between the two men.

"That's Mr. Barnet, all right," Heckmann exclaimed afterward. "He's my customer."

It soon became clear, however, that Heckmann expected to receive a substantial payment for his testimony. When Pulitzer's representatives balked, Heckmann began to waffle. In the end, he refused to cooperate, informing Buchignani that he "would not swear to his identification of Molineux."[5]

HECKMANN THE LAST 'IDENTIFIER' TO FAIL, read a headline in the next morning's *World*. The story—which focused on the two letter box men as well as Emma Miller, the jewelry shop clerk who continued to stick to her "red-bearded man" story—began with a lead that accurately conveyed the disheartened mood of the authorities: "Hope of an identification that will ever be of any value is rapidly fading away. In fact, so far as it depends on any of the persons known to have seen the false Barnet and Cornish and the purchaser of the silver holder, it is already hopeless."[6]

By then—as if matters weren't already complicated enough—another forged letter had turned up.

Written on the familiar robin's-egg-blue, crescent-embossed stationery, it, too, had been sent to a drug firm, Frederick Stearns & Company of Detroit. This time, however, it was not an order for an impotence cure or a sex manual. Rather, it was a note requesting information about a former employee of the firm, a man named Alvin A. Harpster.

A portly, affable fellow with a pronounced fondness for drink, Harpster had worked for Frederick Stearns & Company in the early 1890s. Though hardly an athlete himself, he was an avid sports fan who was eventually fired from his job for being "more interested in the prize fights than the drug business," as his employer put it.[7] Taking a position as clerk in the Knickerbocker Athletic Club, he became friends with Harry Cornish, who, as it happened, was himself an acquaintance of Harpster's former boss, Frederick Stearns. In January 1898, Harpster had left the athletic club and gone to work as a salesman for the Ballantine Brewery.

The letter mailed to the Stearns company read: "Gentlemen—Mr. A. A. Harpster has applied to me for a position as collector. He did not refer to you but mentioned having been in your employ. A line from you would be considered confidential and greatly appreciated." It was signed "Very truly yours, H. C. Cornish" and gave as a return address "1620 Broadway, NYC."

Everything about this letter struck Frederick Stearns as peculiar, beginning with the stationery itself, which seemed far too pretentious for the bluff and down-to-earth athletic director. Since Stearns knew Cornish personally, he was also puzzled by the stiffly formal tone. And why, Stearns wondered, would Cornish be asking for a letter of recommendation? Harpster had already worked at the Knickerbocker Club and his employment record was well known to his friend Cornish.

When Stearns compared the letter with other communications he had received from Harry Cornish, he saw right away that the handwriting was completely different.

Within a day of its discovery in the company files, the "Harpster letter," as it came to be known, was in the possession of Captain McCluskey, who—like Frederick Stearns—believed that it had been mailed by the poisoner for the express purpose of introducing Harpster's name into the case and thus "casting suspicion on an innocent man."[8] It was clear to McCluskey that the fat, easygoing beer salesman had nothing whatsoever to do with the killings. That the authorities never regarded Harpster as a serious suspect, however, did not prevent the yellow papers from plastering his name across the front pages in the most insinuating way—a situation that persisted until Harpster sued Pulitzer for libel and settled for an undisclosed sum.[9]

Harpster wasn't the only one to find himself in the media spotlight in the waning days of January 1899. Felix Gallagher—another former member of the Knickerbocker Athletic Club and a close friend of Roland Molineux's—fell under suspicion after a bartender named Charley White overheard him bad-mouthing Harry Cornish in Jim Wakeley's saloon. And then there was the usual assortment of highly colorful cranks: the mind reader who, in a trance, saw the suspect; the "demented man" from Baltimore who confessed to the murders; the "well-dressed woman" who told police of a sinister "secret society" whose members bore a grudge against Cornish; the "erratic" young fellow named William Koutnik, who claimed that, on the day before Christmas, he had been accosted by a "strange man" on Madison Avenue who asked him to mail a package to Harry Cornish.[10]

Most titillating of all were the allegations by the *World*, which announced that it had unearthed "a startling, almost incredible scandal" involving a group of homosexuals—or, as the paper put it, a "coterie of vicious degenerates"—within the Knickerbocker Athletic Club. Though "supposedly of good social standing," these men existed "in a condition of moral degeneracy so horrible that it can hardly be referred to." For years, "under cover of the Knickerbocker Athletic Club," they had "carried on their vile practices," creating "a noxious state of affairs unparalleled in the history of this city." Fearing that the "terrible truth" was about to be exposed by Henry Barnet and Harry Cornish, they had conspired to poison both men.[11]

All of these claims, accusations, and innuendos, however, proved to be mere sideshows in what was already the greatest media circus of the day. In the end, the police and the press invariably ended up where they began. As the *Herald* put it: "One peculiarity about the Adams case and the Henry C. Barnet case also is that, no matter in what direction newly discovered clews lead, they almost always eventually turn toward a person whose name has been connected with the case very prominently for several weeks."

Once again, the *Herald* judiciously refrained from identifying that person. In the very next paragraph, however, the article noted that the paper had "engaged a handwriting expert of repute to compare specimens of handwriting in its possession with the writing on the poison package sent to Cornish." After completing his analysis, the expert announced that he "had found much similarity between the writing on the various specimens and the writing of Roland B. Molineux."[12]

43

As self-appointed spokesman for the oppressed masses, the multimillionaire William Randolph Hearst never missed an opportunity to attack the high and mighty on behalf of his readers. The official mismanagement of the Adams-Barnet case afforded him a perfect soapbox.

"Imagine a murder committed in a tenement house on the East Side," he thundered in an editorial published in early February, "and the persons believed to have committed it walking about town for six weeks under the eyes of the police without an arrest! If this had happened among people without influence, every person suspected of knowing anything about it would have been locked up before morning and the 'third degree' would have been vigorously applied. . . . But when two deliberate, premeditated murders have been committed by persons with financial and political pull, the whole machinery of justice has been paralyzed."

The time had come, Hearst cried, for the authorities to get to the bottom of the whole "loathsome affair." "Let in the light!" he demanded.[1]

It was a call that District Attorney Asa Bird Gardiner was finally prepared to heed. Already feeling the heat from a reform movement that would soon drive him and the rest of the Tammany crowd from office, Gardiner had suddenly decided to take matters out of the hands of the police. If McCluskey and his men couldn't uncover enough evidence to produce an arrest, there was someone else who could: the Manhattan coroner, Edward H. Hart.

The position of coroner no longer exists in New York City, having been replaced in 1915 by the medical examiner's office. At the time of the Adams-Barnet case, however, it was a centuries-old institution, transported from England during colonial times.

Whenever a suspicious death occurred, it was the coroner's duty to assemble a jury and hold an inquest to determine if a murder had been committed. Though he could find probable cause for an arrest, he was not, as a rule, expected to identify the killer. In almost all instances, his job was limited to establishing whether a sudden death was an accident, a suicide, or the result of foul play. In the latter event, it was left to the police to investigate the crime, track down the suspects, and take them into custody. Since Captain McCluskey's detectives had come up short in the present case, however, it would now be up to Coroner Hart to supply the evidence that would finally bring the perpetrator to justice.

It was a responsibility that Hart took seriously. Aside from his sense of professional duty, he had strong personal feelings on the subject. "Murder by poison must stop," he told reporters. "To me, the crime is cowardly, detestable, abominable."[2] The inquest, he announced, would begin on the first available date on his calendar—Thursday, February 9.

So intense was public fascination with the case that Hart—who generally had trouble finding willing volunteers for his juries—was immediately deluged with applicants. Some hinted that they were in possession of secrets that would "flood with light all the darkness surrounding the case." Others claimed to have "wonderful powers of discernment" that "would do much toward assisting the ferreting out" of the truth. One man wrote that his "great ability to fathom motives" made human psychology seem "as simple as a problem in geometry to a school mathematics teacher." Another sought to demonstrate his qualifications by citing scripture: "Counsel in the heart of man is like deep water; but a man of understanding will draw it out."[3]

While Hart attended to the jury selection, his assistants were busy drawing up subpoenas. Though the coroner refused to identify all the witnesses he intended to call, the papers quickly published a partial list, which included Mrs. Adams's daughter, Florence Rodgers; the physicians who attended the poisoned woman; the letter box men, Heckmann and Koch; Harry Cornish; and, of course, Roland Molineux, who was immediately placed under police surveillance to ensure that he didn't skip town.[4]

Speculation ran high about one name not immediately mentioned by Hart—the witness that both the public and the press were most eager to get a look at. It was not until February 6—just three days before the inquest was slated to begin—that the *World* trumpeted the exciting news: MRS. ROLAND MOLINEUX TO BE CALLED IN POISON CASE.

From her girlhood days, when she first dreamed of becoming a famous singer, Blanche had always hungered for the limelight. Now, she was about to occupy it in a way that she could never have imagined.

Besides demanding an immediate inquest, District Attorney Gardiner made another decision that produced a sensation in the press. Officially, the cause of Henry Barnet's death remained an open question. Though all the evidence pointed to the poisoned Kutnow's Powder, Barnet's physician, Dr. Douglass, continued to insist that the patient had died of diphtheria. With Barnet in the grave, there was only one way to settle the issue.

On Monday, February 6—after receiving a sworn affidavit from undertaker Herbert H. Jackson that no mercury had been used in preparing Barnet's corpse for burial—Gardiner submitted an application to Justice Gildersleeve of the New York State Supreme Court. His request was granted at once.

On Wednesday, February 8—one day before the scheduled start of the coroner's inquest—the body of Henry Crossman Barnet would be exhumed from its resting place in Brooklyn's Green-Wood Cemetery. The corpse would then be dissected and its organs examined for the presence of cyanide of mercury.

"Death's secret," as one headline put it, was "to be wrested from the grave."[5]

SOME STUDIES OF HARRY CORNISH AT THE POISON INQUEST.

Part Four

INQUEST

44

Snow was pelting from a leaden sky when the three carriages reached the gate of Green-Wood Cemetery late on the morning of Wednesday, February 8. The vehicles carried a party of eight officials whose solemn miens matched the grimness of the weather. Among them were Coroner Edward Hart and the coroner's physician, Dr. A. T. Weston; the chemical expert Professor Rudolph Witthaus; Dr. Henry Beaman Douglass; and a representative from the district attorney's office, Colonel Gardiner's assistant, A. E. Bryan.

They were met at the entrance by Eugene Cushman, superintendent of the cemetery. Having been informed in advance of the party's arrival, Cushman had already dispatched a crew of six gravediggers to Henry Barnet's burial site.

Disembarking from their carriages, the men trudged through the snow, with Cushman in the lead. By the time they reached Barnet's grave, the six workmen, wielding mattocks and spades, had already dug halfway down to the coffin. A mound of earth was heaped beside the freshly made hole, the reddish-brown dirt contrasting starkly with the surrounding whiteness.

The excavation took another hour. Coat collars pulled high, hats drawn low, shoulders hunched against the cold, the observers watched in silence. The only sounds were the grunts of the workmen, the crunching of their blades in the frozen ground, the wind whipping the snow through the naked trees.

At last, there was another sound, of metal scraping against wood. The tools were exchanged for heavy ropes and the earth-stained oak coffin was heaved to the surface. It was loaded on a wagon and transported to the premises of a local undertaker named Frank Selle. When the lid was removed, Dr. Douglass was the first to peer inside. The body, he confirmed, was that of his former patient, Barnet. After three months in the wintry earth, the dead man's features were still perfectly recognizable.

The corpse was removed and laid out upon a table. As the rest of the party observed—Dr. Douglass taking copious notes in a little pad—Weston opened up the body and removed the stomach, liver, kidneys, brain, throat, and a portion of the lungs. These organs were placed in jars, sealed, and turned over to Professor Witthaus for chemical analysis.

Gently returned to its coffin, Barnet's hollowed body was then driven back to the cemetery and replaced in its grave. By nightfall, it was hidden by the same spotless white blanket that covered the countless other sleepers all around.[1]

Though the snow had stopped by the following day, the city was in the grip of a brutal cold spell. Even the arctic weather, however, could not deter the curiosity seekers. Hundreds of them, male and female alike, thronged the hallways of the Criminal Court Building on Center Street, hoping to secure a seat at what the papers were already trumpeting as "the Great Inquest."

Their efforts would prove to be futile. Coroner Hart had announced that only those "who have official business there" would be granted admission. And, in truth, the chamber reserved for the inquest offered scant space for superfluous spectators.

Located on the third floor of the building, the room measured just thirty by sixty feet. Its walls, devoid of all adornment, were of rough, naked plaster. At the front stood the coroner's raised desk and, beside it, a little platform holding the witness chair. The jury box—a dozen bow-back chairs surrounded by a wooden railing—occupied the right side of the room beneath a row of tall, narrow windows. There was a plain oak table for the district attorney and another for the representatives of the press. The rest of the chamber was filled with several rows of pewlike benches. Altogether, as one observer put it, it "offered but a bare-looking stage for the first act of one of the most remarkable dramas of modern times."[2]

A uniformed officer stood at the doorway, admitting only those with signed passes from Coroner Hart. By 10:00 A.M.—the hour scheduled for the start of the proceedings—the chamber was full. In addition to the lawyers, witnesses, and newsmen, a few "privileged persons" had been given permission to attend. One of these was J. Herbert Ballantine, owner of the Knickerbocker Athletic Club facilities. Another was his friend, Albert J. Morgan, heir to the Sapolio soap-making fortune.

It was not idle curiosity that had brought Morgan to the inquest. In digging into the rumored love triangle involving Molineux, Blanche, and Henry Barnet, reporters for the yellow papers had learned about the party on board Morgan's yacht, the *Viator*, during which Roland had first met his future wife. Among Morgan's other guests on that fateful August day in 1897 was Walter Sherman Baldwin. Son of a wealthy manufacturer of paper boxes, Baldwin—a handsome, forty-three-year-old bachelor and man about town—was a longtime member of the New York Athletic Club and an old friend of Roland Molineux's. According to rumor, Baldwin had flirted openly with Blanche on that sparkling summer day in the Portland harbor—as, reportedly, had Morgan himself.

Shortly after the *Viator* returned from its cruise along the coast of Maine, Baldwin—who had seemed to be in robust health—suddenly died. Not long afterward, Morgan himself was stricken and came dangerously close to death. The official diagnosis in both cases was typhoid.

In light of subsequent events, it now seemed extremely peculiar to many observers that of the three men on board the *Viator* who had vied for Blanche Chesebrough's attention, only Roland Molineux had escaped the sudden, devastating illness that had struck his two friends.[3]

The star attractions, Roland and Blanche, did not put in an appearance on opening day. But a stir went through the crowd when a distinguished white-haired figure made his way to the front of the room. The elderly gentleman—who still bore himself with an erect, military posture that made him seem much taller than his diminutive height—was, of course, General E. L. Molineux: the "venerable old soldier," as the papers invariably referred to him. He took a seat beside his son's attorneys, Bartow Weeks and George Gordon Battle.

A few minutes later, the "Great Inquest" got under way.

The day's business proceeded so efficiently that, according to one observer, "it was as if the entire action had been carefully rehearsed and its 'playing time' measured with a stage manager's accuracy."[4] Jury selection took less than forty-five minutes. As soon as the twelve men were seated, District Attorney Asa Bird Gardiner rose to address them.

His speech was brief and to the point. The district attorney's office, he explained, was "not a detective bureau. All we can do is present the evidence gathered by the police and all evidence from outside sources, including such as may be furnished by some of our enterprising newspapers." "Anybody who can throw light" on the investigation "will be welcome."

He pointed out that, while the inquiry would focus on the death of Mrs. Adams, it would "necessarily have much bearing on the Barnet case as well." The two, he declared, were completely intertwined. This was a somewhat premature statement for Gardiner to make. Professor Witthaus, after all, had already made it known that he would need at least three weeks to analyze the organs removed from Barnet's exhumed body.

Nevertheless, Gardiner now stated unequivocally that "the same poison was sent to both Cornish and Henry C. Barnet at the Knickerbocker Club, and that poison was cyanide of mercury. It is a very significant fact that this particular poison, which has practically gone out of the pharmacopeia since 1870 or 1871, should be used to kill two persons within a month. Evidently there was deep deliberation on the part of the person who prepared these poisons."

Gardiner himself did not intend to point an accusatory finger at anyone, and he urged the jurors to banish any preconceived notions from their minds. "Nobody has been arrested," he said, "and consequently there is no defendant before you."

By the end of the inquest, however, he expected the "full and complete" truth to emerge. The killer of Mrs. Adams and Henry Barnet must not escape punishment, since poisoning, as Gardiner solemnly declared, was "a form of death that is abhorrent to the American mind" (a somewhat peculiar observation, which seemed to suggest that, along with its other objectionable qualities, there was something effetely European about poison-murder).

Less than ten minutes after he began, Gardiner made a little bow and excused himself, turning the proceedings over to his assistant, James Osborne.[5]

Born and raised on a plantation in North Carolina, the forty-year-old Osborne had attended school in both his home state and Virginia before coming North to earn a law degree at Columbia. After a few years of private practice, he had joined the district attorney's office and quickly earned a reputation as an outstanding trial attorney. As a cross-examiner, he was known to be "sly, and he could be ferocious." He also had a flair for courtroom theatrics—a great gift in the eyes of his superior, Colonel Gardiner, for whom "melodrama was an attribute of successful prosecution."[6]

It was a few minutes after noon when the first witness, Harry Cornish, took the stand. By then, the room was thick with cigar smoke. With the outside temperature hovering around zero, opening a window was out of the question. The pleas of Coroner's Clerk John Kelly—who stood up to announce that he did "not think smoking was nice or that it showed proper respect to the Court"—were unavailing. The atmosphere, lamented one reporter, "soon became positively vile."[7]

Apart from a brief lunch recess, Cornish remained on the stand in that stuffy little room for more than four hours. His suit was of a conservative cut, his collar stiff and high, his cravat neatly tied. In the weeks that had elapsed since he sampled the poisoned bromo-seltzer, he had regained the weight he had lost during his subsequent illness. With his prognathous jaw, bullet-headed dome, and seemingly permanent scowl, he looked as forbidding as ever.

Osborne, however, was not the least bit intimidated. He began by asking Cornish to "tell what you know of the death of Mrs. Kate J. Adams and so much of the facts concerning your own life as is connected with the subject." When Cornish hesitated, staring down at the floor as if collecting his thoughts, Osborne repeated the question so sharply that Cornish seemed taken aback.

"I don't know just where to begin," he said.

"Begin at the receipt of the poison," Osborne replied, as if speaking to a child.

Leaning back in his chair, the athletic director launched into the now familiar story. He had told it so many times before—to the police, to Gardiner and his assistants, to reporters from a half dozen different papers—that he could recite it by rote.

He told of receiving the anonymous gift and assuming it was meant as a gag; of scissoring out and saving the address; of the close call experienced by his friend Harry King, who would have fixed himself a glass of the lethal bromo-seltzer if the water cooler hadn't been empty; of bringing home the items to the flat he shared with Mrs. Adams and Florence Rodgers; of the older woman's terrible death and his own devastating sickness, during which he had lost fifteen pounds in less than forty-eight hours.

At that point, Osborne interrupted and, speaking in an impatient tone, told Cornish not simply to repeat statements he had already made but to "tell the facts as you recall them now."

Again, Cornish seemed nonplussed. He was having trouble responding to such open-ended instructions. He would rather answer specific questions.

Osborne, however, ignored him. "Now, Cornish," he said, "can you suggest anything as a motive in this case?"

Cornish insisted that he had never done anything in his life that would "warrant a thing like this being done."

Osborne seemed skeptical. "Tell me so much of your private affairs as would throw light on this case," he said.

"I can say this much," Cornish answered. "There is absolutely no possibility of there being any reason for a thing of this kind being done on account of my personal affairs, or on account of any woman, or on account of anyone having a reason to be jealous of me, or anything of that kind. If anybody has done anything, it is for some motive I can't understand. I have told the police everything."

"That is what you had better do here," Osborne said in a warning tone.

For a moment, the two men glared at each other while Cornish played with one waxed tip of his mustache.

"Tell me, Cornish," Osborne said, shifting tacks. "Did you know when Barnet died?"

"Why, yes," said the other. "I knew he was dead. I was told he died of typhoid fever."

"While you were superintendent of the club," Osborne asked, "didn't you and Barnet have a little trouble?"

Cornish shrugged. "Not that I know of."

Osborne raised his eyebrows in an expression of mock surprise. "Do you mean to say that you don't remember the time that Barnet complained because he had to walk from his room to the bathroom and the floor wasn't being kept clean?"

"I never heard of that before," Cornish growled.

Abruptly, as if deliberately trying to keep the witness off balance, Osborne reverted to a question about the poison package. "Now, Cornish," he demanded, "tell me any evidence you have that would suggest a motive for sending you that bottle of powder."

"I can't think of anybody who would have a motive to do a thing of that kind," responded Cornish, who seemed intent on establishing that he had led an utterly blameless life.

His voice rising to a near-shout, Osborne said, "I ask you, Cornish, to tell all the facts that may throw light on the case. Tell the jury without any more hemming and hawing about it."

Cornish did not immediately reply. After studying the floor for several moments, he conceded that "charges had twice been preferred against him" by two members of the club.

"What were the names of the two men involved?" demanded Osborne.

"Mr. Molineux," said Cornish, "and Mr. Barnet."

After further prodding by Osborne, he described the incident in which Roland had demanded his resignation after learning that Cornish had been spreading "disparaging" rumors—namely, that Molineux owned buildings in Newark that were used as gambling dens and whorehouses.

As for Barnet, he had complained to the club's Board of Governors after hearing that Cornish had accused him of "improper practices with women."

At this point, the atmosphere in the room underwent an almost palpable change. Up until that point—despite Osborne's efforts to inject some drama into the proceedings—the inquest had simply been a rehash of well-known facts. With the introduction of this "savory new element," as one commentator put it, "the interest in Cornish's testimony had grown in intensity." Everyone seemed to be sitting forward in his seat, eager not to miss a word. For the first time, deliciously titillating revelations were emerging about the sordid secret lives of the upper-class clubmen—"the unpleasant substratum that is believed to underlie the whole awful case."[8]

Hammering away at Cornish, Osborne got him to admit that he had accused Barnet of frequenting a brothel on East Forty-seventh Street run by a madam named Stern.

"Were *you* ever at that house?" demanded Osborne.

Cornish shifted uncomfortably in his seat. "Yes," he said after a brief pause. "I've been there."

"How many times?"

"I don't think more than once," said Cornish, glaring at his inquisitor.

During the remainder of Cornish's time on the witness stand, Osborne continued to hammer away at him, shouting at him, berating him, dispensing with all pretense of politeness and rudely addressing him by his last name alone. The quality of Osborne's interrogation was conveyed in the headline of that evening's *Journal:* CORNISH ON THE RACK!

Interviewed immediately after the inquest was adjourned for the day, District Attorney Gardiner had harsh words to say about the witness. Cornish, he felt, had been extremely evasive. It was clear, however, that he had reason to harbor ill feelings toward both Barnet and Molineux. Since Cornish, according to his own sworn statement, had been the one who gave Mrs. Adams the bottle of poisoned bromo-seltzer, "it behooves him to clear his own skirts. Under the law," Gardiner warned, "his admission of giving her the poison makes it possible to secure his indictment for murder."[9]

During his opening address, Gardiner had made a point of not naming a suspect. Now, it appeared that he had one in mind. And to the astonishment of everyone who had been following the case, it wasn't Roland Molineux.

45

In his usual Barnumesque way, William Randolph Hearst had once again, with great fanfare, assigned the popular writer Julian Hawthorne to cover the case. By an odd coincidence, an earlier and infinitely greater Hawthorne—Nathaniel—had written a famous short story titled "My Kinsman, Major Molineux." Set in pre–Revolutionary War Boston, this tale concerns a naive country lad named Robin whose journey through the labyrinthine streets of the night-shrouded city leads to an unsettling discovery: that lurking beneath their civilized veneer, human beings possess dark and even frightful impulses. Or, as the story puts it, that a man may "have several voices . . . as well as two complexions."

It was a lesson that the real-life Molineux case would illustrate in an especially vivid way.

Friday, February 10, was the coldest day on record in New York City, with the thermometer dropping to six degrees below zero—"Klondike weather," as the papers described it. Frozen pipes left countless apartment dwellers without gaslight or heat, homeless people perished in the streets, and the rivers turned to solid ice, forming "perfect bridges from Jersey to Manhattan, from Manhattan to Long Island."[1]

Once again, however, the little courtroom was filled to capacity when the inquest resumed that frigid morning. At a few minutes before eleven, an excited murmur ran through the crowd. People shifted in their seats and craned their necks for a better view. Some rose to their feet.

Walking beside his father, one hand resting lightly in the crook of the older man's elbow, Roland Molineux had just entered the room.

The two made their way to the places reserved for them up front, where Roland slipped off his fine kidskin gloves, doffed his elegant derby, and removed his costly astrakhan-lined overcoat. Impeccably dressed in a high collar, black tie, and double-breasted coat, he seated himself next to his father. Heads bent close together, the two began to examine the morning papers, chuckling softly over the artists' renditions of Roland, which seemed to exaggerate his features to the point of caricature—the up-tilted nose, the square, dimpled chin, the disdainful curl of his mouth.

When his name was called, he smiled and whispered something to the General, who gave his boy an encouraging clap on the shoulder. Still carrying his tan-colored gloves in one hand, Roland then stepped to the witness chair.

In marked contrast to the gruff Harry Cornish, Molineux struck observers as the epitome of "polished courtesy." He smiled often, spoke in a "soft, cultured voice," replied graciously to all of Osborne's questions.

And yet, along with the suave, agreeable manners, there was something else, something off-putting, even unsavory. "It cannot be said that his appearance recommends him," wrote Julian Hawthorne, who saw in the handsomely groomed socialite "an air of hauteur—a peculiar cold eye."[2]

Another observer detected "a touch of the dangerous, perhaps the sinister" about Molineux. "At the moment when his manners, speech, and general address induced the greatest confidence, there was a look in his eyes, a cast to his face, that stirred doubt." To this observer, the coolly self-possessed Molineux was a dark enigma, "the sort of being that a thousand authors have tried to call up from the world of imagination"—"the flesh-and-blood realization of the Mystery Man."[3]

Molineux's smooth, courteous bearing was matched by Assistant DA Osborne. In his questioning of Harry Cornish, Osborne had been aggressive to the point of hostility. With Molineux, on the other hand, he "was gentle, deferential, apologetic." Whereas he had treated the athletic director with open disdain—consistently calling him "Cornish" without so much as a pretense of politeness—he never once addressed Roland as anything other than "Mr. Molineux."[4]

"Now, Mr. Molineux," Osborne began with a smile. "You're not afraid to tell the truth in this case, are you?"

"I am sworn to tell the truth," Roland replied with a little smile of his own.

"And you are not worried," continued Osborne, "that your examination might at some future time lead to the charge of homicide against you?"

"Not at all," said Roland, still smiling.

"You claim to be innocent of the crime that is charged?" said Osborne.

"Entirely and absolutely innocent," Roland said easily.

Under Osborne's gentle questioning, Roland—the very picture of relaxed self-confidence—proceeded to recount the troubles he had with Cornish. He told of the time he had requested a new set of horizontal bars, only to have Cornish substitute a different brand on the order form; of Cornish's alleged mismanagement of the club facilities; and of the inflammatory letter that Cornish had sent to the track star Bernie Wefers on official club stationery—the precipitating cause of Roland's resignation from the KAC.

"You felt that you wanted Cornish removed?" asked Osborne.

"Yes," said Roland. "I felt it would be best for the club."

"You had a strong feeling against him on account of his conduct?" asked Osborne.

"That was my state of mind at the time," Roland acknowledged.

"A strong, bitter feeling?" Osborne said.

"Yes, sir," Roland calmly replied.

"You thought he had been disrespectful?"

"I knew so," said Roland.

"You thought he had overstepped his bounds as an employee?"

"I knew that, too."

"You thought you were justified in having this feeling toward him?" said Osborne.

"I thought so then," answered Roland, wearing his usual half smile, "and I think so now."

Roland was then asked about a note he had mailed to a friend named William Scheffler, giving his reasons for resigning from the Knickerbocker and denouncing Cornish for having written the offending letter to Bernie Wefers. Surely, said Osborne, sending such a note to Scheffler proved that Roland continued to harbor bitter feelings toward Cornish after quitting the KAC.

"Yes, sir," said Roland without hesitation. "I suppose, for a time, that feeling lingered with me. But my going to the New York Athletic Club—it was a better club and nicer men were in it. And I was a governor there, where I had only been a committeeman in the Knickerbocker Athletic Club."

"So that feeling gradually wore away?" asked Osborne.

"It did," said Roland.

"And Cornish passed out of your life?"

"Yes, sir."

Osborne then shifted his attention to Roland's relationship with Barnet. He had not proceeded far with this line of questioning, when—as though struck with a sudden realization—he interrupted himself.

"Oh, by the way—you must excuse me for the way the examination is going on," he said somewhat sheepishly, "but have you got the original of that letter you wrote to Scheffler about Cornish?"

"You may conduct the examination any way you see fit," Roland said pleasantly. "My counsel has the letter. I've turned everything over to him."

After receiving the letter from Bartow Weeks, Osborne showed it to Roland, who identified it as his "own ordinary handwriting." The letter was then marked and turned over to Coroner Hart.

Roland remained on the witness stand for another hour or so, recounting—in a voice tinged with sadness—his "warm friendship" with the late Henry C. Barnet. Only once was there even a hint of friction between the witness and his interrogator. It happened when Osborne remarked on how strange it seemed that Roland had learned of Barnet's death only by reading about it in the papers.

Roland, unflappable as ever, replied that he saw nothing strange about it.

"And yet," said Osborne, "you told me a moment ago, almost with tears in your eyes, that he was such a warm personal friend."

"I don't think you saw any tears in my eyes," Roland said with a barely suppressed sneer in his voice.

"I said 'almost,'" Osborne replied, reddening visibly. He then asked why Roland had never once visited Barnet during the latter's final illness.

Roland's answer seemed perfectly reasonable. He had heard that his old friend was under quarantine for diphtheria. The sickroom was off limits to visitors.

"Mr. Molineux," said Osborne after a brief pause. "I want to know whether Barnet knew your wife?"

"Do you mean, Mr. Osborne," said Roland, allowing a note of indignation to enter his voice, "when did I present him to her?"

"Yes," said Osborne. "When did you present your wife, Miss Chesebrough?"

"I presented Barnet to Miss Chesebrough at the Metropolitan Opera House," said Roland. "It was the fall of 1897. I don't remember the date, but it was the first concert given by the Banda Rossa."

At this juncture—and much to the disappointment of many of the spectators, who felt that the proceedings had just reached a particularly juicy point—Osborne broke off his questioning, and the inquest was adjourned.[5]

Rising from the witness chair, Roland strolled back to his place, where his beaming father patted him on the back and handed him a big black cigar. As his lawyer, Bartow Weeks, made ready to depart, Roland, always the gentleman, held the older man's coat for him.

Everyone present agreed that they had witnessed a splendid performance. In contrast to Cornish—who had come across as nervous, shifty, furtive—Roland had seemed open, confident, perfectly at ease: a man with nothing either to hide or apologize for.

On his way out of the courtroom, Osborne told reporters that he was, in fact, far more "favorably impressed with" Molineux than he had been with Cornish.

"It is true that it was Cornish who administered the poison that killed Mrs. Adams," he declared. "It is true that he is not a willing witness. It is true that he has made several contradictory statements on the witness stand. I never met a criminal in my life—and I have convicted many—who did not assume that attitude when placed on the witness stand.

"I assure you," he added portentously, "I am by no means through with Cornish."[6]

46

Throughout his testimony, Roland had held on to his elegant kidskin gloves, toying with them, lightly slapping them against his crossed knee or waving them in the air to make a point. It was another pair of kid gloves, however—the metaphorical ones with which Assistant District Attorney Osborne had handled the witness—that drew the sharpest comments from the press.

Predictably, Hearst's *Journal* adopted the most scathing tone. Osborne—the "fearless cross-examiner who had browbeaten Cornish into contradiction and confusion"—had inexplicably become "gentle as a lamb" in his questioning of Molineux. Instead of being "placed upon the rack" and reduced to "a tattered remnant" of himself, the witness had been treated with an almost fawning deference. No wonder Roland and his father had left the courtroom looking "supremely happy." "It was whitewashing day for Molineux," the paper jeered, "and the brush was wielded by Mr. Osborne."[1]

If Osborne was stung by these criticisms, he showed no sign of it when the proceedings resumed on Tuesday, February 14. Over the intervening weekend, the city had been hit with a blizzard of such ferocity that entire streets were blocked with six-foot-high drifts. By Tuesday, however, the skies were clear, and when the doors opened at 10:00 A.M., the little courtroom was quickly filled to overflowing.[2]

Looking "bright and fresh, his face free from worry," Molineux took the stand shortly after eleven, his fine tan gloves held, as before, in his right hand. Throughout his testimony, he was, as one observer noted, the very picture of seemingly "unstudied grace."

By contrast, Harry Cornish—seated near the front where he had an obstructed view of the witness chair—"looked careworn and nervous, as if there was a great load of some kind weighing upon his mind." As he listened to the testimony of his debonair rival, his face took on a "look full of bitterness and hate."[3]

To the delight of the more prurient-minded spectators—who "manifested an air of intense expectancy," according to the papers—Osborne picked up where he had left on Friday, with the matter of Henry Barnet's relationship with Blanche. Those who hoped to see Osborne conduct a more aggressive grilling of the witness, however, were in for a disappointment. If anything, he seemed even more solicitous of Molineux's feelings, prefacing his most probing questions with elaborate apologies.

"I ask these questions with considerable regret, Mr. Molineux," he began. "I have no wish to pry into your personal life, but I must do so in the interest of justice."

"I realize that, Mr. Osborne," Roland said with an understanding smile. "And I will answer you in the same spirit."

Acknowledging Roland's gracious reply with a little bow, Osborne said, "Tell me, Mr. Molineux. After you introduced Mr. Barnet to Miss Chesebrough, did he pay her any attention?"

"He was polite to her," said Roland. "He sent her flowers, took her to dinner—just such attentions as a gentleman would pay to any lady."

"Then I ask you, Mr. Molineux, was your wife in love with Mr. Barnet?"

"I think she admired him as a friend," Roland said with a dismissive little wave of his gloves.

"Did you ever have reason to believe that Mr. Barnet was in love with Miss Chesebrough?" asked Osborne.

"Really, Mr. Osborne," said Roland, as if addressing a child, "I have no way of knowing the state of Mr. Barnet's feelings. If he were," he added gallantly, "I'm sure I wouldn't blame him."

"Did Barnet ever visit your wife at Mrs. Bellinger's house before your marriage?" asked Osborne.

"I think he did," said Roland.

"Was it done with your knowledge and approval?"

"Why, yes, certainly," said Roland, as though the answer were so obvious it hardly needed stating. "He had a perfect right to call upon her."

"Did you ever resent it?"

"Never," said Roland.

Apologizing once more for the necessity of inquiring into Roland's "private and domestic life," Osborne then asked if it was true that he had been turned down once by Blanche before she finally consented to marry him. "There is no intention to insult you," Osborne hastened to assure him.

"I have no such opinion," Roland said with a smile. He then acknowledged that Blanche had indeed rejected his first proposal.

"After you proposed that first time, did you object to Barnet's attention to Miss Chesebrough?"

"Upon what grounds could I object, Mr. Osborne?" replied Roland, in the urbane tone of one man of the world to another. "She certainly had the right to receive the attentions of any man she favored."

"Then you had no reason to be jealous of Mr. Barnet?"

"None whatsoever," said Roland. "Barnet, Miss Chesebrough, and I were all good friends. He called me 'Mollie' and I called him 'Barney.' Miss Chesebrough did, too." There was a hint of sadness in his voice, as though his heart had been pierced by the sudden recollection of happier times.

Osborne paused for a moment to consult his notes. When he resumed, the subject he raised was even more titillating than the reputed romantic triangle involving Mollie, Barney, and Blanche.

Had Roland ever visited the so-called Oriental room described in recent newspapers? Osborne asked.

The question made the spectators sit up in their seats. Osborne was clearly inquiring about one of the most explosive aspects of the whole affair—the rumored "coterie of degenerates" within the Knickerbocker Athletic Club. The ringleader of this sinister bunch, who had never been publicly identified, was said to inhabit an "Oriental apartment fashioned after the rooms occupied by Oscar Wilde"—shocking proof of his depravity.[4]

In response to Osborne's question, Roland now conceded that he had, in fact, once visited the apartment, though he denied that there was "anything Oriental about it."

And what, Osborne asked, had occasioned the visit?

Molineux said that he had gone there to speak to its occupant—Mr. John Adams.

The mention of this name caused a stir in the courtroom. Adams was the secretary of the Knickerbocker Athletic Club. It was Adams who first noticed the supposed similarity between the penmanship on the poison package and the handwriting on Roland's letter of resignation. And it was Adams who first brought this resemblance to Harry Cornish's attention.

Now it appeared—from Osborne's line of questioning—that Adams himself was a person of highly dubious character, a member, if not the leader, of the homosexual gang that had allegedly conspired to eliminate the two men who threatened them with exposure: Harry Cornish and Henry Barnet. Could Adams have pointed the finger of suspicion at Roland in order to deflect attention from the true culprits—that is, himself and his fellow "degenerates"?

"Do you know a young man by the name of Glohr?" asked Osborne.

"Paul Glohr?" said Molineux, as if slightly surprised by the introduction of this name. "Yes, I know him."

"Tell me what you know about him," Osborne said.

Molineux explained that Glohr had been an office boy at the club—and not, in Roland's opinion, a very good one. He had been remiss in his duties and had once used the tip of his forefinger to inscribe an obscenity on the frost of a windowpane facing Forty-fifth Street.

Roland had taken it upon himself to complain about Glohr to John Adams, who had called the boy to his room, presumably to reprimand him. The next thing Roland knew, Glohr had been made a member of the club and was visiting Adams's room almost every evening to receive a "history lesson." Eventually, Adams moved out of the club and took an apartment nearby, bringing the boy to live with him as his "ward." It was this apartment that had reportedly been furnished in the scandalous "Oriental" style.

After questioning Roland about several other boys who had reportedly been taken under Adams's wing, Osborne suddenly changed tack again. This time, he focused on published reports about Roland's own supposedly immoral behavior. As before, however, he seemed almost abashed at having to raise such distasteful matters, apologizing in advance for the "personal questions" he was compelled to ask.

"I shall be glad to answer them if they give me a chance to deny some rumors," said Roland with his usual urbanity.

"Did you ever smoke opium?" asked Osborne.

Roland did not miss a beat. "Yes, over a year ago," he said. "I will qualify that by saying once or twice to see what it was like."

"But you are not an opium fiend?"

Roland chuckled softly. "No, sir. I was in Chinatown sightseeing and wanted to see what opium smoking was like. Just curiosity."

"I'm told," said Osborne, "that you know all the bartenders in Newark, and that you associate with that sort of men. Is that true?"

"It is false," said Roland flatly.

"I'm also told you took your wife out there and introduced her to a bartender," said Osborne.

For the first time, Roland appeared to bristle. "Are you in earnest, Mr. Osborne?"

"Yes."

"It's a lie," Roland said angrily.

"Tell me, if you please, Mr. Molineux," said Osborne. "Have you ever rented a letter box in your life? A private letter box?"

"Never," answered Roland.

"What do you know about cyanide of mercury?"

"I don't think I even knew such a poison existed except perhaps in a general way before this Adams case," Roland said.

"But aren't you a chemist?" Osborne asked.

"A very bad chemist," Roland said with a self-deprecating smile. "My specialty is the study of pigments. I'm merely a color-maker at a factory."

Osborne then asked Roland if he had ever written any requests to patent medicine firms. Roland denied that he had.

Stepping to the counsel's table, Osborne sifted through a stack of documents, then approached the witness box with a single sheet in one hand.

"Have you ever seen paper like this, Mr. Molineux?" asked Osborne, handing him the sheet—a piece of eggshell blue stationery embossed with three interlinked silver crescents.

Roland studied it for a moment before saying, "Not that I remember, Mr. Osborne."

"You have never seen any paper like that in your life?" Osborne repeated. "I mean, with that crest on it?"

"Not that I recall," said Roland.

Shortly afterward, Osborne excused Molineux from the witness stand, thanking him for his cooperation and asking if he would be willing to return for further questioning should the need arise.

"I shall be very glad to come whenever you send for me," Roland said with a smile as he rose from his chair. He then returned to his place, where his father welcomed him with an affectionate little rub on the back.[5]

Interviewed by reporters at the close of the day's proceedings, Osborne, as before, was effusive in his praise for Roland, whose testimony—in contrast to Cornish's grudging answers—had been so frank and forthright.

The warm feelings were reciprocated by Roland and his representatives. Until that moment, Weeks and his co-counsel, George Gordon Battle, had refused to permit their client to supply the authorities with a penmanship sample. Now, believing that the district attorney and his men were focusing their suspicions on the surly athletic director, they agreed.

Late that afternoon, in the presence of his attorneys, Roland sat down at a table in James Osborne's office and, to the dictation of handwriting expert William Kinsley, penned a number of samples. These included the address on the poison package sent to Harry Cornish, which Kinsley read aloud to Roland.

When he was finished, Roland shook hands all around and took his leave, "pleased and confident."

Kinsley carefully put the samples in an envelope. He would need some time to analyze them closely. But even at a glance, he had noticed something interesting.

In writing out the address of the Knickerbocker Athletic Club, Roland had spelled the street number "Fourty Fifth Street," adding a superfluous *u*.

It was the same error made by the anonymous sender of the poisoned bromo-seltzer.[6]

47

As the dominant news story of the day, the Great Poison Mystery continued to inspire copycat crimes, including one whose intended victim was another man named Cornish—Adelbert D. Cornish of Lewiston, Maine, a judge at the municipal court.

In the fall of 1898, a sour-tempered landlord named George W. Pierce was arrested on an assault charge by the town marshal, Herbert Teel, and brought before Judge Cornish. A plea bargain was eventually struck, but Pierce became convinced that he had been "sold out" by his lawyer, W. H. Newell.

A few months later, Judge Cornish found a bag of sugar on his doorstep, ostensibly left there as a gift. His suspicions aroused, he turned it over to a chemistry professor named Robinson at Bowdoin College, who found so much arsenic in the sugar that "a single spoonful would kill a man." Cornish immediately alerted Marshal Teel, who revealed that he, too, had recently received an anonymous gift—a bottle of whiskey. Fortunately for Teel, he had stuck the liquor in a cabinet without sampling any. Upon analysis by Professor Robinson, it also turned out "to contain arsenic in large quantities."

Several juvenile neighbors of Lawyer Newell weren't quite so lucky. Finding a box of candy on the driveway leading to Newell's stables, they snuck a few pieces and came close to dying. In the end, the police determined that the source of all three of these lethal "gifts" was the embittered George Pierce, who was promptly arrested and charged with several counts of attempted murder.[1]

While the small-town judge from Maine suddenly found himself on the front pages—ANOTHER CORNISH IN POISON MYSTERY, trumpeted the headline in the *World*—his namesake in New York was coming under increasing attack by the Manhattan DA's office. Any doubts that District Attorney Asa Bird Gardiner and his assistants were "ranged against Harry Cornish" (as the *Journal* put it) were dispelled on Wednesday, when several witnesses were called to offer damaging testimony against the athletic director.

Rumors that Mrs. Molineux would take the stand brought an extra crush of people to the courthouse that morning. They were destined to be disappointed, since neither Roland nor Blanche put in an appearance. Still, the day was not lacking in interest.

A dramatic high point occurred during the questioning of Dr. Edwin Hitchcock, the first physician to be called to Mrs. Adams's apartment on the day of her death. According to Hitchcock, he had announced at once that "a diabolical crime had been committed" and asked Cornish if he had any enemies who might send him poisoned bromo-seltzer. This was a direct contradiction of Cornish, who was on record as stating that he had not suspected foul play until several days later. Indeed, to more than one observer, the questions addressed to Hitchcock seemed expressly designed to expose Cornish as a liar.[2]

Hitchcock also revealed that Mrs. Adams's daughter, Florence Rodgers, had taken him aside that morning and asked if her mother's death could be "kept as quiet as possible." She seemed particularly anxious that it not be reported by the press.

For anyone closely following the case, Hitchcock's testimony seemed to support one especially lurid theory that had been bandied about in the yellow papers: that the womanizing Harry Cornish and his attractive roommate, Mrs. Rodgers, were involved in an affair and had plotted to eliminate her disapproving mother.

It is no wonder that Cornish himself sat through Hitchcock's testimony scowling at the witness. Or that his elderly parents—who had traveled to New York to offer their moral support—looked so exceedingly glum.

By contrast, General Molineux and his son's attorney, Bartow Weeks, wore expressions of undiluted satisfaction. When the day's proceedings were over, they left the courtroom together with broad smiles on their faces.[3]

In the following days, Osborne called other witnesses who (as one headline put it) gave "the lie to Cornish."[4] John McIntyre—Harry's friend in the district attorney's office—testified that he, too, had immediately suspected foul play in Mrs. Adams's death and had said so to Cornish within hours of her murder. Dr. Hitchcock's colleague, E. S. Potter, went so far as to suggest that Cornish had lied about drinking the poison. Potter declared that he "did not observe any signs of sickness upon Cornish while I was in the house"—a claim supported by another witness, who testified that he had seen Cornish eating an apple that morning.[5]

According to Potter, moreover, he had noticed *two* tumblers on Mrs. Adams's dining room table when he arrived at the apartment. One contained the remainder of the deadly bromo-seltzer solution; the other was filled with what appeared to be water. Potter's implication seemed to be that Cornish had only pretended to sample the lethal concoction, when, in fact, he had actually sipped from the water glass.[6]

By the end of the week, Cornish's credibility was in such tatters that even Hearst's *Journal*—which had, from the start, been relentless in its persecution of Roland Molineux—seemed to have changed its position. On Friday, the paper ran a remarkable piece, deploring the very different kinds of justice meted out to poor black residents of the city and to people like Harry Cornish.

Highlighted within a little box at the top page, the article drew a pointed comparison between two current tragedies. On the one hand, there was the pitiable case of Mrs. Mary Hubbard, a destitute "negress" who had "notified the Charity and Police departments in Brooklyn on Wednesday that she had rolled over on her baby in her sleep and smothered it to death. She alleged that it was an accident and asked for aid to bury the body." And how had the authorities responded to Mrs. Hubbard? "SHE WAS LOCKED UP AT ONCE IN THE GATES AVENUE POLICE STATION ON A CHARGE OF MURDER," the paper exclaimed in capital letters.

In striking contrast, there was the case of Harry Cornish, a well-connected athlete and clubman, who "gave to Mrs. Kate Adams, December 28 last, a dose of poisoned bromo-seltzer, which killed her. His claim is that the stuff had been sent to him by some unknown enemy and that the poisoning of Mrs. Adams was unintentional." And what had happened to Cornish? "HE IS STILL AT LARGE, FIFTY DAYS AFTER THE TRAGEDY!" declared the paper in outraged tones.[7]

By this point, even Cornish—who belonged to the tight-lipped "never-complain-never-explain" school of manhood—was so beleaguered that he felt compelled to issue a public statement. Published in the papers under the headline CORNISH SAYS SOME THINGS LOOK BAD, BUT HE CAN EXPLAIN, the statement perfectly captured the blunt, combative style of the man:

> I appreciate that there are many points brought out in the testimony that make it look bad for me, but I am not losing my head or my nerve, and don't intend to. Remember, I have not had my chance to talk yet, but I am carefully noting all that is said, and matters will look very different when I get through telling my story.
>
> All I want is the chance to tell my story, fully, freely, and without interruption, as Molineux was allowed to tell his. Mr. Osborne has promised me that I shall have that chance.
>
> No, I will not tell now what I will testify to when put on the stand. What I want to do is clear up some things that now look very bad. For instance, much has been made of . . . the testimony of Dr. Potter, that there were two glasses on the table when he got to the Adams flat. That agrees entirely with my statement to the police and my testimony on the stand. Mrs. Adams brought in two glasses, one empty and the other half-filled with water, for me to mix the bromo-seltzer. I put the bromo-seltzer in the empty glass and poured the water in upon it.
>
> Of course, the District Attorney has the right to proceed as he sees fit, but I promise you that when I get on that stand again and tell my story, the atmosphere will be very much cleared.[8]

Cornish would soon have his day in court. But first, the public would finally be treated to an impressive performance by the glamorous star witness they had waited so long to see.

48

In her late-life memoirs, composed nearly forty years after the fact, Blanche describes herself as feeling so anxious and confused on the day of her testimony that her state of mind bordered on panic. Written in a breathless, fragmentary style, the passage is meant to convey both the dizzying unreality of the moment and her own tumultuous emotions:

> There is a low confused murmur of voices. The wave of sound rises, grows louder. There is so much excitement it is confusing. I am in a daze. The coroner reaches over and pounds loudly with his gavel for silence. There before me is the prosecuting attorney; and there, back of him, a blurred sea of faces. How everybody stares! They sit forward in their seats. How crowded it is, and hot. I can hardly breathe. Mr. Osborne is asking me questions. They seem quite rude and impertinent. I wonder if I am coherent. I really don't know in what manner I am replying to him. It becomes confusing, tiresome. I see no point to all the questions. To get away—out of that horrible stuffy courtroom, to escape that crowd. God, how inquisitive and curious they are, all those people! Sensation-seekers, watching to see if I will writhe under the dissecting knife of the State Prosecutor's queries. How long will this inquisition last? What a fantastic, what a grotesque

and impossible contretemps! O God! O my God! I am dreaming it—I *must* be dreaming it![1]

It is a vivid (if characteristically overwrought) self-portrait of Blanche as a young woman teetering on the verge of a nervous collapse as she undergoes an agonizing public ordeal.

Eyewitness accounts of that day, however—Tuesday, February 21, 1899—present a very different picture. Those who saw her on the stand were unanimous in their depiction of Blanche as a person of exceptional poise, whose testimony, far from being tongue-tied or stammering, was so smooth and assured that it struck many observers as carefully rehearsed.

She was waiting in an anteroom with Roland and his parents when Bartow Weeks appeared at the doorway. "It is time, Mrs. Molineux," he said.

Roland offered her his arm. Then, with her in-laws preceding her, she and her husband emerged from the room. The courtroom was only a few steps away, but the hallway was so crammed that a policeman had to clear a pathway through the crowd.

All eyes turned toward her as she entered the courtroom. Her appearance came as a surprise to those whose fantasies had been formed by the suggestive accounts in the yellow press, where she was invariably portrayed as a female of dark and irresistible allure. She was, to begin with, much larger than anyone expected—several inches taller, at five feet ten, than her husband. Though handsomely proportioned, she struck more than one observer as "not especially graceful in carriage or movement." And with her somewhat long face, sharp nose, large mouth, and glass eye, she was by no means conventionally beautiful.[2]

Still, she was dressed in high style, in a fashionable black gown and an elegant black cloak lined with black Persian wool. Her black, turban-shaped hat was trimmed with violets. She wore white kid gloves and carried a large sable muff with several tails dangling from the front.[3]

Taking a seat at the front of the room, she seemed perfectly at ease. When Roland leaned close to whisper something in her ear, she smiled broadly, revealing a set of large, white, perfectly formed teeth. A few moments later, her name was called, and an expectant hush fell over the crowd as she rose from her place.

The image of Blanche as a Circe-like enchantress made for such good copy that some newsmen continued to foster it. According to one reporter, she "swept to the witness chair in a shimmer of silk." And when James Osborne began to question her, she answered in a "voice as low and musical as a lyre." Whether Blanche really possessed the vocal sorcery of a Siren is open to doubt. Still, everyone agreed that she spoke in a clear, well-modulated voice that carried the hint of an affected British accent.[4]

As he had done with her husband, Osborne prefaced his questions with elaborate apologies. It pained him, he said, to pry into such private matters, and he did so only with the greatest reluctance. Indeed, Osborne often seemed genuinely discomfited, resorting to prim circumlocutions that brought audible snickers from the spectators. Early on in his questioning, for example, he wanted to know when Roland "began paying addresses" to Blanche.

"I do not quite know what you mean," Blanche said with a smile.

Osborne seemed slightly flustered. "I don't know how to express myself in any other way," he said.

"Do you mean," Blanche asked, "when did we become engaged?"

"No, not exactly," said Osborne. "I mean, when did he begin paying addresses to you that in your mind led you to think that he might propose to you?"

"We were always very good friends from the time we first met," Blanche said pleasantly.

"Well, when *did* Mr. Molineux first propose to you?" Osborne asked.

"I think it was on Thanksgiving, 1897."

"Was Mr. Barnet paying you attentions at that time?" said Osborne.

"Why, we were all very good friends," Blanche said with a little laugh.

"Yes, I know," said Osborne. "But was Barnet paying you, let us say, heavy attentions?"

Osborne's priggish diction brought another burst of laughter from the spectators, while Blanche raised her sable muff to her lips to conceal her own giggles.

"Now, Mrs. Molineux," said Osborne after a moment. "These questions embarrass me just as much as they do you. Please tell me whether or not, in any sense of the word, Barnet and Molineux were rivals."

"Never," Blanche said.[5]

Throughout her time on the witness stand, Blanche remained utterly self-composed. She spoke easily, without the slightest hesitation, giving replies that completely supported her husband's testimony. Indeed, as more than one observer noted, her answers so closely matched Roland's that she appeared to have been coached. She did not falter even when Osborne turned to the most potentially damaging piece of evidence—the emotional note she had written to Barnet during his final illness.

Osborne began by reading the letter aloud: "'I am distressed to learn of your illness. I arrived home Saturday. I am so exceedingly sorry to know that you have been indisposed. Won't you let me know when you are able to be about? I want so much to see you. Is it that you do not believe me? If you would but let me prove to you my sincerity. Do not be cross any more and accept, I pray you, my very best wishes. Yours, Blanche.'"

Since this letter had been blazoned on the front pages of virtually every newspaper in the city, its contents came as no surprise to the listeners in the courtroom. Nevertheless, in her memoirs, Blanche claims to have been caught completely off guard by Osborne's introduction of this document:

> And now—Good God!—they are questioning me about Barnet! Mr. Osborne has a letter in his hand. It is the letter I wrote Barney while he was ill. A letter written to Barney—what has *that* to do with this, this inquiry into the death of the Adams woman? What possible bearing on all this was my friendship with Henry Barnet? Wait! They are hinting at a love affair between myself and the man who had been Roland's friend! What does it mean? How bewildering it is. I cannot understand.[6]

Again, Blanche's melodramatic account is in striking contrast to the official record. Far from being flustered and confused by Osborne's reading of the letter, she was clearly prepared for it, and parried every question he posed with remarkable finesse.

"What did you mean by writing, 'Is it that you do not believe me?'" asked Osborne when he finished reciting the letter.

"I had no especial meaning," came the breezy reply. "It was simply a form of speech."

"And 'Don't be cross with me anymore'?—what did you mean by that?"

"I had written to him last June and he never sent me a reply," Blanche said in the same offhanded tone. "I did not know whether he was piqued at something or not, but I concluded that there must be something the matter, so I just wrote, 'Don't be cross with me.'"

"Then what does this mean?—'If you would but let me prove my sincerity?'"

"It was just a form of expression, rather awkwardly put," Blanche said.

"You signed yourself 'Blanche,'" said Osborne, as though to imply that such informality indicated an unusual degree of intimacy between the two.

"Yes," Blanche said with a smile. "All three of us—my husband, Barney, and I—called each other by our first names."

After another twenty minutes of similarly unenlightening testimony, Blanche was dismissed and the proceedings adjourned for the day.

For her performance, Blanche received high praise from Roland, his parents, and his attorneys. The press reviews were decidedly more mixed. Everyone agreed that she had comported herself with admirable aplomb. But there was a general consensus that she had done nothing to help clear up the mystery. If anything, her testimony reinforced the popular perception of her as a dangerously cunning female, capable of twisting any susceptible male—in this case, the public prosecutor, James Osborne—around her little finger.

As one reporter, reflecting the casual misogyny of the era, put it, Mrs. Blanche Molineux had shown herself to be "clever beyond the ordinary run of her sex."[7]

49

On Thursday, February 23—exactly two weeks after his first appearance at the inquest—Harry Cornish finally got his chance to take the witness stand again. This time, in stark contrast to the previous occasion, there was nothing tentative or evasive about his testimony. From the moment he began to speak, it was clear that he had come with only one purpose in mind: to deliver what the newspapers would call a "savage assault" on Roland Molineux.

It was close to eleven before the proceedings got under way. Seated near the front of the room, Cornish could be seen tapping one foot impatiently. Assistant District Attorney Osborne, however, appeared to be in no great hurry to begin. For at least ten minutes, he sat at the lawyers' table, leisurely reviewing a stack of memoranda. Finally, he turned to the athletic director, and addressing him as discourteously as ever, said, "Now, Cornish, you can take the stand."

Clutching several sheets of notes in one beefy fist, Cornish strode to the witness chair, then looked at the jury eagerly. Osborne, however, seemed intent on making him wait. Another six or seven minutes elapsed while Osborne held a whispered consultation with his colleague, Assistant DA Maurice Blumenthal. Only then did he turn to the witness and say, "Now, Cornish, can you suggest anything as to a motive in this case by any human being?"

"Yes," said Cornish. "I think I can."

For the next thirty minutes or so—pausing only intermittently to consult his notes—Cornish offered a long, somewhat rambling but unrelievedly bitter denunciation of Roland Molineux. So severe were the aspersions he cast on the latter's moral character that, at several points, General Molineux seemed ready to spring from his chair and set upon his son's accuser.[1]

It was only natural, said Cornish, that he would suspect Molineux of having sent him the poison. No one else had ever harbored such intense and inexplicable animosity toward him. Molineux had "tried to take the bread and butter out of my mouth, and a man who would do that would do anything."[2]

Besides, Cornish was far from alone in suspecting Roland. "There were fifty men in the club who thought the same thing." Indeed, it was general knowledge at the Knickerbocker that Roland was a man of questionable character. He was known, for example, to keep a library of "immoral books" in his room. Among these works was Alexander Dumas's *Celebrated Crimes* (a collection of nonfiction accounts of notorious criminals, including several legendary poisoners), as well as a medical text meant only "for physicians who study the abnormal" and "not intended for laymen." Though Cornish had not seen this volume himself, he had heard from others that it was "obscene." The author's name, he said, sounded something like "Craft Eby"[3]—an obvious reference to Richard von Krafft-Ebing, author of *Psychopathia Sexualis*, a pioneering study of sexual aberration that compiles hundreds of case histories of every known perversion, from fetishism to lust-murder, bestiality to necrophilia. Roland was also rumored to have a collection of pornographic pictures—"photographs of an indescribable character"—that he showed to select friends.[4]

And there were other indications of Roland's "bad mind." According to Cornish, it was Molineux who had originated the stories about the supposed "coterie of degenerates" at the club. Molineux had also spread scurrilous rumors about John Adams, claiming, among other things, that Adams and Herbert Ballantine had been "unusually friendly" while classmates at Cornell.[5]

And why, asked Cornish, had Molineux thought it necessary to hire a lawyer the instant the story broke in the newspapers? "I do not see why anyone who had nothing to fear should do anything of that kind."

There was also the matter of the tangled ties among Roland, Blanche, and Barnet. Cornish had it on good authority that—contrary to Blanche's assertions—her relationship with Barnet had been much more than a mere friendship. It was widely known in the club, for example, that Barnet had made remarks about "kissing her," and that, on at least one occasion, the two had been alone in his room, sharing a bottle of wine.

Roland, moreover, was not nearly as friendly with Barnet as he had claimed. Cornish recounted an incident in the summer of 1898, when Barnet had left for the Atlantic Yacht Club, "ostensibly for a cruise. He came back shortly afterward. A friend said: 'Thought you were going on a cruise.' Barnet said: 'I went to the boat but found that fellow Molineux there, and I would not go.' "

Given the obvious enmity between Molineux and Barnet, it struck Cornish as "very queer" when he heard that Roland "had married Miss Chesebrough."[6]

Cornish was allowed to speak uninterruptedly for nearly a half hour. Reporters covering the inquest agreed that he presented a forceful argument—"like a lawyer summing up a case."[7] The moment he was finished, however, James Osborne—employing the same openly hostile manner as before—began to barrage him with questions whose only apparent purpose was to rattle the witness and subvert his testimony.

His voice raised to a near-shout, Osborne treated the witness (as one reporter put it) "exactly as if Cornish were on trial for poisoning Mrs. Adams." His questions were peppered with sneering remarks: "Oh, come, do you really mean to tell this jury—?" "Do you actually expect this jury to believe—?" "Is that the best explanation you can come up with?" Every small discrepancy and contradiction in Cornish's testimony was flung back in his face. By the end of the day, it seemed to many observers that Osborne had not merely cross-examined Cornish but "pilloried him."[8]

Osborne's demeanor couldn't have been more different the following day, when Roland was called back to the witness stand to answer Cornish's charges. Once again, the assistant district attorney treated Molineux with an almost fawning deference. "Mr. Molineux, I am very sorry to ask you to testify again, but I cannot help it," he began, then proceeded to preface many of his questions with equally abject apologies: "I am sorry to trouble you, Mr. Molineux," "Forgive me for bothering you, Mr. Molineux," and so on. His tone, as one reporter noted, was consistently "helpful, conciliatory, friendly. The one distinct purpose of the examination seemed to be to protect Molineux."[9]

When Osborne asked about the "obscene" books Cornish had referred to, for example, Roland admitted that he owned a copy of Krafft-Ebing's *Psychopathia Sexualis*. Far from treating this admission as a vindication of Cornish's testimony, however, Osborne brushed the whole business off with a joke. "As a matter of fact," he said with a laugh, "I believe everyone in the district attorney's office has a copy. Except me, of course. I understand that Mr. Weeks owns one, too," he added with a wink at Roland's attorney. "I heard he bought it on the day it was published."[10]

By the time the inquest adjourned for the weekend, the audience was "buzzing and speculating upon the curious difference between Osborne's treatment" of the two witnesses. That difference was captured in an acerbic little cartoon that ran in Saturday's *Evening Journal*. It showed two images of Osborne. In one, he is throttling a miniature Cornish while grimacing angrily at the frightened and helpless little figure clutched in his mitts. In the other, he is dandling a doll-size Molineux on his lap while cooing sweetly to the smiling little man.[11]

There was one part of Osborne's examination of Molineux to which the press, while noting, attached little importance. It happened soon after Roland took the stand. After apologizing for troubling him with so trivial a matter, Osborne handed the witness a sheaf of papers and asked if he would mind identifying them for the record. Roland studied them for a moment before confirming that they were, in fact, specimens of his handwriting. Thanking him, Osborne took the papers from his hand and passed them to Coroner Hart.

They were the penmanship samples Roland had produced the previous week in Osborne's office under the supervision of handwriting expert William Kinsley.[12]

50

Something was brewing at the district attorney's office.

Over the weekend, Chief Detective McCluskey—who was supposedly at odds with the DA over his conduct of the case—paid a visit to Colonel Gardiner, accompanied by his two lead investigators, Detective Sergeants Carey and McCafferty. James Osborne was also present at the meeting.

The five men remained shut up in Gardiner's office for nearly two hours—their longest consultation since the start of the inquest. When McCluskey and his men emerged from the meeting, they had little to say to reporters. By then, however, rumors had spread that "a most startling denouement" was about "to occur in the Adams poison mystery." A surprise witness was to be called when the inquest resumed on Monday—someone whose testimony would break the case wide open and "lead to the arrest of one of the suspected men."[1]

Despite McCluskey's refusal to divulge the name of this mystery witness, the yellow papers quickly sniffed it out. It was Nicholas Heckmann, owner of the little advertising business at 257 West Forty-second Street, where the man who called himself H. C. Barnet had rented a private letter box the previous May.

Heckmann, of course, had already been given the opportunity to identify the renter and, in spite of his insistence that he could pick the fake Barnet "out of a million," had failed to do so. Now, however, he admitted that he had deliberately held back, believing that "his information was of value" and that he might be able to peddle it to a newspaper for as much as $1,200. Having finally accepted the regrettable fact that no one would pay him for his testimony, he had nobly resolved to offer it free of charge.

When called to the stand, he declared, he would perform his "duty as a citizen and tell the truth."[2]

There was an air of anticipation in the little courtroom when the inquest got under way on Monday, February 27. Everybody who had read the weekend papers felt sure that something dramatic was about to happen. Even so, the day would deliver a far more stunning surprise than almost anyone expected.

Certainly, Roland Molineux never saw it coming.

The morning began unremarkably enough, with an appearance by Joseph Koch, proprietor of the little shop at 1620 Broadway, who declared that—owing largely to his poor eyesight—he could not identify the man who had rented a private letter box under the name of Cornish in December.

Then, Nicholas Heckmann took the stand.

A wiry little man with sharp eyes and a waxed mustache—its ends curled upward in the French style—Heckmann leaned forward eagerly in his chair. Seated a few yards away beside his father, Roland studied the witness intently, while a tense, suspenseful silence descended on the room.

The audience did not have to wait long for the first moment of high drama in what would turn out to be a morning full of sensational scenes. After querying Heckmann about the nature and location of his business, Osborne asked if he had rented a letter box the previous May "to a person who gave his name as Mr. H. C. Barnet."

Heckmann confirmed that he had.

"About how often did you see that person?"

"About fifteen or twenty times," said Heckmann.

"Would you recognize him if you saw him again?"

Heckmann nodded emphatically. "Yes, sir."

"Do you see him now in court?"

Turning, Heckmann raised his left hand and pointed the forefinger straight at Roland. "Over there," he said.

Accounts of Roland's reaction differ. According to some observers, the color drained from his face and he leapt from his seat, shaking one fist angrily at the witness. Others describe him as barking out a disdainful laugh before rising slowly to his feet. All agree, however, about what he said: "It is a lie. I have never seen that man but once in my life. I have never rented a letter box from him. What he says is a lie."

Ignoring him, Osborne asked Heckmann, "Is the man who just stood up the one who hired the letter box under the name of H. C. Barnet?"

"Yes, sir," said Heckmann.

"Are you positive of that?"

"Yes, sir," Heckmann repeated.

This time, it was Bartow Weeks, Roland's attorney, who sprang from his seat. "I ask, Mr. Coroner," he began, addressing the bench in a quivering voice. "In the interests of justice, I *demand*—"

He was interrupted by District Attorney Gardiner, who was present in the courtroom for the first time since the start of the proceedings. "*I* demand that Mr. Weeks be directed to sit down."

"But I insist that this man, who has offered to sell his identification, be cross-examined!" shouted Weeks.

"And I insist," said Gardiner harshly, "that Mr. Weeks be committed for contempt."

"You must sit down, Mr. Weeks," ordered Coroner Hart.

Weeks vented his outrage for another few moments. Finally, after Hart threatened to expel him from the courtroom, he ceased his protests and lowered himself back into his chair.

By then, Roland had also reseated himself. A change had come over his expression. The supercilious smile and complacent look were gone. Eyes narrowed, nostrils distended, lips tightly drawn, he seemed suddenly wary.

It wasn't Heckmann's testimony that had put him on his guard. Like most people in the courtroom, he had been prepared for that by the weekend newspapers. What had taken him by surprise was the sudden shift in Gardiner's attitude. Up until that moment, the men from the DA's office had treated Roland and his lawyers with perfect, even inordinate, civility.

In reacting to Weeks's outburst, however, Gardiner's tone had been harsh to the point of belligerence.

As Hearst's on-scene reporter, Charles Michelson, wrote:

> This was Molineux's first intimation that there was a trap, that the honeyed words and courteous treatment he had received in so marked a degree were merely a bait to lure him on to his own destruction. Until then, he had borne himself before the Coroner with an air of superiority, confidence, and good humor. But once the trap was sprung, he saw the situation in an instant. There is nothing stupid about Molineux. From that moment on, he was the personification of watchfulness and care. In an instant, there had been a complete change in the attitude and conduct of the Coroner's inquest. From being the shielded, protected, coddled, and stroked friend of the prosecuting officer, Molineux suddenly found himself exposed to the full broadside of that officer's artillery. The manhunters came from behind their cover of soft words and apologies and attacked their quarry as openly as wolf-trappers go after a pelt when their game is in the snare.

Heckmann's positive identification of Molineux was just the first of the day's sensations. "Thenceforward," wrote Michelson, "the inquest was a succession of the most dramatic scenes."[3]

The next one occurred during the testimony of William Kinsley, the handwriting expert who had spent the past week analyzing the penmanship specimens Roland had agreed to provide at the start of the inquest. Under questioning by Osborne, Kinsley declared "positively" that Roland's writing matched that on the fake Barnet and Cornish letters.

"And comparing those specimens with the poison package mailed to Cornish, what is your opinion?" asked Osborne.

"That they were written by one and the same hand," answered Kinsley.

"And that is the hand of whom?"

"It is the hand," said Kinsley, "of Roland B. Molineux."

An excited buzz arose from the crowd. Coroner Hart pounded his gavel for silence.

"I ask you, Mr. Kinsley, how strong is that opinion?" Osborne asked when quiet was restored.

"I am positive of it," said Kinsley. "I haven't got a doubt."

Once more, Weeks sprang from his seat. "Mr. Coroner," he cried in a voice choked with anger. "I presume there can be no question that this testimony by Mr. Kinsley is practically an accusation of crime against Mr. Molineux. I insist that my client has some constitutional rights!"

"And I object to your stump speeches," shouted Gardiner, rising to his feet.

For a few moments, the two men engaged in a shouting match. It was only after he had been threatened, once again, with ejection that Weeks grudgingly resumed his seat.

If Kinsley's testimony was, as one observer wrote, "a knockout blow," the witnesses who followed delivered the coup de grâce.[4] In rapid succession, Osborne put six more handwriting experts on the stand—nationally recognized specialists from different parts of the country, including an official from the U. S. Treasury Department in Washington, D.C., and a gentleman named Ames who had come from San Francisco, where his testimony had helped convict Cordelia Botkin. All declared unequivocally—"without a shadow of a doubt," as several of them put it—that the fake Barnet and Cornish letters, along with the address on the poison package, had been penned by Roland Molineux.

By this point, Roland had regained his usual sangfroid. Arms folded across his chest, his fine kid gloves clenched in one hand, he listened to this damning testimony with a half smile, half sneer on his handsome face. Only his inordinate pallor showed how rattled he really was by this unforeseen turn of events.

Cornish, in the meanwhile, had been slower than Roland to realize what was happening. Now, as it "dawned on him that all the anxiety, all the suffering and outrage he had undergone were only a part of the plan for the confounding of his enemy," his "cheeks grew flushed, and into his eyes there crept a look of triumph."[5]

When the last handwriting expert stepped down from the witness stand, Colonel Gardiner arose to deliver a summation. This was a highly unusual procedure at a coroner's inquest, and the spectators sat forward in their seats, expecting something dramatic.

They were not disappointed.

The DA began by confirming what Roland had, by that point, already surmised. Osborne's controversial conduct of the case—his shockingly disparate treatment of Molineux and Cornish—had all been part of a cunningly laid plot, devised to lull Roland into a false sense of security.

Every other suspect in the case had readily agreed to provide investigators with handwriting samples, explained Gardiner. Only Roland—who alone among the suspects had immediately retained an attorney—refused. As a result the prosecution soon found itself "at a standstill." Clearly, "it was necessary to do something—to disarm the suspect of his suspicions." But how?

It was Captain McCluskey who had come up with the idea. "He suggested that, whenever Molineux was on the stand, he should be treated with utmost courtesy," said Gardiner. Assistant DA Osborne had then carried out the plan to perfection. Whenever it came time to examine Roland, Osborne was "most apologetic. He really appeared to hesitate to ask Molineux a single question." Roland "was made to feel quite at ease."

By contrast, Cornish was deliberately handled harshly. He was even sometimes berated on the witness stand. "From an accusing witness, he was made a suspect himself."

And yet, Gardiner continued, "nobody connected with the prosecution believed for a moment that Cornish was guilty." There were too many "elements in the case which precluded such a belief." Cornish, for example, had taken a near-fatal dose of the lethal bromo-seltzer himself. He had also offered some to his good friend Harry King, who had been saved from death only because the gymnasium water cooler was empty that morning.

Gardiner knew that he and his assistants would come under fire for their "different treatment of the two witnesses"—that his office "would be roundly abused in the papers for its apparent partiality.

"But roundly as we were abused," he continued, "we accomplished our purpose. Molineux was no longer suspicious. He became cooperative. We asked him to write and he wrote—freely and voluntarily. You know the result, gentlemen," said Gardiner, gesturing toward the bench where Kinsley and his colleagues sat. "The experts have told you that young Mr. Molineux has written himself down as the poisoner."

Gardiner paused for a moment to let the weight of this comment sink in. When he resumed, his voice was tinged with sadness. To cast aspersions on members of the Molineux family gave him no pleasure. After all, he declared, "Mr. Molineux's father was my friend in the army." And yet, duty compelled him to make certain less-than-flattering statements about Blanche Molineux—to "show that she was the woman for whom Roland Molineux had committed murder."

At this remark, Roland—ever the gentleman—exclaimed, "*Lady*, if you please, Mr. Gardiner."

Gardiner gave Roland a frosty look. "In polite society now," he said, "*woman* is considered a perfectly proper expression."

Gardiner then went on to describe in the most insinuating way the yachting party on board the *Viator*, during which Blanche and Roland had first become acquainted. After reminding the jurors that the only other female on board the ship was Blanche's sister, Mrs. Stearns—who was there "without her husband"—Gardiner sniffed, "That tells you what kind of woman Blanche is. That fixes her character pretty clearly."

Fists clenched, Roland started to his feet, as if he meant to do physical violence to the district attorney. Weeks had to forcibly restrain him.

Paying no attention to Roland (or to the issue that the jurors were supposed to address, the murder of Mrs. Adams), Gardiner now focused his attention on the death of Henry Barnet. What motive, he asked, lay behind Barnet's poisoning? The same ones that had inspired such crimes "for a thousand years": "jealousy and hate."

"Barnet was on the closest terms of intimacy with Blanche Chesebrough," said Gardiner. "He dined her and wined her. She visited his room in the Knickerbocker Athletic Club. We can only imagine," he added, inviting the twelve male jurors to let their most prurient fantasies run wild, "the scenes that went on there."

In a censorious tone that left no doubt as to his opinion of her moral character, Gardiner again portrayed Blanche as a wayward young woman, who "lived by herself, first in one place, then another," with no "natural supporter," no one to protect or keep an eye on her. "And what were her relations with Barnet?" Gardiner paused for dramatic effect before declaring, in a voice full of scorn, "He was her man."

The implication of this remark—that Blanche had been Barnet's mistress—brought a shout of protest from Roland's father. The "gallant old soldier" (as the newspapers called him) became even more agitated when Gardiner, after reading aloud the infamous "Blanche letter," sneered, "I ask you, gentlemen of the jury. Is that the sort of letter a woman who is about to marry one man would write to another?"

"Yes," shouted the General.

"No!" came Gardiner's retort.

"I say, yes!" the General repeated.

"Again I say no," Gardiner exclaimed. He then turned to Hart and said, "Mr. Coroner, I ask you to order the removal of the persons who are interrupting me if they do so again."

"I shall so order, unless they desist," Hart said.

This time, it was Roland's turn to play pacifier. Leaning toward his father, he took the old man's hand and whispered something in his ear until the General calmed down.

Proceeding with his summation, Gardiner finally said a few words about the attempted murder of Harry Cornish, which had led to the inadvertent poisoning of Katherine Adams. That Molineux was responsible for sending the cyanide-laced bromo-seltzer, said Gardiner, was clear not only from his implacable hatred of Cornish but from the very nature of the crime. No red-blooded male would stoop to such a cowardly, furtive form of murder.

"Poisoning," Gardiner solemnly intoned, "is not a crime that the robust, Anglo-Saxon nature turns to. Poison crimes have been committed almost invariably by women and by men who were degenerates."

There could be little doubt about Roland's degeneracy. The many impotence cures he had sent for proved that he "was a man who had lost his virility." His effeminate character was further shown by his behavior at the time of his final confrontation with Cornish.

"You remember the remark which Cornish made to Molineux on the stairs of the Knickerbocker Athletic Club the night that Molineux resigned from the club?" said Gardiner to the jurors. "The two met on the stairs. Cornish applied that vile epithet to him. What was Molineux's reply? He simply said, 'You win.' Who but a degenerate would not have shown greater resentment to a remark like that?

"This man was also a frequenter of Chinatown," the DA continued. "He went down there and smoked opium. He was an intimate friend of Chuck Connors and men of that character. Besides all this, you have the testimony of the experts. They have told you that all the writing on the letters was in the hand of Roland Burnham Molineux, and they have told you that no one but he could have written the address on the poison package.

"Gentlemen," Gardiner concluded in a thunderous voice, "the case is in your hands. If we have given you enough evidence to create a reasonable belief that Roland B. Molineux is the man who committed this crime, we demand in the name of the People of the State that you shall put the responsibility upon him."[6]

51

As Gardiner took his seat, a "painful silence" fell over the courtroom.[1] Roland, arms still folded over his chest, betrayed no emotion, though his father, seated at his side, wore a stricken expression.

A few moments later, Coroner Hart delivered a brief charge to the jury. It was precisely 6:15 P.M. when the twelve men filed from the room to begin their deliberations.

Expecting a quick verdict, many of the spectators remained in their places. Roland, his father, and their attorneys, however, gathered up their coats and repaired to a nearby restaurant, Holtz's, on Franklin Street and Broadway. They were tailed by Detectives Carey and McCafferty, who were under orders to keep Roland in sight and who took a table near the entrance.

The presence of the detectives did not appear to faze Roland. He calmly studied the menu before ordering a hearty meal, then perused the evening papers while his father and the lawyers conferred. Nor did he react when, ten or fifteen minutes later, Harry Cornish and his parents—accompanied by Colonel Gardiner and Assistant DA Osborne—entered the restaurant and seated themselves a short distance away. The two parties studiously ignored each other. Only once did Molineux and Cornish exchange a look. Roland maintained his usual blasé expression, while Cornish's face, which had seemed fixed in a scowl for the past two weeks, was "wreathed in smiles."[2]

By 8:00 P.M., the two Molineuxs and their counsel were back in the courtroom. Roland was just finishing a cigar when the jury returned.

"Gentlemen, have you agreed upon a verdict?" asked Coroner Hart when the twelve men had reseated themselves.

"We have," replied the foreman, Otto P. Amend.

"What is the verdict?" asked Hart.

Foreman Amend handed the written verdict to the stenographer, but Hart directed him to read it himself. In a voice that resounded in the tense silence of the little courtroom, Amend read, "We find that the said Mrs. Katherine Adams came to her death on the twenty-eighth day of December 1898 by poisoning by mercuric cyanide administered to her by Harry S. Cornish, said poison having been sent in a bottle of bromo-seltzer through the mails by Roland B. Molineux."

A reporter, keeping his eyes on Molineux's face as the judgment was delivered, saw his "lips tremble." Otherwise, Roland remained as stolid as ever.

"The coroner's jury having found that Katherine J. Adams came to her death by poison sent through the mails by Roland Burnham Molineux, it becomes my duty to order his arrest and direct that he be arraigned before me," said Hart, looking and sounding far more nervous than Roland. Though the New York State Code of Criminal Procedure allowed the coroner to issue an arrest warrant, it was a power he rarely had to exercise, and Hart seemed slightly overwhelmed by the gravity of the occasion.[3]

Detectives Carey and McCafferty, who had followed Roland back from the restaurant, sprang from their seats and hurried over to his side. The accused man never winced as the officers placed their hands on his shoulders and ordered him to rise. Spectators at the rear of the courtroom surged forward or stood on their seats, craning their necks for a clearer view.

Coat and derby in hand, Roland was escorted from the courtroom. "They had to settle on someone, so they settled on me," he said to the reporters who thronged around him. "I am innocent. They have no evidence to hold me." In the din that had erupted in the cramped little chamber, the newsmen had to strain to make out the words.

Men who have been charged with sensational murders rarely lack for female admirers. This is true even when the accused is significantly less handsome than Roland Burnham Molineux. As the prisoner disappeared into Coroner Hart's office, a gaggle of young women attempted to push their way inside and had to be forcibly barred by a police officer stationed at the doorway.

Inside the office, while Hart signed the commitment papers, Roland exchanged a few words with his father, who was visibly moved. The prisoner was then taken down one of the elevator cars to the second floor of the building. The General and his lawyers followed in the next car. At the threshold of the doorway leading to the "Bridge of Sighs"—the enclosed walkway that connected the Criminal Court Building to the Tombs—Roland shook his father's hand and said, "Good-bye, Governor."

"Good-bye, boy," said the General, tears welling in his eyes. Then, as his son was led away by the detectives, the old man turned to Bartow Weeks and said, "I wish I was going in there instead." Weeks gave him a consoling pat on the shoulder, and the two men left the building.

The evening papers had lost no time in rushing out special editions. Outside, on the snow-covered streets, newsboys were shouting the headlines: "Molineux arrested!" "Molineux the Poisoner!"[4]

By the time the General arrived home, the news had reached Brooklyn. He found his wife in a state of near collapse. As for Blanche, she had shut herself in her upstairs room, where she lay facedown on her bed, sobbing into her pillow. Anyone overhearing those anguished sounds would have naturally (if mistakenly) assumed that she was weeping for her husband.

After bidding farewell to his father, Roland had spent a few minutes consulting with his attorneys in the office of Warden Hagen. He seemed perfectly composed and not the least bit downhearted. Before being led away, he asked for permission to smoke in his cell, a request Hagen readily granted. Escorted by a guard, Roland was then taken up an iron staircase to "Murderers' Row" on the second tier of the old prison, where he was locked in cell 36.

By the feeble light entering through a narrow barred window set high in one stone wall, Roland inspected his surroundings. This did not require much time. Measuring six feet wide by eight feet long, the cell was just large enough to accommodate a steel-framed bunk bed, a small wooden bench holding a washbasin, and a chamber pot. In the remaining space, a standing man had barely enough room to dress and undress himself.

Extracting a big Havana from the inside pocket of his double-breasted coat, he bit off one end and lit the other with a phosphorous match. But after only a few puffs, he plucked the cigar from his mouth and hurled it onto the cold stone floor.

Then, seating himself on the edge of the bottom cot, he leaned forward, propped his elbows on his knees, and buried his face in his hands.[5]

52

At 5:00 P.M. on Wednesday, March 1, 1899, a grand jury indicted Roland Burnham Molineux on the charge of murder in the first degree for killing Mrs. Katherine J. Adams with twenty grains of cyanide of mercury. Roland learned the news from the evening papers, which he read while standing near the door of his cell, where the gaslight filtering in from the corridor was strongest.

If he had succumbed to a moment of despair two nights earlier when the iron-grated door first clanged shut behind him, he had quickly recovered his composure. By the following morning, he seemed his usual unruffled self. He rose early, performed his ablutions, then dressed in the clothing he had neatly laid out on the unused upper bunk. Inmates of the Tombs were allowed to hold on to their money and purchase special meals from the prison restaurant. For thirty cents, Roland was able to breakfast on a chop, bread, butter, and coffee.

Afterward, he took an hour's exercise with the other prisoners, who strode around and around the second tier of the jail in single file. If Roland—the champion athlete accustomed to working out in the city's most exclusive gymnasiums—felt uncomfortable among the "shambling, shuffling, heel-dragging" crew of pickpockets, thieves, and murderers, he showed no sign of it.[1] By the time Bartow Weeks arrived later that day for a brief consultation, Roland seemed positively chipper. "Brace up, old fellow," he told his worried-looking lawyer, giving Weeks a companionable slap on the back. "Don't look so down in the mouth."[2]

Now, as he stood reading the evening papers, Roland's expression remained impassive, though every now and then his finely molded upper lip would curl into a sneer and a soft, derisive snort would issue from his nostrils. There were dozens of articles about him, ranging from hour-by-hour descriptions of his prison routine to accounts of his courtroom appearances. Many were illustrated with pen-and-ink drawings, depicting him pacing his cell, making up his cot, or taking his daily exercise under the watchful gaze of his jailers. Some were reported with scrupulous accuracy, down to the precise ingredients of his meals. Others were pure fabrications, such as the sensational (and wholly fictitious) report that "extraordinary precautions" were "being taken by the Warden of the Tombs to prevent Roland Molineux from committing suicide in order to escape the threatened ignominy of death in the electric chair."[3]

Editorial opinion was divided along strict class lines on the issue of his arrest and indictment. The yellow papers—each one of which claimed exclusive credit for having fingered Roland from the start—expressed unalloyed satisfaction that this son of wealth and privilege, protected for so long by his father's political influence and the best legal advice money could buy, was finally behind bars. Papers like the *Times*, the *Tribune*, and the *Telegraph*, on the other hand—whose readership belonged to the same social class as the Molineuxs—attacked the district attorney for failing to pursue "other theories of guilt" and, in particular, for not demanding the arrest of Harry Cornish, who was, after all, the person who gave Mrs. Adams the poison.[4]

As Roland continued to leaf through the evening papers, he was astonished by some of the stories. There were several articles about young people who had become so "crazed" by all the publicity surrounding his case that they had been driven to commit horrible crimes themselves. On the last day of February, for example, Frederick Norton of Torrington, Connecticut—a twenty-five-year-old employee of the Excelsior Needle Works, married just eight months—delivered a fatal head blow to his young wife with the butt of his rifle before turning the firearm on himself. He was found dead on his bedroom floor, surrounded by "New York newspapers opened at the pages containing accounts of the inquest into Mrs. Adams's death." According to his grieving mother, Frederick had "never showed any symptoms of insanity until he began reading about the murder of Kate Adams and Henry Barnet."[5]

Equally startling was the case of fourteen-year-old Adeline Harvey of Providence, Rhode Island, who attempted to poison her father by sprinkling creosote over the food in his lunch pail. According to those who knew her, young Adeline "had never shown any sign of degeneracy" until "a misguided interest in the Adams poison mystery temporarily unsettled her mind."[6]

These and similar stories about seemingly ordinary people made mad by the frenzied coverage of his case caused Roland to shake his head in wonder. It was as though the public were in the grip of one of those mass manias Charles Mackay had written about in his famous book on extraordinary popular delusions. To be sure, Roland had been an object of intense fascination since the story first broke two months earlier. But with his arrest and incarceration for what the papers were now calling "the most atrocious crime of the century," a change had occured.[7] He had become something more than a mere curiosity, something for which no phrase had as yet been invented: a media celebrity.

Signs of that change were everywhere—in the bouquets of flowers and gushing letters that arrived daily from female admirers; in the stares he drew from other prisoners whenever he stepped out of his cell; in the jostling mob that showed up when he appeared for a magistrate's hearing, a crowd so large and unruly that the proceedings had to be moved to a different location.[8]

That hearing had produced one of the most remarkable pieces of journalism so far generated by the case, an article headlined GENERAL MOLINEUX, GENTLEMAN. Written by Hearst's famed "sob sister," Annie Laurie (the pen name of chorus-girl-turned-reporter Winifred Black), it was a shamelessly sentimental tribute to Roland's father, who was treated with unqualified reverence even by those papers most antagonistic to his son.

In the article, Laurie described herself as standing in the corridor beside an "old colored woman," waiting for the hearing to begin. Suddenly, General Molineux walked by. Drawing "herself up very straight," the old woman, "eyes shining," turned to the writer and—speaking in the broad Negro dialect popular in the regionalist literature of the time (though it strikes a modern ear as an Amos 'n' Andy travesty)—proceeded to deliver a long speech about the noble old soldier.

"Chile," she began, "we's been lookin' at the quality."

> How do I know he's de quality, de old General? Didn't you see his haid? Carried it some like a mighty proud yearlin' colt does. Not a tear in his eye, an' not a wrinkle in his face, neither. De quality don' cry where folks can see 'em. An' when he met dat boy o' his'n did you see his eye? Jist as proud an' as lovin' as if he was meetin' him at his wedding day, or some big graduatin' time, where all de folks are gettin' mighty proud of him, an' he war rememberin' back when he was a little teeny baby chile. He don' b'leeve no truck about dat boy of his'n an' no poison. He couldn't believe it if he see him droppin' de stuff in a glass an' killin' a dozen folks. De quality don' never b'leeve bad things easy.
>
> Quality folks seems to have some kind o' spirit dat makes 'em keep dey haids up when common folks would be bowed down to de yearth. Laws, chile, money don' make quality, an' not blood always, neither. Now, most always de real quality has good blood, but I'se seen mighty po' trash wid er big name. Dis yer General dat's passed us, he'd be quality even if he didn't have nary a cent, an' if his name war common as turkey tracks.[9]

If Roland was gratified by this paean to his father, he was less pleased by other articles that appeared in the immediate aftermath of his arrest. One paper published an unsubstantiated rumor that he had fathered an illegitimate child. Another printed details of his scandalous adolescence, when at the tender age of fifteen he had been named as a corespondent in the nasty divorce case involving his neighbor, Mrs. Eleanor Kindberg.[10]

Most worrisome of all to Roland, however, was a small piece that appeared in Pulitzer's *World* under the headline MOLINEUX WANTED TO GET RID OF SOMEONE. The source of the story was a somewhat shady character named Joseph Wriggins, a onetime member of the Newark Police Department who had become a private detective after being dismissed from the force for conduct unbecoming an officer. In September 1898, according to

Wriggins, he had heard through an acquaintance that "Molineux had a job for me." Soon afterward, he had gone to the Morris Herrmann factory, where Roland had explained that "there was a party he wanted to get rid of."

Wriggins would say no more about the matter, though he did reveal the name of the acquaintance who had contacted him about the "job." This turned out to be Detective Joseph Farrell, Roland's old friend on the Newark police force. Farrell's story, as reported in the *World*, was that "a girl named Mamie Allen, the daughter of a Bayonne policeman, worked for Molineux for a long time. A short while ago, the Washington Hotel in Newark was raided and Farrell was engaged in the raid. Among the people arrested was Mamie Allen. She gave the name of Mamie Shields at the First Precinct Court. Molineux paid her fine and sent her home. It was then he tried to get Wriggins."[11]

The implication of the article was impossible to miss: that Roland had attempted to hire the disgraced former police detective to dispose of a prostitute named Mamie Allen, a.k.a. "Mamie Shields."

Her real name, of course, was neither Shields nor Allen, as *The New York Times* was the first to discover. "The young woman whom Roland Burnham Molineux is said to have befriended many times while she was in the employ of the Morris Herrmann company and whose whereabouts he was anxious to learn when he was contemplating hiring ex-detective Wriggins is Mary Milander," read a small item in the following day's edition of the *Times*.[12]

It was the first, though by no means the last, time that the name (slightly misspelled) of Roland's former child-mistress, Mary Melando, would appear in the press.

So murky was the light that penetrated his cell from the gas jet in the corridor that even by leaning against the grated door and holding the pages close to his face, reading was a difficult task. After an hour, Roland's eyes were burning. Tossing aside the last of his newspapers, he lay on his cot and waited for his dinner to arrive. When it came—a meal of roast chicken, potatoes, and applesauce that had cost him fifty cents—he ate it with gusto. Afterward, he smoked a cigar and contemplated the dreary months to come.

Of all the articles he had read that day, perhaps the most disheartening was the one that quoted District Attorney Gardiner, who had announced that the trial could not possibly be held "until the early fall." That meant, at a minimum, another six or seven months in the Tombs. It was a grim enough prospect, but there was nothing to be done about it. Roland knew what was required of him. He must assume the air of manly stoicism expected of a Molineux. His father, after all, had endured far worse during the years of the war.

There was one hopeful note, at least. According to the same article, one of Gardiner's underlings had insisted that "when the trial comes, it will be the shortest on record, considering its importance. The District Attorney can put in his entire case in two days."[13]

Neither Roland nor anyone else could possibly know that this remark would prove to be one of the least astute predictions in the annals of American jurisprudence.

Part Five

THE PEOPLE VERSUS MOLINEUX

53

oland wasn't the only principal in the Great Poison Mystery to find himself more famous than ever when the coroner's inquest came to an end.

On Thursday, March 2, the Fifth Annual Sportsman's Show opened in Madison Square Garden. This weeklong extravaganza, which combined Barnumesque spectacle with serious athletic competition, drew enormous crowds to the famous arena, whose interior had been transformed into a stunningly realistic replica of a frontier wilderness.

A panoramic backdrop depicting a snowcapped Rocky Mountain range hung from the ceiling. At its foot stood an actual Indian encampment, surrounded by real trees—spruce, fir, cedar, and pine—and inhabited by several Native American families. A sparkling brook ran through the encampment and terminated in an enormous pool—seventy-five feet long by forty feet wide—disguised to resemble a mountain lake, its sides concealed by sandy beaches and banks of high grass. A game park populated with live elk, deer, and moose occupied one side of the pool, along with a menagerie featuring a pair of mountain lions, several gray wolves, three opossums, five raccoons, and a black bear named Pete. There were taxidermy exhibits and shooting galleries, basket-weaving demonstrations and an aquarium stocked with a vast collection of rare fish, including a thirty-six-pound rainbow trout.

And, of course, there were the thrilling athletic events, among them the National Water Polo Championships, log-rolling contests, and a "clothes race," in which swimmers competed while fully garbed in shoes, trousers, shirts, jackets, and top hats.

Nothing in the show, however—not Nassadao, the six-foot Algonquin Indian and former Rough Rider who paddled a bark canoe around the artificial lake between swimming events, not even the famed female sharpshooter Annie Oakley, there to compete in the clay-pigeon contests held on the rooftop range—generated as much excitement among spectators as the man responsible for managing the show's athletic events: Harry Cornish.

Fresh from his triumphant vindication at the coroner's inquest, Cornish, never averse to publicity, basked in his new notoriety. Wearing a top hat and full evening dress, he stationed himself in a conspicuous place during the aquatic events, drawing more attention than the swimmers themselves. He insisted on starting most of the races, firing the pistol with an extra flourish that delighted the crowds, who rewarded him with thunderous applause.[1]

It was Cornish who came up with one of the most sensational events of the show. Noticing that there was a steel roof girder directly above the pool, he hired a friend—a fearless forty-five-year-old Englishman named Tom Donaldson—to perform a nightly high dive. For fifteen dollars a dive, Donaldson would take a spectacular headfirst plunge into the pool. The distance was fifty-two feet. The pool was eight feet deep. The feat was advertised, not hyperbolically, as the "Drop of Death."

For nearly a week, Donaldson performed the stunt twice a day without sustaining anything more serious than a nosebleed. When he climbed out onto the girder on the afternoon of Wednesday, March 8, however, he appeared a little shaky.

Standing beside Harry Cornish at poolside, the announcer, Peter Prunty, directed the audience's attention to the little figure balanced high above their heads on the narrow girder. Dressed in a pair of loose-fitting American-flag pantaloons and a white jersey, Donaldson acknowledged their applause with a bow.

"Donaldson, are you ready?" called Prunty.

"Yes," came the high-pitched reply.

Prunty looked at Cornish, who cupped his hands to his mouth and shouted, "Go!"

Donaldson seemed to hesitate a moment before raising his hands above his head, leaning down, and plunging forward. Three thousand people held their breath, then broke into a wild ovation as he hit the water. The excitement turned to consternation, however, as Donaldson failed to reappear.

All at once, a shout broke the tense silence that had descended over the arena: "Get him out! He must be hurt!"

Tearing off his coat, Frank Spohn, a Garden employee, jumped into the pool, while Nassadao and another Algonquin leapt into a birch canoe and paddled to the spot where Donaldson had vanished. At almost the same time, Harry Reeder, captain of the Knickerbocker water polo team, dove into the water.

After several attempts, Reeder came up with Donaldson in his arms. With Spohn's help, he swam the unconscious man to the side of the pool, where a hundred hands were waiting to help pull Donaldson from the water. There was an ugly wound on his head where it had struck the bottom of the pool, and blood gushed from his nostrils, mouth, and ears. He was rushed to New York Hospital, where he died of a severe skull fracture the next day.[2]

In the wake of this tragedy, Garden officials decided that they had seen enough of Harry Cornish. Not only was he responsible for the ill-advised stunt; his insistence on making himself such a conspicuous feature of the show was, they felt, "in bad taste, in view of the recent notoriety he had attained" in the Molineux case. From that point on, he was banished to a little office near the Garden entrance.[3]

Once again, Cornish found himself on the defensive, vehemently denying that he had "sought notoriety by exhibiting myself to the crowds" and insisting that Donaldson—who had been making even riskier dives at Manhattan Beach—"had personally superintended" every aspect of the stunt.[4]

Cornish still had plenty of supporters in the athletic world, and few held him to blame for the accident. Still, the more superstitious of his friends began to wonder if some terrible curse had suddenly attached itself to him.

Wherever Cornish went lately, death seemed to follow.

54

Following her appearance at the inquest—and the scandalous picture Gardiner had painted of her in his closing remarks—Blanche could not appear in public without attracting crowds of the morbidly curious. More than ever, she became a prisoner inside the Molineuxs' cheerless home, with its dark paneling, its ponderous furnishings, its heavy draperies perpetually drawn against the prying eyes of passersby.

An intensely social creature, she now found herself in a state of almost total isolation—cut off not only from the outside world, but even from the few other members of the besieged little household. "On Fort Greene Place," she would recall in her memoirs, "we were bound together by a mutual grief; but each of us had to face it alone. We retreated, each in his own way, farther within ourselves. We talked but little. The days became an endless chain, each one linked to the other, drab and colorless."[1]

Her in-laws could offer no comfort. They both put on brave faces, though Mrs. Molineux's hair had turned noticeably whiter in the few months since her son was first implicated in the crimes. As for the General, he did his best to keep up their spirits. "Vindication will come," he would declare. "And when this is ended, we will shake off this strange dream, and with God's help forget it."[2]

But even as he spoke these hopeful words, Blanche observed, his voice would crack and he would turn away and gaze "into the glowing coals of the open fire. I knew it was so we should not see the tears that were in his eyes. He cleared his throat and briskly knocked the ashes from his pipe."[3]

Blanche's only outings were the occasional visits she paid to her husband. These were not made willingly but were done, at the General's insistence, for the sake of appearances. By this point, Blanche had developed a deep resentment of her husband. Decades later, in describing these occasions, her distaste for him was palpable. "There was the necessity for those visits to the Tombs, and one was compelled to see this son of General Molineux there, behind those bars."[4]

What had turned her so violently against Roland was not a sudden loss of faith in his innocence (though by this time she was, in fact, wracked with doubts). Her bitterness toward him stemmed largely from her sense that, after seducing her into marriage with promises of glamorous living—evenings at the opera, summers in Europe, parties with the social elite—he had condemned her to an existence of crushing tedium, public disgrace, and virtual imprisonment.

Making the situation even more galling was his attitude toward his own incarceration. While Blanche experienced her forced seclusion as unremitting torture, Roland seemed to view his life behind bars as an irksome, though temporary, inconvenience. "He was quite stoical," writes Blanche in her memoirs. "There was no betrayal of what lay beneath the surface, his lips taut and hard, and his eyes inscrutable. There was about him a supercilious air of patronizing tolerance, as though he were extremely annoyed, as though he hoped they would hurry up and get done with the whole business so that he might resume normal living."[5]

Blanche's efforts to protect her privacy were, of course, futile, given the relentless sensation-mongering of the yellow press. In early spring, the *Journal* made an explosive charge, claiming that on at least a half dozen occasions between May 1897 and August 1898, Henry Barnet and an unidentified female friend paid periodic visits to a hotel in Jersey City. The couple, who always registered as husband and wife, occupied "the best suite in the house." Generally, "they remained there just one night, though on at least one occasion they lived at the hotel for a week."

Employees of the hotel described Barnet's companion as "a tall, stylish woman, one of whose eyes was faulty." No one knew who she really was, though as the *Journal* was quick to point out, the description "tallies with that of Mrs. Roland B. Molineux, the former Blanche Chesebrough."

During their last overnight stay, the fake Mrs. Barnet had accidentally left behind her parasol, "a dainty, expensive Parisian thing of green plaid, white silk, and lace." The hotel proprietor, Mr. J. B. Hamlin, had placed it for safekeeping in a storage room. Regarding it as a potentially important clue, Captain McCluskey had dispatched Detective McCafferty to Jersey City to retrieve the parasol, along with the register containing the signatures of Barnet and his lover.[6]

One day after Hearst's paper carried this story, Pulitzer's *World* featured a front-page denial signed by Blanche, "her first statement for publication," as the headline trumpeted. The statement read:

> Since the terrible tragedy culminating in the death of Mrs. Adams and throughout the inexpressibly painful scenes that have followed, I have felt it to be my duty to bear in silence the cruel attacks that have been made upon me in the newspapers. I have made no answers to these attacks, nor have I made any effort to set myself right before the world, under the advice of the counsel for my husband, who has been subjected to this infamous and unfounded charge, and whose interests are, of course, next to my heart.
>
> But the statements in the newspapers of today, charging me, by implication, with having visited a hotel in Jersey City with Mr. Barnet are so grossly and atrociously false, that I feel in justice to myself, my husband, and my friends I must now make some statement.
>
> I may say, in the beginning, that the cruel slander uttered by the District Attorney in his address to the Coroner's jury is, I believe, largely responsible for the subsequent attacks upon me. His official position gave his statements a weight that they did not deserve. The public has been slow to believe that a sworn public officer could, without a shadow of proof, vilify and slander the reputation of a woman. But this was done by the District Attorney, and I have suffered in consequence.
>
> There has never been any mystery about my life or move-

ments, nor has there been anything in my life different from that of any other self-respecting woman.

My acquaintance with Mr. Barnet was through the introduction of Mr. Molineux, and my associations with him were merely those of friendship. I was never in Jersey City in my life, except in passing through to take a train.

At the time stated in the newspapers when Mr. Barnet first visited the hotel, May, 1897, I had never met him.

This slander is as baseless as the many others which have been published concerning me.

In simple justice to myself, my family, and my friends, I ask the public press to refrain from printing such wicked accusations, which the slightest investigation would show to be unfounded.[7]

Though Blanche's signature was affixed to this statement, she was not, in fact, its sole author. The General, along with Roland's attorneys, had not only vetted her first draft but made sure to add the line denouncing the "infamous and unfounded charge" that had been leveled against her husband, "whose interests are, of course, next to my heart."

However deeply she resented Roland for entangling her in such a nightmare, it was made abundantly clear to Blanche that for as long as the ordeal lasted, she was expected to play the part of the loyal, loving wife.

55

As Blanche observed during her compulsory visits to the Tombs, Roland had adapted to his life behind bars with a tight-lipped stoicism, comporting himself in a manner that drew admiring words even from his persecutors in the yellow press. "Guilty or innocent, Roland Molineux is a fellow of spirit," the *Journal* conceded. "There is plenty of backbone about this alleged poisoner."[1]

Despite his precipitous comedown from pampered clubman to prison inmate, he showed no trace of self-pity. During the nine months he spent in the Tombs while awaiting the start of his trial, he kept to a meticulous routine. He paid minute attention to his appearance, sponge-bathing twice a day, shaving each morning, neatly combing his hair. He brushed his clothes and shined his shoes "as if he were his own valet."[2] He never failed to wear his necktie. By the time the guard came around with his breakfast, Roland looked, as one newspaper put it, "as if he were about to visit his club."[3]

He always ate his catered meals with relish. Afterward, he would smoke a big cigar—partly to conceal the stink from the chamber pot.

To supplement his daily walks around the second tier, he would often strip off his coat and do whatever calisthenics he could manage in the constricted space of his cell. At other times, he would engage in a bout of shadowboxing.

Each afternoon, he received a visit from his father, who—despite the universal veneration in which he was held—was forced, like everyone else, to undergo the indignity of a search and to relinquish his pocketknife for the duration of his stay.[4] Other family members came, too, particularly Roland's younger brother, Cecil—who on one occasion was made to endure what the papers described as a "vicarious experience of his brother's plight." Receiving permission to see Roland in his cell (instead of the usual visitor's room), Cecil found himself locked behind bars for more than an hour while his brother went off to consult with his lawyers and evidently forgot all about his younger sibling.[5]

The rest of Roland's time was taken up with reading and writing. He was inundated with letters from what the papers referred to as the "morbid type" of woman—what would be known today as a "killer groupie." Not content with merely writing to the dashing alleged poisoner, a number of these women—some bearing gifts of flowers or popular novels—showed up at the Tombs and "importuned the Warden for just one glimpse of Molineux."[6]

Though Roland was not permitted to receive gifts from these female titillation seekers, he was kept well stocked with reading matter by his father. And, of course, he was able to purchase a half dozen different newspapers each day, which he pored over for hours. As a result, he would have been acutely aware of the story that dominated the headlines during the third week of March 1899: the death of Martha Place, the first woman ever executed in the electric chair.

Raised on a hardscrabble farm in rural New Jersey, Martha, whose maiden name was Garretson, knew nothing but endless drudgery and severe emotional deprivation during her early years. To escape the miseries of her home life, she wed a fellow named Wesley Savacool, but they fought bitterly from the start and she soon abandoned him, finding work as a seamstress in a New Brunswick sweatshop. In 1894, at the age of forty, she answered a classified ad placed by an insurance adjuster named William Place—a widower with a twelve-year-old daughter named Ida—who was looking for a housekeeper. Mrs. Savacool, as Martha was then known, was hired on the spot.

Accounts of what happened next vary. According to some reports, the miserly Place eventually proposed marriage so that he could keep Martha as a housekeeper without paying her salary. Others claim that it was Martha who coerced William into marriage by threatening to tell his friends that he had seduced her.[7]

Whatever the case, one thing is certain. In 1895, the two were married; whereupon Martha Place very quickly transformed into a wicked stepmother straight out of a Grimm brothers' story. Venting her resentment of her husband's emotional and financial stinginess on his beloved daughter, Martha began to mercilessly persecute the now teenaged girl.

The culminating horror occurred on Monday, February 7, 1898. Before William left for work that morning, Martha demanded a twenty-dollar household allowance. Place refused.

"I will make this cost you dearly," Martha hissed.

Ignoring the threat, Place kissed his daughter and departed. He was hardly out the door when Martha turned on the girl, viciously berating her. Ida fled upstairs to her bedroom. A short time later, at approximately 8:15 A.M., the "warped, vengeful" woman (as the papers described her) went down to the basement where her husband kept a photographic darkroom. Filling a jar with acid, she carried it up to Ida's bedroom, threw open the door, and hurled the contents into the girl's eyes, blinding her. Then—as the *Journal* reported—"with bony hands which her long years of hard work had made strong and sinewy, she clutched the poor child by the throat and relentlessly strangled the life out of her."[8]

Martha spent the remainder of the day at home. A visitor who arrived that afternoon found her seated calmly in the parlor.

Hours later, at around 6:30 P.M., William returned from work. As he made his way down the hallway to the kitchen, a closet door flew open. Out burst Martha, wielding an ax. She took a vicious swipe at William, who ducked reflexively. The blade buried itself in the woodwork. As William made for the door, Martha yanked the ax free, chased after her husband, and struck him in the arm, opening a savage gash. Bleeding profusely, he staggered into the street, shouting for help.

Several policemen came on the run. While William was taken to the hospital, they searched the house. They found the dead, disfigured girl in bed, clad only in her bloomers. Martha had retreated to her own bedroom, where she had turned on the gas jets in a halfhearted suicide attempt. She was tried and—despite the efforts of her lawyers to portray her as insane—found guilty and sentenced to die in the electric chair, the first woman so condemned.

That grim landmark took place on Monday, March 20, 1899, after Governor Theodore Roosevelt refused to commute the sentence, explaining—in a perverse endorsement of equal rights—that "in the commission of a crime, a woman is deserving of the same blame as a man in a similar case."[9] For days afterward, the newspapers were full of firsthand accounts of Mrs. Place's death, a number of them accompanied by gruesome illustrations showing her strapped into the electric chair at Sing Sing.[10] In the typically hypocritical way of the sensationalistic press, even those papers presumably opposed to her execution found ways to exploit it. While sanctimoniously decrying the state-sanctioned killing of female criminals as a relic of barbarism, for example, Hearst's *Journal* managed to titillate its readers by running an illustrated strip headlined HOW MEN HAVE PUT WOMEN TO DEATH SINCE HISTORY BEGAN, each panel of which depicting a different method of execution, from burning at the stake to beheading to hanging.[11] Hearst knew perfectly well that whatever their avowed attitudes toward capital punishment, giving his readers graphic accounts of a juicy execution was a surefire way to sell papers.

Certainly, it was a story that held great interest for Roland Molineux, whose lawyers were already working desperately to ensure that their client did not suffer the same fate.

56

For a while, events seemed to turn in Roland's favor.

On the last day of March, Bartow Weeks, appearing in the criminal branch of the New York City Supreme Court, moved to quash the indictment against his client. Arguing before a judge with the peculiarly apt name of Pardon C. Williams, Weeks maintained that the evidence presented to the grand jury had been "flimsy and inadequate."

"The sole facts provided by the testimony are these," he said with more than a hint of scorn in his voice. "First, the defendant had a slight difference over club affairs with Cornish a year before the crime charged. And second, three expert witnesses, without giving any reason for their belief and without being cross-examined, declared their opinion that the defendant wrote the superscription upon the package alleged to have contained the poison.

"Is it possible," he exclaimed, "that the life of a human being shall be put in jeopardy and that he shall be subjected to the great expense, terrible disgrace and ignominy of a trial for his life upon such evidence? Would any court allow a jury to bring in a verdict upon such evidence?"[1]

Weeks's argument fell on sympathetic ears. Two weeks later, Justice Williams granted Weeks's motion "on the ground that improper evidence had been submitted to the Grand Jury."[2]

Specifically, Williams ruled that, since the crime in question was the murder of Mrs. Adams, the introduction of evidence related to the death of Henry Barnet had been unjustified. Williams therefore set aside the indictment and ordered the case resubmitted to a new grand jury.

Though Roland would remain in custody, he received the news with expressions of the "heartiest satisfaction." At the Molineux home in Brooklyn, the reaction was much the same. Informed of Williams's decision by a reporter for the *World*, Roland's mother "clapped her hands to her bosom" and tearfully thanked heaven. As for the General, the strain of the preceding few months had finally taken its toll on the old soldier, who was bedridden with one of the incapacitating headaches he had suffered since the war.

After hearing that his son's indictment had been dismissed, however, he was soon back on his feet. The news, he declared, was "the best medicine he could have had."[3]

At the very time that Justice Williams was handing down his decision, another, even more dramatic development occurred in the case. Wholly unexpected, it seemed at first like nothing less than a godsend for Roland.

On Monday, April 10, 1899, newspapers reported that in response to a formal request by his counterpart in Tennessee, Governor Roosevelt had issued a warrant for the arrest and extradition of a man named Percy E. Raymond, a petty thief and con man who had escaped from the Tennessee Penitentiary in April 1893 while serving two years at hard labor for larceny. According to the stories, Raymond had been aided by a young woman named Blanche M. Graham, the daughter of a prominent Southern politician, who had allowed herself to be seduced by the honey-tongued deceiver. After his arrest, she had pawned her jewelry and smuggled the cash to her lover, who had used it to bribe his way out of prison. Raymond had promised Blanche that once he was free, they would run off and get married. Instead, he had absconded to New York, leaving her heartbroken and "ruined."

For years, no one had heard anything about Raymond. Then, in late February, his picture had been widely printed in the newspapers. Though he had adopted a new identity, he was recognized by a Nashville lawyer named A. S. Colyar, Jr., who had immediately notified the authorities. Colyar and Miss Graham had both traveled north to identify Raymond and were now ensconced in a hotel, awaiting his arrest.

Under normal circumstances, this story would not have been deemed particularly newsworthy. As a criminal, Raymond was extremely small fry.

The reward for his return to Tennessee was $25. What propelled it into the headlines was the revelation that, for the past six years, he had been living in New York City, where he was passing himself off as a respectable businessman. The thief, pickpocket, and escaped convict, so it was claimed, was now the proprietor of a private letter box establishment at 257 West Forty-second Street.

The name he went by was Nicholas Heckmann.[4]

Heckmann, of course, had been the single most devastating witness at the coroner's inquest. His identification of Roland as the man who rented box 217 under the name H. C. Barnet had been a moment of high drama. For Molineux and his lawyers, therefore, the news about Heckmann's true identity couldn't have been more welcome. With the principal witness against him exposed as a fugitive, fraud, and inveterate criminal, Roland's prospects seemed brighter than ever.

The rejoicing in Molineux's camp, however, proved to be exceptionally short-lived. Just days after the story broke, the truth came to light. The whole thing turned out to be a bizarre plot concocted by the Nashville attorney, A. S. Colyar. A mentally unstable young man who, it emerged, had done at least two stints in a Knoxville insane asylum, Colyar had seen Heckmann's picture in the papers and—noting a resemblance between the letter box man and the fugitive Raymond—had cooked up a scheme to keep Heckmann from testifying at the trial by having him arrested and shipped to Tennessee. His apparent hope was to earn the gratitude (presumably in pecuniary form) of Roland's wealthy father.

To assist in what District Attorney Gardiner termed "this vile conspiracy," Colyar had enlisted a female acquaintance named Ida Cole to play the role of the betrayed Southern belle Blanche Graham. When Colyar's ruse was exposed, Miss Cole promptly (and more or less literally) bailed out, eluding police officials by jumping off a Manhattan-bound train as it pulled out of the Newark station and vanishing into the night. Colyar was arrested by Detective Sergeant Carey, while to the great relief of the DA and his men, who were busily preparing for the trial, their star witness, Nicholas Heckmann, was fully exonerated.[5]

Though the "Heckmann Plot" (as the newspapers called it) did nothing to help Roland's cause, he seemed chipper enough when he was next seen in public. On the morning of Tuesday, April 25, he was taken in handcuffs from the Tombs and escorted to the county courthouse—a short stroll that led him down Centre Street and through the little park near City Hall. It was the first time that he had been outdoors since his incarceration nearly two months earlier.

Inside the crowded courtroom, he was warmly greeted by his father, who looked, to several observers, perceptibly older than before—haggard and careworn, with hollowed cheeks and dark rings under his eyes. Roland, by contrast, had grown somewhat plump from his purchased prison meals. Dressed in a black diagonal suit, standing collar, and white tie—and holding his tan gloves, as usual, in his left hand—he sat back in his chair and paid close attention to the proceedings.

At issue was Roland's continued detention in the Tombs. Arguing before a judge named Bookstaver, Bartow Weeks insisted that there was no legal justification for keeping his client behind bars, the original indictment for murder having been set aside by Justice Williams. District Attorney Gardiner vehemently disagreed, maintaining that there was nothing in Williams's ruling that authorized Roland's release. Bookstaver ordered both sides to submit briefs, then adjourned the hearing until May 1, when he would render his decision.

Before being led away, Roland conferred briefly with Weeks, who, according to several observers, wore a worried look. And for good reason. For more than a week, the papers had been trumpeting a new and startling discovery related to the case—one that boded very ill for Roland.[4]

At the time of the Molineux affair, dealers in mail-order patent medicine brought in extra income by saving the correspondence they received from customers, then selling these letters to other mail-order firms. In mid-February 1899, Professor F. C. Fowler of Moodus, Connecticut—maker of Dr. Rudolphe's Specific Remedy for Impotence—purchased such a batch of letters from a fellow nostrum peddler, Dr. James Burns, who was giving up his Manhattan-based business and relocating to Detroit.

The job of sorting through the nearly ten thousand letters acquired from Burns and compiling a mailing list of prospective customers for Professor Fowler's snake oil fell to his adult daughter. Ever since one of the fake Barnet orders had turned up in her father's files, this young woman had been paying particularly close attention to the Molineux case. And so she instantly recognized the significance of the one-sentence note she came across as she sat at her worktable on Monday, April 10.

She lost no time in showing the note to her father, who immediately mailed it to Captain McCluskey at the Manhattan Detective Bureau.

The moment McCluskey received it, he fairly leapt to his feet with excitement. He saw at once that he had just come into possession of the single most important piece of evidence that the investigation had yet turned up—"the strongest link in the circumstantial chain being woven about" young Molineux, as *The New York Times* put it.[7]

The letter, mailed to Dr. Burns's offices on Columbus Avenue, consisted of a single line that read: "Please find enclosed 25 cents, for which send remedy, and oblige." It was a request for a sample of Burns's Marvelous Giant Indian Salve, his supposed cure for male "atrophy." The letter was signed Roland Molineux and the return address given as "No. 6 Jersey Street, Newark, New Jersey"—the Morris Herrmann factory, where Roland kept an apartment.

What made the letter so significant, however, wasn't just the signature and return address. It was the stationery itself: robin's-egg blue with an embossed crest of three interlinked silver crescents. The same paper that several of the fake Cornish and Barnet letters had been written on—and that Roland, at the coroner's inquest, had sworn he'd never seen.[8]

57

On Monday, May 1, Justice Bookstaver handed down his decision. Bartow Weeks's motion to obtain the immediate release of his client was denied. Roland would have to remain in jail.[1]

Even as Molineux received this disappointing news, however, powerful backstairs forces were at work to set him free.

Just two days after Bookstaver issued his ruling, Roland's case was resubmitted to a new grand jury. The justice in charge was a gentleman named MacMahon, a former battlefield comrade of Roland's father and, like the General, a longtime member of the Military Order of the Loyal Legion of the United States. Six of the jurors belonged to the same patriotic organization, including the foreman, Colonel William C. Church, who like Justice MacMahon was an old friend of General Molineux's.

On the afternoon of Wednesday, May 10—a week to the day after beginning its deliberations—the grand jury refused to reindict Roland. While the men from the DA's office—James Osborne and Maurice Blumenthal—looked on grimly, Roland was brought to the bar. He was dressed in a black double-breasted sack coat that made the prison pallor of his face stand out in even sharper relief. Despite his somewhat unwholesome appearance, however, he carried his head erect and wore a look of supreme confidence. He permitted himself only the faintest of smiles when—acting on the jury's decision—his father's crony, Justice MacMahon, immediately discharged the prisoner from custody.

Hurrying up to Roland, a beaming Bartow Weeks threw an arm around his shoulder and exclaimed, "I congratulate you!"

Roland seized his lawyer's hand and shook it vigorously before turning to the seated grand jurors. "I thank you, gentlemen," he said with a grave little bow. Then, with Weeks at his side and a mob of reporters at his heels, he headed for the exit.

His freedom lasted only as long as it took him to reach the door.

Hardly had he set foot in the corridor when he was confronted by two burly figures with badges pinned to their coats—his longtime nemeses, Detectives Carey and McCafferty. Holding up one beefy hand, McCafferty ordered Molineux to stop. "You are under arrest," he declared.

Roland, looking startled, halted in his tracks.

"What's going on here?" cried Weeks. "This man has just been discharged!"

Ignoring the lawyer, McCafferty took Roland by the arm. "Come along with me," he said.

"Hold on," demanded Weeks. "Where's your warrant?"

Reaching into a pocket, McCafferty removed a paper and handed it to Weeks, whose face had gone red with anger. He examined it for a moment before emitting a derisive snort. "It is a charge of assault," he explained to Roland. "Against Cornish. Well, we'll see about *that*."

By then, the corridor was jammed with "a hundred or so of men, reporters, witnesses, clerks, and hangers-on about the building," the whole surging mob buzzing with excitement. "Make room here," bawled McCafferty as he and Carey elbowed their way through the crowd.

With a horde of newsmen "tumbling one over another in pursuit," Roland was led down one flight of stairs to the chambers of Police Justice William Travers Jerome. After an hour or so of legal wrangling between Weeks and Osborne, Roland—who had enjoyed approximately three minutes of liberty—was returned to his cell in the Tombs, his bail set at $10,000.[2]

The rearrest of his son did little to dampen the happiness of Roland's father, who, like Bartow Weeks, was confident that the "charge of assault won't amount to anything." His son, he predicted, would soon be a free man. After all, if the grand jurors had refused to indict Roland for murder, they were hardly likely to do so for the lesser charge of assault.[3]

The yellow papers, in the meantime, fumed at this latest turn of events. ACTION IN THE MOLINEUX CASE A PUZZLE, read the headline of Tuesday's *Journal.* WHAT MYSTERIOUS INFLUENCE WORKED TO PREVENT HIS FACING A TRIAL JURY? Hearst himself provided the answer on his editorial page. That the grand jury—stacked with General Molineux's friends and sympathizers—had dismissed the charges against Roland was a flagrant instance of what Hearst decried as "the Triumph of the Pull":

> The most corroding evil in American life today is the power of pulls. In this republic, by the theory of whose government one man is as good as another and has all the rights of any other, there is a discrimination among citizens that can hardly be matched anywhere in the world outside of Turkey. If the schools are overcrowded and some children must be shut out, the parents with influence secure the places. Pulls obtain positions in every branch of the public service; they gain favor in assessments for taxation; they relieve their possessors from jury duty; they secure contracts; they give desirable assignments to officers of the army and navy; and they enable one firm to sell poisonous beef to the Government when another would not be allowed to dispose of goods of the first quality. The pull is rampant in private business, and it has now invaded the courts. . . . When the power of pull can accomplish that much, the plain American citizen may be thankful that he is allowed to live.[4]

The same "mysterious influence" appeared to be at work when, several weeks later, Roland's bail was cut in half. On the afternoon of Friday, June 9, he was taken from the Tombs and escorted to the chief clerk's office, where he received an affectionate greeting and a celebratory cigar from his father, who had just posted the $5,000 cash bail with the city chamberlain.

Once again, however, Assistant District Attorney Osborne had planned for this contingency. As Bartow Weeks led Roland and his father from the office, he spotted Detectives Carey and McCafferty conferring in the corridor. Surmising at once that they were waiting for his client, Weeks motioned for Roland and the General to follow him. Slipping back into the office, the three men quickly crossed the room and filed rapidly up the narrow iron staircase at the rear.

It took a moment for the detectives to realize that Molineux was gone. When they did, they made a mad dash for the stairway. By then, Roland and the others had crossed to the opposite side of the building and gotten into the elevator, which was carrying them down to the lobby. Realizing what was happening, the detectives managed to intercept their quarry before he fled the building.

Grinning at the farcical little chase, Roland was served with another arrest warrant for the murder of Mrs. Adams and, after being taken again before Justice Jerome, returned to his cell in the Tombs.[5]

This time, he had managed to remain free for nearly twice as long as on the previous occasion: just over five minutes.

In mid-July, by the order of Justice Edgar Fursman, the Molineux case was resubmitted to yet another grand jury—the third to take up the case. This time, however, there were no intimates of Roland's father among the jurors. After a three-day investigation, they handed down their decision.

Roland Molineux was indicted on the charge of murder in the first degree for the killing of Katherine Adams. He was arraigned the following day, Friday, July 21, 1899.

Colonel Gardiner felt certain that, this time, the indictment would stick. "I am satisfied that we have sufficient evidence against Molineux to convict him of murder," he declared.[6]

Assistant District Attorney Osborne was positively jubilant. The moment he learned of the indictment, he called for a messenger boy and sent a message to his wife, who was summering upstate in the village of Pawling. The telegram consisted of a single terse but eloquent line: "The people won."[7]

58

With Roland languishing in jail, awaiting the start of his trial, there was little to report about his case. Still, readers of the yellow papers did not lack for diversion. The papers were full of their usual mix of bizarre and sensational stories.

There was the tragic death of Little Aitmarhoke, a pretty ten-year-old "Esquimau girl" brought to New York City in 1895, who had recently died of consumption and whose body—if certain heartless "men of science" had their way—was to be mummified and exhibited at the Museum of Natural History. There was the trial of William G. Peckham of Westfield, New Jersey, charged with one count of cat murder after shooting his neighbor's marauding black tom, Bouncer. There was the arrest of "Jack the Cutter," a young man with a "strange mania" for gashing the arms of female pedestrians on the streets of Manhattan. There was the controversy ignited at the Erster Neu Sandestzer Lodge on Houston Street, when one of its members, Lewis Lowensohn, decided to hold funeral rites for his amputated left leg. "How can he get the society to bury his leg?" protested fellow member Isaac Schmidt. "Suppose he gets well and falls down in front of a trolley car and gets an arm cut off. Will he get his arm buried free, too? He holds only one membership. That entitles him to be buried, but not by piecemeal. He must be buried all at once."[1]

A number of divorces received particular attention, including the marital split between seventeen-year-old Jacob Schoerer and his sixteen-year-old wife, Clara, both of them barely four feet in height (CHILD DWARFS IN DIVORCE SUIT, read the headline), as well as a custody suit filed by Mr. Charles Lee, secretary of the Oriental Benevolent Labor Association, against his spouse, the former Esther Goldberger (CHINAMAN SUES HIS JEW WIFE).[2]

As always, the extravagant doings among the social elite were followed with keen interest. One typical story told of a gala dinner held at the Hotel Marie Antoinette, the "piece de resistance" of which was an enormous pie, out of which emerged an actual one-year-old African-American infant—or, as *The New York Journal* described him, "a little pickanniny." "The advent of the pickanniny was the crowning feature of the dinner," the paper enthused. As the baby crawled out of the gigantic pastry, the celebrated Polish opera singer, Jean de Reszke—"the highest priced tenor in the world"—crooned him a lullaby, after which the hostess "placed a small American flag in the pickanniny's hand" to the "applause of the gracious, brilliant throng."[3]

For several weeks, the city was riveted by the case of eighteen-month-old Marion Clarke, snatched by a kidnapper who signed his ransom notes "Mephisto, King of the American Mafia" and who threatened to "cut, saw, chop, and dismember" the baby "into bits the size of a walnut" unless he received prompt payment of $10,000. Ten days after her disappearance, "Baby Clarke" was found alive and well in an upstate farmhouse. Her abductor—a scoundrel named George Beauregard Barrows with a history of concocting kidnapping plots—was swiftly apprehended and, after a trial that began less than a week after his arrest, convicted and sentenced to fourteen years in Sing Sing.[4]

The seventh anniversary of the ax-murder of Mr. and Mrs. Andrew J. Borden of Fall River, Massachusetts, was commemorated with lengthy features about the current life of the central figure in the case (TODAY, LIZZIE BORDEN IS THE SAME QUIET UNASSUMING PERSON, one headline proclaimed). And there were plenty of other, more recent homicides to satisfy the public's unquenchable appetite for grisly crimes. In the second week of June, various chunks of a male body were found floating in the harbor—the remains, it turned out, of a Swedish sailor named Peterson, murdered after a "row" in a Bowery tenement house, then butchered and dumped in the river. At around the same time, a man named William McCormick, discovering that his sweetheart was cheating on him, found his way to her parlor and managed not only to slit the young woman's throat but to kill her mother as well—a particularly remarkable crime since, as the papers marveled, McCormick was totally blind. There was also the shocking case of nine-year-old Charles Hughes, who stabbed a juvenile playmate to death while playing the battle of San Juan Hill with a bunch of other boys.[5]

And then, of course, there was the usual spate of poisonings: an attempt to kill two Jersey City families by means of deadly dinner rolls; the murder of little Leon Glassburg of Brooklyn by a stranger who gave him lethal candy; the near-fatal illnesses of two private nurses after they shared a pot of poisoned coffee. And more.[6]

Not that Roland ever disappeared completely from the news. From time to time throughout the summer and fall, stories about him would appear in the papers. In late July, the *World* reported that Molineux's months of close confinement in his dimly lit cell had so damaged his eyes that he "must now give up reading entirely or run the risk of permanently defective sight—a sore trial to the prisoner, as his books have been his chief entertainers since his confinement." The following month brought tales of an attempt by a young man named Darwin Messerole—an accused killer who'd undergone a jailhouse conversion—to bring "religion's comfort" to the decidedly secular Molineux. And then there was the day in mid-September when an inmate named Joseph Limberg attempted to hang himself with a rope made from his bedsheet and would surely have succeeded in doing so had not Roland, hearing the "sounds of choking from the cell opposite his own," shouted for a guard.[7]

On the very day that he saved Limberg's life, another newsworthy event happened to Roland. He received a visit from Blanche—the second time she had come to see him since his incarceration six months before.

As far as Blanche was concerned, her forced confinement in the Molineuxs' imposing Brooklyn home was every bit as onerous as Roland's imprisonment in his six-by-eight-foot cell—perhaps even more so, since she had done nothing to deserve it. Thanks to a married friend named Jeanne, however, who owned an estate on the Long Island coast, Blanche was able to enjoy a brief respite.

For several weeks in the summer, she "swam daily in blue waters," "raced on the beach like a child," lunched on the "pleasure boat owned by Jeanne's husband," and basked in the company of a dashing neighbor—a "tall, blond young man" with "hair and skin of the same bronze hue." Possessed of "magnificent horsemanship skills," this captivating figure, who "rode like a centaur," would frequently "arrive in the saddle and stay to dine," lavishing most of his attentions on Blanche, who did nothing to discourage his interest.

As the sun set, Blanche, her friends, and her new conquest would sit "in the half-lighted rooms where the burning candles on the long carved refectory table wavered and flared fitfully in the faint wind from open casements and doors. We lounged over our after dinner coffee, and the men smoked. Before complete darkness came, we would walk the narrow path to the low cliffs, where we could glimpse the full sweep of the ocean. The twilights were long, those summer nights, and they always had a song for me."

By the time she returned to Brooklyn, Blanche's spirits had been much restored. But her tranquil mood quickly evaporated. With each new day, her idyll on Long Island seemed more and more like a sweet but fading dream. By the time she paid her visit to Roland in mid-September, she felt thoroughly "encompassed" again by a nightmare.[8]

On Wednesday, November 1, 1899, Roland Molineux was led into a courtroom crowded with spectators. More than three months had passed since the third grand jury to take up his case had submitted its findings. During that time, Roland's lawyers had made one last, futile attempt to quash the indictment. Now, as Bartow Weeks conceded, there was "nothing left for us to do but go to trial."[9]

Roland looked almost shockingly pale as he entered the courtroom, flanked by two guards. But his mood appeared to be upbeat. He smiled at his father, who was seated at the front of the room and whose eyes shone with pleasure at the sight of his boy.

The business of the day—the setting of a date for Roland's trial—was quickly disposed of. Assistant DA John McIntyre told the court that the people would be "ready to proceed on November 14." Weeks made no objection. "All we want," he declared, "is a speedy trial." Justice Fursman then directed that the "trial be commenced on the date proposed."

The matter having been settled, Roland was allowed to converse with his father. They talked together cheerfully for several minutes before walking out of the courtroom arm in arm.

Afterward, most observers agreed that, in foreseeing a "speedy trial," Weeks was being overly sanguine. The consensus among legal experts was that, given the importance and complexity of the case, the proceedings were bound to be protracted.

Indeed, as one newspaper reported, "it is thought that the trial may last as long as three weeks."[10]

59

Had the electronic media existed back then, the trial of Roland Molineux would have been a round-the-clock extravaganza on the order of the O. J. Simpson circus. But even without cable TV at their disposal, Pulitzer and Hearst—the great pioneers of what would come to be known as tabloid journalism—knew how to whip the public into a frenzy.

The *Journal* in particular pulled out all the stops for the start of the "Great Poison Trial" on Tuesday, November 14. MOLINEUX FIGHTS DESPERATELY FOR HIS LIFE! screamed the front page of the evening edition in letters nearly three inches tall. Though the headlines would get smaller in the coming weeks, the proceedings would continue to dominate the news throughout their duration.

That period of time turned out to be much longer than anticipated. The prognosticators who foresaw a three-week courtroom battle were significantly wide of the mark. In the event, the trial lasted four times as long, beginning a few weeks before Thanksgiving Day 1899, and not coming to an end until early February of the new year.

Presiding at the trial was a ruddy-faced, white-bearded character named John Goff, who held the soon-to-be-obsolete office of recorder. An acid-tongued Irishman and bitter foe of Tammany Hall, Goff was the kind of judge who made no pretense of impartiality. Having "made up his mind as to the guilt or innocence of the accused, . . . he used his discretion with liberality in favor of the side of justice as he saw it."[1] Throughout the Molineux trial, his preferential treatment of the prosecuting attorney, James Osborne, would make it perfectly clear to the jury that, in Goff's view, the defendant deserved to be convicted.

It was nearly half past ten before Goff arrived and took his seat on the bench on opening day. By then, the courtroom was filled to capacity: Many of the spectators were prominent attorneys, who were there to observe what they correctly believed would turn out to be a landmark trial. Some had traveled all the way from the West Coast just to witness the event.

Meanwhile, in the corridor outside, scores of curiosity-seekers begged for admission. Among them were at least a dozen young women, a number of whom had brought their lunches. One of these hopefuls, a "stylishly dressed blonde wearing expensive diamonds," swore that she was a close friend of Roland's. Her pleas, however, did not move the burly court officer standing sentinel at the doorway, and she—like the other "morbid type" of women who had come to moon over the handsome defendant—was turned away.[2]

Roland himself was brought into the courtroom a few minutes after Goff made his entry. After seven months in the Tombs, he looked pale and doughy, though as "faultlessly groomed" as ever in his black single-breasted, tightly buttoned sack coat. His stiff standing collar was so high that, to keep it from crinkling, he was compelled to hold his head thrown back, a posture that made it appear as if he were looking down his nose at the world. His face, though of a waxen pallor, was clean-shaven. His hair was neatly combed and meticulously parted down the middle, with the merest hint of a bald spot in back.

Proceeding to the front of the room, he seated himself beside his father, who had been the first to arrive in the courtroom that morning. The General, who had aged visibly since last seen in public, had exchanged his derby for a black silk skullcap, which he would wear throughout the trial to keep his balding head warm in the unheated room. As Roland sank down beside him, the "white-haired veteran" eagerly grasped his boy by the hand.

"I'm all right, Father," said Roland, who then cast a glance around the room. When he caught sight of Harry Cornish, seated a few rows away, he frowned deeply. Cornish coldly met his stare.[3]

Roland next shook hands with his counsel, Bartow Weeks and Weeks's partner in his Wall Street firm, George Gordon Battle.

A courtly Southerner who had migrated to New York City after the Civil War, Battle had worked in the Manhattan DA's office before entering into private practice. He would go on to have a long and distinguished career in both law and local politics, though he is remembered today, if at all, only because of his controversial namesake. A generous benefactor, Battle, in later years, helped put his office boy, a poor but promising youngster name Sylvester Liddy, through law school. In gratitude, Sylvester would name his firstborn after his mentor: George Gordon Battle Liddy—or as the world came to know him during the Watergate scandal, G. Gordon Liddy.[4]

In trumpeting the start of Roland's trial as an edge-of-the-seat life-or-death struggle, the yellow papers had primed the audience for a thrilling melodrama. What they got instead, at least to begin with, was something much closer to farce.

After an hour or so of procedural bickering between Osborne and Weeks, the two lawyers got down to the first order of business, the selection of a jury. It was a process normally accomplished in a day, two at most. Jurors could be rejected either by mutual consent of the prosecution and defense or by objection of either side. The entire remainder of day one was given over to the questioning of potential jurors, none of whom was deemed acceptable.

Some were excused because they had moral scruples against capital punishment. Others did not appear physically suited for what promised to be a long and demanding task. One fellow complained that he did not wish to serve because, if the trial lasted several weeks, it would "interfere with my health on account of lack of exercise." Another was dismissed because "he had caught a cold while waiting for his name to be called."

For the most part, however, talesmen were disqualified because of their inability to provide suitable answers to the questions posed by Osborne and Weeks.

One prospective juror, a chandelier salesman named Edward N. Sprague, gave an emphatic no when asked if "he would have any trouble convicting a man on the basis of circumstantial evidence." He was then asked to define circumstantial evidence.

"Fictitious and imaginary evidence," was his reply.

As Roland barked out a laugh, Weeks asked incredulously, "Do you mean to say that you would find a verdict of murder in the first degree upon fictitious and imaginary evidence?"

Sprague shrugged as if to say, Why, yes, is there something wrong with that?—at which point he was summarily excused.[5]

Another talesman, a cabbie named Hugh Dougherty, brought down the house when Osborne posed the following query: "Do you understand that, in order to justify legal guilt from circumstantial evidence, the inculpatory facts must be absolutely incompatible with the innocence of the accused?"

"I never heard that while driving my cab," said Dougherty.

As the examination of the talesmen proceeded, the courtroom took on the atmosphere of a comedy show. At one point during his questioning of a hatmaker named Jacob J. Bantler, Weeks asked, "What is turpitude?"

"An all-around man," Bantler replied without a moment's hesitation, provoking another outburst of hilarity from the audience.

Dougherty and Bantler weren't the only ones flummoxed by the high-flown vocabulary and arcane legalese of Osborne and Weeks. Indeed, the lawyers' insistence on framing their questions in the most convoluted way possible brought the first of many reprimands from Goff.

"What would you understand," Weeks asked a gentleman named Albert C. Ayer, "if the court were to say to you that the human mind sometimes acts with such celerity that it is sometimes impossible to measure, and that the deduction of malice from the perpetration of the deed should be drawn after carefully considering all the circumstances?"

As Ayer stared at the attorney in mute bewilderment, Goff said angrily, "I won't allow citizens to be brought here and submitted to ridicule by such questions. You have been asking questions that the most learned of jurists could hardly answer."

"But, Your Honor," Weeks protested, "it is the desire of both the prosecution and of ourselves that men of a high order of intelligence be secured as jurors in this case. That is why we ask these questions."

"But I won't allow it," said Goff. "These citizens are summoned here for their capacity as jurors and not to be made ridiculous by hypothetical conglomerations that nobody could understand. I, too, want to secure good and intelligent jurors, but they can be secured without such questions."

Goff's rebuke had little effect on either Weeks or Osborne, who seemed either incapable of—or unwilling to—ask a straightforward question. Ayers was rejected because he did not understand the terms *hypothesis*, *celerity*, and *morbid propensity*. Likewise, the next talesman, a man named Joseph C. Emsheimer, was excused because he could not give a definition of the words *probative*, *obliquity*, and *turpitude*.

And so it went. By the end of day one, nothing had been accomplished. When Goff adjourned the proceedings at 2:00 P.M., the jury box was still empty.[6]

The story was the same the following day. From 10:30 A.M. until 5:30 P.M., nearly fifty potential jurors—men from all walks of life and with varying degrees of formal education—were called to the front of the courtroom and subjected to questions like: "If the court should charge you that you should keep your mind in a condition of equipoise until all the facts were presented, what would you understand by that?" and "If the court should say to you that the presence of the principal need not be personal—that he need not be personally present in order to be responsible for his act—that the act of another, if by his inducement or authority or direction, would be sufficient—would you understand that?"

Once again, Goff, growing more impatient by the minute, took the lawyers to task, warning them that unless they managed to impanel a jury soon, he would be compelled to hold night sessions. But his threats were unavailing. The day ended again without the selection of a single juror.

By day three, some of the talesmen were so worried about being made into laughingstocks that they showed up with crib sheets—little slips of paper containing written definitions of words like *celerity* and *perfidy*. There was a comical aspect to the sight of these grown, respectable men "looking for all the world like nervous schoolboys, determined not to fail on their English examinations . . . and frightened with the prospect of being forced to spend another year in study."[7] Still, as far as most observers were concerned, the humor had largely drained from the situation. Two men were finally chosen for the jury that day, but only after another thirty-plus candidates had been questioned, bringing the total to nearly one hundred.

By then, the papers were in an uproar. In a withering editorial, *The New York Times* blasted the two attorneys for "wasting both time and the taxpayer's money." By posing questions "that would be more in place in a competitive examination for a professorship of rhetoric than in an endeavor to obtain a fair jury for the trial of a criminal case," Osborne and Weeks had turned the proceedings into a "discreditable spectacle."[8]

The *Sun*, meanwhile, published a scathing satire that described potential jurors fleeing the courtroom in despair after being asked questions like: "Tell me, sir, is your psychological integument sufficiently pachydermatous to obviate the potentiality of the percolation of irrelevant perceptions?" and "Would the juxtaposition of inherently incompatible circumstances in the testimony militate against proper ideation on your part?"[9]

Nothing, however—neither the mockery of the press nor the efforts by Goff to speed things along—seemed to work. The selection of the Molineux jury proceeded at an agonizing pace. Day after day, the papers ran the same disheartening headlines: NO NEW JURORS FOUND TO TRY MOLINEUX, NO NEW JUROR SECURED, MOLINEUX TALESMEN UNACCEPTABLE TODAY, STILL NO MOLINEUX JURY. When, at the start of the second week of the trial, three men were chosen on a single day, the *Brooklyn Eagle* hailed it, unironically, as a "splendid achievement."[10]

With the proceedings mired in tedium and nothing dramatic to report, the yellow papers resorted to a venerable tactic: the promulgation of sensational rumors. On November 22, Hearst's *Evening Journal* featured an explosive charge on its front page: INSANITY TAINT IN BRANCHES OF MOLINEUX FAMILY! The gist of the story was that Roland suffered from hereditary madness and would most likely plead insanity.

People who bothered to read the piece all the way through, however, would have discovered that this depiction of the Molineux clan as a kind of latter-day House of Usher was less than convincing. The supposed "insane streak" that ran through the family consisted of two distant female cousins of Roland's who had reportedly "shown signs" of unspecified "mental trouble" and a woman, Hedda Strack, "wife of Molineux's great grand-uncle on his mother's side," who "was an epileptic."[11]

The next day, Weeks protested in court that the article was prejudicial to his client, then dropped the matter and returned to the seemingly endless business of jury selection. It was November 23, ten days after the start of the trial, and there were still five spots to fill in the jury box.

The process would not be completed until the following week, Wednesday, November 29. At a few minutes before 5:00 P.M.—not long after Goff threatened to continue the session into the night, if necessary—the twelfth man, an employee of the American Book Company named Frederick Crane, took his place in the jury box. A collective sigh of relief went up in the courtroom. It had taken more than two weeks and the examination of 504 talesmen to accomplish the task, though the consensus was that, in the end, the two sides had secured a jury of remarkable caliber—a dozen men "of high standing and unusual intelligence."[12]

The completion of jury selection, however, was not the big story of the day. The event that dominated the headlines was the first genuinely dramatic moment in the trial: a surprise appearance by the leading lady in the drama, Blanche Chesebrough Molineux.

She arrived by carriage shortly after nine in the morning, accompanied by her elderly mother-in-law. The General, who was already waiting at the courthouse, met them in the corridor. The little party was then escorted into the courtroom, where the unexpected entrance of the two women caused an excited stir among the spectators.

Blanche was elegantly dressed in a black cloth gown and a black cloak with a high collarette. Her hands were enveloped in a muff of gray fur and her features partially concealed behind a black veil. She carried herself with her usual air of regal grace, walking to the defense table "with that fine carriage that has always distinguished her."[13] Seating herself at the table, she threw back her veil before extending her hand to Messrs. Weeks and Battle.

When Roland was led into the courtroom nearly an hour later, he appeared to be much startled by the sight of his wife and mother. As he paused to gaze at them, his face (as one newsman reported) "lighted up with joyousness." Then,

> he almost ran across the courtroom, brushing past his lawyers without a greeting. Both his hands were outstretched. He folded his wife in his arms and kissed her. He held her close while he

whispered something to her, and then he kissed her again and again. His face was radiant and she was smiling tearfully. She placed her arms about him and kissed him.

"Mother, too," he said and turned to the older woman and hugged and kissed her in a hearty, earnest, happy way.

"It is a happy day," Molineux said.[14]

Altogether, it was a touching display. What added to its piquancy was the fact that—as the newspapers prominently noted—it had been a year to the day since Blanche and Roland's wedding. According to the story put out by Roland's attorneys, the idea of surprising Roland on their anniversary had originated with Blanche, who couldn't bear the thought of being apart from her husband on such a special day.

The truth, of course, was somewhat different. As Blanche's memoirs make clear, the entire event was contrived by Roland's attorneys, working in conjunction with the General. She herself "considered the idea Machiavellian" and only "agreed to cooperate" because "there was no way out." Far from feeling eager to see Roland, she had to "steel herself for the obligatory reunion and the strong show of affection that was expected."[15]

In any case, she turned in a convincing performance. One observer rated the reunion between husband and wife as "a powerfully moving drama of family ties. . . . No play ever presented a more affecting meeting than this which took place today on a stage of real life, with life and death hanging in the balance."[16] Much to the delight of Weeks and Battle, the jurors—for whose benefit the little scene had been enacted—seemed visibly moved. Assistant DA Osborne, on the other hand, made no effort to conceal his displeasure. His face, wrote one observer, "grew savage" as he saw how the jurors responded, "for he realized how easily their emotions might overweigh all the law and the evidence he might array against the boyish young man."[17]

He would soon have a chance to discover where the sympathies of the jury lay. Following the selection of Frederick Crane, Goff adjourned until Monday, December 4, when the taking of testimony would finally get under way. The hoopla attending the official start of the trial on November 14 had turned out to be greatly overblown. The first two weeks had been a mere prologue. Starting Monday, the newspapers promised, "the greatest murder trial ever held in this city" would really begin.[18]

60

Exactly when the twentieth century began has always been a matter of debate. In the weeks leading up to New Year's Day 1900, "there was sharp division over what was called the 'century question'—whether January 1, 1900, was the first day of the new century, or simply the beginning of the last year of the old." President McKinley and Queen Victoria, for example, "were all quite certain that the twentieth century was still one year away." The German emperor, Kaiser Wilhelm, on the other hand, "hailed the birth of the new century with a thirty-three gun salute."[1] Even fifty years later, when the editors of *Life* magazine chose the first week of January 1950 to publish a special issue commemorating the midpoint of the century, they felt the need to justify their decision by citing historian Mark Sullivan: that January 1, 1900, "seems to the eye and sounds to the ear more like the beginning of a century than January 1, 1901."[2]

If the twentieth century can be defined not strictly by chronology, however, but in terms of its distinctive features, then there is another possibility.[3] In his 1998 book, *Life: The Movie*, culture critic Neal Gabler examines the way the American media have turned all of reality—everything from news and politics to high art and crime—into "a branch of show business, where the overriding objective is getting and satisfying an audience." Gabler sees this "conversion of life into an entertainment medium" as the "single most important cultural transformation in this country in the twentieth century."[4]

If Gabler is right—that the obliteration of the boundaries between real life and show business is the hallmark of our age—then the twentieth century can be said to have begun not on New Year's Day 1900, but a month earlier: on December 4, 1899, when one of New York City's leading newspapers, the *Herald*, assigned its renowned theater critic, Clement Scott, to cover the murder trial of Roland Molineux.

Before coming to America in 1898, Scott was, for thirty years, an enormously influential figure on the English theatrical scene, first as a writer for the London *Sunday Times*, then as chief theater critic of the *Daily Telegraph*, where, among other achievements, he pioneered the publication of opening-night reviews.[5] Brought to New York with great fanfare in 1898, he became the city's most celebrated drama critic at a time—before movies, radio, and TV—when the stage was a major medium of popular entertainment.

The *Herald*'s assignment of Scott to cover the Molineux trial drew a sharp rebuke from at least one rival publication, which bitterly denounced the move as a tasteless stunt:

> Freak journalism has done many curious things in New York, in its enthusiasm to be different. But few of them have been more utterly inappropriate than the action of the *Herald* in sending Clement Scott, its imported dramatic critic, to write up the Molineux trial as a dramatic spectacle. . . . The trial is dramatic but it is not a dramatic spectacle. An admission fee is not charged and there is no occasion for a self-confessed "judge of art" to tout the merits of the trial as a "show." Publicity it must and should have, but appreciation of the issues at stake and familiarity with the other great trials in American courts are better qualifications for writing it than are years spent in describing the tawdry first nights of the make-believe woes of the theater. A murder trial should not be made to wear the aspect of a public diversion.[6]

Though he couldn't know it, of course, the writer of this high-minded editorial was whistling in the wind. To a modern-day reader, his insistence that "a murder trial should not be made to wear the aspect of a public diversion" seems as quaint as the notion that, when escorting a lady down the street, a gentleman should always walk closer to the curb to protect his companion from the mud of passing coaches. In the coming decades, America would witness one judicial extravaganza after another, each generating more media hysteria than the last and bestowing national (at times worldwide) notoriety on its protagonists, from Harry Thaw to Leopold and Loeb, Bruno Richard Hauptmann to O. J. Simpson. And the first of these "trials of the century," coinciding with the start of the century itself, would be that of Roland Molineux.

The scene outside the courtroom was even more clamorous than usual on the morning of Monday, December 4. According to one estimate, fully a thousand men and women crammed the gloomy marble corridor, pressing for admission. "Men of wealth tried to bribe their way in," one newsman reported. "Men about town tried to get in by pull. The women used every art of persuasion they knew. A man with long hair wanted to get in to collect material for a tragedy he was writing. An elderly man in the garb of a clergyman wanted material for a sermon."[7] Apart from those authorized to enter, however—expert witnesses, government officials, members of the press, and various visiting attorneys (including Miss Alice Gerber, one of the city's few female lawyers and the only woman permitted inside)—everyone was turned away.

By 10:30 A.M., when Recorder Goff entered in his billowing black gown, every seat in the spectator section was occupied. Unfortunately, this was not the case in the jury box, where one of the chairs remained conspicuously empty. Word flew around the courtroom: one of the jurors appeared to be out sick. Goff's disbelieving expression as he stared at the vacant chair seemed to mirror the feelings of everyone present. Was it possible that after the torturous delay of the last few weeks the proceedings would have to be postponed yet again? After a few tense minutes, however, Juror Number 9, Frederick Billings, came hurrying into the courtroom, muttering apologies for his tardiness.

As soon as he was seated, the crier called out, "Roland B. Molineux to the bar!"

There was a bustle among the spectators and a collective craning of necks as the door at the rear courtroom opened and Roland entered, escorted by a police captain. He wore a broad grin and walked with such a jaunty step that, as one observer put it, he virtually "danced down the aisle, as he used to into the glare of lights at the Knickerbocker Athletic Club amateur circus, when his trapeze performance was the star feature of the evening."[8] Seating himself at the defense table, he chatted merrily with his father and lawyers. Even when ordered to stand for the reading of the indictment, his smile never left his face.

For the next half hour, both he and the audience were subjected to the clerk's droning recitation of the numbingly repetitive six-count indictment: "And the Grand Jury aforesaid by this indictment further accuse the said Roland Burnham Molineux of the same crime of murder in the first degree, committed as follows: The said Roland Burnham Molineux, late of the Borough of Manhattan of the City of New York in the county of New York aforesaid, on the twenty-eighth day of December in the year one thousand eight hundred and ninety-eight, at the borough and county aforesaid, willfully, feloniously, and with a deliberate and premeditated design to effect the death of one Harry Cornish, in and upon one Katherine J. Adams did give and administer to and cause to be taken and swallowed by her, the said Katherine J. Adams, a large quantity, to wit, twenty grains weight, of a certain deadly poison called cyanide of mercury. . . ." And on and on.

When the clerk reached the point at which the indictment described, in its tortured legalese, the death of Mrs. Adams ("she, the said Katherine J. Adams, then and there became and was mortally sick and distempered in her body and of which said mortal sickness and distemper, she, the said Katherine J. Adams, did then and there die"), Roland could no longer contain his amusement. As his laughter rose up in his throat, he clamped a hand over his mouth, then coughed several times before pulling himself together. It was just the first glimpse of the wildly inappropriate demeanor Roland would display throughout the trial, when he would often be seen throwing back his head and laughing uproariously or whiling away the time playing tic-tac-toe.[9]

It was ten minutes after eleven when Assistant DA Osborne rose to make his opening remarks. He would speak until lunch recess at one, then resume an hour later and continue uninterrupted until nearly four-thirty.

His nearly four-and-a-half-hour address would send Clement Scott into rhapsodies of praise. The fifty-eight-year-old Englishman—sounding less like a distinguished theater critic than a starstruck adolescent—would describe Osborne's statement as "a veritable masterpiece of sustained oratory," "one of the very finest specimens of forensic eloquence and artistic strength that it has ever been my good lot to hear." "Never," Scott gushed, "have I listened to such a masterly exposition of a case, to an orator at once so splendidly virile, so superb in arraignment, such a consummate marshaller of facts, and advocate so good-tempered and so conspicuously fair. Simply with expressive face and speaking hands, Mr. Osborne kept us enthralled morning and noon by an outline of a drama that no actor living could attempt to interpret in such a masterly fashion."[10]

Scott himself would incur considerable ridicule for these effusions, which struck many readers as almost embarrassingly overdone. Still, few disagreed with his larger point: that on the whole, Osborne's opening statement in the Molineux trial was remarkably effective.

He began, in fairly melodramatic fashion, by reminding the jurors that the country was in the grip of a crisis: a life-or-death "fight between society and poisoners." In this war, the poisoner was constantly devising new and ingenious means of destruction: methods of killing that "improved on their predecessors." In the present case, the killer had come up with what "he thought was a particularly clever method."

Fortunately, society was more than capable of fighting back. Armed with only a "few elements of clews," Captain McCluskey and his men had been able to piece together a perfect image of the suspect—"to put the elements together into a personality that is unmistakable, to fasten this crime upon one man.

"And I want to say, gentleman of the jury," Osborne continued, "that each of you in this case will become a judicial Frankenstein. Little by little, you, too, will build up a picture of the man who did the poisoning. We intend to put the evidence before you that will enable you to construct this man piece by piece."

This rather unfortunate analogy—which, in effect, likened the prosecution's case to a lumbering, crudely stitched-together travesty—brought snickers from both Roland and his father. Even District Attorney

Gardiner—who otherwise wore the look of a proud papa watching his child deliver a prizewinning performance at the elementary school talent show—seemed bewildered by Osborne's extremely labored metaphor.

Happily, Osborne eschewed figurative language for the remainder of his presentation, laying out the state's case in a vigorous and straightforward manner.

The man who had unintentionally murdered Mrs. Adams, explained Osborne, had concocted a particularly diabolical scheme for striking at his actual target, Harry Cornish. He had "sent his enemy a holiday present, a beautiful silver bottle holder, and in it a joking allusion to the need for something like bromo-seltzer some men have on the morning after a convivial night. There was nothing suspicious in that, nothing at all—just a nice holiday gift."

Inside this seemingly innocuous package, however, was a rare and especially deadly poison, cyanide of mercury—"a poison that some of our greatest druggists live all their lives without ever seeing. Why, gentlemen, this is only the third case of poisoning by cyanide of mercury on record. The largest chemical firm in the world handled in one year only thirty ounces of the poison.

"Let me tell you something about cyanide of mercury," Osborne went on, emphasizing the level of technical expertise required to procure the lethal substance. "It was discovered by a German chemist named Schuele, while he was experimenting with a color called Prussian blue, a color of which cyanide of mercury is a part. Now, one of the first conclusions Captain McCluskey arrived at was that the man who sent that bottle to Harry S. Cornish must be a man who was engaged in the manufacture of, or who knew something about, Prussian blue. No other person, except a chemist or a color-maker, would have used such a poison."

Osborne next turned his attention to the silver bottle holder. McCluskey's men, he said, had easily "traced it to the store where it was sold to the murderer. Now, where was this store? Where was this holder purchased? Was it bought in Brooklyn or New York? No. It was bought in Hartdegen and Company of Newark, New Jersey. Now who would likely know that Hartdegen and Company of Newark kept silver bottle holders such as this except a man who knew all about that town? But the man must also have lived for part of his life in New York. So we began to look for a man who lived partly in Newark and partly in New York."

Beside the poisoned bromo-seltzer and the telltale bottle holder, the package sent to Cornish had offered another important clue: the handwritten address on the wrapper.

"I want to state to you, gentlemen of the jury, that no handwriting is alike," said Osborne. "Every man's writing has characteristics that belong to no other writing. This man tried to disguise his writing. He tried to write unlike himself or anyone else. But that is where he made a mistake. He tried to write this address in a hand that could not be recognized as his own. But I shall prove to you that the address on that box has the same characteristic as the other handwriting by the man who has been built up from the evidence. I will prove that he wrote the address on the poison package and, though he tried to disguise the writing, the man's characteristics still cling to it."

As Osborne warmed to his subject, his manner became increasingly intense. He jabbed his right forefinger at the jurors, thrust out his combative chin, fixed each of them in turn with a look that seemed to mesmerize them. His voice—never less than "a bellowing, even in its mild and conversational tones"[11]—rose, at points, to thunderous levels.

Having dispensed with the subject of method, he now turned to the question of motive. "Now what is the old motto the Romans applied in all their murder mysteries?" he asked. "It was *Cui bono.* That means, 'For whose good, or to whose advantage?' This was the question the chief detective had to ask himself. Who benefited by the death of Cornish? We looked for motives—who would like Cornish dead? We looked for a man who hated Cornish—not with a hate like a burning house but with a quiet, hidden hate. And, gentlemen of the jury, we found this man."

It was at this moment that the trial took what would prove to be a fateful turn. "Now I am simply painting a picture of this man," said Osborne, placing his palms flat on the table and leaning toward the jurors. "He is, first, a man who lives partly in Newark and partly in New York. He is either a chemist or a color-maker. He is a man who had a motive for killing Harry Cornish. He is a man who knew that Hartdegen and Company kept silver bottle holders. And he is a man with a peculiar style of handwriting.

"But there is another name," he continued. "Another man who figures more largely in this case than almost any other. Even if we were to fail to complete this picture with the evidence I have already mentioned, we could make it perfect by showing you the connection to this other man." That man, of course, was Henry C. Barnet.

At the mention of Barnet's name, Bartow Weeks leapt to his feet and offered a vehement objection, pointing out, quite accurately, that the first indictment against his client had been dismissed precisely because of "the illegality of evidence touching the Barnet case."

"The Barnet murder," he protested, "is another crime."

Goff, however, overruled him. "If it is apparent that circumstances of one crime are relevant to the other," said the recorder, "they are admissible."

Goff's decision was widely regarded at the time as "the greatest blow the defense could possibly receive." In the end, however, it would prove to be quite the opposite.

As Weeks, looking deeply disgruntled, sank back in his chair, Osborne proceeded to describe Barnet's murder and its unmistakable similarities to the poisoning of Katherine Adams. "There is not a man under the sun so stupid," he growled, "who would not know that the same man who perpetrated one crime committed the other."

He then went on to detail other evidence that would be presented in the course of trial: the letter boxes rented under the names of Barnet and Cornish, the robin's-egg-blue stationery with the distinctive silver crest, the various requests for impotence cures.

"Experience of mankind teaches us how a man who writes for such remedies, because he believes himself to be in the condition named, how such a man broods and thinks and plots," said Osborne, suggesting that only a man who had "lost his virility" would resort to a crime as "effeminate" as poison-murder. "If you find that man, gentlemen of the jury, I say that you have found the poisoner."

Thus far, Osborne had not mentioned the defendant by name. Now nearing exhaustion from his three-hour speech, he mustered his strength and, raising his hoarse voice to a near-shout, concluded in a "blaze of passion."

"Who," he thundered, "had in his possession the means of making cyanide of mercury? Roland B. Molineux!

"Who had a hatred of Cornish—not that sudden flaring-up I mentioned but a long, slow-burning hatred? Roland B. Molineux!

"Who lived at the Knickerbocker Athletic Club at the same time that Cornish and Barnet lived there? Roland B. Molineux!

"Whose business was kept partly in New York and partly in Newark? Roland B. Molineux!

"Who knew that Hartdegen and Company had silverware and bottle holders for sale? Roland B. Molineux!

"Who hired the letter boxes in the names of H. C. Barnet and Harry Cornish? Roland B. Molineux!

"Who, in June 1898, wrote to dealers in patent medicines for remedies for the loss of manhood? Roland B. Molineux!

"Who used the peculiar egg-blue paper in writing those letters? Roland B. Molineux!"

On and on went this litany of condemnation until—his voice ragged—Osborne brought his oration to a dramatic close.

"Who in every conceivable way—residence, business, environment, hatred, handwriting—complies with the absolute description of the poisoner? I say to you, gentlemen of the jury, that of all mankind—of all men on earth—there is but one who can fill the bill, who fits into every circumstance of this crime. And that man," said Osborne, leveling a forefinger at Roland, "is the defendant at the bar!"[12]

As Osborne, completely spent, returned to his seat, the spectators closest to Roland studied his face, trying to gauge his reaction. Throughout most of the day, he had worn a supercilious smile that had sometimes turned into a sneer of cold contempt. Now, as Osborne asked the court "out of mercy" for an immediate adjournment, Roland sat there impassively, arms folded across his chest, his emotions impossible to read.

It was Clement Scott—with his highly trained eye for the nuances of facial expression—who offered the most penetrating assessment. Looking Roland "full in the face," the famed theater critic saw "not nonchalance or carelessness or disrespect or contempt." "This wretched young man—and God knows he ought to be wretched after a year of anxiety and horror—is not indifferent or supercilious," Scott would write in his inaugural piece on the trial. "But he wears a mask":

> It is a mask as well defined as that of Comedy or Tragedy assumed by the Greek actors of old. There never was such a mask. It is not Roland B. Molineux. It is a false, unnatural man. The

mask he assumes bulges the forehead, makes the eyes small, inert and insignificant, sharpens the nose and gives a great indented dimple to the hard and somewhat vindictive chin.

Behind this actor's mask, I can see the mind of the wretched man working. When he smiles, don't think he is careless or indifferent. When he assumes a nonchalant air, don't let it convey the idea that he is not weighing every word of Mr. Osborne's tremendous indictment.

He is for the moment two men—the man as he is, and the man in the mask![13]

61

Osborne's Frankenstein analogy proved to be an all-too-accurate description of the sloppily assembled case he would build in the coming weeks. Before the trial was over, he would put more than a hundred witnesses on the stand—doctors and detectives, chemists and clubmen, handwriting analysts and housemaids, postal workers, patent-medicine dealers, bank tellers, bookkeepers, and many more.

There would be no apparent logic to his approach. The order in which the witnesses were called and their testimony taken was so unsystematic as to border on the haphazard. Even the worshipful Clement Scott saw Osborne's case as something crudely "patched and joined," if ultimately compelling: a creation ("like Mrs. Shelley's bogeyman") pieced together from ill-sorted fragments—though no less devastating in the end for its clumsy construction.[1]

The prosecutor's helter-skelter method was evident from the start of testimony. He began conventionally enough by calling a medical witness to prove the corpus delicti.[2] Under Osborne's questioning, Dr. Edwin Hitchcock recapped the graphic account of Katherine Adams's death that he had previously delivered at the inquest.

As everyone listened raptly (everyone, that is, except Roland, who wore a look of extreme ennui), Hitchcock described the grim scene that had greeted him upon his arrival. He had "found Mrs. Adams lying on the sofa in the dining room, with her right arm extended, breathing stertorously." Her face had a ghastly pallor—"a kind of dark bluish color"—and her expression "indicated extreme pain." Touching two fingers to the inside of her wrist, he realized at once that she was "near death." Her skin had a "cold clammy feeling," and he could barely detect a pulse.

He immediately leapt into action, "loosening her clothes," giving her "a hypodermic injection of a heart stimulant," holding "a bottle of ammonia to her nose," and performing "Sylvester's artificial respiration." All to no avail.

"She died while I was working over her," said Hitchcock. "Her lower jaw dropped, and I saw then that it was all over."

Hitchcock then went on to describe Cornish's dire condition and his own sampling of the doctored bromo-seltzer. The instant he had put a "small particle" of the powder on his tongue, he "detected a mercurial taste" and "the odor of almonds" and realized at once that he "was in contact with the most deadly poison that I had ever heard of."

Fearing that he would soon be incapacitated, he had immediately sent for his colleague, Dr. E. Styles Potter. Then—after fortifying himself with some whiskey—he had "started right in again to work over Katherine Adams's body." He realized that his efforts were pointless, but her daughter, Florence Rodgers, "kept imploring me to do more." And so for the next ten minutes, while he waited for Potter to arrive, Hitchcock continued to minister to Mrs. Adams, though he knew "she was perfectly dead."[3]

Hitchcock did not complete his testimony until late in the afternoon, at which point Goff ordered an adjournment. When the proceedings resumed the following morning, the court was in for a surprise.

Normally, the prosecutor in a murder trial would call other witnesses to establish the corpus delicti. Osborne, however, did something unexpected. Instead of putting his other medical experts on the stand, as custom dictated, he called a former employee of the Knickerbocker Athletic Club, Rudolph Heiles. In what the papers would describe as a "crushing blow to the defense," Heiles revealed the existence of yet another bogus letter authored by Roland and intended to embarrass Harry Cornish's friend

Alvin Harpster.[4] Heiles—whose testimony underscored the depth of Roland's malice toward Cornish—was then followed to the stand by the prosecution's chief handwriting analyst, William Kinsley, who identified Roland as the writer of the many requests for impotence remedies mailed under the names of Barnet and Cornish.

Caught off guard by the seemingly incoherent way his opponent was proceeding—with a lay witness sandwiched between a medical expert and a handwriting specialist—Bartow Weeks made a strenuous objection, claiming that Osborne was "flinging away precedent." His objection, however, was overruled. Nor did Weeks succeed in his efforts to damage Kinsley's credibility, though his cross-examination of the eminent chirographer did provide a moment of comic relief.

Under direct questioning by Osborne, Kinsley had described himself as a full-time handwriting expert and editor of the respected trade publication *The Penman's Art Journal.* Now, brandishing the most recent issue of that monthly, Weeks drew the jury's attention to an advertisement Kinsley had placed in its pages. Under a headline touting his "prize-winning stock," the ad offered various breeds of chicken for sale—Minorcas, Plymouth Rocks, and others, "mostly farm-raised and great layers of large white eggs!" It also recommended poultry breeding as a healthy and profitable pastime.

As Weeks read the advertisement aloud in a sardonic tone ("Poultry raising is a pleasant recreation . . . and it pays, too!"), the audience, along with most of the jury, broke into titters. Even Recorder Goff shook with suppressed laughter.

His cheeks burning, Kinsley insisted that chicken raising was "a mere recreation—a hobby."

"Is your work as a handwriting expert a hobby, too?" Weeks sneered.

Weeks proceeded in the same sarcastic vein, at one point openly scoffing at Kinsley's description of handwriting analysis as a "science." In the end, however, his attempt to discredit the witness—who had testified in nearly 150 previous cases—came to nothing.[5]

Of everyone present, Roland seemed the most amused by the revelation of Kinsley's sideline. But then, Roland appeared to be tickled by much of what transpired. In contrast to his father—who sat with a grim expression on his face, clearly "pained by the charges of perversion and moral turpitude" leveled at his son[6]—Roland might have been attending a production of *The Pirates of Penzance* instead of a trial at which his life was at stake. He chuckled and guffawed and occasionally broke into such unconstrained laughter, even when nothing remotely funny was taking place, that the people around him turned to stare at him in bewilderment. But even Roland found nothing to laugh about on the following Monday, when his onetime child-mistress, Mamie Melando, was brought to the stand. Her testimony, though it had to be virtually dragged from her lips, would finally wipe the smile off the face of her former lover.

Captain McCluskey and his men had known about Mamie for many months—almost from the start of their investigation. They had first heard about her from Harry Cornish, who told them of the telephone call Roland had received at the club back in April 1897, after Mamie's arrest at the brothel in Newark.

Traveling to New Jersey, Detectives Carey and McCafferty easily tracked down Mamie, who was residing in Paterson. During a lengthy interview with her, they learned a startling fact. As Carey would write in his memoirs, Mamie explained that "she liked fine stationery, and so one morning while in Molineux's apartment she had picked up from his desk several sheets that caught her eye. It was robin's-egg-blue note paper with three interclasped silver crescents."

Her disclosure was a bombshell. Here was a witness who could tie the defendant directly to some of the most important evidence in the case—who "could put the robin's-egg-blue paper in Molineux's hands," as Carey said.[7] Despite the shabby way Roland had treated her after he took up with Blanche, however, Mamie remained touchingly loyal to him and adamantly refused to go to New York to testify against him. As long as she remained in New Jersey—outside the jurisdiction of the New York City police—there was nothing the prosecution could do to get her on the witness stand.

Or so Roland's defense team believed.

On Thursday, December 8, Mamie and a friend named May Raymond met a pair of handsome young men "with money to burn," who proposed that the four of them travel to New York City to see a show. When Mamie protested that she could not leave New Jersey, the two men—who were actually undercover detectives from Manhattan—suggested that they go to Newark instead.

After a night on the town—which involved, as one news account put it, "opening many bottles"—the foursome boarded a train, presumably bound for Paterson. Mamie, drowsy from drink, placed her head upon the shoulder of her male companion and promptly dozed off.

She was awakened sometime later by her date, who informed her that they had to get off at the next station. They were headed in the wrong direction, he explained, and had to switch trains. No sooner had they disembarked than they were approached by a pair of burly men whom Mamie—even in her bleary state—recognized at once as Detectives Carey and McCafferty, who had been waiting for them on the platform.

"You can't touch me," Mamie cried, as McCafferty reached out for her arm. "We're in New Jersey."

"No," said McCafferty. "This is Suffern, New York."

At that point, according to several accounts, Mamie fainted and her friend tried to stab the detectives with a hat pin. Despite this attempted assault, Miss Raymond was put on the train back to Paterson, while Mamie, placed under arrest, was taken to a hotel in Nyack.

The next morning, she and the two detectives crossed over into Tarrytown, then took the train to the city, where after a long talk with McCluskey, she was placed in the House of Detention to await her courtroom appearance.[8]

The news that Mamie Melando had been "lured to New York" (or "kidnapped," as one paper put it) stirred up such intense excitement that five times the usual number of police officers had to be stationed at the courthouse to keep the mobs at bay on the morning of her scheduled appearance. The windows of the nearby buildings were crowded with people, many armed with field glasses, trying to peer into the courtroom. A member of the U.S. House of Representatives, the Honorable John Raines, showed up to take in the drama. So did Dr. Mary Edwards Walker, winner of the Congressional Medal of Honor for her service as a Civil War surgeon and a feminist pioneer who agitated for women's rights to wear pants. She arrived at the courtroom in her trademark outfit: trousers, frock coat, wing collar, cravat, and top hat.[9]

Mamie made her entrance at a few minutes after 10:00 A.M., immediately after Goff convened the court. The reporters who studied her appearance as she moved down the central aisle were unanimous in their judgment. Though "she might have been pretty when Molineux first met her," there were few apparent traces of whatever physical allure she may once have possessed.

Short and stout ("inclined to embonpoint," as the *Times* delicately put it), she had a heavy jaw, small eyes, "a very bad nose," and a coarse complexion, creased with "the lines that come to a woman's face when she reaches the age of twenty-eight." She was simply dressed, as befitting her station in life, in a round black hat trimmed with white ruching, a black cloth jacket over a green skirt, brown gloves. A pair of cheap silver bangles dangled from one plump wrist.

As she stood beside the jury box waiting to be called, Roland entered, stepping down the aisle with his usual bouncy gait. Spotting Mamie, he paused, smiled, gave her a courtly little bow, then took his place beside his father.

Though Roland attempted to look unconcerned, his face wore an increasingly strained expression as Mamie, under Osborne's questioning, haltingly—at times almost inaudibly—delivered a major blow to the defense. Shown several of the forged Cornish and Barnet letters that had been written on the fancy robin's-egg-blue stationery, she admitted that she had seen a half dozen identical sheets of paper in Roland's "sleeping apartment" in the Morris Herrmann factory. She had found them while looking through a drawer of his sideboard in October 1898. Attracted by their color, she had taken half the stationery, along with all the envelopes. She had subsequently used one of the sheets to write a letter to a plumber named Wilson in Trenton; the other two pieces were lost "in some way."

Before allowing Mamie to leave the stand, Goff himself subjected her to a searching cross-examination, delivered in what one observer described as the recorder's "caustic, satirical style."

He began by asking about her background—her parents and friends, religious upbringing, and work life. Nervously plucking at the fabric of her skirt, Mamie offered a brief and not wholly forthcoming reply. Asked about her means of supporting herself, for example, she insisted that since leaving her job at the factory, she had received "no wages from anybody." As for the occupation that had gotten her nabbed in the raid at the Newark "disorderly house," she remained, understandably enough, mum.

The subject then turned to her relationship with Roland. What, Goff wanted to know, was Mamie doing in his room in the first place? Why had she opened the drawer? Was she "in the habit of" going through his sideboard? Did Molineux know she had taken the paper?

Mamie, growing increasingly agitated, would say only that she had gone to the factory "to see Mr. Molineux"; that she had the "right" to be in his sleeping quarters, having visited him there many times before; that she had opened the unlocked drawer to look for "some books"; and that she had not told Roland about the theft.

As she spoke, she cast an anxious glance at Roland, who fixed her with a look that made her tremble.

"Just look at me, Miss Melando," said Goff. "You have done nothing to be ashamed of, have you?"

"No, sir," came the whispered reply.

"You have always been a good girl, haven't you?" asked Goff.

"I have always tried to be," sniffled Mamie.

"Yes, well, then there is no reason why you should be afraid to speak the truth, is there?"

"No," said Mamie in a voice so low that the jurors had to strain forward in their seats.

"Speak up, please," said Goff, gesturing toward the jury box. "We want all those gentlemen to hear you. Now," he continued, "you were very friendly to Mr. Molineux, were you not?"

"Yes, sir," Mamie answered in a tremulous voice.

"And you still feel very friendly towards him today?"

Fighting back tears, Mamie managed to stammer a yes.

Before Goff could pose his next question, she was overcome with emotion and, burying her face in an embroidered handkerchief, broke into convulsive sobs.

Goff urged her to get hold of herself, but his admonition only made matters worse. Mamie continued to weep for a full two minutes before she regained sufficient control to drink a glass of water. Even then, her hands trembled so badly that she spilled some of the liquid onto her lap.

At length, she was able to resume her testimony, though her voice continued to quake with emotion. She remained on the stand for another half hour before Goff finally told her she was free to go. Rising unsteadily, she slowly made her way to the door in the back of the courtroom, keeping her head bowed and her damp eyes averted from Roland.[10]

Mamie's testimony about the robin's-egg-blue paper was the big story of the day. But her breakdown under Goff's questioning made for even juicier copy, and Hearst in particular proceeded to milk it for every last drop of rank sentimentality. In a Sunday supplement feature titled "Between Love and Duty," the *Journal* described the episode in the overheated style of a Victorian tearjerker. Indeed, according to the paper, the exchange between Goff and Mamie was a scene "worthy of Ouida"—the pen name of Maria Louise de la Ramée, a best-selling English novelist known for her flamboyantly melodramatic tales.

In the *Journal*'s telling, Mamie—a simple young woman "whose sphere was bounded by the caste of her position and the confines of her factory life"—fell hopelessly in love with the dashing Molineux, "the only gentleman who had ever come into her life." Though occupying an infinitely superior station in life, Roland had never treated her with condescension. He "had been good to her," had "never considered her beneath him." At first, she had merely "been grateful to him. Then—it is a way women have—she had adored him." In her worshipful eyes, he became "a god who could do no wrong."

When she discovered that the police wished to question her about "her dear master," she found herself in a terrible dilemma. "Think how she must have felt when she knew that she—who had been almost his slave by her veneration—held in her power the ability to harm or benefit him, this man she most admired in the world!"

In the end, after agonizing over her predicament, she "had sworn to herself not to let out one word that might incriminate her dear, dear Roland.

" 'Let them torture me,' she thought. 'I will not confess!' "

As she entered the courtroom—"her heart bleeding with pity for the white-haired father of her hero and for the hero himself"—her resolve remained firm. Taking the oath, she glanced over at Roland "with such a look as a dumb animal might give his dear master."

On the stand, "she was ready to swear away her soul if need be to protect her master." "At her elbow stood the God of Love, aiming his shafts of devotion at her heart." But in the end, "it was Goff who blunted his arrows."

Under the recorder's "tender and fatherly probing," Mamie's resolve faltered. Finally, her "conscience was awakened and she broke down and wept."

"Before she left the witness stand," the article concluded, "she who was willing to jeopardize her very soul by perjury confessed everything, and in so doing endangered the life of the man she loved—Molineux!"[11]

62

Not to be outdone by his archrival Hearst—who continued to run periodic pieces on the trial by Clement Scott—Joseph Pulitzer brought in his own celebrity commentator from the theatrical world: famed American playwright Bronson Howard, author, among other hits, of the enormously successful Civil War drama *Shenandoah*. In his first article for the *World*—headlined BRONSON HOWARD ON THE DRAMATIC SIDE OF THE MOLINEUX TRIAL—the writer focused on the performances of the principal figures in the case, with particular attention to James Osborne.

Like Scott, Howard was deeply impressed by Osborne's forensic skills, praising him as "a naturally great criminal lawyer." Still, the playwright made it clear that if *he* were directing the show, he would have Osborne tone down his act. The assistant DA had the "wrong conception" of his part. In Howard's view, a prosecuting attorney should feel—or at least convincingly project—a perfect impartiality. As "an officer representing the state," he "should appear deeply anxious that the accused man be proven innocent if the facts in the case warrant it . . . for the state wants no man found guilty. It wants only justice." Osborne, on the other hand, left no doubt of his desire "to prove the guilt of the prisoner."[1]

Howard's criticism—that the prosecutor seemed overly eager to win a conviction—would have been odd in any circumstance. But it seemed especially paradoxical in the case of Osborne, who during the inquest had been attacked on the opposite grounds—for being too soft on Roland. Certainly, few people in the courtroom would have agreed with the playwright. For all of Osborne's "scorn for courtroom conventionalities"—his refusal "to present the evidence in the acceptably logical order"—the intensity, even ferocity, he brought to his task added a welcome jolt of energy to the proceedings.[2]

In his eagerness to put Mamie Melando on the stand, Osborne had broken off his questioning of the state's chief handwriting witness, William Kinsley. Now the assistant DA resumed his examination of the expert chirographer, whose testimony would drag on for another full week.

Day after day, spending much of his time illustrating his points at a blackboard, Kinsley would drone on about the minutiae of lowercase letters, punctuation marks, and word spacing. As he lectured, the fifty-odd reporters covering the trial would scribble away in their notebooks like obedient pupils. To more than one observer, the highly touted Great Poison Trial had rapidly degenerated into pure tedium, with all the drama and excitement of a high school penmanship class.

So soporific was the atmosphere that spectators and court officials alike could be seen snoozing in their seats, while the yellow papers began running satirical pieces recommending a visit to the courtroom as a surefire cure for insomnia.[3]

The most wakeful people in the courtroom were a contingent of Roland's female admirers, who had managed to wangle their way inside. Fifteen or twenty of them occupied the first two rows of the spectator benches, those in front—like considerate theatergoers—removing their bonnets so as not to obstruct the view of the women behind them. Ignoring the witness, they kept their eyes fixed on Roland, who as usual seemed to regard the proceedings as the height of hilarity, "laughing loud and long and very contemptuously" throughout Kinsley's testimony.[4]

His demeanor turned noticeably grimmer when Osborne—interrupting his examination of Kinsley yet again—called Robert S. Holt, Jr., to the stand. The son of Henry Barnet's employer, Holt was asked to authenticate a letter written by Barnet, which Kinsley intended to compare with one of the forgeries. It was a purely perfunctory matter. In the course of the questioning, however, Holt made an unexpected admission.

He revealed that he had once seen Blanche alone with Barnet in the latter's room at the Knickerbocker Athletic Club, a half-empty bottle of champagne on the table between them. It was the first time during the trial that Blanche's name had been invoked, and it offered, as the *Journal* put it, a "startling glimpse of that life of gayety, revelry, wine, love and jealousy in which the prosecutor believes the poison plot had its birth."[5]

Roland's defense team responded with the same tactic they had employed earlier. To demonstrate that Roland had not the slightest cause for jealousy, they immediately trotted out Blanche for another public display of wifely devotion.

She arrived on the morning of December 18 in the company of her mother-in-law. As the audience buzzed with excitement, the two women strolled to the front of the courtroom and took seats at the defense table. When, a few minutes later, Roland crossed over the Bridge of Sighs and entered the chamber, he put on a convincing show of surprise, widening his eyes and smiling brightly. Bounding down the central aisle, he bent low, put one hand behind Blanche's head, and "kissed her fair and square on the lips." Then, after embracing his mother, he seated himself beside his wife.

As always, Blanche was fashionably attired. She wore a black velvet toque trimmed with black tulle that sat far down on her forehead, a tippet and muff of sable, an elaborately embroidered black cloth coat, and white kid gloves. Though most observers conceded that her looks were far from perfect ("Probably Roland Molineux is the only man in the world who could call his wife beautiful," sniffed one reporter), all agreed that she possessed a striking charm. "Altogether," opined one newsman, who might have been describing Henry James's Daisy Miller, "Mrs. Molineux seems to me to be a good, strong, healthy type of American girl: not too intellectual."[6]

Before the trial resumed, Goff had another piece of business to attend to: the case of a teenager named Jacob Berisham who had spent the past four years in the House of Refuge, having murdered a playmate at the age of twelve by bashing in his head with a shovel blade. Blanche appeared keenly interested in the matter, shuddering visibly as the "uncouth youth" was brought before Goff for sentencing.[7]

Her interest—like that of most people in the courtroom—waned considerably when Kinsley returned to the stand for his tenth and final day of testimony. Throughout much of the morning session, she listened to his lecture on slants and curves and curlicues with a look of barely disguised boredom, occasionally holding a whispered exchange with Roland or placing a small cut-glass phial of perfume to her nostrils to offset the air of the packed and stuffy chamber, many of whose male occupants did not, evidently, observe the highest standards of personal hygiene ("the atmosphere," one newsman dryly observed, "is not that of Araby the Blest").[8]

To most of the reporters who studied them, Roland and Blanche seemed the very picture of conjugal happiness. At one point, she placed an arm around her husband, who rested his head on her shoulder—a tender moment captured in a front-page illustration in the following day's edition of Pulitzer's *World.* At other times, Roland slipped his hand beneath the table and gave her knee an affectionate pat. When recess was called and it was time for her to leave, Blanche, in full view of the court, pulled Roland close and kissed him on the mouth.

It was clear, wrote Hearst's reporter, that the couple were "very much in love." Neither he nor anyone else, of course, guessed the truth. As Blanche makes clear in her memoirs, every moment she spent in the courtroom was an agonizing ordeal. By that point, her resentment of Roland had reached such a pitch that she could barely bring herself to utter his name, coldly referring to him as "General Molineux's son." Only her sympathy for her in-laws—along with other pressures brought to bear on her by Roland's family and legal defenders—compelled her to go through with the charade. Once again, as she had done several weeks earlier, Blanche managed to turn in a first-rate performance—one so persuasive that even the famous playwright Bronson Howard failed to realize he was watching an act.

63

Kinsley was followed to the stand by the same parade of handwriting analysts that had appeared at the inquest, among them Daniel T. Ames—recently returned from the Cordelia Botkin trial—and John Tyrell, who in the coming decades would figure in some of the most sensational cases of the twentieth century, including those of the Jazz Age "thrill killers," Leopold and Loeb, and Bruno Richard Hauptmann, convicted kidnapper of the Lindbergh baby.[1]

The highly technical testimony of these experts would prove to be so "slumberous" that, at one point, even Osborne could be seen burying his face in his hands and moaning, "How long, O Lord, how long."[2] All agreed with Kinsley's findings that the fake Barnet and Cornish letters, along with the address on the package received by Harry Cornish, were written by Roland Molineux. Bartow Weeks's cross-examination did little to cast doubt on their opinions, though—as with his gibes at Kinsley's poultry-related pastime—he did manage to provide a bit of diversion in the otherwise dreary proceedings.

It happened during the testimony of Daniel Ames, the oldest of the experts, whose luxuriant white beard endowed him (ironically enough) with the appearance of an Old Testament prophet. Ames, like every other witness, had sworn to the requisite oath before taking the stand, ending with the formulaic affirmation, "So help me God." This purely perfunctory act provided Weeks with a pretext for launching a sneak attack on Ames's credibility.

Approaching the witness stand, Weeks brandished a small green-covered journal. "I have in my hand here, Mr. Ames, a pamphlet," he said.

The witness looked at it quizzically, then nodded. It was a publication called *The Free Thought Magazine.* The cover featured a photograph—clearly taken some years earlier—of its editor, Daniêl T. Ames.

"I see here," Weeks continued, "an article entitled 'Biblical Myths—a Rational Exposition of the Same.' Are you the author of that article?"

"Yes, I am," said Ames.

"You are, eh?" Weeks sneered. "Let me read an excerpt from this article that you are the author of."

He then proceeded to read a passage in which Ames mockingly referred to "Moses, Jehovah & Co.," and wondered how long "human progress was to be stayed throughout Christendom by the ancient barbaric tricks, myths, and frauds under the label of the holy Bible."

Before he had finished, Osborne—his face white with anger—was on his feet, shouting an objection. "This is done for the sole purpose of prejudicing the jury with a degree of unfairness I have never beheld in a courtroom," he cried.

Goff sustained the objection, pointing out to the jurors that, "Our law admits no religious test. The affirmation does not necessarily embrace a declaration of belief in God."

"But, Your Honor," Weeks protested, "I want to show by this blasphemy that the witness—"

"Blasphemy!" yelled Osborne. "You're a nice one to talk about blasphemies!"

"Stop this at once!" Goff admonished the lawyers. He then turned to the jurors again and reminded them that "Mohammedan, Buddhist, or atheist" [or even, as Pulitzer's man couldn't resist adding in the casually racist way of the era, "a Chinaman who makes a pass over the decapitated head of a chicken"] was "equally to be believed in an American court."

"Well, I think I have a right to emphasize this blasphemous utterance," Weeks insisted.

"You must not use such language," said Goff, flushing with anger. He then instructed the jury "to disregard whatever counsel has said on the subject."

Roland, meanwhile, watched the scene with his usual merriment. Even the General—a deeply religious man whose faith had sustained him through the darkest days of the war—wore a satisfied smile, an expression rarely seen anymore on his gaunt and careworn face.[3]

Though his accommodations were a far cry from those he had enjoyed a year earlier—when he and Blanche spent their honeymoon in the bridal suite of the Waldorf-Astoria—Christmas Day 1899 found Roland in high spirits.

Rising early, he took an hour's exercise in the prison yard before breakfasting on poached eggs, fried potatoes, and hot chocolate. He spent the next few hours stretched on the upper cot of his bunk bed, perusing the papers and reading a novel. For his holiday dinner, he treated himself to a veritable feast served up by the prison caterer: oysters on the half shell, roast turkey, cranberry sauce, mashed potatoes, celery, sliced tomatoes, toasted Boston brown bread, ice-cold milk, and mince pie.

Shortly before 3:00 P.M., a closed carriage drawn by two white horses pulled up before the entrance of the Tombs. Out climbed General Molineux, who proceeded to help his wife and daughter in law, both heavily veiled, from the vehicle. The trio were then ushered by Warden Hagen into the counsel room, where they spent more than an hour in a private conference with Roland while the sounds of the religious service conducted by the Reverend Charles C. Proffitt of the Episcopal City Mission Society drifted in from the room across the corridor.

At around four, the prisoner—now sporting a small gold ring set with two diamonds and a crescent that he had not been wearing before—was escorted back to his cell. As his family members left the prison, they were accosted by a photographer who had been alerted to their visit.

"You may take my picture as often as you please," said the General, reaching out a gloved hand and pushing the camera aside. "But you must not take a picture of the ladies."

Ignoring the warning, the photographer again aimed his lens at the ladies. Face flushed, the General lashed out with his walking stick, knocking the camera onto the sidewalk, then striking it repeatedly with the silver handle of his cane until it lay in pieces on the pavement.[4]

Even the yellow press—on whose behalf the cameraman was attempting to snap his pictures of Blanche and the elder Mrs. Molineux—applauded the General's gallantry. No one, however, perceived the incident for what it truly was.

The outraged old warrior's efforts to shield his family's privacy from the intrusions of the popular press—from this forebear of the paparazzi—was not just a dramatic moment but an emblematic one as well: the personification of Victorian propriety waging a brave if ultimately hopeless battle against those forces that were already beginning to turn American society into a nonstop media circus of scandal, gossip, and fifteen-minute fame.

Two days after Christmas, the Molineux trial reached a legal milestone, becoming the longest-running murder trial in the history of New York State. The previous record had been held by the Fleming trial of 1896, which had lasted forty-three days and resulted in the acquittal of its defendant, a middle-aged woman accused of killing her elderly mother with poison-laced clam broth in order to get her hands on a sizable inheritance. As of December 27, 1899, the Molineux trial was already forty-four days old—and the end was nowhere in sight.

What made the situation so disheartening in the view of many observers was how little had been accomplished in all that time. The *Sun* put the matter most forcefully. "In spite of the record being broken," the paper marveled,

> the prosecution has up to the present time failed to prove that a murder was committed, that a package of poison was sent through the mail, or any other of the essentials in a murder trial that are usually proved within three or four days after the trial has begun. The entire time has been spent in getting up a jury and in listening to the testimony of expert handwriting witnesses who have sworn that three sets of letters were written by one person and that the person is Molineux. But in not a solitary one of any of these letters is there a word or pen scratch that has anything to do with the murder of Mrs. Adams; the attempted murder of Harry

> S. Cornish which ended in the murder of Mrs. Adams; with the death of H. C. Barnet, which the prosecution has in newspaper statements connected with the case; or with Mrs. Roland B. Molineux who, the prosecution has hinted, had something to do with the motive for the alleged crime.[5]

One reporter calculated that 1,239,200 words had already been "uttered and recorded" at the trial—almost twice as many as contained in the Old and New Testaments combined.[6] And yet, the state had still not even established that Katherine Adams had been the victim of a homicide.

A turning point came on Thursday, December 28—one year to the day after Katherine Adams's murder—when, in yet another deviation from standard procedure, Osborne called Harry Cornish to the stand.

Rising from his place within the railing, Cornish strode to the rear of the courtroom, where he helped himself to a leisurely drink from the watercooler before proceeding to the witness chair. As he seated himself, he looked squarely at Roland, who gave him a sneer of such open contempt that Cornish grew visibly furious. Two spots of color appeared on his cheeks, his thin lips tightened beneath his stiff, black mustache, and his fingers clenched convulsively. His voice, however, remained cool and controlled as he began to respond to Osborne's examination.

He began by describing his background and education, which included a degree from a business college in Pittsburgh, a stint at the summer school for physical instruction at Harvard, and several courses in anatomy at Columbia College in New York City, where he had participated in the dissection of several cadavers. His goal, he declared, was to "make myself perfect" in "all branches" of learning that related to "cultivating the human body through athletic exercise."

Shown several of the letters for impotence remedies signed with his name, Cornish flatly denied having written them. He also declared that he had never rented a private letter box or laid eyes on the robin's-egg-blue stationery embossed with three interlaced silver crescents until "some time in the early part of this year," when "this case arose."

Speaking in a loud, clear, and unhurried manner, Cornish then proceeded to relate the tale of the anonymous package he had received the previous Christmas, which had led to the death of Mrs. Adams. It was an entirely familiar story, having been repeated countless times in the press for the past twelve months, and Cornish had nothing new to add. Still, the audience sat spellbound throughout his narration, delivered in "straightforward and unvarnished" style and accompanied by an array of expressive hand gestures.[7]

To the theater critics seated in the spectator section, it was Cornish's very lack of polish—his gruff, no-nonsense manner—that made his testimony so compelling. Indeed, Bronson Howard could find only one flaw in his performance. It happened when Osborne handed Cornish the bromo-seltzer bottle and silver holder for identification. "Here," Howard complained, "Cornish and his plain unvarnished story lost some of its effect. He scarcely looked at the bottle and holder before he identified them. It would have been much more theatric and therefore more impressive if he had most carefully examined the two things around which this tragedy turns."[8]

Still, the day came to a satisfactorily dramatic close. Cornish had just reached the point in his narrative when Mrs. Adams collapsed and was carried to the sofa. It was at this "truly tragic climax," wrote Howard, that Goff announced an adjournment and "the curtain fell for the day," leaving "the unfortunate Mrs. Adams dying on her couch."[9]

So many people showed up the next morning to hear Cornish complete his cliff-hanging testimony that extra chairs had to be set up in the aisles to accommodate the crowd. Even so, several hundred hopefuls had to be turned away at the door. It wasn't until after lunch recess, however, that Cornish was called to the witness stand, where he mesmerized listeners with his account of Mrs. Adams's death and his own sufferings after sampling the lethal bromo-seltzer.

Cornish got to show off his skill at pantomime when, late in the afternoon, he was asked to demonstrate precisely how he had prepared the deadly potion for Mrs. Adams. Provided with a tumbler, a teaspoon, an empty bromo-seltzer bottle, and a goblet of water, he stood at a table set up near the witness chair and acted out the procedure. As the spectators watched in rapt silence, he removed the cork from the bottle, measured out a dose of the imaginary powder, placed it in the tumbler, then half filled the glass with water and stirred with the spoon.

"Mrs. Adams picked up the mixture," he explained, "and drank it until there was about this much left in the tumbler." Holding the tumbler over the goblet, he poured out the contents until there was only about a half inch of liquid left.

"Yes, there was about that much left," he said, raising the tumbler to the light. "And then I took a fair-sized swallow myself."

"Show us how much you drank," said Bartow Weeks, who had called for the demonstration.

When Cornish appeared to hesitate for a moment, Osborne wryly interjected, "He doesn't like to drink water"—suggesting, of course, that whiskey was the beverage of choice for the two-fisted athletic director. The comment brought a burst of appreciative laughter from the audience.[10]

Though Osborne's crack elicited a certain amount of tongue-clucking from the press—which decried it as a "cheap joke" that had turned an "intensely dramatic moment" into "horseplay"[11]—it was in keeping with the general perception of Cornish as a red-blooded, all-American male, whose virility was in stark contrast to the dubious masculinity of the defendant. "Molineux's face is weak and effeminate, while Cornish's is strong and manly," declared one reporter, comparing the physiognomies of the two antagonists as they confronted each other in the courtroom. "Cornish's face gives an impression of cruelty and brutality but there is no suggestion of craftiness. He does not look like a man who would send poison through the mail, but rather like a man who would love to feel his fists beat strong against the face of a man he hated. Neither does Molineux look like a crafty murderer, but he does not look like a cool, courageous man who would seek to arbitrate his differences in the open and without forbidden weapons."[12]

Even Weeks's efforts to discredit Cornish during cross-examination only served to highlight the latter's virile nature. In questioning the witness, Roland's lawyer brought out that Cornish's wife had sued him for divorce on the grounds of marital infidelity. Weeks also managed to invoke the name of Mrs. Small—Cornish's longtime mistress who had reportedly died during an illegal abortion—and further suggested that the athletic director had moved into Mrs. Adams's apartment because he was having an affair with her married daughter, Florence Rodgers.

It was Goff who put a stop to these insinuations, declaring that Weeks was raising irrelevant issues of the witness's "private life." "Many a man is not living with his wife whose word is as good as that of any other man," said the recorder. "That is not an act of moral turpitude or moral deformity that would attach any penalty to it whatever."[13]

In any case, it was doubtful that Weeks's efforts to prove Cornish guilty of "moral turpitude" would have carried much weight with the twelve male jurors. From the beginning, the gruff, pugnacious Cornish had widely been seen as something of a cad. But at least he didn't require mail-order remedies for impotence—the certain sign of the sort of "degeneracy" that would lead a man to resort to the effeminate weapon of poison.

64

In the debate over "the century question"—whether 1900 signified the last year of the nineteenth century or the first of the twentieth—almost all the city's dailies took the former position. Even so, there was general agreement that January 1 marked the start of an epoch. "The 1800s are gone forever," exclaimed the *World*, "and the brisk, bright, fresh, altogether new 1900 greets everybody today—good for a clean hundred years before 2000 comes around and you and everybody else now alive are gone."[1]

Certainly, the public pulled out all the stops for the occasion, celebrating the arrival of 1900 with such "noise and jollification that you might have believed it was the new century after all."[2] Though thousands of sober-minded citizens spent New Year's Eve at church—most notably at St. Patrick's Cathedral, where Archbishop Corrigan himself conducted a special midnight mass—most of the celebrants took to the streets.

The scene was especially raucous in lower Manhattan, where an estimated fifteen thousand people gathered around Trinity Church. Armed with tin horns, ratchet rattles, and pistols loaded with blanks (to say nothing of their own whooping, shouting, and bellowing voices), they set up such a racket as the clock approached midnight that the bells ringing in the new year were inaudible over the din. At the height of the festivities, two young men were arrested after getting into a fight and assaulting each other with their five-cent noisemakers. Otherwise, for all its exuberance, the crowd was exceptionally well behaved. When the police announced that the party was over and told everyone to go home, there was an orderly rush for the various lines of transportation. By one o'clock, "lower Broadway was as it always is at that hour of the morning."[3]

The inmates of the Tombs had to wait until New Year's Day itself to enjoy a celebration. On the afternoon of January 1, the famed orchestra leader Frank Banta paid a visit to the prison, accompanied by a crew of his musicians and the singer Annie Hart, star of the vaudeville show *The Bowery Girl*, in which she had introduced the ballad "Little Annie Rooney" to American audiences.

Roland was seated on his bunk reading the papers by candlelight when the performers arrived. Setting up their stands directly across from his cell, they proceeded to delight their listeners with a selection of standards—"The Old Oaken Bucket," "Bonnie Doon," "Ring Out, Wild Bells," "Unfurl the Banner," and more. Some of the players were so curious about the city's most infamous prisoner that, on several occasions, they hit the wrong notes as they glanced up from their music to sneak looks at him. Still, the concert was deemed a smashing success.

Afterward, Miss Hart stood by Roland's door and exchanged a few words with him through the iron grating. Ever the gentleman, Roland offered his heartfelt thanks for the afternoon's entertainment. She, in turn, wished him well and expressed her ardent prayers for his "speedy deliverance."[4]

Harry Cornish completed his testimony when the trial resumed on the following day. He was followed to the stand by several other members of the Knickerbocker Athletic Club, including the "thrice lucky" Harry King, who had escaped certain death only because the custodian had neglected to refill the gymnasium watercooler, and Patrick Fineran, who had suggested that Cornish save the wrapper from the anonymous package in the hope of identifying the sender.

The last witness of the day was the coroner's physician, Albert T. Weston, who gave a concise but graphic account of the autopsy he had performed on Katherine Adams the day after her death, and confirmed his belief that the victim had been poisoned with cyanide of mercury.

"Did you see the body of Mrs. Adams on December 28, 1898?" asked Osborne.

"I did," said Weston.

"And was the body of Mrs. Katherine J. Adams, on which you performed an autopsy on the twenty-ninth, the same body you saw on the twenty-eighth which was identified by Mr. McIntyre as the body of Katherine J. Adams?"

"It was," said Weston.

This brief, seemingly perfunctory exchange was, in fact, a significant moment in the trial. After forty-nine days, the prosecution had finally, as one observer pointed out, "proved the corpus delicti in the case."[5]

Over the next few weeks, Osborne put scores of witnesses on the stand, sometimes as many as a dozen in a single day. By and large, they were a familiar bunch, repeating information that had been conveyed countless times in the press.

The renowned toxicologist Dr. Rudolph Witthaus confirmed that Mrs. Adams had been poisoned with cyanide of mercury. Detectives Herlihy and Carey described the tracing of the silver toothpick holder to Hartdegen's jewelry store. Club members John Yocum and John Adams recalled the bad blood that had existed between Cornish and Molineux. The letter box men, Joseph Koch and Nicholas Heckmann, both identified Roland as the person who had rented private boxes from them under assumed names.[6]

And there were others—Florence Rodgers, who corroborated Cornish's account of her mother's death; Joseph Farrell, the Newark police officer who recounted the time he had run into Roland not far from Hartdegen's; Elsie Gray, the bookkeeper for the Kutnow Brothers Drug Company, who told of discovering the fake Cornish letter written on the distinctive robin's-egg-blue stationery; Carl Trommer, a salesman for a chemical supply company who testified that Roland kept the raw materials for making cyanide of mercury in his lab at the Morris Herrmann factory; and more.

Though each of these witnesses represented an important link in the chain of circumstantial evidence Osborne was attempting to forge, there was nothing new or surprising about their testimony. To the crowds that continued to flock to the courtroom—and to the millions of newspaper readers who had been following the case since its inception—the Great Poison Trial was turning out to be a distinct disappointment, a mere rehash of the widely known facts. Roland himself had reached a point of such supreme boredom that he now spent much of his time playing tic-tac-toe with one of the expert defense witnesses seated at his table.[7] As the prosecution began to wind up its case, it seemed as if the much-ballyhooed trial would end without a single sensational revelation.

And then, nearly ten weeks into the trial, the public finally got the titillation it was itching for.

The session had just opened on Monday morning, January 15, when two African-American women—variously referred to in the papers as "negresses," "colored servants," and "sable-colored witnesses"—were escorted into the courtroom by a pair of detectives. Shortly afterward, Osborne called out the name Rachel Greene. One of the women—a slender figure neatly garbed in a black dress and a large feathered hat—stepped to the front of the room. No one knew who she was—even Roland looked at her idly, "as if she didn't remind him of anything." Still, there was a buzz in the courtroom as she took the stand, as though the audience sensed that they were about to hear "a witness of unusual interest."[8]

After identifying herself, the young woman explained that she was a native of Washington, D.C., and still lived there, at 1633 Sixth Street, N.W. Several years before, however—from the fall of 1897 until early 1898—she had resided in New York City, at a boardinghouse owned by Mrs. Mary Bell on West Seventy-second Street, where she had worked as a chambermaid. "I kept the rooms clean," Miss Greene explained, "and answered the doorbell."

"Did you know the defendant there at the time?" asked Osborne.

The witness paused a moment before replying, "I knew Mr. and Mrs. Chesebrough."

This unexpected answer produced an immediate effect. Everyone in the courtroom—the jurors, the spectators, Roland's attorneys—seemed to snap to attention. Even Roland seemed roused from his usual apathy. He tightened his lips and "looked at the witness intently, as if he knew what was coming."

"Do you see this Mr. Chesebrough in the courtroom?" asked Osborne.

There was absolute silence in the courtroom as the young woman rose from her seat and began scanning the faces of the jurors, the lawyers, the reporters. As it happened, Osborne was blocking her view of the defendant.

"You're in the way," whispered an assistant district attorney named Collins, reaching up to tug at Osborne's sleeve.

As Osborne stepped aside, Rachel Greene's eyes fixed on Roland, who leaned back, looked straight at her, and arranged his mouth into a smile of chilly amusement.

"I think that's the gentleman there," said the witness. "Beside the one with the white hair. Only he don't have any mustache now."

"So he wore a mustache then?" asked Osborne.

"Yes, sir," said Miss Greene.

Suddenly, Goff interrupted. "This won't do," he said. "To say 'that gentleman there' is not a proper identification in a trial of this importance."

Acknowledging Goff's admonition, Osborne instructed the witness to come down from the stand and point out the man she knew as "Mr. Chesebrough."

Her pocketbook clasped in her right hand, Rachel walked slowly to the long defense table and halted directly opposite Roland. Then, as Molineux looked her squarely in the eye, she extended her left forefinger and said, "That's the gentleman."

It was a moment of high drama, one of the very few the trial had offered. A flush of anger came to Roland's cheeks, then quickly drained away, leaving his complexion more pallid than before. Turning to his father, he whispered something in the older man's ear before barking out a bitter laugh.

"Now, Miss Greene," said Osborne, as the witness settled back in her chair, "how long were that man and Miss Chesebrough at the place where you worked?"

"From November 2, 1897, to January of 1898," answered Rachel.

"And what room did they occupy?"

"The front room," said the witness. "One flight up."

"They did not have any other room in the house?"

Miss Greene shook her head emphatically. "No, they lived there together."

"As man and wife?" asked Osborne.

"Yes," said Miss Greene.

Her reply caused a stir among the spectators, who like everyone familiar with the case knew that Roland and Blanche had not been wed until the following November, a year after they began cohabiting in Mrs. Bell's boardinghouse.

"Did Mr. Chesebrough have any of his belongings there?" asked Osborne.

Miss Greene replied that he had kept "his comb and toothbrush and that sort of thing" in the room.

"Anything else?" asked Osborne.

"A man used to bring a dress suitcase there," said the witness.

Turning to the spectator section, Osborne summoned a young man named Fisk, who worked as a valet in the Knickerbocker Athletic Club, and asked him to stand near the witness box.

"Is this the man who used to bring the suitcase?" asked Osborne.

Rachel studied Fisk for a long moment before replying, "It looks like the gentleman, but it seems to me he's got fatter."

The remark elicited some chuckles from the audience. Roland, however, was clearly not amused. Clenched fists thrust beneath his folded arms, he sat there in what one reporter described as a "sort of gray rage"—"powerless to interfere while the negro serving woman made statements about his wife, accusations which would warrant a husband in resorting to violence."

Before letting her go, Osborne asked the witness if she knew where Blanche had gone after moving out of Mary Bell's boardinghouse at the beginning of January 1898.

"I believe she moved on out to West End Avenue," came the reply. "To Mrs. Bellinger's."

Osborne then called the second of the African-American women, Minnie Betts, who picked up the story where Rachel Greene had left off—with Blanche's move to the home of her friend Alice Bellinger. A tall, slender woman who had worked for years as Mrs. Bellinger's maid, Minnie offered testimony every bit as sensational as her predecessor's.

Asked when she had "first seen Molineux," Minnie swore that she had never set eyes on him until he and Blanche were married. During the entire ten months between Blanche's arrival at the Bellinger home in January 1898 and her wedding to Roland shortly before the following Thanksgiving, he had never paid a visit to the house.

"Did someone else call on Miss Chesebrough during that time?" asked Osborne.

"Yes, sir," said Minnie. "There was a young man, but I didn't know who he was."

Stepping to the defense table, Osborne picked up a photograph and handed it to Minnie.

"I show you here a picture," he said, "and I ask you if that is the man who visited Miss Chesebrough in 1898, prior to her marriage to the defendant."

The courtroom was hushed as Minnie studied the photograph.

"Yes," she said at length. "It looks like him."

A ripple of excitement ran through the spectator section. Even without seeing the picture, everyone knew that Minnie Betts had just identified Henry Barnet as Blanche Chesebrough's gentleman caller.

At that moment, Goff spoke up. "What do you propose to show by all this evidence?" he asked Osborne.

"Why, Your Honor," said Osborne, "I will establish the motive. First it's Molineux and Blanche Chesebrough living as husband and wife. Then it is Barnet calling at the house and not Molineux. Then Barnet dies of poison. It's clear that Barnet stepped in between Molineux and Miss Chesebrough. That was the motive for killing Barnet."

"But this defendant is not on trial for the murder of Barnet," said Goff.

"No," said Osborne. "But I want to show that the man who hated Barnet also hated Cornish. We find letters written for certain remedies in Barnet's name. We also find letters in Cornish's name. This shows the workings of the defendant's mind. Barnet died of cyanide of mercury, just as Cornish was to have died. It's the same sort of plot, and as such should be allowed in evidence."

A long moment passed while Goff considered this argument. Then he spoke three words that would have momentous consequences for Roland Molineux.

"You may continue."[9]

The testimony of the two chambermaids provided just the jolt of sensationalism the yellow papers were waiting for. It wasn't Rachel Greene or Minnie Betts, however, whose image was blazoned on the front pages but Blanche Molineux—"the most fascinating and mysterious figure of all the case," as the *Journal* described her. Under headlines such as BARNET CROSSED ROLAND MOLINEUX IN LOVE and WIFE'S NAME DRAGGED IN AT MOLINEUX TRIAL, the papers dished up the whole salacious story of Blanche's scandalous living arrangement with Roland and her affair with another man in the months before her marriage.

Even while Hearst and Pulitzer were gleefully exploiting these lurid revelations, one newspaper was expressing concern over the chambermaids' testimony. In an editorial published on Wednesday, January 17, the *Brooklyn Eagle* acknowledged that, in establishing the connections between Barnet's death and the attempt on Cornish's life, Osborne had managed to "show a plot outdoing Poe in its gruesomeness"—one that "quite justified the use of the term Frankenstein which has figured so largely in the case." But by "admitting testimony tending to show a motive for the murder of Barnet," Recorder Goff had almost guaranteed that the long-drawn-out case would not be resolved anytime soon.

Up until two days earlier, it seemed as if a verdict might be reached within the next few weeks. But Goff's decision to allow evidence relating to another crime—one for which the defendant had never been charged—had opened up a "grave possibility": that if Roland were convicted and the case went to the court of appeals, it would "have to be tried all over again."[10]

65

On the afternoon of Thursday, January 18—to the great relief of everyone involved in the seemingly interminable trial—James Osborne declared that he would wrap up the state's case on the following day after tying up a few "tag ends."[1]

The announcement allowed trial-watchers to assess Osborne's overall performance. There was general agreement that he had succeeded in establishing a number of crucial points: that the bogus Barnet and Cornish letters, as well as the address on the poison package, were all written by Molineux. That Roland, under the two assumed names, had rented a pair of private letter boxes, where he had received material from various patent-medicine dealers, including a sample tin of Kutnow's Powder. That the description given on the "diagnosis blank" mailed to the Marston Remedy Company by the person who signed himself "H. C. Barnet" corresponded far more closely to Roland than to the ostensible sender. That Roland was familiar with Hartdegen's jewelry store, where the silver toothpick holder sent to Cornish was purchased. That, as a chemist, Roland had both the means and the know-how to obtain or concoct cyanide of mercury.

Most observers agreed, however, that on one key point, Osborne had failed to make a particularly convincing case: Roland's motive for wanting Harry Cornish dead. The assistant DA had certainly shown that there was no love lost between the two men. But the conflicts described by the witnesses—disputes over gym equipment and the state of the swimming pool and an insulting letter written about a member of a rival club—hardly seemed sufficient to explain such a dastardly crime. That darker, more malevolent impulses might have been operating in the depths of Roland's mind—that the swaggering Cornish might, for example, have been an unconscious surrogate for another figure of formidable manhood whom Roland had spent a lifetime trying, and failing, to measure up to—would not have occurred to anyone in that pre-Freudian era.

Osborne had clearly recognized this problem and had sought to get around it by arguing that the man who tried to kill Cornish had also poisoned Barnet. It was much easier to prove motive in the Barnet case; sexual jealousy was something every male juror could understand. Everyone agreed that the assistant DA had been extremely "adroit in connecting the cases together so inseparably that evidence in one has been applied to the other as if the two were the same." Indeed, as one newspaper put it, "if Molineux were on trial for the murder of Barnet, the case would be so strong that the jury almost certainly would return a verdict of guilty."

There was only one problem: the murder of Henry Barnet was "a crime which was not charged against Molineux in the indictment."[2]

Osborne's announcement turned out to be premature. As it happened, he would not be ready to conclude his case until the following Wednesday, January 24.

There was an air of expectancy in the courtroom that morning. The previous afternoon, Osborne had let it be known that the state would require only a half hour more to complete the questioning of its final witness, yet another handwriting expert, this one a Philadelphian named Percival Fraser. The "long-heralded end" of the prosecution's case appeared to be at hand.

Before the proceedings could begin on Wednesday morning, however, Recorder Goff was handed a message informing him that one of the jurors, a gentleman named Manheim Brown, had "taken sick" and was confined to bed. According to the sender—Brown's physician, Dr. Sigmund Tynberg—the patient's "indisposition was not of a serious nature and a prolonged delay on his account was unlikely." Goff had no choice but to adjourn the case until the morrow.

Audible groans of disappointment arose from the spectator section. Still, given the ungodly length of the trial, the severity of the weather, and the terrible ventilation in the courtroom, most observers agreed that it was "remarkable that none of those concerned in the case had succumbed before this."[3]

Dr. Tynberg's prognosis, as it turned out, was overly sanguine. By the following Monday, January 29, Brown had still not returned to the trial. His condition, claimed the doctor, could be blamed directly on the conditions in the courtroom.

"It is a wonder to me that Mr. Brown did not give way sooner," Tynberg told a reporter for the *Journal.* "The morning that he took to his bed, he stopped in my office on his way to court. He was then suffering from bronchitis, grippe, and rheumatism. It was with difficulty that he managed to return to his home, and when I saw him an hour later, he was in a high fever and great pain."

Tynberg went on to blame Brown's illness on the "drafts from the partly opened window in the courtroom behind the jury box." Brown had "frequently complained to the Court of the danger in which he was placed" but was told that "there was no remedy," since "there were no adequate means of ventilating the room without having the window open."

"It occurs to me," the doctor concluded, "that the city is liable to Mr. Brown for damages."[4]

It was not until Monday, February 5—after a nearly two-week delay in the trial—that Brown was able to return to the courtroom. Looking exceedingly frail and supporting himself with a crutch, he was the last juror to take his seat. Throughout the day, he kept a woolen shawl wrapped around his body, while his wife, who had accompanied him to court in a closed carriage, kept a watchful eye on him from the front row of the spectator section.

The final thirty minutes of expert testimony that Osborne claimed he would require stretched into three hours. Finally, at 2:00 P.M., the prosecution rested its case.

At that point, the Molineux trial had been going on for nearly twice as long as the previous record holder. Since the start of the proceedings on November 14, eighty-three days had elapsed.

And—as one observer somewhat ruefully noted—the defense was "yet to be heard from."[5]

66

Anticipation ran high on the morning of Tuesday, February 6. Once again, extra chairs had to be set up in the aisles to accommodate the crowd, which included an unusually large number of lawyers who had come to see what sort of defense Roland's highly paid attorneys would mount.

There had already been much speculation on that subject in the press. Citing an anonymous informant, the *World* confidently predicted that the defense would last between six and eight weeks. In what promised to be a "savage assault" upon the prosecution's case—and particularly its star toxicologist, Dr. Rudolph Witthaus—a "long list of experts" would be called to testify that Mrs. Adams's death had not been caused by cyanide of mercury at all. Instead, the defense intended to prove that the bromo-seltzer alone, if allowed to go stale, could degrade into a noxious substance capable of producing "very serious and possible fatal results."

To bolster this argument, Roland's defense team intended to call a "fifteen-year-old girl of good family," one Ida Halporn of East Fifty-fifth Street. The previous March, this "healthy and full-blooded girl" had taken a dose of bromo-seltzer from a bottle that had been sitting on a shelf for more than a year. Within minutes of drinking the effervescent mixture, she had fallen so seriously ill that even now, nearly twelve months later, she remained "frail and weak in comparison with her former self." A

$50,000 lawsuit brought by her parents against the Emerson Drug Company was presently pending in the United States District Court.

The sensational possibility had also been raised that Molineux himself might be put on the stand. In any event, there seemed little doubt that, after two months of remaining "supine"—of "awaiting attack and repelling it as best it could"—Roland's defense team was now ready to launch a fierce attack of its own.[1]

Given the lurid picture the prosecution had been allowed to paint of Blanche's relationship with Barnet, it was hardly surprising that, once again, she was dragged into court for another conspicuous show of conjugal devotion. She and her mother-in-law arrived with the General at 9:30 A.M. on Tuesday. A half hour later, Roland entered, eyes "dancing with merriment" and "lips quivering," as though he were struggling to suppress his amusement at some private joke.

Spotting his wife and mother at the defense table, he made his way down the aisle with a "quick, springy stride," then threw himself into Blanche's welcoming arms. As he bent his face to hers, she kissed him repeatedly on the mouth—a charade intended to make a mockery of the state's contention that sexual rivalry had driven Roland to poison Barnet. Clearly, no woman so passionately in love with her husband could ever have given him the slightest cause for jealousy.[2]

Goff appeared a few moments later. Everyone rose and remained standing until the recorder bowed and took his seat on the bench. The jurors were then polled. All were in attendance, including Manheim Brown, who sat with his lower body swaddled in a woolen lap robe.

Then, clutching a sheaf of papers in one hand, Roland's chief counsel, Bartow Weeks, got slowly to his feet.

His eyes were bloodshot and his face unusually pale. Afterward, he would confess that he had spent a sleepless night debating the wisdom of the startling course of action he was about to take.

In a solemn voice that betrayed the slightest hint of a tremor, Weeks looked at Goff and said, "If Your Honor please, after making a thorough study of the evidence in this case, I am convinced that the prosecution has utterly failed to prove its charge against the defendant. Therefore, we are content to rest the case of the defense upon the evidence offered by the state."

He then stepped back to the defense table and reseated himself.

There was a stunned silence in the courtroom that lasted for more than a minute. When the full import of this statement finally sank in, an excited murmur erupted from the spectator section. Goff rapped his gavel for order, while Roland, arms folded across his chest, looked on with a satisfied smile. At the prosecution table, Osborne exchanged astonished looks with his associates.

Roland's counsel had sprung the most shocking surprise of the trial.

After all the speculation about their intended strategy, Weeks and his partner—with the full approval of the General—had opted for a tactic that no one had foreseen. Not a single witness would be called to testify on their client's behalf. Roland Molineux's lawyers had chosen to rest their case without offering a defense.[3]

67

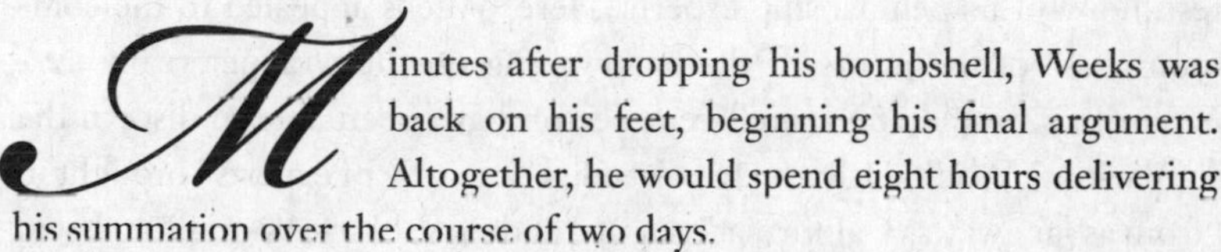

Minutes after dropping his bombshell, Weeks was back on his feet, beginning his final argument. Altogether, he would spend eight hours delivering his summation over the course of two days.

Weeks was not an especially compelling speaker. He refrained from oratorical flourishes; used few, if any, gestures; and, with his thick shoulders, bull neck, and heavy limbs, cut a somewhat lumbering figure. His voice, lacking sonority under the best of circumstances, was rendered even less melodious than usual by a slight case of laryngitis. Nevertheless, his climactic plea was regarded by most observers as a powerful, at times even brilliant, effort.[1]

After apologizing for the "harsh and disagreeable" sound of his voice, he reminded the jurors of the charge against his client—that Molineux had mailed a bottle of poisoned bromo-seltzer along with a silver holder to Harry Cornish, who then gave some of the lethal powder to Mrs. Katherine Adams, killing her more or less instantly. Thus, the entire case really boiled down to a single question: "Whether this defendant sent that package to Harry S. Cornish on the twenty-third of December 1898. As you determine that issue, you determine this case."

He began by insisting that the state had offered "not a syllable" of proof connecting his client to any of the items employed in the crime—not the Tiffany box nor the bromo-seltzer nor the manila paper the package was wrapped in. As for the silver toothpick holder, there was the positive statement of the Hartdegen bookkeeper, Emma Miller, who testified that it had been purchased, not by Molineux, but by a man with a reddish "Van Dyke beard." Weeks scoffed at the notion that Molineux might have relied on an accomplice. "Men who are secretive, men of the sort who will commit murder by poison, do not take others into their confidence."

Nor had the prosecution established that Molineux had ever been in possession of cyanide of mercury. The claim that as a chemist he could have concocted the poison himself was undercut by evidence which showed that of the two key ingredients needed to produce the deadly substance, Roland kept only one in his private laboratory at the Morris Herrmann factory.

Since "not one of the articles" in the poison package had been convincingly tied to the defendant, the state had been forced to rely on the testimony of its penmanship experts. Here, Weeks appealed to the common sense of the jurors. If the handwriting on the wrapper really *were* Molineux's, wouldn't an intelligent person have been able to discern the similarities? Would Osborne have needed "an army of experts" brought in "from as far away as California," put up "at the Waldorf-Astoria," and paid "thousands of dollars" to "convince you of it?" Were the jurors prepared to find the defendant guilty and "send him to the electric chair" strictly "on the testimony of these *experts*?" asked Weeks, placing a particularly sardonic emphasis on the final word.

Weeks paused for a sip of water. When he resumed, he cast a pointed look at Harry Cornish, who was seated near the front of the courtroom, chewing ruminatively on the point of a pencil, his chair tilted back on its rear legs.

After insisting that he had "no wish to accuse any person of the commission of these crimes," Weeks, in his lawyerly way, proceeded to do just that by deflecting suspicion onto Roland's archenemy. Apart from Cornish's testimony, Weeks pointed out, there was not a shred of evidence that the poison package had actually arrived by post. Perhaps, he implied, the athletic director had lied about receiving it from an anonymous source and had actually planted it in his club mailbox himself. And wasn't it odd that Cornish had been able to travel around the city for several hours after supposedly taking a drink of the lethal mixture? And how to explain the peculiar coincidence that the toothpick holder purchased at Hartdegen's bore a design almost identical to the one on the silver toiletry articles on Florence Rodgers's dresser? Was it possible that *Cornish* had been the mysterious red-bearded man who had bought the holder?

"Why," Weeks wondered, "wasn't Cornish investigated?" After all, he was "the man who had administered the dose that killed Mrs. Adams." And what about Cornish's rumored affair with Florence Rodgers—his "role in her separation and divorce"?

"Do you believe that Mrs. Adams approved of Cornish's relationship with her daughter?" asked Weeks, suggesting a reason why Cornish might have wanted the older woman out of the way.

By this point, Weeks's voice had grown so hoarse that he was barely able to make himself heard. After heaping scorn on the two letter box men, Heckmann and Koch—rank opportunists, he charged, who had tried to cash in by peddling their testimony to the yellow papers—Weeks "begged leave to discontinue." The request was promptly granted and the trial was adjourned for the day.[2]

Among his professional peers, the consensus seemed to be that Weeks had done the right thing in making no defense.

It was true, said a prominent Manhattan attorney named Emanuel Friend, that the prosecution had "introduced a mass of evidence." But "it was not the kind upon which an intelligent juror will send a man to the chair. It lacked directness, and the motive was never at any time brought out with sufficient strength and clearness." From a strictly legal point of view, moreover, Friend did "not think that the corpus delicti was proved—at least, there was not sufficient evidence to show that Mrs. Adams died from the poison alleged."

Other lawyers polled by the papers agreed that "the people had not made out a case against Molineux," and that Weeks had "acted wisely in resting his case without the introduction of evidence."

There were a few dissenters. While conceding that Weeks had made "a bold move indeed," William Howe—the oldest criminal lawyer then practicing at the New York City bar—expressed his belief "that it would have been more satisfactory to have had Mr. Molineux take the stand and personally deny having written those letters the experts place at his door."

In the end, of course, as Howe very sensibly noted, the wisdom of

Weeks's strategy would be judged by the outcome of the trial. "It is one of those cases where, should the lawyer succeed in securing an acquittal or hanging the jury, his friends will unite in saying it was a clever defense.

"If, on the other hand, the jury should find the defendant guilty," said Howe, "the condemnation of Mr. Weeks will be long and loud."[3]

68

Following Tuesday's adjournment, the members of the jury, at Goff's orders, were taken to the Astor House, where they were put up in handsomely appointed rooms and "provided with every comfort and convenience." It was the first time that they had been sequestered. Goff made his decision after the newspapers printed stories that one of the men, while dining with "business associates," remarked that "he would not hang a yellow dog on the evidence that has been presented."

As the jurors had never been separated from their families in the three months since the start of the trial, the court did its best to accommodate their relatives the following morning. When Wednesday's session began, "a large part of the crowd that was packed into the courtroom" consisted of the wives, children, and elderly parents of the twelve jurors.[1]

Those seated in the rear had to strain to hear Roland's attorney when he resumed his summation at approximately 10:30 A.M. Even after a night's rest, Weeks had not recovered the full use of his voice. Still, apart from a ninety-minute lunch recess, he managed to speak continuously until nearly five in the afternoon.

He picked up where he had left off the previous day, with a savage denunciation of the letter box men. He then proceeded to cast doubt on the testimony of Mamie Melando and to deride the entire field of handwriting analysis by invoking the Dreyfus affair—a case in which "a man spent five years on Devil's Island because the handwriting experts were mistaken."

Moving on to the issue of motive, he sneered at the notion that any man would commit murder for the reasons alleged by the prosecution—petty disputes over gym equipment and a nasty letter written on official club stationery. "Would the defendant imperil his life, ruin his family, drag them to dishonor and disgrace for such a trifling motive as that?"

His harshest attacks, however, were reserved for his opponent. He reminded the jurors that Osborne, during his opening speech, had promised to expose the defendant as a kind of "Frankenstein monster"—a "man sicklied o'er with the pale cast of sexual perversion." "But has the district attorney done so?" demanded Weeks. "No! He has not introduced a syllable of evidence in support of this cruel assertion."

But Osborne had acted in an even more deplorable manner, Weeks charged. Not content with vilifying the defendant as a moral degenerate, he had stooped to defaming Roland's wife.

"That old father and mother you see there lost a son when he was carried off to the Tombs," said Weeks, gesturing toward the table where Roland sat between Blanche and his parents. "All through the eleven months of his imprisonment, while their boy has been away from them, their daughter-in-law has been with them as a comfort and a solace. Was the burden of the father and mother not already heavy enough when their dear son was imprisoned? *No!*" cried Weeks, his voice quaking with indignation. "The district attorney was not satisfied with the effort to deprive the defendant of his life. He also sought to deprive the defendant's wife of her honor!"

Turning toward the prosecution table, Weeks proceeded (as one reporter put it) to "verbally flay" the prosecutor for calling the two "colored servant girls" to testify that "Barnet had supplanted the defendant" in Blanche's affection.

"Why did you do it?" he demanded, stabbing a finger in Osborne's direction. "You knew the foul and scandalous accusation had nothing to do with the case. It was unnecessary. It was unworthy. It was untrue!"

"Then why didn't you deny it?" sneered Osborne.

"Why should I have to deny such infamous lies?" Weeks exploded. "What business did you have introducing it? You knew you couldn't connect it to the death of Mrs. Adams—yet you brought it in anyway. How dare you produce it?"

Weeks took a moment to regain his composure. Then, after offering one final dig at the state's handwriting experts, who had failed to show any "forcible similarity" between Roland's penmanship and the "poison package address," he launched into his peroration.

"My task is done," he began. "The decision of the case and the fate of the prisoner is in your hands," he solemnly intoned. "You are to consign him to a disgraceful death or you are to restore him to his family and freedom. I ask you to consider carefully, conscientiously, and mercifully before you bring in a verdict of guilty, a verdict which is to cut asunder the ties of this married life, a verdict that will bring disgrace and dishonor to his family."

He praised their acumen, expressing his confidence that, after considering the great mass of evidence that had been presented to them, they would "sift the chaff from the wheat" and arrive at the only reasonable verdict—"a verdict that will restore this young man to his family, restore his good name, and set him free after his long period of imprisonment."

He urged them to listen to their conscience, and if they found themselves wavering, to "err on humanity's side." "The wrong you do can never be restored," he cautioned. "Gentlemen, in a case of doubt, when the scales are oscillating, let them turn in the favor of the prisoner. It is a terrible thing to destroy the temple of an immortal soul."

In graphic terms, he reminded the jurors of the awful responsibility that had been imposed upon them. "I know the district attorney will tell you that it will not be you who will take this man's life if you find him guilty. That it will not be you who will touch the button that sends the electric shock through his body, burning his nerves and disfiguring him. But it *will* be you. It will be you, gentlemen, who will have to say whether he lives or dies. You will have to say whether or not the evidence has convinced you beyond a reasonable doubt that he is guilty."

By then, Weeks's voice had almost given out. After a few final flattering remarks about their common sense and conscience, he declared his absolute confidence in their verdict. "We ask no maudlin sympathy," he said. "We ask no favor. We ask only as a man to his fellow man—'Do unto others as you would have them do unto you.' In doing that, we are sure of your verdict."[2]

Throughout Weeks's final appeal, reporters kept their eyes on Roland and his family, attempting to gauge their reactions. At no point did Roland display the slightest emotion. He maintained the indifferent demeanor he always wore when he wasn't smirking or looking bored. His parents, too, sat there stonily, though stress and anxiety were etched on their faces.

Blanche alone put on a show. When Weeks described the horrors of the electric chair, she let out a cry of distress, buried her face in her hands, and broke into loud sobs. At least one observer found her outburst somewhat "ostentatiously done"—marked by a certain degree of "theatrical exaggeration."[3] But apart from this cold-eyed critic, Blanche's impersonation of a caring wife fooled everyone.

69

That evening, a few hours after Bartow Weeks completed his impassioned plea, the Loyal Legion held a gala dinner in the cavernous banquet hall of Delmonico's restaurant. Between four and five hundred people were present, having come to pay tribute to the nation's most celebrated military figure, Admiral George Dewey.

The previous fall, Dewey—"the Hero of Manila"—had arrived back in the States to a tumultuous welcome. In New York City, a public holiday was declared in his honor. The Brooklyn Bridge was strung with several thousand electric lights spelling out his name in thirty-six-foot-high letters, a floating chorus of more than twelve hundred singers serenaded him aboard his flagship *Olympia*, a "Dewey Triumphal Arch" was erected in Madison Square Park, and—following a massive parade watched by nearly a million wildly cheering spectators—the mayor presented him with a solid gold loving cup on the steps of City Hall.[1]

The scene was the same in Washington, D.C., where he was marched to the Capitol building at the head of a grand parade, presented with a commemorative jeweled sword voted to him by Congress, and feted at the largest dinner party in the history of White House social functions.[2] The whole country appeared to be in the grip of what was dubbed a "Dewey craze"—a frenzied adulation of the sort that would not be seen again until 1927, when Charles Lindbergh returned home following his transatlantic triumph. Dozens of the admiral's closest associates urged him to run for president, and there was little doubt, as *The New York Times* wrote, that "Dewey would be elected no matter by what party he was nominated."[3]

The hero worship remained just as intense five months later when the Loyal Legion held its dinner at Delmonico's on Wednesday evening, February 7. Before the food was served the members conducted their regular meeting. It was still in progress when Dewey arrived to "a storm of applause." Taking his place at the head of the banquet hall, the admiral sat and listened politely while General Horatio C. King read his paper, "The Shenandoah Valley During the Civil War."

In the course of his speech, King made special mention of one of the notables present that evening: Brigadier General Edward Leslie Molineux, who had come to Delmonico's straight from the courtroom where his son's murder trial was in its final stages. As King described the "brilliant and daring work" General Molineux had performed during the Shenandoah Valley campaign, everyone present—not only the veterans in the main body of the hall but the ladies seated in the balcony—rose from their chairs and gave him an ovation that lasted five full minutes, considerably longer than the one accorded Dewey.

As the applause subsided, one of the listeners called out, "Repeat!" The cry was immediately taken up from table to table, until the entire hall was filled with the chant. Happy to comply, King reread the portion of his lecture dealing with the General's contributions to the war. No sooner had he concluded than the crowd again burst into wild cheers, rose to its feet, and toasted "the long life and health of General Molineux."[4]

It was an extraordinary demonstration of the high regard in which the elder Molineux was held by his peers. Indeed, the sight of the valiant old warrior maintaining his proud demeanor in the face of his dreadful ordeal moved more than one of the attendees to tears. The question of his son's guilt or innocence—the possibility that the General's middle child might be a degenerate killer—had no bearing at all on the profound admiration, even reverence, felt for the father.

Perhaps because it was the public's last chance to attend the hottest show in town, the scene outside the courtroom was especially chaotic on the morning of Thursday, February 8. A jostling horde of several hundred people—"men who had evidently played football and women trained at the department store bargain counter," cracked one writer—tried to elbow their way inside, many insisting that they were relatives of one or another of the principals. Twenty policemen struggled with the crowd, trying to clear a path for the arriving jurors. But it was a losing battle. As fast as the officers shoved people aside, the seething mob re-formed itself. In the end, the jurors were forced to enter the chamber through the anteroom used by the defendant.

When the doors opened at ten-thirty to admit the press corps, the crowd surged forward with a roar, nearly knocking down and trampling the policemen. Infuriated, the officers formed a cordon in front of the entrance and refused to let anyone enter without official authorization. As a result, when the proceedings got under way at eleven, the spectator section was emptier than at any time since the trial began.[5]

Unlike Bartow Weeks—who had delivered his closing remarks in a subdued, deliberate manner, standing in one spot and using few gestures—Assistant DA Osborne prowled the floor with a "tigerish mien" during his summation, gesticulating dramatically and attacking the defense in a voice that often rose to an angry shout.[6]

He bitterly denounced the defense for attempting to shift the blame onto Harry Cornish. "Consider, gentlemen, the circumstances of the murder," he said, leaning forward on the railing of the jury box and looking at each of the twelve men in turn. "Mrs. Adams takes the poison administered to her by Cornish. It is administered openly, in the presence of her daughter. Cornish then runs for a doctor and turns over to him all the evidence. Is such a course consistent with guilt on the part of Cornish? And yet, Mr. Weeks tries to bring a charge against him that would lead to his death. My God! Isn't it enough that the defendant tried to poison him with cyanide of mercury? Isn't it enough that he was made the unwitting instrument in one of the greatest crimes in history?"

At this last, hyperbolic statement, Osborne threw a savage look at Molineux, who responded with a mocking smile.

Osborne's most scathing remarks were directed at Weeks's failure to mount a defense. "Do you realize, gentlemen, that not one word has been said by the defendant in his own behalf? What would *you* do if you were innocent? You would say, 'My reputation is ruined. The brand of Cain has been put on my brow. I must defend myself.' Think of all the witnesses Mr. Weeks could have called if his client were innocent. There must be two or three hundred people in New York City who know the defendant's handwriting. He is a prolific writer of letters. And yet, in the great city of New York, not a solitary human being could be brought down here who would testify that the defendant did not write those letters. That is the fact. That is the cold, undisguised, naked fact. Why, if he were innocent, a troop of soldiers with Gatling guns could not have kept those witnesses away from the courtroom."

Turning toward the defense table, Osborne fairly shouted at Weeks, "If you knew of a single witness who could have aided the theory of the defendant's innocence and did not call him, you have violated your oath as a counselor. Your action is a plea of guilty!"

His cheeks flushing, Weeks made a strenuous objection, but Goff refused to instruct the jury to disregard the remark.

Gesturing toward the General and his wife, who were watching him grimly, Osborne sneered that Weeks's only defense was to put "that old gray-haired father and that sweet-faced mother" on display in an effort to elicit the sympathy of the jury. He acknowledged that he himself had initially been reluctant to suspect Roland "because he was General Edward Leslie Molineux's son." The same was true of Captain McCluskey and everyone else involved in Roland's arrest. "We were all sorry to think that a son of General Molineux's should have turned out bad," Osborne said. "But what could we do?" The chain of circumstantial evidence put together by the investigators was "the strongest ever forged against one man."[7]

Osborne spoke until 1:00 P.M., at which point Goff ordered a ninety-minute lunch recess. It seemed likely that the prosecutor would complete his summation when the proceedings resumed and that the case would be in the hands of the jury by the end of the day.

When the court reconvened at two-thirty, however, something was conspicuously absent—the entire jury. Rumors quickly spread that juror number 10—Manheim Brown—had suffered a relapse during lunch and had retreated to his room in the Astor House. Since, by Goff's order, all of the jurors had to be sequestered together, none could return until Brown was back on his feet.

At 4:30 P.M., with the jury still absent, the courtroom was cleared. By then, Goff had received a telephone message informing him that Brown had been stricken with an attack of sciatica. How long he might be bedridden no one could say. Given his fragile condition, it seemed conceivable that he might not recover for days, possibly longer.

The idea of another protracted delay was almost too distressing to contemplate, though it wasn't the worst possibility. If Brown were unable to return at all, Goff would be forced to declare a mistrial. After eighty-five days and a cost to New York County of $200,000—a sum that translates into more than $4,000,000 today—the trial would have to be "started all over again as if it has never once begun."

It was a prospect that filled the prosecution with "feelings of unmingled horror."[8]

70

To the profound relief of Osborne and his associates, Manheim Brown was sufficiently recuperated by the next morning to make it to court. To ensure that he would suffer no discomfort, his regular straight-backed wooden seat had been replaced with a big leather armchair. Lowering himself onto the thickly padded cushion, he arranged a heavy worsted shawl around his body, then sank so far down in the chair that he was almost reclining. From the main body of the courtroom, only his face was visible.[1]

It was close to eleven-thirty by the time Osborne took the floor. He resumed where he had left off, insisting that it pained him deeply to prosecute the son of General Molineux. "I had hoped from my very soul," he declared in earnest tones, "that Mr. Weeks might appear as a second Moses and smite the rock with his staff for the truth to gush forth. I had hoped that he might be able to write boldly in letters of fire, even as vivid as the writing on the wall, 'Molineux is innocent.' I had hoped that the finger of guilt might be turned away from the son of this heroic old soldier." Here, he paused to emit a dramatic sigh. "But it was not to be."

He then returned to Weeks's failure to mount a defense. It was, proclaimed Osborne, "one of primeval principles of human nature to say, when you are accused of a crime: 'I am not guilty! See, here are my witnesses!' " And yet, the defense had been unable to produce a single person to support its case.

"Why, if this defendant were innocent," cried Osborne, "if the writing on that poison package and in the Barnet letters weren't his handwriting, there would be such an army of witnesses at that door that the officer would call out: 'Stand back! No room!' And you would hear that crowd cry out: 'What? The son of General Molineux accused of such a crime, and we who can clear him to be stopped at the door?' And you would have seen that officer overpowered, and the door broken in!"

Osborne spent several hours reviewing the particulars of the state's case against Molineux. There was nothing flat or perfunctory about his presentation. It was a characteristically riveting performance, delivered with the zeal of a revivalist preacher. At the defense table, Blanche and her in-laws watched with taut expressions—"the air of people who have bought seats for a show and are determined to sit through it."[2] Roland, on the other hand, spent much of the time smirking. When, at one point, he burst into outright laughter, Osborne turned on him fiercely.

Scoffing at Weeks's attempts to incriminate Cornish, Osborne insisted that the bare-knuckled athletic director—a "rough, rugged man"—was hardly the type to "resort to poisoning" as a way of dealing with an adversary. "No," said Osborne, in a voice heavy with scorn. "It is the furtive nature of the prisoner to which we must look—this laughing prisoner. Laughing when? Laughing here in open court while we described the death of his friend, Barnet. Laughing when we described the death agonies of Mrs. Adams. Laughing and smiling when he knows that, come what may, he has broken the heart of his father and mother. It is this attitude, gentlemen, which shows that the defendant has an entire absence of soul."

Roland's ridiculing manner—his tendency to treat the trial as a lark—was, Osborne suggested, just one sign of his "warped" nature. For the first time, the assistant DA suggested that at the root of Molineux's obsession with Cornish there lay dark, "perverted" impulses.

"What sort of a man must we look for as the person to commit this crime?" he asked. "Truly, it is an outré, strange, abnormal crime. We must therefore look for a man who is outré, strange, abnormal. Somebody who looked on life with warped eyes. There was something psychologically queer about this man's hatred of Cornish. It was a controlling thing in his life." Though Osborne could not have known the term—which had only been coined a few years earlier—he was, in effect, describing Roland as a psychopath: a conscienceless killer driven by vicious compulsions.

For sheer sensationalism, the high point of Osborne's summation came when he turned his attention to the murder of Henry Barnet. "It is practically conceded," he declared, "that the man who tried to poison Cornish was the same man who sent the Kutnow Powders to Barnet. How can anyone have knowledge of the two crimes and not be convinced that they were conceived by the same brain? Look at it—effervescent salts, cyanide of mercury, letters, poison sent through the mails. Can you separate them?

"Now, what sort of man was this Barnet?" Osborne continued. "Handsome, gentlemanly, fond of the ladies. He gets sick. He receives a bouquet from a lady, accompanied by a note. The note is signed Blanche. And who is Blanche? The defendant's wife.

"Now, you must remember, gentlemen, that the defendant was married on November 19, 1898. Barnet died on November 10, 1898. The defendant has testified before the coroner's jury that he had wanted to marry Blanche Chesebrough since January of that year. She refuses to marry him. The plain, cold facts are that she would not marry him while Barnet was alive. But when Barnet was cold in his grave, she marries the defendant, and marries him immediately.

"Gentlemen," Osborne said with great solemnity, "it is not often that a motive assumes a real, concrete personality. This one is endowed with flesh and blood. It has the form of a human being. And there," he suddenly cried, swiveling toward the defense table and leveling an accusing finger at Blanche, who was flanked by her husband and the General—"there the motive sits!"

Weeks was on his feet in an instant, offering a strenuous objection.

"Let the galled jade wince," sneered Osborne, waxing Shakespearean. "I don't blame Mr. Weeks for not wanting to hear those remarks. God knows, I didn't want to bring this woman's name out in court. I have the feelings of an American gentleman. But I was duty bound to do so. If anyone should feel ashamed, it is Mr. Weeks, for bringing this lady into court while I am making this speech."

Refusing to cower under Osborne's assault, Blanche raised a hand to her mouth and pretended to stifle a yawn. The gesture, so fraught with contempt, unleashed "a flood of passion" in Osborne, who ended his peroration on a particularly lurid note, invoking an image straight out of a Gothic potboiler.

"Like a bloated spider in his web," he thundered, "the poisoner spun out his filaments to the outer world. We must trace from the end of these filaments back to the center. Here's a line running out to Barnet; we trace it back, and at the other end is the mind of Molineux. A line running out to Cornish, and tracing it back to the web's center, we find the mind of Molineux. At the end of another line, we find the blue crested paper, and in the center connected with it, the mind of Molineux. A line terminating in the remedy for impotence, the mind of Molineux at the other end. A line stretching to 1620 Broadway, a line stretching to Heckmann's letter box, a line stretching to the diagnosis blank's description, and at the center of the web to which all these lines extend we find, spinning its deadly plots, the mind of Molineux.

"Gentlemen of the jury," he continued in the same melodramatic vein, "in your hands are the lives of our wives and children, of the people of this community. It is your duty and mine to protect them. Suppose that on this evidence you refuse to convict. You thereby say to the defendant: 'Go forth and do it again as often as you please. Kill! Kill! Kill!' "

By this point Osborne's voice had risen to a shout. "I say that this defendant has degraded his race. I say that he is chargeable with the death of Mrs. Adams and the death of Barnet. I say that the evidence from every direction points to that conclusion, and I leave this case in your hands, knowing that you will find your verdict in the sight of God, in the sight of man, without fear and without favor."

Altogether—excluding a ninety-minute lunch recess and a midafternoon break—the day's session had lasted nearly six hours. It was almost seven-thirty by the time Osborne finished, at which point Goff ordered an adjournment.

At ten-thirty the next morning, when the proceedings resumed, the recorder would deliver his charge, and the fate of Roland Burnham Molineux would be placed in the hands of the jury.[3]

71

Though the police guards were under strict orders to keep out all curiosity seekers on Saturday morning, February 10, at least one unauthorized person—Anna Held, the city's brightest musical star and the wife of impresario Florenz Ziegfeld—wangled her way into the courtroom on the strength of her celebrity. When the General, his wife, and Blanche arrived a short time later, the officers cleared a path for them through the crowd and helped them to their seats. Roland was the next to arrive. Wearing a carefree smile, he stepped jauntily to the front of the chamber, where he embraced his wife and mother and gave his father's hand a hearty shake. If he was at all concerned that, before the day was through, "the twelve men of the jury might doom him to death," he gave no sign of it.[1]

It was eleven—a half hour later than usual—before Recorder Goff arrived. In the moments before he began to speak, the courtroom was so hushed that, when a wagon rattled by on the street three stories below, "it sounded as loud as the rumble of artillery."[2]

Upon convening the court, Goff immediately launched into his charge. He instructed the jurors that they were to base their verdict on "four main propositions": "first, that the defendant directed and sent to Harry Cornish a package which Molineux knew to contain a deadly poison; second, that the defendant sent the package with the premeditated intent to kill Cornish; third, that Cornish received the package and gave a portion of it to Mrs. Katherine J. Adams; and fourth, that Mrs. Adams drank a portion of the poison contained in the package and died from the effects of it.

"If you are satisfied that these four facts are sufficiently proven," said Goff, speaking in such a soft voice that those in the rear of the chamber could barely hear him, "then you may bring in a verdict of guilty of murder in the first degree. But if you believe that they are not proven beyond a reasonable doubt, then you are to bring in a verdict of not guilty."

Given the enormous mass of testimony that had been presented during the foregoing three months, Goff proposed to "briefly sum up some of the most prominent features of the case." He then proceeded to review the evidence in such elaborate detail that his remarks lasted more than four hours.

It was 3:04 P.M. when Goff concluded by reminding the jurors "that they must not permit their feelings for the defendant's family to affect their verdict," particularly "their sympathies for the defendant's distinguished father, who bears such an honored name and position. His honored father," Goff stressed, "is not on trial."

In the company of seven officers assigned to guard them, the jurors then made their way out of the courtroom, with Manheim Brown—moving slowly with the aid of a cane—bringing up the rear.

As soon as the anteroom door closed behind the jurors, Roland rose, bid farewell to his family, and was led back to his cell. Blanche and her mother-in-law retired for a while to a judge's chamber. In the unheated room, the two women sat shivering in their furs. Eventually, the General came in and urged them to go back home to Brooklyn. He would follow "as soon as it was all over." He then escorted them to their carriage and watched as the two women drove away from the shadow of the Tombs.

Blanche was only too happy to escape from the nerve-racking courthouse and the morbid throng cramming its hallways. Back in Fort Greene Place, she and the elder Mrs. Molineux settled themselves in the parlor, where a maid brought them a silver tray holding a decanter of sherry and a plateful of sandwiches that they left untouched. Face cupped in the palm of one hand, Roland's mother stared at the flaming logs in the hearth, while Blanche silently wondered "what pictures she saw in the fire."

Leaning her head back on the pillows of her chair, Blanche soon lost track of the time. All at once, she was startled from her reveries by the chiming of the mantelpiece clock. Two hours had passed since they had returned from the courthouse. It suddenly occurred to her that, at any moment, the front door might open and in walk "the General, perhaps a friend or two, possibly the lawyers, and—Roland!"

After a nightmarish, yearlong separation, she might, that very evening, be reunited with her husband. Given her feelings about Roland—a man she had come to regard with a distaste that bordered on revulsion—it was a prospect that made her heart sink.[3]

After seeing his wife and daughter-in-law off, the General had gone back upstairs to the courtroom. Outside the door, several elderly gentlemen greeted him warmly. They were fellow members of the Loyal Legion, there to lend their moral support.

"It's a pretty nervous time, eh, General?" said one of the men in a commiserating tone.

"No, no, I'm not nervous," Molineux said heartily. "It'll come out all right."

"That's the spirit," said another of the white-bearded veterans. "We'll wait here with you, Molineux, and shout hurrah when it's all over."[4]

The General's friends weren't the only ones convinced that the jury would come back with an acquittal. The consensus among the crowd in the corridor was that—whether Roland was guilty or not—"the evidence hardly justified a verdict against him."[5] The same opinion prevailed in the city's big poolrooms, where there was more betting on the outcome of the Molineux trial than on the horse races. The average odds offered by bookmakers were two to one on conviction, even money on a hung jury, and seven to ten on acquittal.[6]

Back in the courtroom, the General sat at the defense table with his oldest son, Leslie—a balding, red-bearded man who bore little resemblance to the rest of the clan—and Cecil, the youngest son, an even handsomer version of Roland. Puffing incessantly on cigars, the old soldier cast occasional glances at the wall clock but otherwise showed few signs of nervousness.

In the spectator section—where the people lucky enough to get seats stayed put for fear of losing their places—rumors buzzed throughout the afternoon. At around four-thirty, the opening of the door to the jury room created an excited stir in the chamber: the twelve men had reached a verdict! But the excitement quickly died away. The famished jurors were just sending out for sandwiches and seltzer water.

Like the jurors, General Molineux hadn't eaten since breakfast. At around seven-thirty, he and his sons stepped out for a quick bite. As they left the room, Captain McCluskey—watching the General march down the aisle—remarked to James Osborne that the elder Molineux was "the grandest man I ever saw." Osborne agreed. "For his sake," confessed the man who had so fiercely prosecuted Roland, "I could almost wish for an acquittal."[7]

Throughout the evening, suspense continued to build, until "every man and woman was reduced to a bundle of nerves."[8] The tension was made even more unbearable by several false alarms.

At around 9:00 P.M., word flew around the courthouse that the jury was about to come in. Roland, looking "jaunty as ever," arrived a few minutes later. He shook hands with his brothers and patted his father on the back before seating himself between his two lawyers. The twelve jurors then filed into the courtroom and took their usual places.

It quickly became apparent, however, that the long-awaited climax was not yet at hand. Rising from his seat, Foreman Matthias Martin explained to Recorder Goff that the jury members wished to examine all the handwriting specimens, particularly the fake Cornish and Barnet letters and the poison package address. The request was granted and the twelve men soon returned to their deliberations.

At precisely 10:27 P.M., another stir from the direction of the jury room sent a wave of excitement through the courthouse. Once again, word quickly spread that a verdict had been reached—and once again, the information proved to be wrong. The jurors had not yet come to agreement; they were merely sending out another request for several additional pieces of evidence, including a photograph of Roland's private chemical lab in the Morris Herrmann factory.

Just ten minutes later, however, news swept through the courtroom that the jury had arrived at a verdict. And this time, it was true.

As the jury filed into the courtroom—with Manheim Brown limping painfully and leaning on the arm of a court officer—the atmosphere in the courtroom was "vibrant with suspense." In the spectator section, men plucked nervously at their mustaches, while the women sat wringing their handkerchiefs. At the defense table, Roland's lawyers studied the faces of the jurors, their own faces wrought into expressions of intense concern.

They had reason to be worried. To a man, the twelve jurors—haggard and ashen—refused to so much as glance at the defendant. They all kept their heads bowed or stared fixedly ahead.

Five excruciating minutes passed before Goff appeared and took his seat. During that time, the grim-faced jurors looked up at the ceiling or over at the recorder's vacant chair or down at their own hands clasped tightly in their laps—anywhere but at Roland.

General Molineux, seated next to Roland, pressed even closer to his son. Though neither man showed a trace of fear, their somber looks made it clear that they knew what was coming.

After a few preliminaries, the court clerk, James Brophy—a portly fellow with a voice as sonorous as a pipe organ—said, "Gentlemen of the jury, have you reached a verdict?"

"We have," said Foreman Martin, rising slowly from his seat. His expression was pained, his complexion drained of color.

"Defendant, please rise," said Brophy. It was a command he had delivered countless times before. On this occasion, however, his rich voice shook slightly as he spoke it.

Roland sprang to his feet. He stood very erect, his shoulders squared, his thumbs hooked in his trouser pockets.

"Jurors, look upon the defendant," said Brophy. "Defendant, look upon the jurors."

Roland gazed steadily at the jury. Some of the men managed to meet his eyes. Others, however, looked away. At least one of them, William Post, was clearly fighting to hold back his tears.

"How say you, gentlemen of the jury?" said Brophy. "Do you find the defendant guilty or not guilty?"

Martin's voice was low but—in the absolute hush of the courtroom—perfectly distinct. "Guilty of murder in the first degree," he said.

Roland's only response was to hold his head higher. Nor did his father flinch when the foreman pronounced Roland's doom.

Slipping over to the chair beside his son, the General looked up at him and whispered, "Never mind, my boy. You'll be all right."

"I know," said Roland. "I'll stand it, all right. Keep your courage up, Father."

The date for the sentencing was set for the following Friday, February 16. Goff then ordered that the defendant be removed to his cell. Grasping each other's hands, Roland and his father exchanged words of comfort. Before being led away by the jailer, Roland paused to say a consoling word to Bartow Weeks, who looked far more devastated than either of the Molineuxs. Patting him on the back, Roland assured his lawyer that he knew Weeks had done the best he could.

Goff then thanked the jury for the "commendable manner" in which they had attended to their "arduous duties." By that point, William Post had lost his struggle to subdue his emotions and was weeping openly, while his fellow juror William Thompson seemed on the verge of collapse. Others, too, were wiping their eyes. Manheim Brown was in such a sorry condition that he had to be carried from the jury box by two court officials.

At Weeks's request, Goff granted the General permission to see his son before Roland was locked up again. Grabbing his coat and hat, the General hurried downstairs, followed by a crowd of several hundred people who had been waiting all day in the hallway outside the courtroom. The General reached his son just as Roland was about to be led across the Bridge of Sighs. As the two shook hands once again, someone in the crowd shouted, "Three cheers for General Molineux!" and an enormous roar went up. There were cheers for Roland, too, though they were considerably less fervent.

By then, word of the verdict had reached the street, where "fully two thousand persons were shouting 'Guilty! Guilty!' " The motormen on the trolley cars coming down Centre Street stopped for the news, and passengers disembarked to join the throng in front of the courthouse.[9] The following morning, the outcome of "the greatest criminal case of the generation" would be trumpeted on front pages throughout the country.

Harry Cornish had spent the evening in Madison Square Garden, where he was serving as a referee at the Knickerbocker Athletic Club's annual tournament. He got the news about the verdict from a reporter for the *Sun*, who found Cornish standing at the main entrance of the building, smoking a cigar and conversing with some friends.

"My God, are you sure?" exclaimed Cornish, who refused to give the newsman a statement until he had confirmed the news.

Leading Cornish to a nearby hotel, the reporter telephoned his office and asked for the city editor, who assured the athletic director that Molineux had indeed been found guilty. Cornish, who seemed very agitated, then repaired to the nearest bar, where, after downing a glass of whiskey, he asked for a pencil and paper and wrote out a statement that would be widely circulated on the following day: "I can't see how any twelve men could hear that evidence and return any other verdict."[10]

While the General hurried out to say a final word of comfort to Roland, his older son, Leslie, remained behind to speak to the crush of reporters who were clamoring for a statement from a member of the Molineux family. An employee of the Lehigh Railway Company, the bald, bewhiskered Leslie might not have resembled his brothers, but, like them, he had been brought up to face any crisis with the fortitude befitting a son of the celebrated war hero.

"You can say for my father and myself," he announced in a voice that rang with confidence, "that we have no fear as to the ultimate outcome of the case. My brother is innocent, and justice will eventually triumph. This is the beginning, not the ending."[11]

72

The Molineux verdict was the talk of the town on Sunday, February 11. "All over the city, the principal topic of conversation wherever men met together was the finding of the jury declaring Roland B. Molineux guilty of murder in the first degree. On street corners and in the cars the name of Molineux went from lip to lip. Hotel lobbies buzzed with it, club gossip centered around it, and in the big poolrooms bets are already being made as to the possible reversal of judgment by the Court of Appeals."[1]

In churches, too, ministers invoked Molineux's name from the pulpit. After bitterly denouncing the jury for basing its decision "on intuition rather than evidence," the Reverend Joseph A. Fisher of the Riverhead Congregational Church closed his sermon with an earnest petition for young Molineux. Dr. David Gregg of the Lafayette Avenue Presbyterian Church ended the afternoon rally at the Brooklyn YMCA Hall with a similar heartfelt prayer. "O God, help us all in such a way that we may not be put on trial for having committed a sin," he implored. "We pray for the young man who has been on trial. We have been waiting and watching for the verdict. Now that it has come, we pray for the poor young man upon whom the verdict has been pronounced by his fellow men. We pray for the aged father—the stricken father."

At another revival service, this one held at the First Baptist Church in Brooklyn, the Reverend John D. Wells drew a stern moral lesson from the case. "Think of that young man who has been condemned to death," he admonished the congregation, "and who, unless there is a reversal by the Court of Appeals, must suffer the penalty. That is the condition of the unbeliever. Don't believe there is any pardon for your sins after death, for there is not. Unless you are one with Christ, you are lost."[2]

Roland himself took an unusually active part in the Sunday religious services, as if to demonstrate to the world that—contrary to the insinuations of men such as the Reverend Wells—he was no infidel. After enjoying a perfectly untroubled night's sleep, he awoke on Sunday morning—"his first day as a convicted murderer in the shadow of the death chair"—as "cheery and chipper as a cricket." After consuming his usual breakfast of rolls, coffee, and two soft-boiled eggs, he took his morning constitutional in the prison yard, then attended the prayer meeting conducted by the prison chaplain, the Reverend J. J. Munroe. Reverend Munroe's text was taken from the third chapter of John, verses eighteen and nineteen: "He who believeth in Him is not condemned, but he who believeth not is condemned already because he hath not believed in the name of the only begotten Son of God. And this is the condemnation, that the light has come into the world and men loved darkness rather than light because their deeds were evil."

Molineux listened intently, then joined enthusiastically in the hymn "Nearer My God to Thee."

When the service ended, Roland was led back to his cell, where he was visited by Reverend Munroe. Reaching his hand through the grating of his door, Roland shook the chaplain's hand and assured him, "I *am* a believer. And I have firm faith in God as to the outcome of my case."[3]

And indeed, in the immediate aftermath of the verdict, Roland behaved like a man who fully expected to be exonerated and not at all like a man who, as Warden Hagen put it, "has been convicted of one of the greatest crimes of the age, and who has only the Court of Appeals between himself and the electric chair."

"I have seen many prisoners of all kinds and stations of life in homicide cases," Hagen told a reporter for the *Sun*, "and there has always been some change after a verdict of guilty, particularly if they were found guilty of murder in the first degree. They have grown morose or sullen or nervous. With Molineux, there is nothing of the kind. I can't see that the verdict has made the slightest difference in him. In all my experience, I never saw a man bear himself so calmly."[4]

As the venerable criminal attorney William Howe had predicted, there was much second-guessing of the gamble taken by Roland's defense team. One of the city's most respected citizens, General Ferdinand P. Earle, spoke for many when he told the *World*, "I think Mr. Weeks made a sad mistake in letting the case rest on the evidence brought by the prosecution." The editorial page of *The New York Times* leveled a similar charge, declaring that "it was a grave error of the counsel for the defense not to introduce expert evidence to contradict the testimony of the prosecution's handwriting experts."[5]

The belief that Weeks had made a fatal miscalculation was confirmed by one of the jurors, James J. Hynes. In an interview with one of Hearst's reporters, Hynes asserted that the outcome of the trial might have been very different had Roland's counsel "put in a defense. If Molineux had friends, or if his lawyers had witnesses who could have testified in his behalf, why weren't they called?" It was Hynes's firm belief that, "had the defense introduced evidence to refute the other side, it might at least have led to a mistrial." Like many others, Hynes was also puzzled by the defense's decision not to put Roland himself on the stand, given his impressive performance as a witness during the coroner's inquest.[6]

The widespread feeling that Roland should have been allowed to testify on his own behalf was powerfully reinforced on Friday, February 16, the morning of his sentencing. Called to the bar before Recorder Goff and a judge named Foster, Roland was granted permission to deliver a brief statement. Standing before the two jurists—shoulders back, chin up, voice clear and unwavering—he declared himself "absolutely and entirely innocent." The evidence presented by the state "did not point in the direction of guilt on my part," he insisted, particularly the testimony of Emma Miller, who had stuck to her story that Roland was not the man who had purchased the silver toothpick holder. Nor could Roland conceive "how any honest man could believe the testimony of Nicholas Heckmann," who had initially refused to identify Molineux without payment. "Yellow journalism put a price upon my head," Roland proclaimed. "It was an invitation to every blackmailer, every perjurer, every rogue, every man without principle but with a price. And to that invitation, Heckmann responded."

Roland stoutly denied that he had ever possessed "any one of the articles used in the commission of this crime. Nor did I have at any time the least motive."

As for the handwriting analysts, he pointed out that such supposed experts had made "mistakes before"—most notoriously in the Dreyfus affair, one of the "great injustices of history"—and "they have repeated them here."

"Your Honor," said Roland, "the handwriting experts who have testified against me may give their opinion, they may give their reasons, what they believe, what they think. But I know," he continued, raising his hands, palms out, as though displaying them to the judges, "that these hands never put pen to paper to address that poison package or to write the disputed letters."

Up until then, Roland had spoken in a calm, measured tone. Now, his voice began to grow louder and angrier until it had risen to a shout. "Your Honor," he cried, "all this is as nothing compared to what is in my heart at this moment. Above all and beyond everything else, I denounce and despise the action of the district attorney in attempting to vilify and attack the character of the pure and lovely woman who bears my name. It was the act of a blackguard! It was a damnable act! It was a dastardly and villainous lie!"

Roland paused briefly to regain his composure. When he spoke again, the fury had drained from his voice, though his words carried a distinct note of defiance. "Your Honor," he said, "I am now ready to hear the sentence. I am not afraid—for I am not guilty."

Watching Roland's performance, Clement Scott, the drama critic assigned by the *Herald* to cover the trial, found it "a wonderful exhibition of nerves, the most wonderful I have ever seen. There isn't an actor in this city who isn't more rattled every time he has to go on in his part."[7] Another commentator, reporting for *The New York Times*, believed that, "had the Court not warned the crowd against any demonstration," the audience might have delivered a standing ovation. As it was, "a deep, long-drawn sigh came from the spectators" that "seemed almost like an inward applause."[8]

Recorder Goff, however, was unmoved. Addressing the defendant in even tones, he said, "All the matters which you have referred to have been thoroughly sifted. They were examined by twelve men of as high a type of intelligence and honesty as ever sat in a jury box in this County of New

York. Your devoted counsel, for two days without rest, with logic and reason and acuteness of argument, presented all these points to the jury, and that jury, rendering a conscientious verdict, found you guilty on the evidence presented. So far as this court is concerned, that is the last word. The court has but a duty to perform, and that is to pronounce sentence upon you as provided by law."

Every person in the courtroom seemed to hold his breath as Goff spoke the next portentous words:

"The judgment of the Court," he declared, "is that you, Roland Burnham Molineux, for murder in the first degree of Katherine J. Adams, whereof you are convicted, be, and hereby are, sentenced to the punishment of death.

"And it is ordered," Goff continued in the absolute hush of the courtroom, "that within ten days after this day's session of the Court, the Sheriff of the County of New York deliver you together with the warrant of this Court, to the agent and warden of the state prison of the State of New York at Sing Sing, where you shall be kept in solitary confinement until the week beginning Monday, the twenty-sixth of March 1900, and upon some day within the week so appointed, the said agent and warden of the state prison of the State of New York at Sing Sing is commanded to do execution upon you, Roland Burnham Molineux, in the manner and mode prescribed by the laws of the State of New York."

Molineux remained perfectly still, staring straight into the eyes of the recorder, while the sentence was pronounced. He then bowed gravely, swiveled on his heels, and strode from the courtroom. His exit, declared *The New York Times*, "marked the close of the most famous criminal trial of modern times."[9]

Surrounded by officers, Molineux passed swiftly down the corridor to the doorway leading to the Bridge of Sighs. Before he descended the stairway, he was accosted by his old chum, Chuck Connors, who tried to shake his hand but was kept back by the guards. As Roland vanished down the stairwell, the self-appointed "mayor" of the Bowery became teary-eyed and shouted after him "broken asseverations of belief in his innocence."[10]

Inside the Tombs, Molineux was met by Sheriff Grell and his deputies, Daniel G. Kelly and Daniel J. Harris, who escorted him at once to his old cell. There, Molineux sat down on his bunk and awaited his transfer to Sing Sing.[11]

73

Though the sentence mandated that Roland's transfer be accomplished within ten days, Sheriff Grell, in consultation with Bartow Weeks, decided not to wait. At approximately 1:00 P.M., just a few hours after the sentencing, a closed carriage drawn by two horses rolled into the prison yard. Inside his cell, Roland—who had just consumed a last catered luncheon of pork chops and boiled potatoes—bid a genial farewell to Warden Hagen. Then, with his right wrist cuffed to Deputy Kelly's left, he was escorted into the waiting vehicle.

By that point, a crowd of an estimated two thousand people had congregated outside the prison. As the carriage passed through the wide-flung wagon gate, they surged forward, hoping for a glimpse of the nation's most famous criminal. Two dozen officers under the command of Police Captain Titus fought to keep them back. Once the vehicle made its way through the mob, the driver applied his whip to the horses and the coach went clattering up Elm Street.

Forty minutes later—after slowing down at Madison Square to give Roland a chance to view the Dewey Arch he had read so much about—the vehicle arrived at Grand Central Station, where another horde had gathered at the main entrance. At Sheriff Grell's direction, the driver pulled the coach around to the exit on Forty-second Street, where the party quickly alighted and passed through the baggage room and onto the train.

Still handcuffed to Kelly, Molineux was led to the smoking car, where his father and older brother, Leslie—who had arrived a half hour earlier—were waiting. "Hello, my boy," said the General, reaching out his right hand. Noticing the steel bracelet shackling his son to the deputy, the old man mustered a smile and said, "Well, my boy, I suppose I will have to shake you by the left hand."

"That's all right, Governor," said Roland, grasping his father's extended hand and giving it a squeeze.

Reaching into the inside pocket of his coat, the General then extracted a leather case and offered cigars to Roland and his guards, all of whom gratefully accepted.

Outside on the platform, as a squad of policemen struggled to maintain order, an enormous throng pressed close to the train, straining to peer through the windows. Reaching up his free left hand, Roland pulled down the curtain, then settled back to read the newspapers his father had brought him. He was much amused by a front-page illustration in the *Evening World*, showing him with his nose stuck in the air as he denounced James Osborne. "Look at this," he chuckled. "They always make me look as if I were trying to balance a broomstick on my chin."

In the meantime, a steady parade of railroad employees—clerks, conductors, engineers, brakemen, ticket takers—began to troop through the car "like the stream of humanity that winds itself around the bier of a dead hero."[1] The car became so crammed with these curiosity seekers that Captain Price, in charge of the station house in the depot, posted guards at either end with orders not to admit anyone without a ticket.

Moments before the train started, Roland's attorney George Gordon Battle hurried on board. The car being full, General Molineux gave up his seat and perched himself on the lap of his oldest son, Leslie, where he remained until the train reached Tarrytown.

At every stop along the way, dozens of men and women—many of whom had purchased tickets just so they could get a look at Roland—marched down the aisle. Some paused to bid him good luck. Roland was unfailingly polite to these well-wishers. For the most part, however, he did his best to ignore the gawking procession. He chatted easily with his father, brother, and lawyer, or peered out the window, commenting on the beauty of the Hudson River landscape. When the walls of Sing Sing finally came into sight just after 3:00 P.M., he "looked at it unconcernedly and yawned."[2]

So many people had gathered at the station to see the prisoner disembark from the train that it seemed to one observer "as though the entire town had turned out."[3] Three coaches were waiting to transport the party to the prison. A half dozen reporters from the New York City press made a rush for the first, while the General, Leslie, and lawyer Battle climbed into the second. As they sped off, Sheriff Grell and his deputies led Roland to the rear car of the train and hurried him into the third carriage, which followed at some distance behind the others.

Another horde of locals, many armed with cameras, was milling around the entrance of the prison when the first two vehicles arrived. Principal Keeper James Connaughton was there, too, waiting to escort the prisoner inside.

Stepping down from his carriage with Leslie Molineux close behind him, George Gordon Battle introduced himself to the keeper, then, gesturing at Roland's older brother, said, "This is Mr. Molineux."

"All right, Molineux," said Connaughton, "come along with me." Grabbing Leslie by the arm, the burly keeper hurried him through the crowd and down the big stone stairway, where a sentry swung open a barred iron gate. In another instant, Leslie was hustled inside the prison and the gate clanged shut behind him.

Connaughton marched the baffled man into the reception room, where a state detective named Jackson was seated at his desk.

"Here's Molineux," said the keeper, releasing his hold on Leslie.

"That's not Molineux," said Jackson, who had seen Roland on several occasions. "Molineux's a slim fellow, without a beard."

"I'm his brother," said Leslie to Connaughton, whose face had gone instantly red.

"Oh hell," said the keeper, grabbing Leslie again and ushering him unceremoniously out of the room. Just as they approached the barred iron gate, Roland and his escort appeared on the opposite side. The gate was opened again, Roland and his warders were admitted, and the brothers enjoyed a laugh over the comedy of errors before Leslie was let outside.

The gate had just banged to again when the General appeared. Peering through the bars, he called out, "Roland!"

Roland, who had been freed from his handcuffs, stepped up to the gate and extended his right hand between the bars.

"Good-bye, Governor," he said, giving his father's hand a hearty shake.

"Good-bye, my boy," said the General, his voice husky. "God bless you."

As Roland was led away, the old man turned and mounted the stone steps, shaking his head and saying softly, "Well, well, well." With Leslie and Battle beside him, he returned to his coach and was driven back to the station, where he and his companions took the 4:41 train back to the city.

By then, Roland Molineux—freshly bathed and dressed in his prison suit of black sackcloth—was already in his cell in the Death House.[4]

74

Later that day, after returning to Brooklyn from Sing Sing, General Molineux—who, on the advice of counsel, had refrained from making any public statements during the trial—released a letter to the press. Under various headlines—STIRRING PLEA OF THE OLD WARRIOR, GENERAL MOLINEUX DECLARES HIS SON'S INNOCENCE, FATHER MAKES PUBLIC APPEAL—it appeared the next morning on the front pages of virtually every newspaper in the city.[1]

Stories had circulated that legal expenses had driven the General—a wealthy, self-made man, though hardly a member of Mrs. Astor's 400—to near bankruptcy. Several morning newspapers had proposed setting up a fund to assist him in defending his son, and had already begun receiving contributions from scores of old soldiers, eager to help. After expressing his thanks for the outpouring of sympathy he had received "from all sections of the country," the General hastened to assure the public that he required no financial aid.

It was not pride, he insisted, that prevented him from "accepting such assistance, for the reason that I should not myself hesitate to offer it to any person who needed it, and I should never be ashamed to receive what I should not be ashamed to offer. But I owe no man a dollar, and I neither need nor desire any assistance of such a character. I feel, and am amply able in health, strength and in courage natural to a man, to sustain all the burdens that God has placed upon me until He wills otherwise."

But if the General had no need of monetary support, he did need—and appealed for—"the prayers of all those of every denomination and faith who, like myself, feel that my son is innocent and the victim of persecution." He appealed, moreover, "to every man who is a man" to assist him in his struggle to "shield and protect" his "sorely afflicted" daughter-in-law "from unnecessary and intrusive curiosity." Though he had no intention of addressing any legal questions raised by the trial, the General could not refrain from denouncing Assistant District Attorney James Osborne, whose "vile insinuations" against Blanche had been an assault upon the very "sanctity" of "noble American womanhood." That a "sworn public prosecutor, a man educated in an American college and associating with American men," could behave so shamefully toward the "wedded wife of a defendant" was beyond the General's comprehension.

If Blanche required the "heartfelt support" of "all who resent injustice and revere womanhood," Roland himself required no "maudlin sympathy." His son, said the General, was "a strong man, able to bear his own sorrow and responsible for his own acts"—a man "with the strength to live and die bravely." But the charges made against his child had been so outrageous that the General could no longer remain silent on the subject.

"I have seen my son Roland asleep as a child by his mother's side," wrote the General, conjuring up an image guaranteed to tug at the heartstrings of all but the most callous of readers. "I have seen him asleep in his cell after the verdict of death had been pronounced. Who better able than I, his father, to judge whether that sleep was the natural sleep of innocence?" He was not alone, moreover, in these feelings. Everyone who had come into contact with Roland during his incarceration would attest to his innocence. "Ask the prison attendants," wrote the General. "Ask those ministers of religion and of charity who serve the wants of those poor prisoners whether the behavior of Roland Burnham Molineux has been that of a brave and innocent man rather than that of a dastardly poisoner. They will, I know, speak for him."

The very idea that his son might commit a crime as heinous as poisoning was too outlandish to entertain. Roland had "never done a despicable or a cowardly thing. It is not in him. He has always been ready to take his punishment like a man. If whipped, he has acknowledged the fact and has been ready to meet his foe face to face, without malice. Like his father he is not faultless. But he also has much of the better and kindlier nature of his mother. He a pervert, a degenerate, and a vicious poisoner? It is impossible and absurd!"[2] Eloquent and moving—infused with the sense of decency, justice, and faith that had made Edward Molineux such a beloved figure—the General's open letter was a release of long-suppressed feelings. But it was also something more: an assertion of his fighting spirit, of his refusal to surrender—the opening salvo in the old warrior's last and most desperate battle.

Part Six

THE MAN INSIDE

75

Besides Roland, there were eight condemned men in the death house at Sing Sing. Of these the most notorious was Dr. Samuel Kennedy, whose case—thanks to its irresistible mix of sex, scandal, and gruesome violence—had generated intense lip-smacking coverage in the New York City press. A darkly handsome young dentist with a thriving practice, a loving wife, and a newborn son, Kennedy had been convicted of killing his twenty-one-year-old mistress, Emeline "Dolly" Reynolds, whose brutalized corpse, the skull crushed with an iron bludgeon, was found in a Manhattan hotel room in August 1898.[1]

The other death row cells were occupied by a motley assortment of killers, awaiting execution for the kind of small-time savageries that make the headlines for a day or two, then disappear from the news: stabbing a man in a bar fight, strangling a jealous wife, shooting a dry goods clerk during a holdup. A convict named Fritz Meyer—a denizen of the Bowery slums who had gunned down a policeman while robbing a church poor box—had been there the longest, slightly more than two years, while his appeal made its way through the courts. The others—Edward Wise, William Neufeld, Joseph Mullen, Benjamin Pugh, and two recent emigrants from Italy, Lorenzo "Larry" Priori and Antonio Ferraro, nicknamed "Shorty"—had been languishing in their solitary steel cages for periods ranging from three to twenty-one months.

Though conditions at Sing Sing had improved considerably since its earliest days—when prisoners were forced to march in lockstep, forbidden from making eye contact or uttering a sound in each other's presence, and routinely subjected to such medieval tortures as the "Chinese water cure" and the "crucifix"[2]—life in the Death House remained unrelievedly grim. Each man was confined to a tiny, windowless cell—three stone walls and an iron-barred door—barely large enough to accommodate a cot, a table, a hard wooden chair, and a chamber pot. Outside the bars hung a net of steel to ensure that no visitor could make physical contact with the prisoner.

It was always light in the Death House. Glass skylights provided illumination by day. At night, gas and electric lights burned continuously, throwing their beams into every corner of the cell. A pair of keepers, wearing felt-soled shoes to maintain a sepulchral silence, patrolled the corridor day and night. Privacy was impossible, even for a moment. It was, as Roland put it, like living, eating, sleeping, and going to the bathroom "in a searchlight."[3]

The monotony was crushing. No newspapers were allowed. Mail, both incoming and outgoing, was inspected by an official and strictly censored. Once a day, for a half hour, each man was allowed to walk up and down the narrow corridor, while curtains were drawn in front of the other cells to prevent the inmates from setting eyes on one another. Meals were barely palatable—some tasteless hash or glutinous stew or unidentifiable meat, precut so that it could be eaten with the only utensil permitted to inmates, a pewter spoon. Cigarettes and cigars were prohibited, though the men were provided with coarse "State" tobacco and corncob pipes in which to smoke it. For excitement, there was the weekly bath and shave.

For Roland, it was "like being alive, yet buried in a glass coffin." Each newly condemned man would be brought into the Death House, exist for a year or so "in a noiseless purgatory," and then—if his appeal failed—be led one morning through a door at the opposite end of the corridor from which he never emerged. The inmates, who passed and repassed that door each day during their thirty-minute exercise, did their best not to think about the terrors it concealed, and never referred to what lay on the other side by its proper name: the execution chamber.

They called it "the room with the little door."[4]

There were some consolations. Though reading matter from the outside world was strictly forbidden, the condemned men had access to all the books in the prison's extensive library. And while the wire nettings outside their cells kept their loved ones just beyond reach—"no hand clasps, no kisses," sighed Roland—the prisoners could receive extended biweekly visits from their relatives.[5]

Within twenty-four hours of Roland's incarceration, his brothers, parents, and chief counsel, Bartow Weeks, had already come to see him. Several days later, General Molineux announced that he had "engaged quarters" at a house within sight of the prison, where his wife and daughter-in-law would live for the duration of Roland's internment.

It was Blanche, so the General intimated to the press, who had insisted on renting rooms in the village, so that she could visit her dear husband as often as possible and lend him her loving support during his darkest hours.[6]

76

It was only at the General's urging that Blanche agreed to make the move to the village of Sing Sing.[1]

He had confronted her on the day after Roland's sentencing, as she sat in the parlor of the Molineux home on Fort Greene Place—"the house of gloom," as she had taken to calling it.[2]

She was seated on a horsehair divan, gazing dully into the fireplace, when he lowered himself onto the cushion beside her. "How are you feeling, my dear?" he asked.

"Tired," she said in a tremulous voice.

Taking her hand in both of his, the General said, "I know how hard this must be for you, my child. But"—here, his own voice broke—"think how much worse it is for my boy."

He had never looked—or sounded—so tired, so worn. At the sight of the "fine and splendid and brave" old man reduced to "sudden helplessness," Blanche felt a wrenching in her heart, and tears welled in her eyes.

"I think," said the General after a moment, "that your feelings for Roland have changed. I know they have. But you must promise me that you won't do anything rash."

Gazing into his face, Blanche saw—along with his grief—something like real fear. It was a look she had never expected to see in the proud old warrior, and it shocked her.

At that moment, he sprang to his feet and began pacing the floor.

"Just because they've convicted him doesn't mean that he's guilty," he said. "You know he's innocent, don't you?" There was, Blanche thought, a peculiar inflection in his voice—a note of uncertainty—as though he were addressing the question to himself.

Blanche merely repeated, "I'm so tired. I feel it's never going to end."

Pausing before her, fists clenched at his sides, the General cried, "We must not weaken! And so much depends on you. If you were to leave him—"

Blanche buried her face in her hands. "I won't," she groaned, though her muffled words were audible only to herself.

A few days later—her pity for the General bolstered by his assurances that, so long as she stuck by Roland, she would never lack for financial security—Blanche and her mother-in-law took the train up to Sing Sing, where they moved into the home of Mr. Henry G. Miller at 157 Spring Street, just a short carriage ride away from the prison.[3]

Though it was still the dead of winter when she arrived in the upstate village of Sing Sing, Blanche felt a "stirring of new life" as she stepped from the train. Raw as it was, the fresh country air seemed to carry a foretaste of spring. As the coach carried her and Roland's mother to their new quarters in town, Blanche could see—"through the bare branches of trees etched in inky black against the western sky"—a "lovely vista of the Hudson." The sight made her spirits rise. Just being away from the suffocating gloom of the Molineux home felt wonderfully liberating.

Her pleasant mood wasn't destined to last. Through the windows of her second-story room the "massive gray pile of the old prison" was visible in the distance. The "feeling of uplift" she had experienced upon her arrival vanished as she gazed out at it.

"There, challenging me, defying me," she would recall in her memoirs, "were those dark frowning walls, and the knowledge of what they held."

She paid her first visit to Roland the next afternoon. She insisted on going alone. She "could not bear that anyone should witness that meeting."

Accompanied by the warden, she crossed the inner courtyard, then "passed through endless corridors, shut off from those we had first traversed by steel and iron-barred doors. As these clanged behind us, we went on into what seemed a vast fortress of solid stone."

Eventually, she stood at the entrance to the steel door that led into the Death House. The keeper released the "formidable bars" and let her into "the innermost vault."

For a long moment, she stood looking down that gaslit oblong chamber, with its row of cells on either side, and the metal screen barriers fronting the padlocked, iron-barred doors.

"The third on this side, Mrs. Molineux," said the guard, pointing to one of the cells.

Blanche crossed the gray stone flagging in the direction he had indicated. Pausing, she tried to peer inside the cell, past the metal netting and the heavy grating of the door. Suddenly, from the shadows inside the cell, someone rose from his cot and pressed close to the bars to greet her. It was Roland. The sight of him gave her a start.

"He was smiling, but he was ashen. His lips were very white—drained and bloodless. And his eyes—they were dead and expressionless, set in a stone mask that was immovable. The soul of him was dead—it had gone out of him."

Roland spoke and she tried to answer, but her voice "died in my throat." The guard brought her a chair and a glass of water. Soon, she and Roland were chatting, but their words were "perfunctory," "without meaning." His entire existence, Blanche saw, had narrowed to a single "obsession"—"release from the predicament in which he found himself."

As for her, she knew "at that moment that the end of all things between us had come." She felt nothing for her husband except pity. Still, she could "not tell him or anyone" her thoughts. Her "faith in Roland Molineux must appear unshakable." She had promised the General that she would play the faithful wife, and until Roland's fate was decided, she was bound and determined to keep up that "ghastly pretense."[4]

77

Blanche's move to the little white house in Sing Sing—calculated to impress the world with her selfless devotion to Roland—did nothing to stop the press from portraying her in the most scandalous light. Little more than a week after her arrival, a highly sensationalized story appeared in newspapers throughout the country. Written by Hearst's popular sob sister Winifred Black, a.k.a. Annie Laurie, the article purported to be a biography of Blanche—"the great puzzle mystery of the Molineux case"—based on interviews conducted with the subject herself.

Written in the floridly sentimental style Black was famous for, the article told of the "poor little one-eyed country girl" who "came to New York some ten years ago to earn an honest living by singing in a church choir," and who had ended up leading a shocking double life: modest young lady by day, shameless voluptuary after dark:

> Blanche Molineux . . . the woman who wore the quietest little gowns and the plainest hats on Sunday, and who dressed in gorgeousness and diamonds on week days.
>
> The woman who thanked the Sunday school superintendent for a 10 cent bunch of wild flowers, and then went home to an apartment heavy with the perfume of hot house roses at $10 a dozen.

> The woman who drank lemonade at the Sunday school picnic at Williamsburg, and who served champagne in silver buckets at her home in New York.

Even more inflammatory than this portrayal of Blanche as a woman of highly questionable morals—her luxurious life funded by wealthy male "friends"—were Black's insinuations concerning Roland. Describing Blanche's first encounter with her future husband on the yacht *Viator*, the article claimed that there were three men aboard the boat: Roland, Henry Barnet, and a "rich bachelor," never identified by name. During that magically romantic excursion, "with its moonlight, its wealth of flowers, and its plenteous supply of champagne," all three men fell "very much in love with Blanche Chesebrough."

Just a few weeks later, however, two of those three died, "one of cyanide of mercury poisoning and the other of some cause that brought a quick and sudden end." Blanche was left free to marry the only survivor—Roland Molineux.[1]

The widespread dissemination of the article (which appeared first in the *Denver Post*, then ran in *The Philadelphia Inquirer* before showing up in the *New York Journal*) brought a prompt and impassioned reply, published over Blanche's signature, though both General Molineux and Bartow Weeks had a hand in its composition. In it, Blanche decries Black's "villainous assault" upon her character, an act of perfidy made even more unforgivable for having been written by a woman. "It surpasses my understanding," Blanche exclaims, "that any woman can so cruelly and falsely vilify without a shadow of foundation a sister woman on whom the shadow of affliction has already fallen so heavily."

Denouncing the article as a collection of "baseless calumnies," "wicked lies," "infamous innuendoes," she proceeds to set the record straight, denying that, as a single woman, she had ever "lived luxuriously in gorgeous apartments in upper New York," and describing the fateful yachting party as a perfectly innocent occasion, during which she was chaperoned by her older sister.

As for the "gross and atrocious falsehoods" concerning Roland, Blanche proclaims her "absolute confidence" in her "noble husband," who "is wholly innocent of the frightful crime with which he is charged":

> I know this, not only from the fact that no evidence save that of paid experts and venal witnesses of the lowest character has been brought against him, but also and chiefly from my knowledge of his own character. I know him to be brave, strong, and true—the last man to commit a crime of cunning, malice, and cowardice. He might strike in anger and hot blood, but the stealth and premeditation of the poisoner are foreign to his nature.

After a bitter attack on James Osborne, who had so scurrilously suggested that her relationship with Henry Barnet was "something more than an ordinary friendship," the letter concludes with a heartfelt appeal to "the women of this land—the wives, the daughters of this American nation":

> I ask you to feel for me, for one moment put yourself in my place, and you wonder that I break the silence so long enforced upon me; that I cry against the malicious, the cruel, the wanton lies? Shall a man, because he is vested with the power of public office, because he is the prosecuting official in a charge brought against the unfortunate husband of one American woman, shall he, I say, be permitted to make that hapless wife the target of his merciless invective, his unfounded and unproven accusations? Is she to be defamed and robbed of her fair name? Is her honor, her dignity, her character, to be wantonly sullied?[2]

Blanche's reply received exactly the kind of attention the General was counting on: front-page coverage in virtually every New York City daily. He himself followed up with an attack on James Osborne, a native of North Carolina who was even then visiting his aged mother in his hometown, Charlotte. Osborne, said the General in a widely reprinted statement, was a man who made a mockery of the proud tradition "of Southern chivalry. I have fought Southerners, and I know they are brave men. I thought it was always said of them that they never attacked women. I understand that Mr. Osborne is a Southerner—of what sort can now be judged, after his characterization of my daughter-in-law.

"I say to all the world," the General vowed in conclusion, "that she is my daughter, and that I shall protect her to the end."[3]

Given the public's prurient fascination with Blanche, it was only a matter of time before the General was called upon to make good on that pledge. Not long after the appearance of Mrs. Black's spurious biography, stories began to circulate in the papers that Blanche had returned to the city, where she was seen dining at Rector's restaurant on Broadway and Forty-fifth Street with a male companion, clearly not her husband.

Once again, General Molineux found it necessary to issue a statement, attacking the story as "entirely without foundation." On "the night in question," his daughter-in-law "was at Sing Sing with my wife and other relatives." She had not been to Rector's restaurant "at any time since her husband's arrest"; indeed, "to the best of her recollection," she had "never been there in her life." After reconfirming his faith in Blanche, the General warned that we would "take prompt measures" against anyone who published such "cruel libels" in the future.[4]

While General Molineux did battle with Blanche's detractors, Roland's lawyers were engaged on another front. In early March, they filed a notice of appeal. Roland's death sentence—officially slated for the last week of the month—was put on indefinite hold. A few weeks later, to argue the case before the Court of Appeals, they retained one of the country's most prominent attorneys, John G. Milburn of Buffalo.

It was a canny choice. The Court of Appeals sat in Buffalo, and Milburn—a top corporate lawyer who had successfully represented many appellants (including John D. Rockefeller)—was arguably the city's leading resident. Just shy of his fiftieth birthday, he was an imposing six-footer, famed for his "golden-voiced" eloquence and commanding presence.[5]

At the time he agreed to represent Roland Molineux, much of his attention was focused on a project that had dominated his life for the past several years, the great Buffalo World's Fair (officially known as the Pan-American Exposition) scheduled to open the following May. As the head of the exposition's board of directors, Milburn had countless details to attend to, including preparations for a planned visit by President McKinley himself.

Milburn had frequently played host to visiting dignitaries, including

Vice President Roosevelt and the French ambassador, both of whom had been recent guests at his stately home on Delaware Avenue. McKinley's visit to the Buffalo exposition was still more than a year away, and no official date had been set. But there was little doubt that, when he came to town, the president would stay at the Milburn residence.

78

In the Death House, time crawled. Roland busied himself as best he could. For the past year, he had been making notes about his experiences, first in the Tombs and now in Sing Sing—observations about life behind bars, anecdotes about the colorful characters he had encountered, ruminations on the justice system, even bits of doggerel, such as a satirical verse about the handwriting analyst/poultry farmer William Kinsley, whose testimony had been so instrumental in his conviction:

> I'm an expert. I raise chickens, so I know about a "quill."
> How it writes and what you think of when you sign a note
> or bill.
> I'll appear against or for you; either side without regard,
> I can tell my favorite rooster by his claw marks in the yard.
> Like him, I love to scratch in dirt. I'm crooked as his walk,
> I plume myself, and like my hens I cackle when I talk.
> I'm hatching out a plot just now, really it's very funny,
> It's all a guess—ridiculous—but then, I need the money.[1]

When he wasn't jotting notes or composing letters, he was availing himself of the offerings in the prison library. After finishing *Les Misérables*, he plunged into *Paradise Lost*, then made his way through Washington Irving's *Sketch Book*, Sir Walter Scott's *Quentin Durward*, and a novel called *His Father's Son* by the critic, playwright, and Columbia University English professor Brander Matthews. Though published in 1896, two years before Roland Molineux became a household name, Matthews's book prefigures certain aspects of the Molineux affair in almost uncanny ways. Its protagonist is a powerful elderly man named Ezra Pierce who has made a fortune on Wall Street and whose handsome, ne'er-do-well son, Winslow, winds up in trouble that threatens to land him in Sing Sing.

"Father," pleads Winslow when the police first get wind of his activities. "I've got something to tell you—something you won't like either. I'm in a scrape—a very bad scrape, indeed—and you've got to help me out. . . . If you don't want me to go to Sing Sing, you must help me!"[2]

Reading and writing, of course, were a pitiful defense against the miseries of the Death House. Like other condemned men, Roland found it hard to keep thoughts of suicide at bay. In Sing Sing, extraordinary measures were taken to keep the inmates from "cheating the chair." Their clothing was "of such quality" that it could not be turned into a rope, and they were permitted to wear only felt slippers, "as all other shoes have a small piece of steel under the instep which can be taken out and used in a suicide attempt."

Their weekly shaves were administered "by a prison trusty under the watchful eye of a keeper," and their fingernails frequently trimmed "as long nails could be used to cut the arteries of the wrist." Matches, of course, were not allowed—the inmates' corncob pipes were lit upon request by the guards—and all electric lights were located outside the cells "to prevent their being broken and used with suicidal intentions."[3]

Despite these and other precautions, the occasional inmate found some ingenious way to do himself in. One "prisoner saved bits of cotton used in applying medicine to his eyes and made a short rope" with which he succeeded in hanging himself.[4] And another, "under the very eyes of his keepers, without any privacy or apparatus, manufactured the poison with which he ended his life." That, at any rate, was the story Roland heard during his first few weeks in Sing Sing.

According to this tale, a quiet, seemingly gentle convict—German by nationality and nicknamed the Professor because of his thick-lensed eyeglasses—had managed, after months of patient effort, to trap a mouse in his cell. He then proceeded to teach his new pet all manner of tricks—to eat from his hand, to come when it was called, to sleep cuddled under his chin.

Six or eight months went by. Then, one summer day, the Professor heard that his appeal had been denied and the date for his execution set. That very night, his pet mouse died. Shortly thereafter, the Professor himself fell ill and took to his bed. The prison doctor came, took one look at the ailing man, and decided that he was simply prostrate with fear. "Let him alone," he told the keeper.

A few days later, before his execution could be carried out, the Professor died in his cell. The cause was discovered when his corpse was stripped bare for an autopsy.

After receiving the bad news about his appeal, the Professor, it seems, had snapped the neck of his pet mouse and used the creatures' needle-like incisors to inflict several long scratches on his own chest. Then, he had pressed the dead rodent's corpse to the open wound and left it there to putrefy, leading to the blood poisoning that killed him.[5]

As Roland's confinement stretched on, he grew increasingly morbid—obsessed with "the story of the little dead mouse." Whether that story was true or apocryphal he could not say. In either case, he resolved to try the same method on himself should his own appeal fail.[6]

His suicidal fantasies became particularly intense on those awful occasions when an execution loomed. For Roland, as for all the condemned, sharing in the final hours of a fellow inmate whose time had run out was "the greatest horror we are called upon to bear." Isolated in their cages, curtains blocking the bars, the prisoners could only hear what was happening. But the sounds were appalling enough: the shuffling of the doomed man's slippered feet as he was transferred to the cell adjacent to the execution chamber; the tearful farewells to loved ones; the murmuring of prayers as the last rites were administered; the hum of the dynamo as the electric chair was readied; the rapid march of the procession into the death chamber; the clang of "the hungry little door as it closed"—"even the noise made by the drills and saws used in the autopsy immediately following the execution."[7]

Seven times during his incarceration in Sing Sing, Roland lived through this experience.[8]

The fall of 1900 brought one encouraging development. A week before Thanksgiving, Dr. Samuel Kennedy—the New York City dentist convicted of killing his pretty blond mistress, Dolly Reynolds—was granted a new trial. The Court of Appeals had found that certain testimony offered at Kennedy's first trial "should have been excluded as hearsay evidence."

To many legal observers, the ruling—coming in the wake of other, similar decisions—seemed to evince "a disposition on the part of the present Court of Appeals to do away entirely with the death penalty." One prominent criminal lawyer, cited in *The New York Times*, declared that, in reversing Dr. Kennedy's conviction, the Court of Appeals had established a precedent which would have direct bearing on the Molineux case: "The evidence in the Kennedy case, though circumstantial, tended to establish guilt to the exclusion of any other hypothesis," said this gentleman. "In the Molineux case, the evidence is not so strong. If the Court of Appeals is willing to set aside the Kennedy verdict, it is fair to assume that it will perhaps reach the same conclusion in the Molineux case."[9] It is little wonder that, when news of the decision spread through the condemned cells, Roland was jubilant. Or that, as the newspapers reported, he devoured his Thanksgiving dinner one week later—mince pie, cheese, apples, bread, and tea with milk and sugar—with renewed gusto.[10]

Still, his case dragged on. By January 1901—nearly a year after he entered the Death House—the Court of Appeals in Buffalo had still not received the papers submitted by his attorneys. The delay brought outraged protests from the public, the press, and—most heatedly of all, of course—from Roland's father.

In a newspaper interview conducted a few days after the start of the new year, "the old fighter" charged Recorder Goff with professional negligence, cried out against the "barbarism" of his son's protracted confinement, and suggested that there was a deliberate conspiracy to "drive Roland mad before we can set him free." His voice quaking with fury, he announced his intention to go directly to the state legislature and demand an investigation into the "unconscionable delay."[11]

As always, General Molineux received widespread support. Editorial writers joined him in condemning the situation as a "public scandal," while ordinary citizens bombarded the newspapers with sympathetic letters. One writer declared that Molineux would have received more humane treatment among the ancient Aztecs, whose legal code required that appeals be submitted to the "higher judicature" within eighty days.[12]

The outcry, however, did little to expedite matters. Another half year would pass before the appeal was finally heard.

By then—mid-June 1901—Roland had spent fifteen seemingly endless months among the condemned.

79

President McKinley's visit to the Pan-American Exposition was originally scheduled for the second week of June 1901. The plan was put on hold, however, when his beloved wife, Ida, a chronic invalid who suffered from a host of maladies, including petit mal epilepsy, fell seriously ill in mid-May.

At his sprawling home in Buffalo, John G. Milburn, the McKinleys' designated host, received the news with mixed feelings. Though distressed to learn of the first lady's condition, he privately welcomed the postponement. Without the presidential party to attend to, he would be able to concentrate all his energies on a pressing legal matter.[1]

After nearly a year and a half of unprecedented delay, the Molineux case had finally been placed on the calendar of the Court of Appeals. Arguments would begin on Monday, June 17.

A crowd many times larger than the courtroom could accommodate packed the hallway that morning. Bailiffs barred the door, admitting only the "privileged few" by a private entrance. Accompanied by Bartow Weeks and George Gordon Battle, General Molineux made his way to the defense table, walking with a pronounced limp. He had arrived in Buffalo the previous night and had twisted his ankle so badly while alighting from the train that he had to be carried to a cab.[2]

John Milburn entered a few minutes later alongside his opponent, David B. Hill. A former United States senator, ex-governor of New York, and a candidate for the Democratic nomination for president in 1892, Hill had been enlisted by the district attorney to argue the case for the state. Like prizefighters shaking hands before a bout, the two lawyers exchanged greetings at the doorway before taking their respective places.

At ten, the seven black-robed judges filed in and seated themselves at the bench. Preliminaries were quickly dispatched. Both Milburn and Hill requested—and were granted—extensions of the two-hour limit usually allotted for arguments. At 10:37 A.M., Milburn rose from his seat, and the "battle of giants"—as newspapers touted the event—was under way.[3]

Milburn's address would continue uninterruptedly until the 2:00 P.M. adjournment and not conclude until the following day. After describing the key figures in the case (with special mention of General Molineux, "a gallant soldier who never fought a braver battle than this last fight he is making for the life of his son"), the famed Buffalo attorney spent nearly two and a half hours in an attempt to dismantle the arguments that James Osborne had made at the trial.

He ridiculed the notion that the "little club squabbles" between Molineux and Harry Cornish would have driven Roland to murder; denounced the letter box man, Nicholas Heckmann, as a mercenary fraud; disparaged the testimony of the handwriting experts; and even while insisting that he "was not seeking to indicate that any other person is guilty of this crime," cast suspicion on Harry Cornish by suggesting that the athletic director had been conducting an illicit affair with Florence Rodgers and thus had a motive for wanting her mother, Mrs. Adams, out of the way. He also pointed out that, according to the sworn testimony of Emma Miller, Molineux had not been the purchaser of the silver holder and insisted that the embossed robin's-egg-blue stationery to which the prosecution had attached so much significance was "in general use" and might have belonged to anybody.

Proceeding to the legal phase of the appeal, Milburn argued strenuously that Henry Barnet's death should never have been brought up in the trial, the two cases having no connection. It was the admission of evidence relating to Blanche Molineux's moral character, however, that drew Milburn's bitterest words. His voice ringing with outrage, he excoriated Recorder Goff for allowing Rachel Greene, the former chambermaid at

Mary Bell's boardinghouse, to testify that Blanche and Roland had lived together as husband and wife months before their marriage.

"No incident in this trial," he cried, "dealt such a blow to this defendant as this, which went straight at the woman he had married and blasted her reputation for the purposes of this case. On what ground was it admissible? This—this is on the verge of the horrible!

"This defendant," said Milburn, "had not a fair trial."[4]

Altogether, Milburn would address the judges for slightly more than five hours. It was nearly noon on Tuesday, June 18, before ex-senator David Hill rose to speak.

Like Milburn, he began by acknowledging General Molineux's presence in the courtroom. Instead of paying the usual tribute to the old soldier's gallantry, however, Hill insisted that the father's eminence should have no bearing on the case. "This court, we know, is a court of justice," he said, "in which the meanest pauper in the land stands just as high and has just as many rights as the son of a general or the son of a judge."

The thrust of Hill's argument was that the conviction should not be overturned because of technicalities. The key issue was Molineux's guilt, which had been established during the trial by "overwhelming evidence." Even John Milburn had not claimed "that his client is innocent." During the five hours he had addressed the court, "the word innocent never once passed his lips."

Recognizing that the appeal would hinge, to a large extent, on the issue of the Barnet evidence, Hill insisted that the state "had a perfect legal right to show the facts connected with the death of Barnet. Here was a man who was a member of the Knickerbocker Athletic Club, where Cornish was employed. The poison that killed him was sent through the mails, just as it was sent to Cornish. It was the same poison in both cases. All the circumstances were alike. The lives of both men were plotted against by the same assassin. Who was it who desired to destroy them? Someone who was jealous of them. Someone who had quarreled with them. And who was that man? This defendant. He was jealous of Barnet; he had quarreled with Cornish."

As for the testimony related to Blanche that had elicited such outrage from Milburn, Hill declared that the state had every right to introduce it during the trial. In scathing tones, Hill read aloud the notorious letter Blanche had written to Barnet on his deathbed and declared it to be the communication of "a lover." He then read portions of a note that Roland had sent to a friend shortly after Barnet's death, announcing his engagement to Blanche. "It is all so sudden a romance," Roland had written. "I am so happy."

"*Romance*," snorted Hill, tossing the letter onto the table. "It was no romance. It was a tragedy. His rival had been removed."

At that moment, General Molineux abruptly rose from his seat. The relentless attack on his son's character by a man as prominent as David Hill had shaken him badly. Tears streaming down his face, the old man made his way out of the courtroom.

Hill, however, was unmoved by the piteous spectacle. Addressing a question that Milburn had raised—why would Roland have tried to murder Cornish over some petty "club squabbles"?—Hill offered a psychological explanation, suggesting that Roland's "malady," sexual impotence, had driven him into a state of "melancholia" that had mentally unbalanced him.

Despite the defense's efforts to "avert suspicion from their client" by casting it onto Cornish, there was no mistaking the true culprit.

"If it was not Molineux," Hill declared, "it was nobody."[5]

Hill ended his argument at 1:35 P.M. on Wednesday. After a fifteen-minute reply by Milburn, the appeal was formally submitted. The court's decision would be handed down during its fall session.

Afterward, General Molineux—who refused to speak to ex-senator Hill when the two encountered each other as they were leaving the building—made a statement to the press. For the first time, there seemed to be a heartbreaking vulnerability about the old soldier, "whose loyalty to his son," wrote one observer, "has been pathetic."[6] "I must be patient," said the General softly, as though addressing himself. "It will come out all right. I must get my boy back."[7] A few minutes later, he boarded the train back to Manhattan, while John G. Milburn returned to his duties as president of the Pan-American Exposition, the great world's fair designed to showcase Buffalo as one of the nation's leading cities.

80

President McKinley and his wife spent the summer of 1901 in their modest home in Canton, Ohio, where Ida enjoyed a steady recuperation, while her husband indulged in the simple relaxations of a placid Midwestern town—picnics, drives in the family buggy, excursions to nearby county fairs, and an occasional game of euchre. As the summer progressed and Ida continued to improve, his plans to visit Buffalo were renewed. By late August, newspapers around the country were announcing that President's Day at the Pan-American Exposition had been officially rescheduled for Thursday, September 5.

At precisely 5:00 P.M. on Tuesday, September, 3, the president's three-car private train pulled into Buffalo's Terrace Railroad Station overlooking Lake Erie. The following day, McKinley toured the fair then, after a brief rest at the Milburn mansion, attended an evening concert by John Philip Sousa's band.

Thursday began with an early sightseeing trip to Niagara Falls. Following lunch, McKinley returned to Buffalo for his final appearance at the exposition—a public reception held in the Temple of Music, a gaudy, byzantine structure on the north side of the fairgrounds, where he would personally greet the well-wishers who had lined up by the thousand to shake him by the hand.

In accordance with instructions given by McKinley's fiercely devoted personal secretary, George Cortelyou, extra precautions had been taken to ensure the president's safety. In addition to the three Secret Service men who routinely watched over him, a squad of exposition policemen had been stationed at the entrance and a contingent of Buffalo detectives posted in the aisle. Ten enlisted artillerymen and a corporal, all in full-dress uniform, had also been called in, with orders to prevent any suspicious-looking persons from approaching McKinley. Altogether, more than fifty guards were there to keep an eye on the crowd. For the handshaking, McKinley stood between Cortelyou and John Milburn. Four soldiers flanked them, two on each side.[1]

In spite of these heightened security measures, one cardinal rule for protecting the president was flagrantly disregarded. No visitor was supposed to get close to the chief executive unless both hands were plainly visible and completely empty. It was an unusually warm and humid day, however, and the crammed reception hall was sweltering—at least ninety degrees. Sweat poured from every brow, and so many handkerchiefs were in evidence that the guards simply paid no attention to them.

At 4:07 P.M.—just a few minutes after the reception began—a slender, mild-looking young man reached the front of the line. Like so many other people, he was clutching a big white handkerchief. Or so it appeared. In reality, the hankie was wrapped around his right hand, concealing a loaded .32-caliber Iver Johnson revolver. As McKinley reached out to greet him, the young man—a self-professed anarchist named Leon Czolgosz—lunged forward and fired twice into the president's body.

A moment of stunned silence followed the shots. Then pandemonium erupted. While the president staggered back into the arms of the men around him, Cszolgosz was pounced upon by the soldiers and guards, who knocked him to the floor and began to beat him with their rifle butts and fists. One tried to stab him with a bayonet.

"Go easy on him, boys," cried McKinley, now seated in a chair, his face drained of color and a spreading red stain on his shirtfront.

While Cszolgosz was hauled to his feet and dragged to an inner office, the Temple was cleared. A few minutes later, an ambulance clanged up to the entrance and the desperately wounded president was carried out on a litter, loaded into the vehicle, and driven to the exposition hospital.

Housed in a small gray building a quarter mile from the Temple of Music, the hospital was, in actuality, little more than an emergency first-aid center. Exactly eighteen minutes after the shooting, McKinley—fully conscious, though in severe shock—was carried into the rudimentary operating room and laid on the table.

As the nurses began to undress him, one of the bullets, which had glanced off his breastbone, causing only a scratch, fell from his underclothing. Even at a glance, however, it was clear that the other wound was far more serious, perhaps even fatal. It had torn through McKinley's abdomen, approximately five inches below his left nipple.

The first and most urgent order of business was to round up the best physicians available. Dr. Roswell Park, the exposition's medical director and a man with long experience in the treatment of gunshot wounds, was the obvious choice to take charge. But Park was in Niagara Falls, operating on a lymphoma patient. Arrangements were quickly made to rush him back to Buffalo at the earliest possible moment. In the meantime, John Milburn took command. Upon his orders, the president's life was put into the hands of another prominent Buffalo physician, Dr. Matthew Mann.

A short, gray-bearded fifty-six-year-old, Mann had a worldwide reputation. He had trained in the United States and Europe, served on the staff of the Yale Medical School, and authored a standard textbook. Unfortunately, his specialty was gynecology, not abdominal surgery. Nevertheless, he was deemed the most qualified surgeon available at that moment of crisis.

Though the city of Buffalo had recently opened a state-of-the-art general hospital, Mann chose to operate without delay. At 5:20 P.M., the life-and-death procedure began under the least favorable conditions imaginable. Mann, who had arrived without his surgical case, had to work with borrowed instruments. No one wore a cap or gauze mask. Though the fairgrounds blazed each evening with the brilliance of countless incandescent bulbs, there were no electric lights in the operating room. As the daylight waned, the doctors were reduced to using a mirror to reflect the light of the setting sun onto the incision in McKinley's abdominal wall.

Exploring the president's wound, Mann discovered that the bullet had gone straight through the stomach, puncturing both the front and rear walls. He couldn't find the bullet itself, though. An X-ray machine was on display at the fair, but Mann declined to use it. The two holes in the stomach were sutured, the abdominal cavity was flushed with saline solution, and McKinley was stitched back up with the missing bullet still inside him.

At 7:20 P.M.—two hours after the operation began—the groaning, corpse-pale president was taken from the hospital and transported back to John Milburn's residence.

Over the course of the next week, a steady stream of increasingly hopeful communiqués issued from Buffalo. On Friday, September 6, the doctors reported that McKinley was "rallying satisfactorily and resting comfortably." On Saturday, a bulletin described his condition as "quite encouraging." On Sunday, one of his physicians characterized the president as "first rate." The official word on Monday was that his "condition was becoming more and more satisfactory." By Tuesday, newspapers across the country were proclaiming that the president was "on the high road to recovery." The following day, September 11, Dr. Charles McBurney, a prominent New York surgeon, paid lavish tribute to his colleague, Matthew Mann, telling reporters that "the judgment of Dr. Mann in operating as he did within an hour of the shooting in all probability saved the President's life."

But the president's life had not been saved. At 5:00 P.M. on Friday, September 13, the venerated leader suffered a heart attack.

Nine hours later—his stomach, pancreas, and one kidney poisoned by the gangrene that had spread along the path of the unfound bullet—William McKinley died in John Milburn's home after gasping out his final words: "Good-bye all, good-bye. It is God's way. His will be done."[2]

81

The Pan-American Exposition came to an official end on Saturday, November 2. At the stroke of midnight, while ten buglers sounded taps from the Electric Tower, John Milburn threw a switch, and the sprawling fairgrounds—illuminated by 160,000 incandescent lights—went dark forever. To some observers, however, the ceremony seemed slightly redundant. The murder of the president two months earlier had already cast a deep shadow over the "Rainbow City" from which it had never fully emerged.[1]

By then, Leon Czolgosz was dead, electrocuted four days earlier at the state prison in Auburn, New York. Immediately after his execution, the top of his skull had been sawed off and his brain examined for signs of mental impairment. His corpse was then stuck inside a black-stained pine box, doused with sulfuric acid (to obliterate his identity), and buried in an unmarked grave in the prison cemetery.[2]

From the moment of the assassin's capture to the day of his death and ignominious disposal, less than two months had elapsed—a striking contrast to the situation of Roland Molineux, who, at the time of Czolgosz's execution, had been behind bars for more than two years, awaiting a final disposition of his case.

Still, Roland and his father no longer had cause for complaint. On Tuesday, October 15, the Court of Appeals had finally handed down its decision. In his battle against ex-senator Hill, John Milburn had triumphed. Had the great world's fair he had helped shepherd into existence not climaxed in catastrophe, he, too, would have had every reason to celebrate.

The decision in the Molineux appeal—trumpeted on the front pages of newspapers across the country—would prove to be a judicial landmark, defining the conditions under which prosecutors could introduce evidence of previous crimes at a defendant's trial. Generally speaking, wrote Justice William E. Werner in a formulation that even today is known as the "Molineux rule," the state "cannot prove against a defendant any crime not alleged in the indictment." This rule was intended as a constitutional safeguard, protecting a defendant from "the assumption that [he] was guilty of the crime charged because he had committed other, similar crimes in the past."

To be sure, there were exceptions, instances where evidence of prior offenses might be admitted. For example, the prosecution could introduce "proof of another crime" if it helped to establish motive in "the specific crime charged." In Roland's case, however, neither this nor any other exception applied.

The motive for attempting to kill Cornish was, according to Werner, "hatred, engendered by quarrels between them." The motive for poisoning Barnet, on the other hand, was "jealousy caused by the latter's intervention in the love affair of the former." Since the two motives had "no relation to each other," evidence pertaining to the murder of Barnet threw "no light upon the motive which actuated the attempt upon the life of Cornish" and was therefore inadmissible.[3]

Based on this principle, the prevailing opinion held that Recorder Goff had erred in admitting testimony related to the death of Henry Barnet. The judgment of conviction against Roland Burnham Molineux was reversed and a new trial granted.[4]

82

General Molineux was at his office at the Devoe and Raynolds paint factory when the news reached him. He was still beaming with joy a half hour later when a flock of newsmen arrived to hear his reaction.

"Just what I expected, but thank God the strain is over," said the General, offering cigars all around. "I tell you, boys, this has added years to my life."

And what about the rumors, asked one reporter, that the district attorney might decide to forego another trial and simply set Roland free?

"That wouldn't please me at all," said General Molineux. "This thing has gone too far. To let him off would brand him for life with suspicion. I'd rather see my son pass through the ordeal of another trial than have him set free without a complete vindication."

But what if he were to be convicted again? someone asked.

"Impossible," snorted the General. "Why, even on the evidence that sent him to the death cell, he should have been acquitted."

A short time later, he was on the train to Sing Sing. He arrived too late to see Roland, who received the happy news early the next morning from Warden Johnson.

Roland was awake and standing expectantly by the barred door of his cell when Johnson entered the Death House at 6:30 A.M., Wednesday,

October 16. "Well, Roland, I have good news for you," he said. "The Court of Appeals has granted you a new trial."

For a moment, Roland made no reply, "as if he did not realize the full purport of the information." Finally, he let out a laugh and said, "It seems too good to be true." He then thanked Johnson for bringing him the news, while the inmates in the adjoining cells called out their congratulations.[1]

Just before noon the following day, word reached Warden Johnson that a police officer had left New York City with a requisition for Molineux. Preparations for the transfer were immediately begun. At 3:00 P.M., a rickety hack pulled up at the prison gate and discharged Detective Sergeant Robert McNaught, along with General Molineux and George Gordon Battle. The three were immediately ushered into the office of Keeper Connaughton.

A few minutes later, Roland—freshly shaved and wearing a new black serge suit and a pair of tan shoes in place of his prison slippers—was brought into the room. At the sight of his father, he broke into a broad grin, then threw himself into the old man's arms. They embraced and kissed each other's cheeks before stepping back and shaking hands.

"You don't know how good it feels to get hold of you," said Roland, eyes glistening.

"Your grip is as strong as ever, my boy," said the General, clutching his son's hand in both his own. "There's many a good fight left in us yet. We'll stick it out, all right, and the next time we take a journey together, it will be back home to Brooklyn."[2]

A few minutes later, Roland, looking dapper in a black fedora and overcoat provided by the General, emerged from the gray walls of Sing Sing. Outside the gates, he climbed into the ramshackle coach with his father, lawyer, and Detective Sergeant McNaught. They had traveled only half the distance to the railway station when the rear springs gave way and the body of the coach came down with a crash between the wheels.

Roland was the first out and helped his father to crawl through the door, followed by McNaught and Battle. After ascertaining that no one was hurt, the foursome walked the rest of the way to the station, Roland cracking jokes about his bumpy return to the real world.[3]

The platform was packed with villagers when the party strolled up to the station. Roland and the others pushed their way through the gawkers to the waiting room. Inside, Roland was greeted by the stationmaster and other railroad officials, who shook his hand and congratulated him on his release. A few minutes later, the train—known as the "Croton local"—drew up and the party boarded one of the smoking cars. Settling into a forward seat, his father beside him and the two other men directly behind, Roland pushed open the window and let the autumn air wash over him all the way back to New York City.

After arriving at Grand Central station, the four men piled into a cab and drove straight to the Tombs. By nightfall, Roland Molineux was back in his former second-tier cell, which had been whitewashed and furnished with a new bed in preparation for his return.[4]

Two nights later, veterans of the 159th New York State Volunteers—about seventy-five of the grizzled old soldiers, all told—gathered at the Molineux home in Fort Greene Place for their annual reunion. It was the thirty-seventh anniversary, to the day, of the Battle of Cedar Creek, in which Edward Molineux and his brigade had acquitted themselves so heroically. Following the meal, General Horatio C. King, recipient of the Congressional Medal of Honor, rose and delivered a speech in which he paid tribute to the "exceptional and brilliant part" General Molineux had played in that "desperate struggle"—a fight that had ended with the "complete rout" of the enemy forces.

"But we are here not to celebrate that victory alone," King continued, while his listeners—lawyers, judges, congressmen, and other members of the social and political elite of Brooklyn—sat raptly at their tables. "The hearts of your comrades have warmed to you even more than they did in that mighty conflict because of the terrible battle for another's life which you have so heroically made in the past two years or more. Out of the valley of the shadow of death, the boy who is dearer to you than your own life has emerged with another and fairer opportunity to establish his innocence. We, your comrades and friends, who love you and believe in the innocence of your son, are here to congratulate you most fervently, and to pray for an early and complete sweeping away of the dark clouds which have so long hung over your beloved house."

An outburst of thunderous applause interrupted King at this point. He waited until the ovation subsided before bringing his address to a rousing close. "We renew to you the pledge of our friendship and our confidence. In sunshine and shadow, in weal or woe, we are your comrades now as we were when shot and shell made gruesome music in our ears; and the comradeship formed under such conditions can never weaken or fail."[5]

Backing up their vows of support with direct and practical action, the General's old comrades joined together in offering financial help to defray his enormous and ever-mounting legal expenses. "It is well known," read a declaration issued by the veterans, "that by reason of unfortunate circumstances involving the good name of General Molineux and his family, great sacrifices have been made in order to maintain their reputation unsullied. To a younger man, the opportunity to recuperate financially might present itself, but at the age of nearly three score and ten, it would seem almost too late for the General to retrieve his fortune."

The proud old warrior, however, would have none of it. Conveying his heartfelt thanks to his "boys," he graciously declined the offer. He "was not, thank God, down to that necessity. I have said that I would spend my last dollar in the defense of my son," he declared, "and I will. That last dollar has not yet been reached."[6]

The General's willingness to sacrifice his fortune on behalf of his son only enhanced his already lofty reputation among the public. Even his former enemies in the South rallied to his side. "I faced you in battle, but I congratulate you on the prospective release of your son," one ex–Confederate officer wrote to him. "Your brave and generous heart deserves it. I believe in the vindication of your son." He received sympathetic letters from other onetime foes, including a major from the Fifth Georgia Regiment, who denounced Assistant DA Osborne for insulting the General's daughter-in-law and offered to horsewhip the scoundrel should he ever show his face down South.[7]

The General, of course, had always been an object of admiration, even reverence. The outpouring of sympathy for his cause in the wake of Roland's release from Sing Sing, however, was something new. Even the yellow papers, which had tried and convicted Roland in their pages, had lost their taste for attacking the gallant old General's son.

As one observer would put it, "the hostile tide against Roland had begun to ebb."[8]

83

Despite public statements from both Roland and his father that they would settle for nothing less than the complete vindication of an acquittal, the Molineux defense team quickly mounted an effort to quash the murder indictment and have their client set free without a second trial.[1] To argue their case, Weeks and Battle called in Frank S. Black, who had served a term as governor of New York before resuming private practice in Manhattan. Opposing him was another former New York governor, David B. Hill, who had unsuccessfully represented the state before the Court of Appeals.

This time, Hill emerged victorious. On December 6, 1901, Judge Joseph Newburger rendered a decision denying the motion to dismiss the indictment. Roland Molineux would have to be tried again, quite as if the first trial—one of the longest and most costly criminal proceedings in the history of the state—had never taken place.[2]

Roland would spend another year in the Tombs waiting for his trial to begin. Still, he had little to complain about. Despite a smallpox scare in March 1902 that necessitated the immediate vaccination of all 392 inmates,[3] life in the city prison was a holiday after the hell of the Sing Sing Death House. Roland could exercise in the open air, enjoy catered meals, read newspapers to his heart's content, and see friends and relatives on a daily basis. His parents and brothers took full advantage of the liberal visitation policy.

The story was different with Blanche.

The previous fall, within days of Roland's return to the Tombs, she had gone to see him in the company of the General. The meeting took place in the warden's office. Roland, brought down from his cell on Murderer's Row, immediately threw his arms about his wife and kissed her. To observers, Blanche seemed "nervous at first," though she managed a smile and was soon chatting warmly enough with her husband. They remained in each other's company for an hour.

Afterward, in an interview with reporters, she reiterated her belief in Roland's innocence and angrily denied rumors that she had "grown tired of" her marriage and planned to abandon him.

"It is all false!" she cried. "I would gladly give my life in an instant to see Roland happy."[4]

In the following months, however, her visits became less and less frequent until, by the spring of 1902, they had ceased altogether. A few weeks later, she moved out of the Molineux brownstone.

By then, relations between Blanche and her in-laws had grown unbearably tense. With Roland's prospects looking brighter than at any time since his arrest, the General finally agreed to give her a bit of freedom. At first, she was allowed to make afternoon jaunts into Manhattan, where after years of social starvation she hungrily took in shows and concerts and luncheons with friends.

The taste of these pleasures only strengthened her determination to escape the stifling household once and for all. In August 1902, she moved into an airy corner suite at a residential hotel in the Murray Hill section of Manhattan. Her rent was paid by the General, who also provided her with a generous monthly allowance.

In return, Blanche agreed to only one stipulation: during Roland's second trial, she would be at his side in the courtroom.

The General wasn't taking any chances. To be sure, he had every reason to feel optimistic. Even James Osborne acknowledged that public sentiment had changed and that many people, formerly against young Molineux, now "believed he has been punished sufficiently."[5]

Still, Roland wasn't free yet. Appearances must be maintained. The scandalous rumors about Blanche, suggesting that she had lost faith in her husband, would be put to rest. The jury would see for itself just how much she loved and believed in her husband.[6]

84

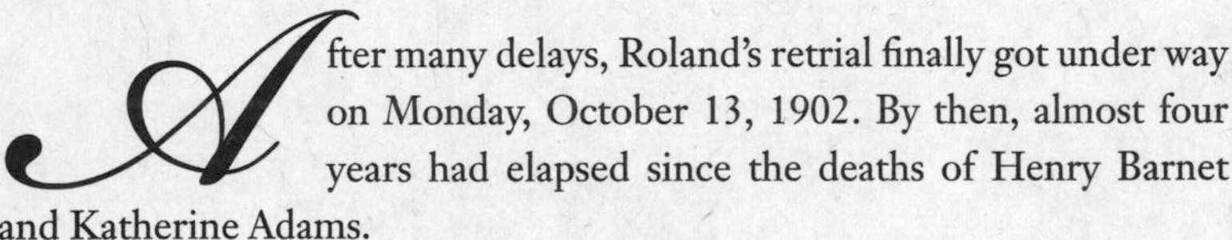

After many delays, Roland's retrial finally got under way on Monday, October 13, 1902. By then, almost four years had elapsed since the deaths of Henry Barnet and Katherine Adams.

New York had not lacked for lurid crimes during that time. Only recently, in fact, the city had been riveted by a particularly sensational murder. Less than a month before the start of Roland's second trial, the mutilated body of a young Manhattan woman named Anna Pulitzer had been found in a canal near Jersey City. What made the murder so newsworthy, beyond its sheer grisliness, was the pedigree of the killer: Brigham Young's grandson, William Hooper Young, who—so the papers claimed—had committed the crime in accordance with the doctrine of "blood atonement" preached by the Mormon leader.[1]

Even with such titillating fare to distract them, the public remained fascinated by the Great Poison Mystery. The crowds who turned out for Molineux's second trial were nearly as large as those who had flocked to the first. What they ended up seeing was a mix of the deeply familiar and the dramatically new.

The cast of characters had changed in certain notable ways. Though Bartow Weeks was present throughout the proceedings, former New York governor Frank S. Black was brought in to serve as lead counsel for the defense. And in place of Recorder Goff (whose rulings had generally favored the prosecution), a judge named John A. Lambert (who turned out to be far more sympathetic to the defense) was called in to preside.

It was largely owing to Lambert's businesslike approach—his "insistence upon cutting out every superfluous word or gesture"[2]—that the second trial moved with such impressive speed. Jury selection, which had originally required more than two weeks, was now completed within twelve hours. James Osborne's opening address lasted only ninety minutes instead of four and a half hours (and was mercifully free of any labored analogies to the Frankenstein monster). And on the first day of testimony, no fewer than thirteen witnesses were examined. As one headline proclaimed, it was ALL HUSTLE, NO NONSENSE IN MOLINEUX CASE.[3]

Though the prosecution witnesses were, by and large, a familiar crew, a number of key figures were missing. Elsie Gray, the bookkeeper for the Kutnow brothers who had discovered one of the bogus Cornish letters, had died shortly after the first trial. And Roland's former child-mistress, Mamie Melando—still smarting from her virtual abduction by Detectives Carey and McCafferty three years earlier—refused to leave New Jersey.[4]

The intervening years had not been kind to other witnesses, including Harry Cornish. Gaunt and hollow-cheeked, his few remaining strands of hair having gone prematurely gray, Cornish no longer made his living as a sportsman. His onetime employer, the Knickerbocker Athletic Club—where the lives of Roland Molineux and Henry Barnet and Cornish himself had so fatefully collided—had recently gone out of business, brought down by the financial troubles of its owner, J. Herbert Ballantine. Cornish, once a celebrity in the city's amateur sporting world, now worked for a bakery.[5]

Still, his manner remained as gruff and uningratiating as ever. He alternately snarled and shouted at ex-governor Black, who subjected him to a ferocious cross-examination. Over Osborne's objections, Black was allowed to interrogate the witness about his marital infidelities, as well as his current relationship with Florence Rodgers, who—so the lawyer intimated—had become Cornish's mistress since her mother's death.

Black also asked pointed questions about the classes Cornish had attended at Columbia Medical College. Cornish explained that he had gone there strictly to "study anatomy," so that he could learn more about the muscular system and improve his performance as a coach. Black, however, insisted that Cornish had "studied medicine"—thus implying that Roland Molineux wasn't the only one with a technical background in chemistry.[6]

When Cornish finally left the stand, he "heaved a deep sigh," as though relieved to be done with the ordeal. At the defense table, Roland—dapper in a double-breasted black sack coat, high collar, silk four-in-hand necktie, and pearl stickpin—watched his rival's discomfiture with a smirk.[7]

In the aftermath of the first trial, Bartow Weeks had been roundly criticized for not putting Roland on the stand. Frank S. Black was not about to repeat that error. When the defense opened its case on Friday, October 31, Roland B. Molineux was the first witness called.

It had taken a contingent of twenty police officers to control the crowd that showed up that morning. When the courtroom doors opened at 9:30 A.M., more than three hundred people—many of them women—managed to fight their way inside. Within minutes, all the seats had been taken, including the two usually reserved for Roland and his father, who upon their arrival a half hour later had to stand until extra chairs could be brought in from another room.[8]

After an opening address that lasted less than five minutes—a "record-breaker in brevity for a case of such importance and scope"[9]—Black launched into his direct examination of the star witness. Roland's voice, which had not been heard in court since the coroner's inquest three years before, was strong and steady. It had, observers felt, "the ring of sincerity in it."[10]

Indeed, everyone who saw him on the stand that day agreed that Roland turned in a remarkable performance. Calmly, clearly, courteously, with no discernible hesitation and a demeanor that struck spectators as perfectly frank and forthcoming, he gave a detailed account of his quarrels with Harry Cornish but insisted that, angry as he was at the time, he had gotten over his animosity long before his marriage.

He emphatically denied that he had bought the silver toothpick holder, rented a private letter box, written the bogus letters, or mailed the poison package. He claimed that he did not know how to make cyanide of mercury and, indeed, had never even heard of the poison until charges were brought against him. He acknowledged that he had sent away for Dr. Burns's Marvelous Giant Indian Salve but insisted that he had used the ointment not for impotence, but for a knee injury sustained in a bicycling accident. He described his relationship with Mamie Melando as that of "employer and employee, solely." He swore that he was "absolutely innocent of any part in or knowledge of" Mrs. Adams's murder.

Black ended his direct examination at 11:55 A.M. It had lasted just sixty-five minutes. By contrast, James Osborne would grill the witness for five hours. In the end, the cross-examination would be a "complete victory" for Roland.[11]

"A marvel of alertness and skill," he calmly parried every attack the prosecutor aimed at him, never seemed rattled or evasive, projected an air of absolute confidence and candor. "To every question he had an easy, ready answer. He smiled and waved his hand, and exhibited complete suavity and ease."[12]

At four-thirty, having utterly failed to extract any damaging admissions from the witness, an exhausted James Osborne begged the judge for an adjournment. "If Your Honor please. I believe I am tired to death, and I would like to say, this being rather, you know, an important matter to both Mr. Molineux and myself, and he is probably tired, too—"

"I am not tired," Roland broke in. "I would just as soon stay here."

Judge Lambert ordered Osborne to continue. He managed to go on for another hour before he "gave out entirely" and collapsed into his chair. Roland, looking as fresh and chipper as ever, left the stand with a smile and returned to his seat, where his father patted him on the back and said, "Good boy."[13]

Speaking to reporters when the day's session was over, Osborne tried to put the best face on the matter, insisting that he "was perfectly satisfied with the cross-examination of Molineux." Nevertheless, even he was forced to concede that Roland was "one of the most wonderful men I ever examined—of more than ordinary intellectual power, quick, resourceful, alert, with an able and flexible mind."

The General gave Roland the ultimate accolade: his son, he proudly told reporters, had borne "himself under fire like a true Molineux."[14]

One person was not there to witness Roland's triumph: his ostensibly devoted wife, Blanche.

When the trial had opened on October 13, the General, in response to a query from reporters, had explained that, while his daughter-in-law would undoubtedly not sit through the entire proceedings, he expected her to be there for the start of each day's session.[15] Since he made that remark, the trial had been going on for more than two weeks. And Blanche had yet to put in a single appearance.

85

It is a cliché of courtroom melodramas: the surprise witness, appearing at the eleventh hour, who offers a startling revelation that settles the defendant's fate. In real life, of course (as opposed to the typical Perry Mason mystery), such a thing rarely occurs. But it did at the second trial of Roland Molineux.

Just a few days after Roland took the stand, stories began to circulate that the defense was planning to call "an entirely new witness," someone whose very existence had never been mentioned in the four years since the story broke, and whose testimony would provide a "sensationally dramatic ending" to the trial. The yellow papers even revealed her identity: Mrs. Anna C. Stephenson, the fifty-five-year-old wife of a veteran Brooklyn police officer, John Stephenson.

Asked about these reports, Black initially waved them off as idle gossip—the "creation of newspapers."[1] When court opened on Thursday, November 6, however, all eyes were immediately drawn to a gaunt, gray-haired woman seated in the section reserved for witnesses. An excited buzz ran through the spectator section: it was Mrs. Stephenson!

For hours, the spectators—some of whom had brought along picnic baskets—waited eagerly for the promised sensation. Her testimony, when she was finally called to the stand at 4:00 P.M., did not disappoint.

Though clearly nervous under the gaze of the crowd, the soft-spoken, self-declared "good Christian woman" explained, with all apparent sincerity, that on December 23, 1898—the day the poison package had been mailed to Harry Cornish—she had traveled to Manhattan from her home in Brooklyn to shop at the Washington Market. She had brought along a Christmas package to mail to her sister in Illinois.

At approximately 4:15 P.M., on her way to the general post office, she paused at the corner of Vesey Street and Broadway, waiting to cross the traffic-clogged thoroughfare. As she stood there, she felt "something pressing against me."

"Looking around," Mrs. Stephenson recalled, "I saw a man very close to me with a package in his overcoat pocket. He seemed very nervous, and I wondered what was the matter with him. He took the package out of his pocket, and just out of curiosity, I glanced at it. I saw the words 'Mr. Harry Cornish, Knickerbocker—' That is all I remember.

"In a moment, the man crossed the street," she continued. "As I had a package to mail, I thought that I would follow him and mail my package where he mailed his. I did follow him and saw him mail his package, and I mailed mine immediately afterwards. The man then went out of the general post office, and I did not see him again."

When, in the days following Katherine Adams's death, the newspapers published a facsimile of the poison package address, Mrs. Stephenson (so she claimed) had immediately realized the significance of what she had seen. She "discussed the matter with her husband," but he advised her "not to get mixed in the case."

Black then turned to the defense table. "Molineux, stand up," he commanded.

Roland sprang to his feet and looked squarely at the witness.

"Now, look at this defendant," Black said to Mrs. Stephenson, "and tell me if he is the man who mailed the poison package."

"He is not," came the unhesitating reply.

"Are you sure?" asked Black.

"Perfectly sure," said Mrs. Stephenson.[2]

As Black took his seat with a smile, James Osborne rose. He, too, was smiling, though far more grimly. Asking Harry Cornish to stand, he turned to Mrs. Stephenson and asked, "Is *this* the man who had the package?"

Osborne's move was clearly meant to confound the witness. But (as another young prosecutor would discover during the last great murder trial of the twentieth century, when he asked the defendant to try on the killer's gloves in full view of the jury) such dramatic courtroom demonstrations sometimes backfire.

"It looks very much like him," said Mrs. Stephenson.

Osborne, reddening, said, "Are you sure of that?"

"Well, I am pretty sure he's the man," answered the witness.

Osborne did his best to recover from this blunder. Under his polite but insistent cross-examination, Mrs. Stephenson revealed that she was unable to read without glasses, which by her own admission she hadn't been wearing on the day in question; that she suffered from "nervous prostration"; and that her decision to testify on Molineux's behalf had been influenced by "divine guidance." Osborne also called her policeman-husband to the stand, who testified that he "did not put much stock" in her story.[3]

Afterward, when reporters asked for his opinion on Mrs. Stephenson, Osborne snorted and said, "I believe the woman thought she was telling the truth. But she is laboring under a delusion such as is common to women of her time of life. She says that she could read the poison address at about 4:30 o'clock on that day. Well, as a matter of fact, the sun set at around 4:30 that day. The street was already dark. It scarcely seems credible that this woman could have read the address at that time with her bad eyesight."

"Do you think the jury will agree with you?" someone asked.

"Oh, I don't believe she made much of an impression on the jury," replied Osborne—a remark that struck more than one observer as a case of wishful thinking.[4]

Mrs. Stephenson wasn't Black's only surprise witness. Barton Huff, a traveling salesman from Battle Creek, Michigan, swore that, a few days before Christmas 1898, he had gone into Hartdegen's jewelry store to inquire about a watch fob he had seen in the window. As he approached the counter, a man rushed into the shop, pushed his way to the front, and told the saleswoman that "he wanted to buy a silver bottle holder to match some dresser articles that a woman friend of his had." The man was about five feet ten inches tall, weighed approximately 175 pounds, and wore "a pointed sandy beard." He bore no resemblance at all, said Huff, to Roland Molineux.[5]

Professor Herman Vulte of Columbia Medical College, another defense witness never heard from before, testified that on the afternoon of

December 23, 1898—the time when the poison package was mailed from the general post office in lower Manhattan—Roland had been in his company the entire afternoon. They did not part until 4:45 P.M. Even if Roland had caught the nearest trolley, then transferred to an elevated car and proceeded directly downtown, he could not possibly have arrived at the general post office before it closed.[6] Vulte was one of nineteen witnesses to take the stand on Friday, November 7. Their testimony marked the end of the defense case. Final arguments would begin the following Monday, after which Roland's fate would be in the hands of the jury.

On the following afternoon, Saturday, November 8, a reporter for Pulitzer's *World* wangled an interview with Blanche at her suite in the Murray Hill Hotel. Why, he wondered, had she not attended a single minute of the trial?

Blanche would only say that she didn't "think a courtroom is the proper place for a woman." Of course, things would have been different if her husband—"Mr. Molineux," as she referred to him—had "nobody else in the world to cheer him up." But with his "dear old father at his side," she didn't see any pressing reason to be there.

Asked her opinion of the trial, she declared that "Mr. Molineux" was bound to be acquitted. But the prospect seemed to fill her with little joy. It was her own long ordeal that she harped on. "You cannot know what a woman suffers when she sees her good name dragged into the gutter by cruel heartless creatures who do not care what lies they tell about a defenseless person," she said bitterly. "I often wonder how I have borne it all."

When the reporter asked about her future with her husband, Blanche gave a strikingly evasive reply. "The future? No matter what the future may be, nothing can repay me for all that I, an innocent woman, have suffered."

It was, of course, a disingenuous reply. Blanche knew very clearly what her future held. She hinted at it in her next remark.

"For four long years," she said, "I have felt like an inhabitant of the infernal regions. At last, I feel as though I can see the first gleam of light—as though the gates of the inferno were about to open, permitting me to escape."[7]

86

The size of the crowd that showed up at the courthouse on Monday, November 10, 1902—the penultimate day of the Molineux trial—was difficult to measure, though a conservative estimate put the number at nearly two thousand.[1] It required fifty policemen to impose a semblance of order on the clamorous mob in the hallway. No sooner did the doors open at 9:30 A.M. than "every seat was occupied, the reporters' tables were overwhelmed, chairs blocked the aisles, and the passageway from the justice's chambers to the bench behind the jury box was packed solidly with spectators."

Unable to find seats, "a solid mass of more than two hundred people stood in the rear of the room." When Molineux entered at ten o'clock, "smiling and unconcerned," court officers could not find a seat for him. The problem "was settled by General Molineux, who gave up his seat to his son," then perched on a chair beside the reporter for the *Times*.[2]

Nearly the entirety of the day was given over to Black's summation. He began in a voice so low that it was "barely audible a few feet away," though it grew in both volume and intensity as he proceeded.

He began by insisting that it was "one of the duties of society to punish the guilty, but even greater is the duty of society to protect the innocent. If there is one innocent hair on the head of the man who stands before you accused of this crime, then you must acquit him."

Black branded as "preposterous" the notion that Molineux would buy the silver holder at a store where he was sure to be recognized, and reminded the jurors that both the Hartdegen clerk, Emma Miller, and the traveling salesman, Barton Huff, had sworn that Roland was not the purchaser. He castigated the letter box man Joseph Koch as someone who "peddled his story and his eternal soul at the same time"; denounced the handwriting experts as "stupendous frauds"; and insisted that, far from being a substance that only a chemist could acquire, cyanide of mercury was commonly available to anyone.

He acknowledged the scandal that had caused Roland's banishment to the West at the age of fifteen. But he asked the jurors "as experienced men, men who have lived in the world, to consider whether in such a case it is the boy of fifteen years or the married woman who is the betrayer." In any event, Black continued, "since that time, you have seen him as a successful businessman with not one blemish against his character until this unfortunate occurrence. He has never done anything since he was fifteen years old to make him unworthy of the affection of the worthiest and bravest, the kindest, most honorable and loyal old man that I have ever known."

At this invocation of the sacred person of General Molineux, a number of spectators burst into applause but were quickly silenced by the court officers.

The bulk of Black's summation dealt with the issue of motive, and here he was helped immeasurably by the exclusion of all evidence relating to the death of Henry Barnet. He was "almost ashamed," said Black, to waste the juror's time in reviewing "the flimsy thing which is considered to be the motive that prompted this dastardly crime.

"Mr. Molineux was a member of the Knickerbocker Athletic Club," Black continued. "Cornish was athletic director there. Molineux had a host of friends there. And you are asked to believe that into the midst of these friends, with no way of knowing whom it would reach, he sent a poisonous drug. And on what grounds are you asked to believe this?

"Because," said Black in an incredulous tone, "Molineux didn't like Cornish. This is all that you have as a motive for this frightful crime."

Here, Black shook his head, as though in amazement. "Between every man on this jury and a hundred other men," he said, "there are greater motives than this for a crime. In every church, in every family, a more serious motive for a crime could be found than this one. Yet on this and this alone, you are asked to single out this one man and say that he is a murderer."

Leaning so far over the jury box that his extended forefinger was within an inch of the foreman's nose, Black declared, "When a man is bent on murdering his enemy does he shoot into a crowd? Does he wreck a train because the object of his hatred is on that train? Would Molineux, to kill Cornish, send into a club where any man might taste it, where many of his friends might be endangered, a poisonous drug? No, gentlemen. I say that Molineux never did it."

Here, Black stepped back from the jury box and paused for a moment, as though for dramatic effect.

"But there *was* a murder here," he continued at length. "And there was a motive. All the evidence in this case points away from Molineux and to another man. It points to that man just as surely as the needle points to the North Star. Gentlemen, I am not here to brand any man, to open any sore. But a crime has been committed here, and my plain duty is before me."

There seemed to be a collective intake of breath at this sudden shift in Black's speech. Everyone knew, of course, that he was referring to Harry Cornish, who—as the newspapers wrote—had been "put on the rack" during his examination by Black. Even so, there was surprise, even shock, that the ex-governor's closing remarks would turn into an open accusation of Roland's old foe.

In a voice heavy with disdain, Black began with a description of Cornish's checkered past: the adulteries that had led his wife to divorce him, and his affair with the Chicago woman, Mrs. Small, which ended in her reported death from an abortion.

"And what does Cornish do then?" asked Black. "He comes to New York and immediately hunts up Mrs. Rodgers. He says in his testimony that Mrs. Rodgers was then living with her husband. But what happens? Why, Mr. Rodgers suddenly disappears and institutes divorce proceedings, and Cornish goes to live on Eighty-fourth Street, on one side of Columbus Avenue, while on the other side Mrs. Rodgers resides. After that, they moved to the flat at Sixty-sixth Street and Park Avenue, and there Mrs. Rodgers and Cornish were in the same house, the same flat. From that minute in September 1898, until last September, fifteen days before this trial was begun, Mrs. Rodgers and Cornish have always lived in the same house."

And what about the murder victim herself, the "good, kind, honest old woman," Mrs. Adams? "Do you believe this old mother would sit by complacent while these things were happening under her eyes?" asked

Black. "That she looked upon Cornish's relations with her daughter with favor? No! From the moment Cornish came to New York, the trail of this creature was on the track of Mrs. Adams and her daughter. Would she let that viper into her home without protest? Would she let them be together if she could prevent them?"

Here at last—in Mrs. Adams's ostensible objection to Cornish's affair with her daughter—Black had come to the "secret, stealthy motive for this crime—the secret, consuming fire that burned into murderous hate."

"Remember, gentlemen," said Black, his voice ringing with indignation, his language growing increasingly colorful, if not positively lurid. "Passion of this kind is the thing that has disrupted kingdoms. It is the greatest force in all the things of this world. Trouble with the management of a circus? Trouble with a horizontal bar? Hah! *Here* is a motive which compared with these is as the vomiting of the volcano of St. Martinique compared with the soft rising of the tide at the base of the Statue of Liberty! The passion that actuated Cornish is stronger than any other motive that could be assigned for murder. When that passion rages, it violates all vows! It burns virtue and honesty like the raging fire that destroys the grass of the prairie! Not a motive to kill this old lady? Why, it was she who sought to protect her daughter. She watched over her until this man, spotted with the slime of immorality, crept into her home. No motive, you say? *There* is your motive!"

While Cornish himself, seated up front between his elderly parents, barked out a contemptuous laugh, Black continued with his assault. Had the prosecution been allowed to introduce testimony relating to Henry Barnet's death, of course, his argument would have seemed far less persuasive. Only one man, after all, had a motive for killing Barnet, and it wasn't Harry Cornish. As matters stood, however, there was a superficial plausibility to Black's accusations.

He cited Emma Miller's claim that the man who purchased the toothpick holder had asked for one "that matched the silver toiletry articles on a lady's dresser." The holder, as the jurors had seen for themselves during the trial, had a "peculiar beaded pattern" that did, in fact, resemble the design on Mrs. Rodgers's toilet articles.

"Where is the living man except Cornish who knew it would match?" thundered Black.

And why, he asked, had Cornish brought the bottle of bromo-seltzer back to the apartment at all? "He testified that he never used bromo himself. Mrs. Rodgers said on the stand that she had never tasted bromo. And yet, he was so anxious to get it home that he broke open his desk to get it. Oh, yes, he got it home just in time. He knew that Mrs. Adams was subject to headaches, and twelve hours after the bromo reached the flat, Mrs. Adams had taken it. She was gone.

"Now there was nothing to stand in the way of that unlimited passion which burns cities and destroys empires!" Black said, his lip curled in disgust.

By this point, he had been speaking for more than four hours. It was nearly 3:00 P.M. before he brought his assault on Harry Cornish to an end.

"With all these circumstances pointing at Mr. Cornish, with every damning fact pointing at Mr. Cornish," said Black, "he has never up to this hour felt the tap of a policeman's hand on his shoulder, nor has he been for one single hour deprived of his liberty. Every single fact in this case points towards Cornish, and not a single fact connects Molineux with this case. It is not for you to say whether Cornish is guilty or not. I ask you only to say that Molineux is not guilty. The character and life of Roland B. Molineux must prevail against the weak and unworthy picture we have been shown of Harry S. Cornish."[3]

No sooner had Black taken his seat than prosecutor James Osborne arose and launched into his own closing statement. It would continue until adjournment and resume the following morning.

Black's blistering attack forced Osborne to devote much of his summation to a defense of Harry Cornish. He pointed out the absurdities and distortions in Black's accusations. Why, for example, would Cornish have concocted such an elaborate plan to do away with Mrs. Adams when "he had every day, hourly, opportunities to slip poison in her coffee?" Why, after tossing it in the wastebasket, would he have "let his friend Fineran persuade him to preserve the wrapper" with the potentially incriminating handwriting? Nothing in Cornish's actions—from his own sampling of the poison, to his immediate summoning of a physician, to his complete cooperation with investigators—was consistent with the behavior of a guilty man.

As for the scandalous insinuations about Cornish's relationship with Mrs. Rodgers, Osborne pointed out that the two were "cousins, first cousins," and that while they did indeed live under the same roof in a Manhattan boardinghouse, Cornish actually shared a room there with Florence Rodgers's older brother, Howard.

His ultimate argument, however—hardly flattering to the man he sought to defend—was that Cornish simply wasn't clever enough to be the killer. To concoct such a diabolical scheme required "a man of intellectuality, of cunning," said Osborne. "Now I ask you, can you make a poisoner out of that material such as Cornish?"

No, Osborne said to the jurors, the accusations hurled against Cornish were simply Black's desperate effort "to cloud your minds." The proof was overwhelming that Molineux—here he turned and jabbed a finger in Roland's direction—was the guilty man.

Hamstrung by his inability to refer to the Barnet murder, Osborne did his best to address the issue of motive, insisting that—far from having put his quarrels with Cornish behind him—Molineux, as the evidence proved, continued to brood about the athletic director, until his "jealousy and bitterness crystallized into action." He refuted Black's assertion about the easy availability of cyanide of mercury, insisting that no one but a chemist would know how to obtain, or concoct, such an uncommon poison. He dwelt on the testimony of several cashiers at Roland's bank, who had identified the handwriting on the poison wrapper as consistent with Molineux's signature.

"I say to you," Osborne concluded, "that the prosecution bears no malice toward this defendant. But it asks you not to swerve from your duty. You are compelled to give the defendant the benefit of your doubt. But we ask you not to be timid, not to shrink because of your natural indisposition to cause harm to a fellow being.

"If you do," he said, his voice rising to a thunderous level, "all through your life you will hear that still small voice of conscience taunting you: 'Coward, coward, coward!' "[4]

It was a few minutes past noon, Tuesday, November 11, when an exhausted Osborne sat down. Judge Lambert then called a lunch recess. When court resumed at one-fifteen, Lambert immediately launched into his charge, which lasted two hours. At 3:14 P.M., the jury retired.

Thirteen minutes later, they were back.

87

Seated between his youngest and eldest sons, Cecil and Leslie, General Molineux nervously scanned the faces of the jurors as the twelve men resumed their places. For the first time, the stoic old soldier seemed overcome with anxiety. His face twitched, he tugged at his white goatee and rubbed his balding dome. He could not remain still for an instant.

To judge from their grave expressions, there was cause for concern. Not one of the jurors would meet Roland's eyes. All kept their gazes on the floor.

The excited buzz that had filled the courtroom when the jurors reentered had subsided into a tense, protracted silence, which was finally broken by Judge Lambert.

"Upon rendition of this verdict," he cautioned, "every person is forbidden to make any demonstration of approval or disapproval. Any person disregarding this admonition will be promptly brought to this bar and punished. When this verdict is rendered, I wish every person to disperse quietly."

At that, the clerk addressed the jurors.

"Please rise, gentlemen," he said, then turned to Roland. "The defendant will rise. Jurors, look upon the prisoner. Prisoner, look upon the jurors."

Molineux shot to his feet and stood so rigidly erect that he appeared to be "almost on tiptoe."[1] He stared hard at the jurors, but though all twelve men had turned in his direction, they seemed to be looking past him.

"Gentlemen of the jury, have you agreed upon a verdict?" asked the clerk.

"We have," replied the foreman, gazing down at the floor.

"What say you, guilty or not guilty as charged in the indictment?"

He seemed to hesitate for a moment before answering: "Not guilty."

Seated beside General Molineux, his business partner, Mr. Devoe, let out an excited yelp and threw out his hands so wildly that he struck the General in the face. But the old man never noticed. Leaping from his chair, he grabbed his boy's hand and held it tightly, while Bartow Weeks leaned forward from his seat and seized Roland's other hand.[2]

Roland—still standing as "erect as a West Point cadet on parade"—showed no reaction at first. All at once, a radiant smile "broadened his prison-pale cheeks and deepened the dimple in his chin," and his eyes danced with happiness.

Intent upon obeying the formalities, the clerk addressed the jurors. "So say you all?" he asked.

The twelve men nodded gravely, then resumed their seats while—in defiance of Judge Lambert's warning—the crowd went wild.

Men cheered and tossed their hats in the air, women clapped and squealed, and a small mob of both sexes surged toward Roland, who was already surrounded by his lawyers, brothers, friends, and other well-wishers. The scene, wrote one reporter, "resembled a football rush." Everyone wanted to shake his hand or (in the case of more than one of his fashionably attired female fans) embrace him.

The heartiest congratulations, however, were reserved for the General; "the old warrior had spent all the savings of a lifetime, given all the energy of the last years of a long and honorable career to the defense of his son." For every handshake Roland received, his father seemed to receive three or four.

The celebration went on for five full minutes before the pounding of Judge Lambert's gavel and the shouts of the court officers restored order to the chaotic scene.

Addressing the district attorney, Lambert asked if there was "any further charge against this defendant."

"There is not," said the DA.

"Then," said the judge, "I declare the defendant discharged."

As the tumult around Roland resumed, jurors filed from the courtroom. Passing a dejected-looking James Osborne, several of them offered consoling remarks.

"We had to go against you," said Foreman Young, "but you went down with flying colors."[3]

Harry Cornish, on learning of the verdict, bitterly declared his belief that the outcome was inevitable, given Judge Lambert's obvious bias. "I want to congratulate the judge on his defense of the accused," he said with heavy sarcasm.[4]

Meanwhile, at the front of the courtroom, the General was besieged by reporters. What were his emotions when he heard the verdict? "Here, give me a pencil and a slip of paper," said the General, "and I will write down just what I feel."

Someone handed him the items and the old man, leaning down to the nearest table, quickly scribbled two lines. They appeared on the front pages the following day—a paraphrase of a famous hymn:

> The strife is o'er, the battle done,
> And Might has lost but Right has won.[5]

As Roland, his father, and their supporters left the courtroom, they were greeted by a deafening yell. The upper floors of the building, which "looked down upon the main hall like so many balconies in the opera house," were thronged with cheering people.

Out on the street, an even more massive crowd burst into a "tremendous wave of applause" at their first glimpse of Roland and the General. People in passing trolley cars waved handkerchiefs from the windows, while, on the fire escapes of the nearby tenements, women and children joined in the general rejoicing.

A few moments later, a closed carriage drew up before the courthouse, and Roland, his father, Bartow Weeks, and George Gordon Battle climbed aboard. Immediately, the crowd closed around it. People reached inside the open windows, attempting to grab Roland's hand, and a few men actually tried to jump inside before the door was yanked shut and secured.

As the driver applied his whip, a squad of several dozen policemen struggled to clear a way through the crowd. Several hundred men and boys pursued the carriage, cheering all the while. At every corner, more people joined the procession. By the time the carriage reached the entrance to the Brooklyn Bridge, an estimated fifteen hundred people followed in its wake.

On the Brooklyn side, the carriage clattered up Fulton Street and past Borough Hall, where another five hundred people had assembled. Roland leaned out the window and waved his hat in response to the cheering mob.

By the time the carriage approached Roland's home, the news had reached Fort Greene Place. Every stoop was lined with men, women, and children. Every open window seemed to frame an excited face. As the police cleared a path on the packed street, the carriage drew up in front of the Molineux residence. Roland was the first out, his father close behind him.

"Three cheers for Roland Molineux!" someone shouted, and the crowd let out a roar.

Roland took off his hat and bowed. Suddenly, the front door opened and his elderly mother, wearing a plain linen cap, stood in the entranceway.

Bounding up the steps, Roland took her in his arms.

"My boy!" she cried, hugging him.

A reverential silence descended on the crowd, as Roland and his mother held their embrace for a full minute. By the time they parted, the General had joined them at the top of the stairs.

"Well, Mother," he said. "I have kept my word. I told you I would bring the boy home."

As Roland and his mother disappeared inside the house, the General turned to the crowd.

"Three cheers for General Molineux, the best father that ever lived!" came another shout. The jubilation that erupted was "such as was never heard in quiet old-fashioned Fort Greene Place." A street band suddenly materialized and struck up a rousing rendition of "Won't You Come Home, Bill Bailey?"[6]

Glowing with happiness—looking "as though he had grown twenty-five years younger in a day"—the General bowed right and left. The sheer intensity of the outpouring confirmed a belief that many commentators would assert for years to come: that "Roland Burnham Molineux was indicted and tried for murder and General Edward Leslie Molineux was acquitted."[7]

Little by little, the crowd dispersed, leaving the Molineuxs to enjoy their reunion in private. But at least one observer had noticed something odd. There appeared to be "one member of the family who was not there to greet Molineux upon his dramatic homecoming," wrote the reporter for the *Brooklyn Eagle*.

"It was his wife."[8]

88

Though most of the crowd had long since dispersed, a dozen or so newsmen were still congregated outside the Molineux home when, at around 6:00 P.M., the front door opened and George Gordon Battle emerged. He was immediately surrounded by the reporters, who bombarded him with questions. The ever-gracious Battle took a moment to explain that, at the family's request, he was on his way to the Murray Hill Hotel to escort Roland's wife home. A moment later, he had boarded a waiting carriage and was gone.[1]

By the time he arrived at the door of her suite, Blanche had already heard the news. Entering, he announced with a smile, "Roland is free."

From her seat in the parlor, Blanche merely looked at him, her face taut. Battle was no fool. He had known for a long time where matters stood between Blanche and her husband.

"You needn't tell me—I think I know," he said as her silence continued. "I appreciate how hard it's been for you. But you must go on a bit longer."

When Blanche finally spoke, there was such bitterness in her voice that even she felt "as though it came from another's throat." "Their son is returned to them. They have him. They don't need me any longer."

Battle's tone was pure gentle persuasion. "But you're wrong. They do need you. It's imperative that you should be in the General's home at this time. You can see why. The newspapers will blow it into a tremendous sensation if they learn you have not rejoined the family."

Blanche struggled to control the emotions that threatened to engulf her: anger, resentment, despair. Nowhere among them was the slightest pleasure or relief at Roland's acquittal.

"Oh, can't I have my own life now?" she cried. "Or what's left of it?"

"But think of the old General," Battle urged.

Blanche was sobbing now. "I don't want to hurt him," she managed to say. "Only please, don't ask me to go back. Let me go away!"[2]

But Battle persisted until, regaining a measure of control, Blanche made herself ready and allowed herself to be led down to the carriage. Throughout the drive to Brooklyn, she stared blankly out the window. She felt, as she would record in her memoirs, "quite dead."

Beside her on the cushion lay a large bouquet of American Beauty roses. Battle had purchased them from a florist's shop, so that Blanche would have something to present to Roland when she saw him—a token of her joy at their reunion.[3]

When the coach drew up at 117 Fort Greene Place, Blanche—handsomely dressed in a big feathered hat, dove-colored shirtwaist, black skirt, with a boa around her neck[4]—stepped onto the sidewalk and, ignoring the shouted questions of the newsmen, ran up the high stoop. Battle followed at her heels. In the excitement of the moment, he did not see that, either by accident or design, she had left the roses behind. By the time he noticed, the coach had already driven away.[5]

The front door was opened by the General, who held out his arms in welcome. Blanche, however, was so eager to see her husband that she rushed past her father-in-law and into the front parlor. At the sight of her, Roland—who had been seated in a chair reading congratulatory telegrams—sprang to his feet and the pair flew into each other's arms. They spent the next several hours in loving communion behind the closed doors of the parlor, while the rest of the family left them discreetly alone.

That, at any rate, was the account that appeared in the next day's newspapers.[6] Blanche's memoirs tell a different story.

Upon entering the Molineux home—her "dead heart carried inside me"—she strode directly "through the high ceilinged and paneled halls" and, without so much as a word to Roland or any other member of the family, proceeded straight "upstairs to my former sleeping chamber."

Removing her wraps and hat but otherwise remaining fully clothed, she sank into an easy chair beside a window. From below stairs, voices floated up to her. "Roland was there with his family. The world believed I was lying in his arms. Yet I sat in my room alone, all night."

By the time the "first faint streak of gray light" showed in the east, she had made her final decision. Moving to the desk, she took a sheet of stationery from a leather portfolio and began a letter.

It was addressed, not to her husband, but to the General. In it, she described "the slow death that had left me numb and cold. I wrote him of my hopes for their happiness, of my love and respect for himself, and my prayer that God would bless him."

As for his son, "I left no word for him"—though she did not fail to deliver an eloquent message.

After sealing the letter with wax, she placed it on the mahogany table. Then she pulled off her wedding ring and set it on top of her farewell note.[7]

When the sun had fully risen, Blanche snuck downstairs and boarded a carriage that took her back to Manhattan.

She never saw Roland Molineux again.

Part Seven

AFTERMATH

89

he story broke on Tuesday, November 18, exactly one week after Roland's acquittal: MRS. MOLINEUX SEEKS A DAKOTA DIVORCE.

The morning after absconding from the Molineux home, Blanche had boarded a train at Grand Central Station and decamped for Sioux Falls, South Dakota—in those days, the quickie-divorce capital of the USA (a position later assumed by Reno, Nevada). She took a room in the Cataract Hotel, the most luxurious lodging in town, though hardly princely in comparison with the accommodations she had enjoyed in Murray Hill. One newspaper described it as "a rather sordid habitation, filled with ill-mannered men and chemically complexioned women seeking the same end as Mrs. Molineux."[1]

Given the nationwide notoriety of the Molineux case, her presence generated a great deal of excitement in the little town. For the most part, Blanche kept a low profile. Despite early reports that she planned to hire "an automobile and make extensive sightseeing trips throughout the surrounding country," she spent most of her time "immured in her modest apartment, reading bundles of New York newspapers, writing, and glancing over the magazines."[2]

As soon as her whereabouts became known, reporters descended on Sioux Falls. For the first time, she openly admitted what many had long suspected: that "her apparent loyalty and love for her husband were all for appearances' sake."

"For four years I have been waiting, living in an agony, to see what would be done with that man," she declared in her first published interview. "Now it's all over and I want to rest. I made myself a martyr for the sake of General Molineux. I love the General, and for his sake I buried myself for four years. There is not another member of his family that I would have done so much for. I promised him I would wait until he had done all possible to save that man."[3]

Her plan, she explained, was to remain in Sioux Falls for the six months required to establish legal residency. She would then promptly file for divorce. She had already engaged a local firm, Kittredge, Kinans & Scott, to represent her. The grounds for the suit would be extreme mental cruelty.[4]

Informed of her statement by reporters back in Brooklyn, General Molineux—for the first time since the long ordeal had begun—became "speechless with rage." It was not until the following morning that he could bring himself to speak about his daughter-in-law. Even then he had little to say, though his tone left no doubt that he viewed her desertion of Roland as an act of the rankest treachery.

"I'm not going to talk about this matter until I see my lawyer," he said. "So far as I can see, the only thing she has against her husband is that he was in prison for four years and she was deprived of some pleasure and enjoyment in that time.

"So she refers to my son as 'that man,' does she?" he continued bitterly. "Well, I have always referred to her as 'that lady.' She has had the first say in this matter. Perhaps she will have the last word—and perhaps not."[5]

For a while, there was talk that Roland might contest the divorce. In the end, however, he chose to let the matter go. By the following September, Blanche was a free woman.

Less than two months later, she married again. Her new husband was Wallace D. Scott—the young attorney who had handled her divorce.[6]

Just a few weeks after her marriage, Blanche—intent on pursuing her aborted stage career—traveled to New York City for a meeting with representatives of vaudeville producer F. F. Proctor. On November 15, 1903, *The New York Times* reported that she had signed a contract for the unprecedented sum of $1,000 per week to perform at Proctor's flagship theater on Twenty-third Street. She would sing "twice daily and also at the Sunday concerts," beginning on Monday, November 23.

The article noted that Blanche was known to possess "a cultivated contralto voice of such quality that it was once praised by Madame Melba."[7] Even Blanche, however, understood that Proctor was counting on her notoriety, not her singing voice, to pull in the crowds. To make sure no one missed the point, the ads for her engagement billed her as "Blanche Molineux Scott."

Neither Blanche nor Proctor, however, had reckoned on the General, who let it be known that he would seek an immediate restraining order to prevent his proud family name from being sullied in such a fashion. The threat was sufficient. Even before she could debut, her contract was canceled and Blanche was soon on her way back to Sioux Falls.[8]

Blanche wasn't the only person to try to capitalize on the Molineux case. As early as 1899, a writer named Randall Irving Tyler had dashed off a book called *The Blind Goddess*—a potboiler that anticipates by a hundred years those TV melodramas whose plotlines are "ripped from the headlines."

The novel involves a statuesque beauty named Helen Brownell, who receives a mysterious gift from an anonymous sender: a Tiffany box containing an expensive "holder with a socket resembling a candlestick" and "a bottle of effervescent headache powder." That very night, while Helen attends a dinner party, her father and a friend named David West—both suffering from mild headaches—sample the medicine and immediately drop dead. The book features many other elements drawn from the Molineux affair, including a lengthy coroner's inquest, private letter boxes, handwriting experts, and an unscrupulous press that "found in the Brownell poisoning case material for the greatest sensation the city had known."[9]

An even trashier piece of pop exploitation appeared less than a month after Roland's acquittal. On December 2, 1902, a preposterously contrived stage melodrama, *The Great Poison Mystery* by one Victor C. Calvert, opened in a theater in Jersey City before making its New York premiere one week later at Blaney's Theater on Driggs Avenue, Williamsburg.

The play makes not the slightest effort to disguise its real-life inspiration. On the contrary, the names of its principal characters are—as one reviewer put it—"libelously like the names of the people they are meant to represent."[10] The dramatis personae consist of a young chemist named Robert Milando and his father, General Milando; Robert's fiancée, Blanche Marlboro; his archenemy, Harrison Cornwall, athletic director of the Metropolitan Sporting Club; Cornwall's elderly aunt, Mrs. Adamson, who dies when she drinks a glass of headache powder spiked with cyanide of mercury; and assorted subsidiary figures, including Assistant District Attorney James Osgood and ex-governor Blackstone, chief counsel for the defense.[11]

Decried by critics as a "ridiculous paraphrase of the famous murder case," Calvert's play presents Milando as an innocent victim, framed by the villainous Cornwall—a character so one-dimensional as to make Snidely Whiplash seem like Iago. Constantly uttering cackling asides ("I have an idea—a brilliant idea, Robert Milando, and it means your ruin!" "Ha! Ha! Never shall she be his bride!"), Cornwall, as one reviewer reported, comes off as so "ridiculously comical" that the first-night audience could not even bring itself to hiss him. All "he got was a continuous roar of hilarious guffaws."[12]

Though *The New York Times* praised the "thrilling climax"—in which Cornwall, reaping his just rewards, plunges to his death from the newly erected East River Bridge—other papers were merciless in their derision ("when the curtain fell, everyone in the audience cheered—because the play was over"). Calvert's play had a deservedly brief run, closing before it reached Broadway.[13]

For hacks like Tyler and Calvert, the Molineux affair was simply a ripe subject for commercial exploitation. But to another American writer, one of our country's greatest novelists, it seemed powerfully emblematic, a story with the potential to be transformed into great tragic art.

Theodore Dreiser was just putting the finishing touches on his scandalous first novel, *Sister Carrie*, when the Molineux story broke. Obsessed with themes of lust, money, and power, the young author was determined to write a book dealing with what he regarded as a peculiarly American brand of crime: a murder committed by a young man whose lethal act is sparked by an explosive mix of sexual hunger and social ambition. In the Molineux case, Dreiser felt he had found the perfect real-life basis for such a tale and began to compile a research file, composed largely of clippings from the *World*, along with painstakingly transcribed copies of other newspaper accounts.[14]

Years would pass before he began work on the manuscript, which he titled *The "Rake."*[15] Its protagonist is young Anstey Bellinger (a name Dreiser took from the real-life Alice Bellinger, Blanche's friend and landlady). The son of a revered Civil War hero, Colonel Bellinger (a "dapper little man" of "Spartan" mettle), Anstey possesses many of Roland Molineux's traits. He works as a chemist and color maker; is a singular combination of dandy and champion athlete; engages in sexual dalliances with factory girls; falls in love with one Celeste Martzo, "a girl of rare beauty but of a very nebulous character"; and belongs to an exclusive Manhattan athletic club whose physical director, Victor Quimby, bears more than a passing resemblance to Harry Cornish ("His eyes were of a steely gray-blue, fixed and steady, not unlike those of a bull-dog, his hair was brown but a little thin above the forehead, his chin full, pugnacious, thick, like the broad end of an egg.")[16]

After producing seven rough-draft chapters, however, Dreiser abandoned the project. In the end, he "had trouble reconciling the Molineux crime with the kind of murder he wanted to portray." What Dreiser wanted was a case involving "a young man whose social ambitions lead to murder." To be sure, Roland Molineux was not lacking in social pretensions. Ultimately, however, he was too upper middle class—not enough of an outsider—to suit Dreiser's fictional needs.[17]

Four years after Roland's acquittal, a young man named Chester Gillette drowned his pregnant girlfriend, Grace Brown, in an Adirondacks lake. It was the ideal crime for Dreiser's purposes, and from it he would forge his masterpiece, *An American Tragedy*.[18]

On the evening of Friday, January 9, 1903, just two months after Roland's acquittal, General Molineux, his wife, and his son Cecil went into Manhattan to dine with friends. At around 10:30 P.M., they started for home. There was a trolley stop not far from their friends' home, at Broadway and Eleventh, right in front of the St. Denis Hotel. The night was clear but piercingly cold. Taking refuge in the entranceway to the hotel, the Molineuxs waited for the trolley to arrive.

When it finally pulled up a few minutes later, the General assisted his wife onto the car. Cecil boarded next. The General had just placed his foot on the step and begun to mount the trolley when the conductor rang the bell, and the car started forward with a violent jerk.

The sudden motion caused the General to lose his footing and fall from the car. Reflexively holding on to the hand bar, he was dragged along the street.

Cecil, looking around and seeing that his father was not behind him, shouted for the conductor to stop, but the trolley continued another full block before coming to a halt. By then, the General had released his grip and was lying in the middle of Broadway, a crowd already gathering around him.

Cecil leapt from the car, followed closely by his mother. By the time they reached him, the General—protesting that he was all right—was attempting to get to his feet with the help of several bystanders. He was loaded into a cab and driven home, where the family physician was immediately summoned. According to the news accounts that appeared the following day, one of the old man's "kneecaps was badly injured and several of his ribs were crushed in."[19]

It took him months to recuperate. The following October, he was still not well enough to attend the seventieth-birthday celebration given in his honor by his old comrades from the 159th Brigade. Cecil and Leslie were there on their father's behalf to accept the various tributes, which included a handsome floral shield of chrysanthemums, roses, and lilies of the valley (meant to symbolize the General's role as a "shield for the preservation of his country's honor" during wartime) and a commemorative tablet consisting of a framed photographic portrait of the General and a Maltese cross inscribed with the names of the battles in which he had distinguished himself.[20]

The old man, however, was nothing if not resilient. By February 1904, he was well enough to perform yet another act of heroism, when a gas pipe broke in the Devoe & Raynolds paint factory and the General—who was working in his office at the time—led a rescue party down into the cellar to save several unconscious workers.[21] In succeeding years, each of his birthdays was celebrated by his (progressively dwindling) band of former comrades, who would arrive at his Fort Greene Place home with floral tributes, speeches, and occasional poems:

And on your shield, my gallant Ned
(I claim the right to speak)
Shall ever shine in letters gold
The name of Cedar Creek,
And history will ever enshrine,
While ages come and go,
With that unique and brilliant fight,
The name of Molineux![22]

The newspapers, too, took note of his birthdays. In October 1912, when Admiral George Dewey turned seventy-five, the *New York World*, in an editorial headlined A HERO OF THE REPUBLIC, reminded its readers "that there are other distinguished men living in the past who have served the Republic splendidly.

"Of these," the editorial continued,

> it may be safely said, none hold a higher place in the public esteem than General Edward L. Molineux, who has just reached his seventy-ninth year. With the details of General Molineux's career in the Civil War our readers are familiar. That career is part of the History of the United States. It shows that patriotism is capable, when emergency arises, of performing deeds of great valor, and that, too, from the loftiest motive. We know of no man whose life affords greater inspiration or a better example than that of General Molineux. That life is replete with honor and distinction, of triumph over difficulties and a stern adherence to high ideals worthy of the sincerest admiration.[23]

It seemed that, after a life filled with such tumult and strife, the General would finally enjoy the serene and honored old age he deserved.

But fate—in the form of his erratic son, Roland—wasn't done with him yet.

Following his release from prison, Roland set about trying to readjust to life as he had known it before his arrest. He joined a gym in Brooklyn Heights in an effort "to recover his old skill and activity as a gymnast."

Within two weeks, he was "able to do some of his old stunts on the horizontal bar," albeit "not with his former vim and vigor."[24] At the General's urging, he also returned to his work as a chemist, this time in his father's paint factory, putting his color-making skills to use in the laboratory.

His true ambition, however—developed during his years behind bars—was to become a man of letters.

In January 1903, just a few months after his acquittal, the New York City publishing firm F. W. Dillingham brought out his first book, *The Room with the Little Door.* Dedicated "To My Father General Edward Leslie Molineux, with Reverence," the volume is a hodgepodge of sketches, poems, and ruminations about life in both the Tombs and the Sing Sing Death House. The reviews were less than glowing. The *World* damned the book with faint praise, describing it as "not lacking in such literary merit as lies in the simplest possible telling."[25] And while the critic for the *Times* conceded that it contained "certain touches of humor," as well as a degree of "unforced pathos," his final judgment was withering. In the end, he declared, "the book reveals nothing new touching prison, can serve no purpose (unless its sales are large enough to put money in its author's pocket), and one cannot help but wishing it had never been written."[26]

Undaunted, Roland turned his hand to fiction. The following September saw the publication of his novel, *The Vice Admiral of the Blue.* At a time when authors such as James, Twain, Dreiser, and Crane were producing some of the masterworks of American realism, Roland's tome—the supposed late-life memoirs of Lord Horatio Nelson's close friend Thomas Masterman Hardy—is a hopelessly overwrought bodice ripper, featuring the usual cast of Victorian stereotypes, from mustachio-twirling villains to bosom-heaving damsels in distress. ("He clasped her once more in his arms, once more lingeringly kissed her, once more whispered to her, 'I love you!' Then, pressing a handkerchief to the mouth he had just touched so fiercely with his own, he carried her through the secret doorway into the gloom beyond. As he did so, the drooping limbs and closed eyes told him that she had fainted!")[27]

In addition to this fluff, he devoted himself to more serious matters, especially the cause of penal reform. Allying himself with famed social crusader Kate Bernard, Roland published a pamphlet urging the creation of "Courts of Rehabilitation": tribunals that would vote to release a convict from prison only when he gave convincing proof of rehabilitation.

Such a system, Roland argued, would serve society far better than the current method of predetermined sentences, which did nothing to encourage criminals to reform.[28]

As an author, however, Roland achieved his greatest success in the field of playwriting. As far back as 1903, he had taken a stab at drama, composing a one-act play, *Was It a Dream?* that had a short run at Proctor's Twenty-third Street theater in March of that year. An insipid fantasy about socially mismatched young lovers who are finally able to wed thanks to the help of a crystal ball, the play was dismissed by the reviewer for the *Times* as a "mediocrity" whose "characters talk a good deal but say little that is of interest to anyone save themselves."[29]

Roland persisted, however, and by 1912 had turned out a full-length drama, *The Man Inside.* That year, Roland's parents, through the intervention of friends, obtained an interview with Broadway impresario David Belasco, who recalled the meeting in his memoirs:

> His mother said to me, "My boy's life has been ruined. His health is gone—he has never been the same since he was released from prison. He has written a play which he believes will do great good, and he has set his heart on getting it acted. If he is disappointed in this, on top of all the rest that he has suffered, we fear that he will die. If his play should be a success, it might open a new life to him. Will you read it and help us if you can?"

Belasco, who "had been tremendously impressed by General Molineux's great fight for his son," agreed to read the play and produce it, "if practicable."

When the manuscript arrived, Belasco found it "long and crude, but I saw possibilities in it and told the parents I would produce it. Their gratitude was very touching. Soon afterward, I met young Molineux, gave him several interviews and went to work to knock his play into shape."[30]

The two continued to work on the play throughout the summer and into the early fall of 1913. On Saturday, November 8, three days before its scheduled premiere, Roland, then forty-seven years old, hastily wed a pretty twenty-eight-year-old play broker named Margaret Connell at City Hall, explaining to reporters that "his mother was dying and that it was her wish that the marriage should take place at once."

By a bizarre coincidence, the deputy clerk who issued the license was none other than Edward Hart—the onetime coroner who had presided at the inquest into Katherine Adams's death more than a decade earlier. Partly as a result of his perceived mishandling of the Molineux affair, Hart had been removed from the coroner's office and was now a lowly functionary in the Marriage License Bureau. Apart from exchanging the few perfunctory words necessary to complete the transaction, both he and Roland did their best to ignore each other during their unexpected reunion.[31]

The Man Inside debuted at the Criterion Theater on Monday, November 10, 1913. Judging from its title, critics expected it to be a frank, even shocking exposé based on the author's personal experience as an inmate of the Sing Sing Death House. What they saw instead was a contrived melodrama about a handsome young district attorney named Richard Gordon who—intent on plumbing the criminal mind—descends into the urban underworld where he falls in love with the beautiful daughter of a small-time crook. Periodically, the action comes to a dead halt so that the hero can deliver a long speech about penal reform.

The reviews were not kind. Though the *Times* praised the grittily realistic sets and "exceptional cast" and conceded that there was a "certain suspensive interest to the proceedings," the paper dismissed the play as hopelessly didactic and predictable—"mere sentimental rubbish." It lasted only sixty-three performances, and its closing marked the end of Roland Molineux's literary career.[32]

By then, however, the failure of his play was the least of his problems.

Even while *The Man Inside* was in rehearsal, Belasco had noticed alarming changes in Roland's behavior. From a willing collaborator, he suddenly "turned sullen and very ugly," the producer wrote in his memoirs. "Sometimes, instead of working, he would sit and roll his eyes or glare at me; and, what was very dreadful, he gave off a horrible, sickening odor like that of a wild beast."

There soon came a point where Belasco began to fear for his safety:

> I shall never forget the last night I ever had with him. He was furious because of the changes I was making, and I am sure he was going to attack me. Suddenly, I stopped arguing with him and,

> picking up a heavy walking stick, I said: "See here, Molineux, stop looking at me like that; I'm not afraid of you. If you had brought me a finished play instead of a lot of words, I wouldn't have had to change your manuscript. Now it's hot and I'm tired, so we'll call the whole thing off for tonight, and you can go home and think it over." He pulled himself together then and tried to apologize and say how much he appreciated all I was doing, but I wouldn't have it and just showed him out of my studio as quickly as I could—and I took care *he* should walk in front of me all the way. There wasn't another soul in the place, except the night watchman, away down at the stagedoor. I never let him come near me again.[33]

Roland continued to deteriorate. During a dress rehearsal he was allowed to attend, he sat quietly and attentively through the first act. As soon as the curtain came down for intermission, however, Roland "became so violently excited and created so much disturbance" that Belasco had him forcibly ejected from the theater. "It was hard to do," the producer recalled, "but it had to be done. I really expected the man would break out and kill somebody."

By the time the play premiered in November 1913, Roland had been shipped off to a "rest farm" in Babylon, Long Island. According to a statement released by his family, he had suffered a nervous breakdown.

Ten months later, in the early morning hours of Sunday, September 6, 1914, Roland—still residing in the sanitarium—escaped into town. He was clad in a bathrobe and shirt but no trousers. As he ran madly down the main street of Babylon, several people stopped to watch him. Roland rushed up to one man, seized him by the arm, and began to shriek incoherently.

The man was so badly frightened that he shouted for help. His cries brought Constable Luke Devin running. At first, Roland appeared to calm down. Suddenly, "he flew into a screaming rage and struck out right and left." It took several men, including Devin and a burly youth named Ray De Garmo, to subdue him. Roland was finally bundled into a car, driven to the Babylon police station, and locked in a cell, where he hurled himself against the bars and jabbered wildly about lending money to the federal government. A few hours later he was arraigned on a charge of disorderly conduct.[34]

By Sunday afternoon, Dr. W. J. Cruikshank, the Molineux family physician, and a Brooklyn psychiatrist (or "alienist," in the jargon of the day) named Arthur C. Brush had been dispatched to Babylon. After interviewing Roland in his cell, they pronounced him insane. "Roland Molineux, defendant in one of the most sensational murder cases this country has ever known," reported the *World*, "is a raving maniac."[35]

The following morning, Roland's father, older brother, and new wife, Margaret, traveled out to Babylon, where—along with doctors Cruikshank and Brush and the family lawyer, Hugo Hirsh—they met with a judge named Nicoll. The disorderly conduct charge was dropped, and—deemed "a person dangerous to be at large"—Roland was committed to the State Hospital for the Insane at King's Park, Long Island.

As Roland—still raving about his stupendous wealth—was placed in a motorcar and driven off to the asylum, General Molineux wept openly. For the first time in his life, the old man, according to one observer, seemed "broken."[36]

Less than one year later, on the evening of Thursday, June 10, 1915, General E. L. Molineux—just a few months shy of his eighty-second birthday—died of complications following surgery at the Roosevelt Hospital. Until he went into the hospital, he was at his office every day, actively attending to business. "So he may be said to have died in the harness of daily duty," wrote one of his many eulogists, "a departure doubtless suited to his indomitable military spirit."[37]

His will, like every other document he put his hand to, speaks loudly of the man's fundamental decency—of that unwavering sense of rectitude that, with the advent of the modern era, was already an anachronism.

It is a simple, straightforward document, barely three typed pages long. The first provisions are charitable bequests, offered in memory of his "beloved wife, Harriet," who had died in February 1914: one to St. Mary's Roman Catholic Church; one to the Brooklyn Home for Blind, Crippled, and Defective Children; the third—and largest—to the Jewish Hospital of Brooklyn.[38] There are also several donations, made in his own name, to his beloved veterans' organizations "for the benefit of needy members."

The bulk of his estate—or what was left of it after the financial toll exacted by his four-year defense of Roland—was divided equally among Leslie, Cecil, and Roland's wife, Margaret, "by her to be used for the maintenance of herself, my said son Roland B. Molineux, and any child that may be born" to them.

The General left another, equally revealing document—a handwritten note, inscribed on Devoe & Raynolds Company letterhead, declaring his "personal desire that my funeral be very simple and without any ceremony except that of a Christian burial." He gives two reasons for his wish, both reflecting his characteristic concern for the welfare of others. First, "funerals of a public character would take hard-earned wages from employees of all sorts by loss of time." Second, such elaborate ceremonies often prove a strain on "feeble and aged persons"—like the General's much-reduced band of Civil War brethren—leading to "subsequent illness and distress."

"I believe I have quite a number of friends, faithful and true," the letter ends, "and I want to remain where I am now—in their hearts—while my body will be resting under a simple and small Cross with the short inscription:

EDWARD L MOLINEUX
A VOLUNTEER OF 1861–5.
"PEACE & GOOD WILL TO ALL."[39]

In accordance with his wishes, the General was given a funeral "of the simplest kind." At 2:00 P.M. on Sunday, June 13, his casket was borne to the First Presbyterian Church on Henry Street in Brooklyn Heights, where the Reverend L. Mason Clarke read from the Scriptures and offered prayer. No eulogy was given. A quartet sang two of the General's favorite hymns. Then a bugler blew taps.

Afterward, the casket was taken to Scarsdale, New York, for burial beside the grave of the General's wife in the churchyard of St. James the Less.[40]

Every paper in the city ran a worshipful obituary of the "great soldier and great man." Nearly all limited themselves to a description of his brilliant military career and subsequent life in business and politics.

Only one editorialist, in referring to the crime that had riveted the nation fifteen years earlier, conveyed the sense of pity and consternation that so many people had felt throughout the General's long ordeal. "That tragedy should have come to such a man in the struggle to save his son, Roland B. Molineux, from a charge of murder, was one of the freaks of fate."[41]

Just two and a half years later, on November 2, 1917, Roland B. Molineux, age fifty-one, followed his father to the grave.

At the time of his commitment to the insane asylum, newspapers had attributed his mental collapse to strains brought by "overwork on his play recently produced by David Belasco."[42] The autopsy told a far more sordid story.

Roland, according to his death certificate, had died of "syphilitic infection." His descent into insanity had been a consequence of that insidious disease. Left untreated, syphilis leads to extreme neurological damage, known as general paresis. As the nerves of the brain deteriorate, the victim displays increasingly severe symptoms of abnormal mental functioning, including marked personality changes and impaired ethical judgment. Eventually, he (or she) succumbs to complete dementia.

Since paresis can take decades to develop after the initial infection, it is possible that the disease had already begun to work its devastating effects on Roland Molineux at the time of the murders of Henry Barnet and Katherine Adams. Certainly, the shattered health that his mother described to David Belasco—and that Belasco himself witnessed firsthand—was not, as she believed, the result of his imprisonment but of advanced untreated syphilis.[43]

Besides the "Molineux Rule"—still frequently invoked in New York State courtrooms—Roland's case produced other changes in the law, from the abolition of private letter boxes to a bill mandating that all medications containing toxic ingredients be sold in specially designed bottles.[44] But its most significant ramifications were cultural.

As the first media-driven crime circus of the twentieth century, it set the pattern for all the carnivalesque "trials of the century" to follow, from those of Leopold and Loeb and the Lindbergh baby kidnapper to that of O. J. Simpson. Hack works like *The Blind Goddess* and *The Great Poison*

Mystery were precursors of the instant books and made-for-TV movies that rush to exploit the public's fascination with the latest sensational crime. The general shamelessness that seems to characterize everyone associated with a notorious murderer nowadays—the former girlfriend who poses for *Playboy*, the sibling who quickly signs a contract for a tell-all book—was foreshadowed by Blanche's attempts to turn her notoriety into a vaudeville career. Roland's own efforts to cash in on his infamy—so strikingly at variance with his father's fiercely maintained sense of dignity and family honor—was a sign of the coming new era, when cheap celebrity, often based on scandal, would supplant traditional concepts of glory and hard-won fame.

Even the unbridled litigiousness of contemporary America—where stranded motorists sue the Samaritans who stop to help them and the morbidly obese bring action against their favorite restaurants for making them fat—was presaged by the Molineux case. Immediately after the end of Roland's first trial, Manheim Brown, the juror who had nearly derailed the proceedings after catching a cold, sued the city for fifty thousand dollars, claiming that his health had been ruined by the poor ventilation in the courtroom. For nearly thirty more years—long after Brown's death in 1913—his family carried on the fight. It was not until 1928—when the state legislature turned down a bill that would have given Brown's widow financial compensation—that the matter was finally dropped.[45]

Harry Cornish also sought redress through litigation. Not long after Roland's acquittal, he sued *The New York Times* for $30,000, claiming that at the height of the Molineux investigation in 1899, the paper had libelously identified him as a man who had purchased cyanide of mercury from a druggist in New Haven, Connecticut, thus "branding him as the murderer of Mrs. Adams or an accessory to the crime." In the end, however, Cornish was no more successful than Manheim Brown's widow. At a trial held before Justice W. S. Andrews in March 1904, the jury agreed with the defense that the article was "a legitimate news publication, fair to the plaintiff, and not of the character set forth in the complaint."[46]

Four years later, in May 1908, Cornish got remarried—not to Florence Rodgers, his alleged longtime lover, but to a thirty-six-year-old resident of Newark, New Jersey, named Mary M. Waite. At the time, Cornish gave his profession as "brass manufacturer." The news of the wedding did not become public until the middle of July.

Less than two weeks later, a sensational item appeared in papers on both coasts. CORNISH'S BODY FOUND IN BAY, read the headline. According to the story, the remains of a man had been found floating in the waters off Coney Island on the evening of July 27, 1908. The victim had a large gash in his head, apparently made with an ax. While "there was some conflicting evidence as to the identification of the body," the coroner was convinced that it was Harry Cornish. "It is thought," read the article, "that Cornish went on the bay in a yacht with a party and that while on the yacht the murder was committed."[47]

The coroner, however, was wrong. Though Cornish would vanish from public view, he wouldn't die for many years to come. He and his wife eventually moved to Los Angeles, where he worked as a mechanical engineer. He died of acute congestive failure in the Los Angeles County General Hospital on the afternoon of January 11, 1947, at the age of eighty-four.[48]

Blanche would outlive them all.

In 1905, after another unsuccessful stab at a singing career (this time under the name Blanche Chesebrough Scott), she and her husband, Wallace, moved to New York City.[49] Apart from an eighteen-month hiatus during which Blanche finally achieved her dream of traveling through Europe, they spent the next eight years in Manhattan before returning to Sioux Falls in 1913. By then, they had a son named Roger, whom Blanche—a decidedly indifferent mother—consistently referred to as "Boy."

In 1915, Wallace journeyed to Minneapolis to try a case and liked the city so well that he decided to stay. Shortly thereafter, Blanche sued him for divorce on the grounds of nonsupport. Their split, however, didn't last. In 1916, the divorce was legally vacated. For the next five years, Blanche and Wallace lived together in a big house on Minneapolis's Park Avenue, while "Boy" was shipped off to a boarding school on the East Coast.

Blanche's marriage to Wallace continued to be as tumultuous as ever, and in January 1921 she filed another petition for divorce. The papers claimed that he "struck, bruised, and choked [her], and that he has used towards her profane, indecent language, and called her many disreputable names . . . as a result thereof, her health has become affected, and her nervous system has been impaired, and to longer live with the defendant would endanger her life." Blanche sought monthly alimony payments of $250, a share of the household furnishings, and custody of their son. Before the divorce could be finalized, however, "Boy," then fifteen years old, contracted rheumatic fever and died.[50]

Blanche and Wallace were divorced for a second time in December 1921. Wallace briefly remarried, while Blanche decamped for New York City, where she lived with her older sister, Izcennia, by then also divorced. In 1926, however, Blanche and Wallace were reconciled once again. She returned to the big house in Minneapolis. For the next four years, they lived together in apparent harmony. In 1930, while returning from a business trip in St. Joseph, Missouri, Wallace was killed in an automobile accident in Iowa. "It may perhaps be said," a newspaper article commented at the time of her husband's death, "that Mrs. Scott has drained life's cup to the last bitter dreg."[51]

She would survive for nearly another quarter century—an increasingly grotesque-looking old woman who dyed her hair a garish red, wore clownish amounts of mascara and rouge, dressed in outlandishly youthful garments, and affected a flamboyantly "cultured" conversational style, heavily peppered with French phrases. Living in a succession of progressively shabby rented rooms, she relied for sustenance on welfare and a dwindling number of friends. She died alone in 1954 at the age of eighty—a relic of an age that, even for her, had long since passed into myth.

NOTES

So many newspapers covered the Molineux story (not only in New York but around the country), and the case went on for so long (four years from Katherine Adams's murder to Roland's acquittal), that, for the sake of completing my research and actually writing the book, I limited myself to five of the city's principal dailies—the *World*, the *Journal*, the *Herald*, the *Sun*, and the *Times*—plus the *Brooklyn Eagle*, which, because of the Molineux family's long association with Brooklyn, covered the case in great detail. Even so, I ended up with several thousand Xeroxed pages, most copied from microfilm machines at the main branch of the New York Public Library. (Thankfully, both the *Times* and the *Brooklyn Eagle* are available online.)

The *Eagle* also ran many articles on Edward Molineux's civic, political, and military activities, extending back to the 1860s. For information about his earlier years I relied entirely on documents—his journals, letters, etc.—in the possession of his great-grandson, Will Molineux.

Throughout the writing of the book I scrupulously avoided the New Journalistic techniques pioneered by Capote *et al*—inventing dialogue, imagining what people were thinking, fleshing out scenes with atmospheric touches, etc. The most novelistic portions of the book are those dealing with Blanche, but everything in them comes directly from her memoirs, provided to me by Jane Pejsa, whose mother, Irene Hauser, befriended Blanche in the last years of her life.

I have also refrained, in the body of the book, from offering a tidy answer to the question of Roland's innocence or guilt. Like the Lizzie Borden and O. J. Simpson cases, the Molineux affair will forever be marked by a degree of ambiguity. Crime buffs have been debating the matter for a century. Entries on Roland are routinely found in crime encyclopedias such as *The Mammoth Book of Murder* (New York: Carroll & Graf, 1989) and *The Greatest Criminals of All Time* (New York: Stein and Day, 1982), whose authors do not hesitate to rank him with the country's most notorious homicidal maniacs. On the other hand, there are those like George P. LeBrun—former New York City coroner and author of *It's Time to Tell* (New York: William Morrow, 1962)—who unequivocally assert Roland's innocence.

As for me, I've always been struck by the fact that, in the century following the slaughter of Andrew and Abby Borden, there were a number of highly sensational murder trials in the United States involving wealthy and prominent citizens accused of committing spectacularly savage acts of violence that were totally anomalous in their otherwise law-abiding lives (the Hall-Mills case of the 1920s is another instance). In each of these cases—owing partly to the skills of the high-powered legal "dream teams" retained by the defendants and partly, perhaps, to the reluctance of jurors to attribute such barbarity to admired, respectable individuals with no criminal backgrounds—the defendants ultimately went free.

My own opinion, based on my long immersion in the details of the Molineux affair, as well as my beliefs about the dark potentialities of human nature, is that the jury at Roland's first trial rendered the correct verdict.

PROLOGUE

1. Mark Essig, *Edison & the Electric Chair: A Story of Light and Death* (New York: Walker & Company, 2003), p. 253.
2. Daniel Allen Hearn, *Legal Executions in New York State, 1639–1963* (Jefferson, North Carolina: McFarland, 1997), pp. 81–92; *New York World*, March 21, 1899, p. 1.
3. Hearn, p. 94.
4. *New York World*, February 24, 1900, p. 12.
5. Roland Molineux, *The Room with the Little Door* (New York: G. W. Dillingham, 1902), pp. 26–32; *New York Times*, February 27, 1900, p. 14.

CHAPTER ONE

1. Edward Molineux's scrapbooks are owned by his great-grandson, Will Molineux.
2. From an unsigned note among the Molineux family papers.
3. The source of this legend is Nellie Zada Rice Molyneux, *History, genealogical and biographical, of the Molyneux families* (Syracuse, NY: C. W. Bardeen, 1904), pp. 17–18.
4. All information regarding Edward Molineux and the Tiemanns comes from the unpublished reminiscences of William Tiemann, a copy of which is owned by Will Molineux.
5. Even before the formation of the 159th Brigade, Edward had already taken part in the war, having been a volunteer member of the storied Seventh Regiment New York State Militia that hurried to the defense of Washington, D.C., immediately after the fall of Fort Sumter.
6. Among them, Port Hudson, Donaldsonville, Martinsville, New Iberia, Pine Mill, Marksville, Halltown, Winchester, Markettown, Cedar Creek, Fisher Hill, Charlestown, and Berryville.
7. "The New Major General," *Brooklyn Eagle*, March 25, 1869, p. 2.
8. From a speech made by William F. Tiemann on October 19, 1896, on the thirty-second anniversary of the Battle of Cedar Creek. A typed transcript is among the ELM papers.
9. As he did in a speech to surviving veterans of the 159th in April, 1902. See "Gathering of Veterans," *Brooklyn Eagle*, April 15, 1902, p. 5.

CHAPTER TWO

1. In June 1884—during a controversy over Governor Grover Cleveland's appointment of ELM as major general of the Second Division of National

Guard—the *Brooklyn Eagle* noted that "General Molineux has been in the West for some time." The reasons for ELM's trip—i.e., to bring Roland home after his two-year exile—were, of course, unknown to the public. See *Brooklyn Eagle*, June 6, 1884, p. 4.

2. Edward Leslie Molineux, *Physical and Military Exercise in Public Schools: A National Necessity*, p. 9.
3. Quoted in John Rickards Betts, *America's Sporting Heritage: 1850–1950* (Reading, MA: Addison-Wesley Publishing Co., 1974), p. 52.
4. J. Willis and R. Wettan. "Social Stratification in New York City Athletic Clubs, 1865–1915," *Journal of Sports History*, 24 (Spring 1997), p. 54.
5. Willis and Wettan, p. 54. See also Malcolm W. Ford, "The New York Athletic Club," *Outing* (Vol. XXXIII), December 1898, pp. 248 ff., and Bob Considine and Fred G. Jarvis, *The First Hundred Years : A Portrait of the NYAC* (London: Collier-Macmillan, 1969).
6. Eric Homberger, *Mrs. Astor's New York: Money and Social Power in a Gilded Age* (New Haven: Yale University Press, 2002), p. 212.
7. Theodore Dreiser, *The "Rake", Papers on Language & Literature*, 27 (spring 1991), 148–49.
8. There were two very different versions of this scandalous incident, one told by Mr. Edward O. Kindberg, the other by his wife, Eleanor. According to the former, his wife had been involved in an adulterous affair with the rakish, fifteen-year-old Molineux. Mrs. Kindberg, on the other hand, claimed that her husband had set her up. According to an affidavit she filed during their exceptionally ugly divorce, on the evening of February 24, 1883, the teenaged Molineux—"a friend and companion of her husband"—called upon her at her apartment at 292 Henry Street, Brooklyn, and "remained in the house until 10 P.M.," innocently chatting with her. About fifteen minutes after his departure, "her husband and several men broke into her room while she was in bed, lighted the gas, and her husband said, 'Now, we've got you, you must sign this paper. We will write for you.' " With one man seated on each side of the bed, she was threatened and "compelled to sign a blank piece of paper," which was later filled in with a fake confession of her own supposed adulterous behavior, to be used as evidence in denying her alimony. See *New York World*, January 12, 1899, p. 12.
9. See *Brooklyn Eagle*, April 7, 1889, p. 1, and February 17, 1891, p. 6.

CHAPTER THREE

1. See Jane Pejsa, *The Molineux Affair* (Minneapolis: Kenwood Publishing, 1983), p. 86. The description of ELM's parenting style is an extrapolation, based on Will Molineux's written memories of his own grandfather, Leslie Edward, the General's oldest son. This seems to me a valid approach, since—as Will Molineux notes—"men are apt to be like their fathers."
2. The information about Leslie Edward comes from Will Molineux's written "Remembrances of my grandfather."
3. Pejsa, p. 29.
4. Samuel Klaus, ed., *The Molineux Case* (New York: Alfred A. Knopf, 1929), p. 230.

5. Klaus, p. 223.
6. Pejsa, p. 30.

CHAPTER FOUR

1. Joseph E. Cornish, *The History and Genealogy of the Cornish Families in America* (Boston: Geo. H. Ellis Co., 1907), p. 128.
2. Klaus, *The Molineux Case*, p. 3.
3. *Brooklyn Eagle*, February 10, 1899, p. 1.
4. *New York Times*, December 18, 1895, p. 15.

CHAPTER FIVE

1. *Brooklyn Eagle*, April 7, 1889, p. 1.
2. Klaus, p. 11.
3. *New York Journal*, February 15, 1899, p. 2 ; *New York World*, February 15, 1899, p. 2.
4. *New York Journal*, February 15, 1899, p. 2.
5. Ibid.
6. *New York World*, February 12, 1899, p. 2; Klaus, p. 8.

CHAPTER SIX

1. Lloyd Morris, *Incredible New York: High Life and Low Life of the Last Hundred Years* (New York: Random House, 1951), p. 208.
2. Pejsa, p. 31; Klaus, p. 19.

CHAPTER SEVEN

1. *New York World*, March 5, 1899, p. 1.
2. This story is impossible to verify. Indeed, it is not at all clear that Blanche really had an artificial eye. Some observers insisted that she did (see, for example, the *New York World*, February 22, 1899, p. 2). Others, however, claimed that her left eye simply had a peculiar cast which, in certain lights, made it look like glass (see Pejsa, pp. 137–38). It appears to be true, however, that whatever was wrong with her eye, Blanche was self-conscious about it. At the time of the first Molineux trial, despite relentless efforts by reporters, only one photograph of her could be found, a group portrait taken when she was a member of the Rubinstein Musical Society and in which she is hardly visible. In her only other surviving photograph—published in the August 27, 1905, issue of *The Chicago Tribune*—she sits with her left side turned away from the camera, as though deliberately concealing it from sight.
3. The unpublished memoirs of Blanche Molineux Scott were provided to me by Jane Pejsa, whose used them as the basis for her own book, *The Molineux Affair*. They will hereafter be referred to as "Scott."
4. Scott, p. 16.
5. Ibid., p. 17.
6. Ibid., p. 18.
7. Ibid., pp. 21–22.
8. Ibid.

CHAPTER EIGHT

1. *New York World*, March 5, 1899, p. 1; Scott, p. 19.
2. Details in this passage—evoking the sights that Blanche would have seen on her strolls along Broadway—are taken from Theodore Dreiser's *Sister Carrie* (New York: Norton, 1970), pp. 226–27.
3. *New York Journal*, February 11, 1900, p. 28; *New York Sun*, February 4, 1900, p. 2.
4. Lucius Beebe, *The Big Spenders* (New York: Random House, 1966), pp. 115–16, and M. H. Dunlop, *Gilded City* (New York: William Morrow, 2000), pp. 20f.
5. Scott, p. 25.
6. Ibid., pp. 24–25.
7. Ibid., pp. 30–32.
8. Ibid., p. 37.

CHAPTER NINE

1. Dunlop, *Gilded City*, p. 124.
2. *New York World*, February 22, 1899.
3. There is an extant portrait of Lois, done by one of Boston's leading painters of society women, William M. Paxton. Titled *Portrait of a Woman in Black (Mrs. Howard Oakie)*. It shows a quite beautiful woman, perhaps thirty years old, with lush deep-brown hair, large dark eyes, a strong nose, full mouth, and elegant throat. She wears no ornamentation beyond a lace scarf draped over the shoulders of her rich, black velvet gown. Despite her subdued garb, there is a physical vibrancy to Mrs. Oakie, a radiant sensuality that, by all accounts, all three Chesebrough sisters shared and that—in addition to their other attributes of intellect and charm—clearly accounted for the attraction they exerted on men.
4. Scott, p. 36.
5. Ibid., p. 37.
6. Ibid., 40–41.
7. Sidney Sutherland, "The Mystery of the Poison Christmas Gift," *Liberty*, March 9, 1929, p 45.
8. Scott, p. 62.
9. Ibid., p. 42.
10. Ibid., p. 61.
11. Ibid., p. 62.

CHAPTER TEN

1. John S. Haller and Robin M. Haller, *The Physician and Sexuality in Victorian America* (New York: Norton, 1977), pp. 108–10; S. Pancoast, *Pancoast's Tokology and Ladies Medical Guide: A Complete Instructor in All the Delicate and Wonderful Matters Pertaining to Women* (Chicago: Thomas & Thomas, 1901), p. 35.
2. For a fascinating discussion of the class of single young women to which Blanche was perceived to belong, see Haller, pp. 246–47.
3. Scott, p. 60.
4. *New York World*, March 3, 1899, p. 1.

5. Scott, p. 44.
6. Ibid., pp. 45–46.
7. Ibid., p. 46.
8. Ibid., p. 47.
9. Ibid.

CHAPTER ELEVEN

1. Scott, p. 49.
2. Ibid., p. 48.
3. Ibid.
4. Ibid.
5. Ibid., pp. 49–50.
6. Klaus, p. 12.

CHAPTER TWELVE

1. Scott, p. 52.
2. Pejsa, p. 31.
3. Scott, p. 52.
4. In her memoir, Blanche mentions these as places she went to dine with Roland. My description of a typical night at these fashionable eateries derives from Lloyd Morris's *Incredible New York: High Life and Low Life of the Last Hundred Years* (New York: Random House, 1951), pp. 260–61.
5. Ibid., p. 60.
6. Klaus, pp. 277–78.
7. Scott, p. 61.
8. Ibid.

CHAPTER THIRTEEN

1. Klaus, p.11.
2. *New York World*, February 11, 1899, p. 2.
3. *New York Journal*, February 22, 1899, p. 2.
4. Scott, p. 58.
5. Ibid., p. 59.
6. Ibid.
7. Ibid., p. 61.
8. Ibid.
9. Ibid., p. 64.
10. Ibid.

CHAPTER FOURTEEN

1. *New York Journal*, February 10, 1899, p. 3.
2. Klaus, p. 10.
3. Pejsa, p. 57.
4. Ibid.

CHAPTER FIFTEEN

1. *New York Journal*, February 10, 1899, p. 2.
2. Subsequent quotations in this chapter are taken from Scott, pp. 65–77.

CHAPTER SIXTEEN

1. All quotations in this chapter are taken from Scott, pp. 80–86.

CHAPTER SEVENTEEN

1. "On the Universal Tendency to Debasement in the Sphere of Love," in *The Standard Edition of the Complete Psychological Works of Sigmund Freud*, Volume XI, trans. James Strachey (London: The Hogarth Press, 1957), p. 183. In Freud's experience, psychical impotence was—next to "the many forms of anxiety"—the disorder that most frequently drove men to seek psychoanalytic help. Unsurprisingly, he traces this disturbance to unconscious incestuous wishes.
2. Pejsa, p. 71.
3. Luc Sante, *Low Life* (New York: Vintage Books, 1992), pp. 126–28. Also, see George Chauncey, *Gay New York* (New York: Basic Books, 1994), pp. 33–40.
4. See Stephen Crane, "Opium's Varied Dreams," in *Stephen Crane: Prose and Poetry*, J.C. Levenson, ed. (New York: Library of America, 1984), pp. 853–59.
5. Scott, p. 63.
6. Ibid., p. 67.
7. Ibid., pp. 87–88.

CHAPTER EIGHTEEN

1. Klaus, p. 302.
2. Ibid., pp. 312–13. Also see *The People of the State of New York, Respondents, against Roland B. Molineux, Appellant. Case on Appeal from the Court of General Sessions of the Peace, in and for the county of New York. Court of Appeals of the State of New York* (New York, 1901), pp. 3222–25.
3. See advertisement in the *New York Sun*, September 24, 1899, p. 6.
4. *People of the State of New York, Respondents, against Roland B. Molineux, Appellant*, p. 3265.

CHAPTER NINETEEN

1. Klaus, pp. 315–16.

CHAPTER TWENTY

1. All quotes in this chapter are taken from Scott, pp. 92–95.

CHAPTER TWENTY-ONE

1. *New York Morning Journal*, January 9, 1899, pp. 1–2.
2. Klaus, p. 135.

3. One of the many ads for Kutnow's can be found in the *New York Journal*, April 30, 1899, p. 3.
4. Klaus, p. 138.
5. Ibid., p. 202.
6. Ibid., p. 206.
7. See *Merck's 1899 Manual of the Materia Medica, Together with a Summary of Therapeutic Indications and a Classification of Medicaments: A Ready-Reference Pocket Book for the Practicing Physician* (New York: Merck & Co., 1899).

CHAPTER TWENTY-TWO

1. Scott, p. 98.
2. Ibid.
3. *New York World*, January 9, 1899, p. 2.
4. Ibid.
5. *New York Times*, November 12, 1898, p. 7.
6. "Brooklyn Society," *Brooklyn Eagle*, November 30, 1898, p. 5. The current Episcopal Church of the Heavenly Rest, located uptown at Fifth Avenue and Ninetieth Street, was not built until the late 1920s. Roland chose to be married in the original church partly because it was close to his club and partly, no doubt, for his usual snobbish reasons, since it was frequented by the city's elite.

CHAPTER TWENTY-THREE

1. Ezra Bowen, ed., *This Fabulous Century: 1870–1900* (New York: Time-Life Books, 1970), p. 166.
2. George Juergens, *Joseph Pulitzer and the New York World* (Princeton: Princeton University Press, 1966), pp. 6 and 51.
3. Bowen, p. 168.
4. Ibid.
5. Juergens, pp. 51–52.
6. John D. Stevens, *Sensationalism and the New York Press* (New York: Columbia University Press, 1991), p. 70.
7. Juergens, pp. 67–69.
8. Denis Brian, *Pulitzer: A Life* (New York: John Wiley & Sons, 2001), p. 74.
9. Ibid., p. 55.
10. W. W. Swanberg, *Citizen Hearst* (New York: Scribner's, 1961), p. 41.
11. Ibid., p. 47.
12. Ben Procter, *William Randolph Hearst: The Early Years, 1863–1910* (New York: Oxford University Press, 1998), p. 41.
13. Swanberg, p. 43.
14. Ibid., p. 193.
15. Ibid., p. 49.

CHAPTER TWENTY-FOUR

1. Sidney Kobre, *The Yellow Press and Gilded Age Journalism* (Tallahassee: Florida State University, 1964), p. 62.

2. Among the staffers he stole away was cartoonist R. F. Outcault, creator of the enormously popular comic strip "The Yellow Kid," starring a bald, jug-eared slum urchin dressed in a yellow nightgown. In retaliation, Pulitzer hired another cartoonist, George Luks, to continue producing "The Yellow Kid" for the *World*. The competing garishly colored comic strips supplied the name that would forever be associated with Hearst and Pulitzer's brand of newspaper sensationalism: "yellow journalism."
3. Swanberg, p. 68.
4. Ibid., p. 66.
5. *New York Journal*, December 29, 1895. See Kobre, p. 73.
6. Swanberg, pp. 124–25.
7. In this sense, our obsession with knife- (or ax- or chain-saw-) wielding psychos—as well as with scalpel-wielding TV medical examiners—is the flip side of our fantasy that our bodies can be made indestructible through exercise: a grim reminder from the unconscious depths that, no matter how many crunches we do, we are made of all-too-perishable flesh.

CHAPTER TWENTY-FIVE

1. Roger Lane, *Murder in America* (Columbus: Ohio State University Press, 1997), p. 320.
2. Mark Regan Essig, *Science and Sensation: Poison Murder and Forensic Medicine in Nineteenth-Century America*. (Unpublished Ph.D. dissertation. Cornell University, January 2000, p. 5.)
3. *New York Sun*, March 3, 1899; *New York World*, March 11, 1899; *New York World*, March 16, 1899; *New York World*, April 2, 1899; *New York World*, April 7, 1899.
4. Edward H. Smith, *Famous Poison Mysteries* (New York: The Dial Press, 1927), p. 30.
5. Ibid., p. 31.
6. Ibid., p. 22.

CHAPTER TWENTY-SIX

1. Klaus, pp. 151–70; *New York World*, February 10, 1899, p. 2.
2. Mrs. Adams's other child, her adult son, Howard, also lived there occasionally, though at this time he was in Connecticut, nursing a broken leg. See Klaus, p. 221.
3. *New York Evening Journal*, December 12, 1898, p. 2.
4. Klaus, pp. 258–69. There is a slight discrepancy between the testimony of Harry Cornish and Florence Rodgers. According to the latter, she called for Cornish's help *after* her mother had collapsed. Cornish testified that he had just reached the bathroom when Mrs. Adams collapsed "like six foot of chain."
5. *New York World*, February 10, 1899, p. 3.
6. Klaus, pp. 51–56; *New York Herald*, February 16, 1899, p. 2; *New York Journal*, February 16, 1899; *New York World*, February 18, 1899.

CHAPTER TWENTY-SEVEN

1. Klaus, p. 157.
2. Ibid., p. 183.
3. Ibid., p. 158.
4. Ibid., p. 128.
5. Ibid.
6. *New York Sun*, February 24, 1899, p. 2.

CHAPTER TWENTY-EIGHT

1. *Evening Journal*, December 28, 1898, p. 2.
2. *New York Journal*, "Gave Poison to a Dozen to Kill One," December 27, 1898, p. 1.
3. *New York Journal*, December 29, 1899, p. 1.
4. *New York World*, December 29, 1898, p. 1.
5. *New York Journal*, December 29, 1899, p. 2; *New York World*, December 19, 1899, p. 2.
6. Jürgen Thorwald, *The Century of the Detective* (New York: Harcourt, Brace & World, 1964), p. 14.
7. Ibid., p. 19.
8. Ibid., pp. 53–54; Jackson Morley, ed., *Crimes and Punishment: A Pictorial Encyclopedia of Aberrant Behavior* (London: BPC Publishing, 1974), Vol. 9, pp. 128–29.
9. Thorwald, p. 100.
10. Louis Menand, "She Had to Have It," *The New Yorker* (April 23 & 30, 2001), pp. 62–70, and Russell R. Bradford and Ralph B. Bradford, *Introduction to Handwriting Examination and Identification* (Chicago: Nelson-Hall, 1992), p. 2.
11. *New York Evening Journal*, December 29, 1899, p. 1.
12. See, for example, the lead story on page 1 of *The New York Herald*, December 29, 1899, which declared that the poison was most probably sent to Cornish by a "woman inspired by jealousy." Also *The New York Times*, December 29, 1899, p. 1.

CHAPTER TWENTY-NINE

1. Klaus, p. 158.
2. Arthur Carey, *Memoirs of a Murder Man* (Garden City, NY: Doubleday, Doran and Company, 1930), p. 45.
3. *New York Journal*, December 30, 1898, p. 1.
4. *New York World*, December 30, 1898, p. 3.
5. *New York Evening Journal*, December 29, 1897, p. 2.
6. *New York World*, December 30, 1898, p. 2.
7. *New York Herald*, December 30, 1898, p. 4.
8. Ibid.
9. *New York Times*, December 30, 1898, p. 1.
10. Ibid.
11. *New York Herald*, December 30, 1898, p. 5.

12. Ibid., p. 3.
13. *New York Journal*, December 30, 1898, pp. 1–2.
14. *New York Times*, December 30, 1898, p. 2.
15. Klaus, pp. 154 and 159; *New York Herald*, February 18, 1899, p. 1.

CHAPTER THIRTY

1. *New York Journal*, December 31, 1898, pp. 1 and 2.
2. Carey, p. 1.
3. Ibid., pp. 2–9.
4. Ibid., pp. 38 ff.
5. *New York Journal*, December 31, 1898, pp. 1 and 3; *New York Herald*, December 31, 1898, p. 1; *New York World*, December 31, 1898, p. 1; Klaus, pp. 179–80; Carey, pp. 76–77.
6. *New York World*, December 31, 1898, p. 1.
7. *New York Journal*, December 31, 1898, p. 1; *New York Herald*, December 31, 1898, p. 1; *New York World*, December 31, 1898, p. 2.
8. *New York Times*, January 1, 1898, p. 2.
9. *New York Journal*, December 31, 1898, p. 2.
10. *New York Herald*, December 31, 1898, p. 4.
11. *New York Herald*, February 21, 1898, p. 1.
12. *New York World*, January 1, 1898, p. 1.
13. Ibid., p. 2.
14. Brian Burrell, *Postcards from the Brain Museum* (New York: Broadway Books, 2004), pp. 135–39.
15. *New York World*, January 2, 1898, p. 2.
16. *New York World*, January 1, 1898, p. 2.
17. Chauncey, pp. 170–73.
18. *New York World*, January 1, 1898, p. 1.

CHAPTER THIRTY-ONE

1. Scott, p. 103.
2. Pejsa, p. 100.
3. Scott, p. 104. The material in this chapter, including all dialogue and direct quotes, is from Scott, pp. 104–10.
4. *New York World*, January 2, 1899, p. 3.

CHAPTER THIRTY-TWO

1. Klaus, p. 312; *Brooklyn Eagle*, January 3, 1899, p. 16.
2. *New York World*, January 3, 1899, p. 2.
3. Ibid.
4. *Brooklyn Eagle*, January 3, 1899, p. 16.
5. Ibid.
6. *New York Herald*, January 3, 1899, p. 4.
7. Klaus, p. 7.
8. Scott, pp. 111–12.

CHAPTER THIRTY-THREE

1. *New York Sun*, January 1, 1899, p. 1
2. Carey, p. 77.
3. *New York Journal*, January 3, 1899, p. 3.
4. Carey, p. 78.
5. *New York Herald*, January 3, 1899, p. 4.
6. *New York Journal*, January 6, 1899, p. 1.
7. Carey, p. 81.
8. Ibid.
9. Ibid., pp. 81–82; Klaus, pp. 212–14.

CHAPTER THIRTY-FOUR

1. *New York Journal*, January 4, 1899, p. 1.
2. *New York World*, January 2, 1899, pp. 1 and 3.
3. At the coroner's inquest into the Adams murder, Roland freely admitted that he was friendly with Connors and his wife. See, for example, *New York World*, February 15, 1899, p. 2. For more on Connors, see Sante, especially pp. 125–30.
4. *New York Journal*, January 4, 1899, p. 2; *New York World*, January 4, 1899, p. 2.
5. Carey, p. 80.
6. Ibid.
7. *New York Times*, January 5, 1899, p. 1.
8. Ibid.
9. Ibid.; *New York Herald*, January 5, 1899, p. 1.
10. For more on the "murder squad," see Swanberg, pp. 124–25.
11. *New York Journal*, January 5, 1899, pp. 1 and 2.
12. Ibid., p. 1.
13. *New York Herald*, January 7, 1899, p. 2.
14. Ibid.; *New York World*, January 7, 1899, p. 2.
15. *New York Herald*, January 7, 1899, p. 2.
16. *New York World*, January 7, 1899, p. 2.
17. *New York World*, January 6, 1899, p. 2.

CHAPTER THIRTY-FIVE

1. *New York World*, January 1, 1899, p. 2.
2. *New York Times*, January 24, 1899, p. 7, and January 25, 1899, p. 12.
3. *New York Journal*, January 5, 1899, p. 2.
4. See Klaus, p. 269.
5. *New York World*, January 4, 1899, p. 2.
6. Ibid.
7. *New York World*, January 13, 1899, p. 1.
8. Ibid., p. 12.
9. *New York World*, January 18, 1899, p. 2.
10. Ibid., p. 1.
11. *New York World*, January 19, 1899, p. 4.

CHAPTER THIRTY-SIX

1. *New York World*, January 2, 1899, p. 1, and December 30, 1898, p. 2.
2. *New York World*, January 4, 1899, p. 2.
3. *New York Herald*, January 5, 1899, p. 1.
4. Carey, p. 83.
5. *New York Journal*, January 9, 1899, p. 2; Klaus, p. 215f.
6. *New York Journal*, January 7, 1899, p. 1, and January 9, 1899, p. 2.

CHAPTER THIRTY-SEVEN

1. Scott, pp. 52, 58, and 118.
2. Ibid., p. 118.
3. Ibid., p. 121.
4. *New York World*, January 8, 1899, p. 2, and January 9, 1899, p. 2.
5. Stevens, pp. 83–84.
6. *New York World Sunday Supplement*, January 8, 1899, p. 21.
7. *New York Journal Sunday Supplement*, January 15, 1899, p. 10.
8. *New York Journal*, January 9, 1899, p. 3.
9. *New York World*, January 8, 1899, p. 3.
10. *New York Journal*, January 6, 1899, p. 2.
11. *New York Journal*, January 7, 1899, p. 2.
12. *New York World*, January 7, 1899, p. 2.
13. Scott, p. 119.

CHAPTER THIRTY-EIGHT

1. *New York Journal Sunday Supplement*, January 15, 1899, p. 10.
2. *New York Journal*, January 13, 1899, p. 5.
3. *New York Journal*, January 14, 1899, p. 6.
4. *New York Journal*, January 16, 1899, p. 6.
5. *New York Journal*, January 11, 1899, p. 2.
6. *New York World*, January 15, 1899, p. 14; *New York Journal*, January 10, 1899, p. 2; *New York Evening Journal*, January 10, 1899, p. 1.
7. *New York Journal*, January 7, 1899, p. 2, and January 9, 1899, p. 6.
8. *New York Sun*, January 7, 1899, p. 1.
9. *New York Journal*, January 7, 1899, p. 2; Pejsa, p. 124.
10. *New York Times*, January 10, 1899, p. 8.
11. *New York Sun*, January 7, 1899, p. 8.
12. *New York Journal*, January 25, 1899, p. 1.

CHAPTER THIRTY-NINE

1. *New York Journal*, January 22, 1899, p. 2.
2. Ibid.
3. Klaus, pp. 241–42.
4. Ibid.
5. *New York World*, January 4, 1899, p. 2.
6. Carey, pp. 84–85.

CHAPTER FORTY

1. Klaus, p. 290.
2. *New York Journal*, January 25, 1899, p. 1.
3. *New York Times*, January 25, 1899, p. 2.
4. Ibid.
5. *New York Times*, January 26, 1899, p. 2; *New York Herald*, January 26, 1899, p. 1; *New York Journal*, January 26, 1899, p. 1.
6. Early reports described the letter as having been written on "stationery such as a woman might use." See *New York Herald*, January 26, 1899, p. 2.

CHAPTER FORTY-ONE

1. As Albert Borowitz summarizes this case: "During the weeks before Christmas [1898] . . . Mrs. Margaret E. Cody went on trial for attempted blackmail of the heirs of robber-baron Jay Gould through threats to disclose that Gould had fathered an illegitimate daughter. Despite the testimony of handwriting expert David Carvalho that Gould's name on the baptismal record of his reputed child had been clumsily forged, the jury could not agree on a verdict." See Borowitz, "Packaged Death: Forerunners of the Tylenol Poisonings," *American Bar Association Journal*, March 1983, p. 282.
2. *New York Herald*, January 26, 1899, p 1.
3. *New York Herald*, January 27, 1899, pp. 1–2.
4. Ibid., p. 2.
5. Ibid.
6. Ibid., p. 1.
7. Carey, p. 87.

CHAPTER FORTY-TWO

1. Klaus, p. 292.
2. *New York Herald*, January 27, 1899, p. 2.
3. *New York World*, January 27, 1899, p. 2.
4. *New York Journal*, January 27, 1899, p. 2, and *New York World*, February 1, 1899, p. 2.
5. Klaus, pp. 305–7, and *New York World*, February 1, 1899, p. 2.
6. *New York World*, February 1, 1899, p. 2.
7. *New York World*, January 30, 1899, p. 2.
8. Ibid.
9. *New York World*, January 27, 28, and 29, 1899, p. 1; *New York Journal*, January 30, 1899, p. 1; and Klaus, p. 8.
10. *New York Journal*, January 27, 1899, p. 2; *New York Sun*, January 4, 1899, p. 2; *New York World*, January 31, 1899; *New York Herald*, January 30, 1899, p. 1.
11. *New York World*, February 2 and 3, 1899, pp. 1–2; *New York Journal*, February 2, 1899, p. 1.
12. *New York Herald*, January 29, 1899, p. 1.

CHAPTER FORTY-THREE

1. *New York Journal*, February 4, 1899, p. 6.
2. *New York Journal*, January 11, 1899, p. 4.
3. *Brooklyn Eagle*, February 3, 1899, p. 1.
4. *New York Journal*, February 3, 1899, p. 3.
5. *New York World*, February 7, 1899, p. 14.

CHAPTER FORTY-FOUR

1. *New York Journal*, February 9, 1899, p. 3; *New York Herald*, February 9, 1899, p. 3; *New York World*, February 9, 1899, p. 2.
2. *New York Journal*, February 10, 1899, p. 1.
3. *New York Herald*, February 8, 1899, p. 3; *New York Journal*, February 9, 1899. After a cursory investigation, the district attorney's office announced that there "was nothing to connect [Baldwin's death] in any way with the death of Mrs. Adams or to show that poison had been given to Mr. Baldwin during or after the trip on the *Viator*." There the matter rested. See *New York Journal*, February 10, 1899, p. 4.
4. *New York Journal*, February 10, 1899, p. 2.
5. Ibid., pp. 1 and 2; *New York World*, February 10, 1899, pp. 1 and 2; *New York Herald*, February 10, 1899, pp. 1 and 2; *New York Sun*, February 10, 1899, pp. 1 and 2; *Brooklyn Eagle*, February 10, 1899, p. 1.
6. Klaus, p. 15.
7. *New York Journal*, February 10, 1899, p. 2.
8. Ibid.
9. Ibid.; *New York Herald*, February 10, 1899, p. 2.

CHAPTER FORTY-FIVE

1. *New York World*, February 11, 1899, pp. 1–2.
2. *New York Journal*, February 11, 1899, p. 1.
3. *New York Times*, February 11, 1899, p. 3.
4. Klaus, p. 15.
5. *New York Journal*, *New York World*, *New York Sun*, February 11, 1899, pp. 1–2.
6. *New York World*, February 13, 1899, p. 3.

CHAPTER FORTY-SIX

1. *New York Journal*, February 13, 1899, p. 1.
2. The great "Blizzard of '99" was an event of such magnitude that it became known in meteorological lore as "the Storm King." See *New York World*, February 14, 1899, p. 1.
3. *New York Journal*, February 15, 1899, p. 1.
4. *New York World*, February 12, 1899, p. 2; Klaus, p. 8.
5. *New York Journal*, *New York World*, *New York Sun*, *New York Herald*, February 15, 1899, pp. 1–2.
6. Carey, p. 91.

CHAPTER FORTY-SEVEN

1. *New York Journal*, February 18, 1899, p. 5; *New York World*, February 19, 1899, p. 1.
2. *New York Herald*, February 16, 1899, p. 3.
3. *New York Journal*, February 16, 1899, p. 5.
4. *New York Herald*, February 18, 1899, p. 3.
5. *New York Journal*, February 18, 1899, p. 5; *New York World*, February 19, 1899, p. 3.
6. Ibid.
7. *New York Journal*, February 17, 1899, p. 5.
8. *New York World*, February 19, 1899, p. 3.

CHAPTER FORTY-EIGHT

1. Scott, pp. 131–32.
2. *New York World*, February 22, 1899, pp. 1 and 2.
3. *New York Sun*, February 22, 1899, p. 2.
4. *New York Herald*, February 22, 1899, p. 1.
5. All quotes from Blanche's testimony are taken from the *New York Sun*, February 22, 1899, p. 2.
6. Scott, p. 132.
7. *New York Journal*, February 22, 1899, p. 5.

CHAPTER FORTY-NINE

1. *Brooklyn Eagle*, February 23, 1899, p. 1.
2. *New York Times*, February 24, 1899, p. 3.
3. *New York Journal*, February 25, 1899, p. 3
4. *New York Journal*, February 24, 1899, p. 4.
5. *New York Herald*, February 24, 1899, p. 4.
6. Ibid.
7. *New York Journal*, February 24, 1899, p. 2.
8. Ibid.
9. *New York Journal*, February 25, 1899, p. 5.
10. Ibid.
11. *New York Evening Journal*, February 25, 1899, p. 2.
12. *New York Journal*, February 25, 1899, p. 5.

CHAPTER FIFTY

1. *New York Herald*, February 26, 1899, p. 1.
2. *New York World*, February 24, 1899, p. 12.
3. *New York Journal*, February 28, 1899, p. 1.
4. Ibid.
5. Ibid.
6. *New York World*, February 28, 1899, pp. 1–2.

CHAPTER FIFTY-ONE

1. *New York World*, February 28, 1899, p. 2.
2. *New York Herald*, February 28, 1899, p. 2.
3. *New York Journal*, February 2, 1899, p. 2.
4. *New York World*, *New York Journal*, *New York Herald*, *New York Sun*, February 28, 1899, pp. 1–2.
5. *New York Journal*, February 28, 1899, p. 2.

CHAPTER FIFTY-TWO

1. *New York World*, March 1, 1899, p. 2.
2. *New York Sun*, March 2, 1899, p. 2.
3. *New York Evening Journal*, March 4, 1899, p. 1.
4. Klaus, p. 18.
5. *New York World*, March 2, 1899, p. 4.
6. *New York Journal*, March 7, 1899, p. 7.
7. *New York Journal*, March 1, 1899, p. 1.
8. *New York Sun*, March 5, 1899, p. 3; *New York Journal*, March 1, 1899, p. 2, and March 2, 1899, p. 1; *New York World*, March 3, 1899, p. 2; *Brooklyn Eagle*, March 2, 1899, p. 1.
9. *New York Journal*, March 5, 1899, p. 12.
10. *New York World*, March 2, 1899, p. 2.
11. *New York World*, March 1, 1899, p. 2.
12. *New York Times*, March 3, 1899, p. 2.
13. *New York Journal*, March 7, 1899, p. 1.

CHAPTER FIFTY-THREE

1. *New York World*, March 10, 1899, p. 4.
2. *New York Journal*, March 9, 1899, p. 3.
3. *New York World*, March 10, 1899, p. 4.
4. Ibid.

CHAPTER FIFTY-FOUR

1. Scott, pp. 135–36.
2. Ibid.
3. Scott, p. 134.
4. Ibid.
5. Ibid.
6. *New York Journal*, March 24, 1899, p. 4.
7. *New York World*, March 25, 1899, p. 1.

CHAPTER FIFTY-FIVE

1. *New York Journal*, March 2, 1899, p. 1.
2. *New York World*, March 2, 1899, p. 2.

3. *New York Herald*, March 3, 1899, p. 2.
4. *New York World*, March 17, 1899, p. 5.
5. *New York Journal*, March 14, 1899, p. 6.
6. *New York Journal*, March 9, 1899, p. 7.
7. Jay Robert Nash, *Murder, America* (London: Harrap, 1980), p. 150; *New York Journal*, March 21, 1899, p. 3.
8. *New York Journal*, March 21, 1899, p. 3.
9. Ann Jones, *Women Who Kill* (New York: Fawcett, 1980), p. 279.
10. See, for example, *New York Journal*, March 20, 1899, p. 4. This image anticipates, by thirty years, the single most infamous picture in the history of tabloid journalism, the front-page *Daily News* photograph of the murderess Ruth Snyder at the instant of her electrocution on January 12, 1928.
11. *New York Evening Journal*, March 20, 1899, p. 3.

CHAPTER FIFTY-SIX

1. *New York World*, April 1, 1899, p. 3.
2. *Brooklyn Eagle*, April 13, 1899, p. 6.
3. *New York World*, April 13, 1899, pp. 1 and 3.
4. *New York World*, April 9, 1899, p. 1; *Brooklyn Eagle*, April 10, 1899, p. 1.
5. *New York World*, April 12, 1899, p. 2, and April 13, 1899, p.2; *New York Journal*, April 12, 1899, p. 1.
6. *New York Evening Journal*, April 25, 1899, p. 2; *New York Journal*, April 26, 1899, p. 5; *New York World*, April 26, 1889, p. 3.
7. *New York Times*, April 14, 1899, p. 3.
8. *Brooklyn Eagle*, April 13, 1899, p. 1; *New York Journal*, April 14, 1899, pp. 1 and 5; *New York Sun*, April 14, 1899, p. 1; *New York World*, April 14, 1899, p. 1.

CHAPTER FIFTY-SEVEN

1. *New York World*, May 2, 1899, p. 2.
2. *New York World*, May 10, 1899, pp. 1 and 2; *New York Journal*, May 10, 1899, pp. 1 and 2; *New York Times*, May 10, 1899, p. 1.
3. *New York Sun*, May 11, 1899, p. 2.
4. *New York Journal*, May 11, 1899, p. 1, and May 10, 1899, p. 5.
5. *Brooklyn Eagle*, June 9, 1899, p. 1; *New York Journal*, June 10, 1899, p. 5; *New York Times*, June 10, 1899, p. 3.
6. *New York World*, July 21, 1899, p. 1; *New York Times*, July 21, 1899, p. 12.
7. *New York Journal*, July 21, 1899, p. 1.

CHAPTER FIFTY-EIGHT

1. *New York Journal*, July 15, 1899, p. 3; *New York Sun*, July 16, 1899, p. 5; *New York Journal*, July 1, 1899, p. 1; *New York World*, July 10, 1899, p. 7.
2. *New York World*, July 21, 1899, p. 5; *New York Sun*, July 19, 1899, p. 5.
3. *New York Journal*, August 16, 1899, p. 3.
4. See all issues of *New York World*, May 23, 1899, through June 17, 1899, p. 1.

5. *New York World*, July 30, 1899, fifth section, p. 1; *New York Journal*, August 13, 1899, p. 1; *New York Sun*, July 4, 1899, p. 1; *New York World*, July 7, 1899, p. 1.
6. *New York World*, July 28, 1899, p. 12, August 27, 1899, p. 7, August 28, 1899, p. 10.
7. *New York World*, July 28, 1899, p. 5; *New York Journal*, August 24, 1899, p. 3; *Brooklyn Eagle*, September 14, 1899, p. 7.
8. Scott, pp. 137–38.
9. *New York World*, August 2, 1899, p. 3.
10. *New York World*, November 2, 1899, p. 2.

CHAPTER FIFTY-NINE

1. Klaus, p. 23.
2. *New York World*, November 15, 1899, p. 2.
3. Ibid.
4. Author's telephone interview with G. Gordon Liddy, May 19, 2004. See also G. Gordon Liddy, *Will* (New York: St. Martin's, 1980), pp. 18–21.
5. *New York World*, November 15, 1899, p. 2.
6. *New York Journal*, November 15, 1899, pp. 1–2.
7. *Brooklyn Eagle*, November 16, 1899, p. 2.
8. *New York Times*, November 21, 1899, p. 6.
9. *New York Sun*, November 20, 1899, p. 3.
10. *Brooklyn Eagle*, November 20, 1899, p. 1.
11. *New York Evening Journal*, November 22, 1899, p. 1.
12. *New York World*, November 30, 1899, p. 2.
13. Ibid.
14. Ibid.
15. Pejsa, p. 183. Adding to the charade was the fact that November 29, 1899, was *not* their wedding anniversary. Roland and Blanche had been married on November 19 of the previous year.
16. *New York Evening Journal*, November 29, 1899, p. 1.
17. *New York World*, November 30, 1899, p. 2.
18. *New York Evening Journal*, December 2, 1899, p. 1.

CHAPTER SIXTY

1. Judy Crichton, *America 1900: The Turning Point* (New York: Henry Holt, 1998), p. 3.
2. *Life*, Vol. 28, No. 1 (January 2, 1950), p. 3.
3. Just as the period we call the sixties did not begin until roughly 1963, with the advent of the Beatles, and ended, arguably, on December 6, 1969, with the debacle of Altamont.
4. Neal Gabler, *Life: The Movie* (New York: Vintage Books, 2000), pp. 7 and 4.
5. Until then, it was common for critics to wait a few days after the first night before publishing reviews to give the production a chance to iron out any wrinkles—a function subsequently served, in the wake of Scott's innovation, by out-of-town tryouts and previews.

6. *Brooklyn Eagle*, December 5, 1899, p. 4.
7. *New York Sun*, December 5, 1899, p. 4.
8. *New York Journal*, December 5, 1899, p. 5.
9. Klaus, pp. 24–25.
10. *New York Herald*, December 5, 1899, p. 1.
11. Klaus, p. 23.
12. This account of Osborne's speech is drawn from the following sources: *New York World*, December 5, 1899, pp. 1–2; *New York Times*, December 5, 1899, p. 14; *New York Journal*, December 5, 1899, p. 16; *Brooklyn Eagle*, December 5, 1899, p. 4.
13. *New York Herald*, December 5, 1899, p. 1.

CHAPTER SIXTY-ONE

1. *New York World*, December 5, 1899. At the end of the first week of testimony, Osborne's conduct of the case already seemed so incoherent that, according to the *New York Sun*, "if the entire testimony . . . were put together in a book and given to the cleverest man that ever lived to read . . . he might read it from end to end and never suspect that he was reading the evidence in a murder trial" (December 9, 1899, p. 1).
2. Though often misunderstood as a literal corpse—the actual body of the victim without which, supposedly, no crime can be proved—the term *corpus delicti* actually means "the body or substance of the offense." In homicide cases, this means the evidence which shows "that a human being was killed, that the death was the result of a criminal act, and that the killing occurred within the jurisdiction of the court." These basic facts must be established before the trial can proceed. See Michael Kurland, *How to Try a Murder* (Edison, New Jersey: Castle Books, 2002), p. 68.
3. Klaus, pp. 51–58.
4. The letter was actually penned by Heiles, though dictated by Roland. It was sent, under a pseudonym, to Frederick Stearns & Company of Detroit, and—like the earlier letter mailed to the same company—sought confidential information about Harpster, a former salesman for Stearns who had subsequently gone to work for J. Herbert Ballantine. According to Heiles's testimony, Roland—who hated Harpster because of the latter's friendship with Cornish—was hoping to obtain compromising information about Harpster's employment record "with a view to getting him dismissed from his place in Ballantine's brewery office." See *New York Journal*, December 6, 1899, p. 1.
5. *Brooklyn Eagle*, December 7, 1899, p. 2; *New York Journal*, December 8, 1899, p. 2; *New York Sun*, December 8, 1899, p. 2.
6. *Brooklyn Eagle*, December 5, 1899, p. 2.
7. Carey, p. 92.
8. *New York World* and *New York Sun*, December 9, 1899, p. 1.
9. *New York Sun*, December 11, 1899, p. 1.
10. *New York Times*, *New York Journal*, *New York World*, December 12, 1899, pp. 1–2; *Brooklyn Eagle*, December 11, 1899, p. 1.
11. *New York Journal Sunday Supplement*, December 17, 1899, p. 18.

CHAPTER SIXTY-TWO

1. *New York World*, December 16, 1899, p. 1.
2. *Brooklyn Eagle*, December 12, 1899, p. 1.
3. *New York World*, December 27, 1899, p. 2.
4. *Brooklyn Eagle*, December 12, 1899, p. 1.
5. *New York Journal*, December 14, 1899.
6. *New York World*, December 19, 1899, p. 2.
7. *New York Journal*, December 19, 1899, p. 1.
8. *New York World*, December 19, 1899, p. 2.

CHAPTER SIXTY-THREE

1. See Bradford and Bradford, p. 8.
2. *New York Sun*, December 27, 1899, p. 1.
3. *New York World* and *New York Journal*, December 28, 1899, pp. 1–2.
4. *New York World*, December 26, 1899, p. 5; *New York Times*, December 26, 1899, p. 8; *New York Journal*, December 26, 1899, p. 14.
5. *New York Sun*, December 27, 1899, p. 3.
6. *New York World*, December 31, 1899, p. 16.
7. *Brooklyn Eagle*, December 28, 1899, p. 1; *New York Times*, December 29, 1899, p. 1; *New York World*, December 29, 1899, p. 1; Klaus, pp. 148 ff.
8. *New York World*, December 29, 1899, p. 1.
9. Ibid., p. 2.
10. *New York World*, December 30, 1899, p. 1.
11. *New York Journal*, December 30, 1899, p. 1.
12. *Brooklyn Eagle*, December 29, 1899, p. 1.
13. Klaus, pp. 159–60.

CHAPTER SIXTY-FOUR

1. *New York World*, January 1, 1900, p. 1.
2. Ibid.
3. *New York Sun*, January 1, 1900, p. 1.
4. *New York Times*, January 2, 1900, p. 8.
5. *New York Sun*, January 3, 1900, p. 3.
6. Koch "positively connected" Molineux to the private letter box by identifying him as the man who had come to his store in the third week of December 1898 and inquired about the price of a rental. According to Koch, however, it was another man who had appeared a few days later and rented the box under Cornish's name, suggesting that Roland may have had an accomplice. See *New York Journal*, January 17, 1900, p. 5, and *New York World*, January 17, 1900, p. 14.
7. See *New York World*, January 24, 1900, p. 3.
8. All details about the testimony of Rachel Greene and Minnie Betts come from the following sources: *Brooklyn Eagle*, January 15, 1900; *New York Journal*, January 16, 1900, pp. 1–2; *New York World*, January 16, 1900, p. 4; Klaus, pp. 277–82.
9. Even before the joint appearance of Rachel Greene and Minnie Betts, Osborne had been allowed to introduce evidence related to the death of Barnet. On

January 4, for instance, both Barnet's doctor and valet described the sufferings he had endured after taking some of the sample Kutnow's Powder. Their testimony occupied such a significant chunk of the day that the *New York Sun* was led to remark that "the title of the case seemed to have changed to the People Against Roland Molineux for the Murder of Henry Crossman Barnet" (January 5, 1900, p. 4).

10. *Brooklyn Eagle,* January 17, 1900, p. 8.

CHAPTER SIXTY-FIVE

1. *New York Sun,* January 19, 1900, p. 3.
2. *Brooklyn Eagle,* January 19, 1900, p. 2.
3. *Brooklyn Eagle,* January 24, 1900, p. 1.
4. *New York Journal,* January 29, 1900, p. 5.
5. *New York Journal,* February 6, 1900, p. 16.

CHAPTER SIXTY-SIX

1. *New York World,* January 28, 1900, p. 5.
2. *New York World,* February 7, 1900, p. 1.
3. *Brooklyn Eagle,* February 6, 1900, p. 1; *New York Journal,* February 7, 1900, p. 1; *New York World,* February 7, 1900, p. 1; *New York Times,* February 7, 1900, p. 4.

CHAPTER SIXTY-SEVEN

1. Klaus, p. 26; *Brooklyn Eagle,* February 7, 1900, p. 1; *New York World,* February 8, 1900, p. 1.
2. *Brooklyn Eagle,* February 6, 1900, p. 1; *New York Journal,* February 7, 1900, pp. 1–2; *New York World,* February 7, 1900, pp. 1–2.
3. *New York World,* February 7, 1900, p. 2.

CHAPTER SIXTY-EIGHT

1. *Brooklyn Eagle,* February 7, 1900, p. 1.
2. *New York World,* February 8, 1900, pp. 1–2.
3. Ibid., p. 2.

CHAPTER SIXTY-NINE

1. *New York Times,* September 29, 1899, p. 1, September 30, 1899, p. 1, October 1, 1899, p. 6; *New York World,* September 30, 1899, pp. 1–2, and October 1, 1899, pp. 1–2.
2. *New York Times,* October 3, 1899, p. 2.
3. *New York Times,* September 29, 1899, p. 4.
4. *New York Journal,* February 8, 1900, p. 1.
5. *Brooklyn Eagle,* February 8, 1900, p. 2; *New York Journal,* February 9, 1900, p. 16.
6. *New York Journal,* February 9, 1900, p. 16.
7. *Brooklyn Eagle,* February 8, 1900, p. 2; *New York World,* February 9, 1900, p. 1; *New York Sun,* February 9, 1900, p. 1.
8. *New York Journal,* February 9, 1900, p. 16.

CHAPTER SEVENTY

1. *Brooklyn Eagle*, February 9, 1900, p. 2; *New York Sun*, February 10, 1900, p. 1.
2. *New York World*, February 10, 1900, p. 1.
3. *Brooklyn Eagle*, February 9, 1900, p. 2; *New York Sun*, February 10, 1900, pp. 1–2; *New York Journal*, February 10, 1900, pp. 1–2; *New York World*, February 10, 1900, pp. 1–2.

CHAPTER SEVENTY-ONE

1. *Brooklyn Eagle*, February 10, 1900, p. 1.
2. *New York World*, February 11, 1900, p. 2.
3. Scott, pp. 163–65.
4. *New York Sun*, February 11, 1900, p. 2.
5. *New York World*, February 11, 1900, p. 2.
6. *New York Sun*, February 11, 1900, p. 2.
7. *New York World*, February 11, 1900, p. 2.
8. *New York Times*, February 11, 1900, p. 1.
9. *New York Sun*, February 11, 1900, p. 2.
10. Ibid.
11. *Brooklyn Eagle*, February 10, 1900, pp. 1–2; *New York World*, February 11, 1900, pp. 1–2; *New York Journal*, February 11, 1900, pp. 1–2; *New York Sun*, February 11, 1900, pp. 1–2; *New York Times*, February 11, 1900, p. 1.

CHAPTER SEVENTY-TWO

1. *New York Sun*, February 12, 1900, p. 1.
2. *New York World*, February 12, 1900, p. 2, and February 13, 1900, p. 2.
3. *New York World*, February 12, 1900, p. 1.
4. *New York Sun*, February 12, 1900, p. 1.
5. *New York Sun*, February 12, 1900, p. 2; *New York Times*, February 12, 1900, p. 6.
6. *New York Journal*, February 13, 1900, p. 16.
7. *New York Herald*, February 17, 1900, p. 2.
8. *New York Times*, February 17, 1900, p. 2.
9. Ibid.
10. *New York Sun*, February 17, 1900, p. 2.
11. *Brooklyn Eagle*, February 16, 1900, p. 1; *New York Times*, February 17, 1900, p. 2; *New York Journal*, February 17, 1900, pp. 1 and 2; *New York Sun*, February 17, 1900, pp. 1 and 2; *New York Journal*, February 17, 1900, pp. 1 and 2; *New York World*, February 17, 1900, pp. 1 and 2.

CHAPTER SEVENTY-THREE

1. *New York Times*, February 17, 1900, p. 2.
2. *New York World*, February 17, 1900, p. 2.
3. Ibid.
4. *New York Journal*, February 17, 1900, p. 2; *New York World*, February 17, 1900, p. 2; *New York Times*, February 17, 1900, p. 2; *New York Sun*, February 17, 1900, p. 2.

CHAPTER SEVENTY-FOUR

1. *New York Journal*, February 17, 1900, p. 1; *New York Times*, February 17, 1900, p. 1; *New York Sun*, February 17, 1900, p. 1.
2. Ibid.

CHAPTER SEVENTY-FIVE

1. *New York Times*, August 27, 1898, p. 11, April 1, 1899, p. 12.
2. Denis Brian, *Sing Sing* (Amherst, New York: Prometheus Books, 2005, p. 22).
3. Roland Molineux, *The Room with the Little Door* (New York: G.W. Dillingham, 1902), p. 21.
4. Ibid., p. 25.
5. Ibid., p. 20.
6. *New York Journal*, February 20, 1900, p. 4; *New York World*, February 20, 1900, p. 14.

CHAPTER SEVENTY-SIX

1. In 1901, to distinguish it from its notorious prison, the village changed its name to Ossining. At the time of Roland's arrival, however, it was still known as Sing Sing.
2. Scott, p. 169.
3. Scott, pp. 169–71; Pejsa, pp. 220–21.
4. Scott, pp. 173–78.

CHAPTER SEVENTY-SEVEN

1. *Brooklyn Eagle*, March 3, 1900, p. 12.
2. *New York Sun*, March 3, 1900, p. 1.
3. *New York Journal*, March 5, 1900, p. 3.
4. *Brooklyn Eagle*, June 11, 1900, p. 5.
5. A vivid description of Milburn can be found in a memorial address delivered by Chief Judge Benjamin Cardozo of the Court of Appeals in December 1930 and privately printed by the Carnegie Corporation. See also the profile of Milburn in the *Brooklyn Eagle*, September 15, 1901, p. 15.

CHAPTER SEVENTY-EIGHT

1. Molineux, *The Room with the Little Door*, p. 52.
2. Brander Matthews, *His Father's Son* (New York: Harper & Brothers, 1896), pp. 211–12.
3. Lewis Lawes, *Life and Death in Sing Sing* (Garden City, New York: Doubleday, Doran & Company, 1928), pp. 163–64.
4. Ibid.
5. Molineux, *The Room with the Little Door*, pp. 26–29.
6. Ibid., p. 209.
7. Ibid., pp. 198–207; Lawes, p. 161.
8. For a list of the men put to death in Sing Sing between February 1900 and

August 1901, see Scott Christianson, *Condemned: Inside the Sing Sing Death House* (New York: New York University Press, 2000), p. 148.

9. *New York Times*, November 23, 1900, p. 14. Kennedy would be tried two more times, in February and June 1901. Each trial resulted in a hung jury, and the indictment was finally dismissed with the consent of the district attorney. Kennedy returned to his home in New Dorp, Staten Island, where he practiced dentistry for another fifty-seven years before his death in August 1948 at the age of eighty-one. See *New York Times*, August 26, 1948, p. 4.
10. *New York Times*, November 30, 1900, p. 3.
11. *New York World*, January 5, 1901, p. 3.
12. *New York Times*, January 7, 1901, p. 6, and June 16, 1901, p. 15.

CHAPTER SEVENTY-NINE

1. Margaret Leech, *In the Days of McKinley* (New York: Harper & Brothers, 1959), pp. 575–85.
2. *New York Times*, June 17, 1901, p. 3.
3. *Brooklyn Eagle*, June 17, 1901, p. 1.
4. *New York World*, June 18, 1901, p. 2; *Brooklyn Eagle*, June 18, 1901, p. 3.
5. *Brooklyn Eagle*, June 19, 1901, p. 1; *New York World*, June 19, 1901, p. 3, and June 20, 1901, p. 4; *New York Times*, June 20, 1901, p. 3.
6. *Brooklyn Eagle*, June 19, 1901, p. 1.
7. *New York World*, June 20, 1901, p. 4.

CHAPTER EIGHTY

1. Robert J. Donovan, "The Man Who Didn't Shake Hands," *New Yorker*, Vol. 29 (November 28, 1953), p. 122.
2. Leech, pp. 589 ff.; Mark Goldman, *High Hopes* (Albany: State University of New York Press, 1983), pp. 3–12.

CHAPTER EIGHTY-ONE

1. With its ubiquitous red-tiled roofs and wildly eclectic mix of architectural elements—from Islamic minarets to Italian loggias—the Pan-American Exposition was a baroque fantasyland of riotous color and garish design: a "Rainbow City" (as it was immediately dubbed) in striking contrast to the marble-like splendor of Chicago's great "White City" of 1893.
2. *New York World*, October 30, 1901, p. 1; *New York Times*, October 30, 1901, p. 3.
3. Several of the judges dissented from Werner's strict interpretation of the "uncharged misconduct" rule (as it has come to be known), arguing that there are additional circumstances when evidence of previous crimes is admissible. All seven agreed, however, that the testimony of Dr. Henry Beaman Douglass—who stated that Barnet had told him of having been sickened by the Kutnow's Powder he received through the mail—was hearsay and should not have been allowed. See *The People of the State of New York, Respondents, against Roland B. Molineux, Appellant;* Thomas J. Reed, "How the Uncharged Misconduct Rule was Born,"

2003; Joseph O'Shea, "The Molineux Rule," Joseph O'Shea, 1990; and Marvin Schechter, "Molineux Unleashed," 1998.

4. *Brooklyn Eagle*, October 15, 1901, p. 1; *New York World*, October 16, 1901, p. 1; *New York Times*, October 16, 1901, p. 1; *New York Journal*, October 16, 1901, p. 1.

CHAPTER EIGHTY-TWO

1. *New York Times*, October 17, 1901, p. 5; *New York World*, October 17, 1901, p. 1.
2. *New York World*, October 18, 1901, p. 1.
3. *New York Times*, October 18, 1901, p. 5.
4. *Brooklyn Eagle*, October 16, 1901, p. 1.
5. *Brooklyn Eagle*, October 20, 1901, p. 3. A signed typescript of General King's speech exists among Edward Molineux's personal papers, now in possession of his great-grandson, Will Molineux.
6. *Brooklyn Eagle*, November 11, 1901, p. 7.
7. *Brooklyn Eagle*, November 12, 1901, p. 5.
8. See Forest Davis, "12 Trials that Gripped New York: How Gallant Old General Molineux Led a Lost Cause and Won," *New York Telegram Sunday Supplement*, January 13, 1931, p. 1.

CHAPTER EIGHTY-THREE

1. At the time of his release from Sing Sing, Roland, like the General, told reporters that "nothing but an acquittal will satisfy me now." See *New York Sun*, October 17, 1901, p. 1.
2. *New York World*, December 7, 1901, p. 1.
3. *New York Times*, March 11, 1902, p. 6.
4. *New York World*, October 19, 1901, p. 3.
5. *New York World*, September 14, 1902, p. 17.
6. Scott, p. 180; Pejsa, p. 227; Klaus, p. 40.

CHAPTER EIGHTY-FOUR

1. *New York Sun*, September 20, 1902, p. 1; *New York Times*, September 20, 1902, p. 1, and September 21, 1902, p. 3.
2. *New York World*, October 21, 1902, p. 1.
3. Ibid.
4. *New York World*, September 14, 1902, p. 8, and October 2, 1902, p. 6.
5. *New York Times*, August 10, 1902, p. 11; *New York World*, September 14, 1902, p. 16.
6. *Brooklyn Eagle*, October 21, 1902, p. 1.
7. *New York World*, October 22, 1902, p. 2.
8. *Brooklyn Eagle*, October 31, 1902, p. 1.
9. *New York Sun*, November 1, 1902, p. 1.
10. Ibid., p. 2.
11. Klaus, p. 36.
12. Ibid.
13. *New York Sun*, November 1, 1902, p. 1; *Brooklyn Eagle*, November 1, 1901, p. 1.

14. *New York World,* November 2, 1902, p. 1, and November 1, 1902, p. 1.
15. *Brooklyn Eagle,* October 13, 1902, p. 1.

CHAPTER EIGHTY-FIVE

1. *Brooklyn Eagle,* November 3, 1902, pp. 1 and 24.
2. *New York Sun,* November 7, 1902, pp. 1–2.
3. *New York World,* November 7, 1902, pp. 1–2.
4. *New York Times,* November 7, 1902, p. 1.
5. *New York Sun,* November 7, 1902, p. 2.
6. *New York World,* November 8, 1902, p. 2.
7. *New York World,* November 9, 1902, p. 16.

CHAPTER EIGHTY-SIX

1. *New York Sun,* November 11, 1902, p. 1.
2. *Brooklyn Eagle,* November 10, 1902, p. 1.
3. *New York World,* November 11, 1902, pp. 1–2.
4. *Brooklyn Eagle,* November 11, 1902, p. 1; *New York Sun,* November 11, 1902, p. 1.

CHAPTER EIGHTY-SEVEN

1. *New York World,* November 12, 1902, p. 1.
2. Ibid., p. 2.
3. *New York Times,* November 12, 1902, p. 1.
4. *New York World,* November 12, 1902, p. 1.
5. Ibid.
6. Ibid.
7. Klaus, p. 40.
8. *Brooklyn Eagle,* November 12, 1902, p. 2.

CHAPTER EIGHTY-EIGHT

1. *Brooklyn Eagle,* November 12, 1902, p. 1.
2. Scott, pp. 182–83.
3. Pejsa, p. 9.
4. *New York World,* November 12, 1902, p. 2.
5. *New York Times,* November 12, 1902, p. 1.
6. *New York World,* November 12, 1902, p. 2.
7. Scott, pp. 184–86.

CHAPTER EIGHTY-NINE

1. *New York World,* November 20, 1902, p. 1.
2. *Brooklyn Eagle,* November 18, 1902, p. 1; *New York World,* November 20, 1902, p. 1.
3. *Brooklyn Eagle,* November 18, 1902, p. 1; *New York Times,* November 18, 1902, p. 1.
4. *New York World,* November 20, 1902, p. 1.

5. *Brooklyn Eagle*, November 18, 1902, p. 2.
6. *New York Times*, November 3, 1903, p. 1; Pejsa, p. 236.
7. *New York Times*, November 15, 1903, p. 21.
8. Klaus, p. 41; Pejsa, p. 236.
9. Randall Irving Tyler, *The Blind Goddess* (New York: Stuyvesant Publishing Company, 1899), pp. 11, 24, 44, 65, and 73. In coming decades, the Molineux affair would inspire other popular works, most famously Anthony Berkley's celebrated 1929 mystery novel, *The Poisoned Chocolates Case*.
10. *Brooklyn Eagle*, December 9, 1902, p. 7.
11. Victor C. Calvert, *The Great Poison Mystery*, 1902.
12. *Brooklyn Eagle*, December 9, 1902, p. 7.
13. *New York Times*, December 2, 1902, p. 3; *Brooklyn Eagle*, December 9, 1902, p. 7.
14. Kathryn M. Plank, "Introduction to *The 'Rake*,'" *Papers on Language & Literature*, 27 (Spring 1991), p. 140.
15. According to Plank, Dreiser began to compose his novel in January 1915. As far back as 1901, he had worked on a book with the same title. Plank, however, along with other Dreiser scholars, believes that this first manuscript was an early version of Dreiser's autobiographical book, *The Genius*, entirely different from the later, Molineux-based work. See Plank, p. 140, n.1.
16. Plank, pp. 145–73.
17. Ibid., pp. 141 and 143.
18. The most complete account of the Chester Gillette-Grace Brown case (which also includes some interesting material on Dreiser and *The "Rake"*) is Craig Brown, *Murder in the Adirondacks* (Utica, NY: North Country Books, 1986).
19. *New York World*, January 11, 1903, Section E, p. 7.
20. *Brooklyn Eagle*, October 12, 1903, p. 2.
21. *New York Times*, February 20, 1904, p. 1.
22. *New York World*, October 15, 1908, p. 8.
23. *New York World*, October 14, 1911, p. 7.
24. *Brooklyn Eagle*, December 31, 1902, p. 1.
25. *New York World*, January 17, 1903, p. 16.
26. *New York Times*, February 14, 1903, p. 12.
27. Roland Molineux, *Vice Admiral of the Blue* (New York: G. W. Dillingham Company, 1903), p. 97.
28. Roland Molineux, "The Court of Rehabilitation," privately printed, 1907, thirty pages. Also see *New York Times*, September 29, 1907, p. 5.
29. *New York Times*, March 10, 1903, p. 9.
30. William Winter, *The Life of David Belasco*, Vol. 2 (New York: Moffat, Yard and Company, 1918), pp. 389–90.
31. *New York Times*, November 8, 1913, p. 6; *New York World*, November 8, 1913, p. 5.
32. *New York Times*, November 12, 1913, p. 9.
33. Winter, pp. 390–91.
34. *New York World*, September 7, 1914, p. 14; *New York Times*, September 7, 1914, p. 12.
35. Ibid.

36. Winter, p. 391.
37. *New York World*, June 11, 1915, p. 12.
38. The last of these gifts stands in stark contrast to Roland's reputed anti-Semitic sentiments. See Pejsa, p. 30.
39. ELM's private papers.
40. *Brooklyn Eagle*, June 11, 1915, p. 4, and June 13, 1915, p. 1.
41. *New York World*, June 12, 1915, p. 11.
42. *New York Times*, September 7, 1914, p. 12.
43. *New York World*, November 3, 1917, p. 12.
44. *New York Journal*, April 2, 1899, p. 42; *New York Times*, January 28, 1899, p. 13.
45. *New York Times*, May 13, 1905, p. 16, and March 14, 1916, p. 7; Klaus, pp. 27–28.
46. *New York Times*, March 30, 1904, p. 9.
47. *Los Angeles Times*, July 7, 1908, p. 1.
48. Death certificate, obtained from the registrar-recorder/county clerk, County of Los Angeles.
49. Under the headline "Former Mrs. Molineux to Go on Stage," the *Chicago Daily Tribune* of August 27, 1905, ran a piece about Blanche's renewed plans to "appear before the footlights in vaudeville." The article is accompanied by a rare photograph of Blanche, posing as though for a portrait by John Singer Sargent (p. 5). Also, see *New York Times*, April 15, 1905, p. 1, and September 20, 1905, p. 2.
50. The information in this section comes from various documents, including a copy of Blanche's divorce complaint against Wallace Scott, provided to me by Jane Pejsa.
51. *Sioux Falls Daily Argus-Leader*, October 19, 1930, p. 1.

BIBLIOGRAPHY

Adelman, Melvin L. *A Sporting Time: New York City and the Rise of Modern Athletics, 1820–70.* Urbana and Chicago: University of Illinois Press, 1986.

Beebe, Lucius. *The Big Spenders.* Garden City, NY: Doubleday & Co., 1966.

Berkeley, Anthony. *The Poisoned Chocolates Case.* Garden City, NY: Doubleday, Page & Co., 1929.

Betts, John Rickards Betts. *America's Sporting Heritage: 1850–1950.* Reading, MA: Addison-Wesley Publishing, 1974.

Borowitz, Albert I. "Packaged Death: Forerunners of the Tylenol Poisonings." *American Bar Association Journal,* March 1983, pp. 282–86.

Bradford, Russell R. and Ralph B. Bradford. *Introduction to Handwriting Examination and Identification.* Chicago: Nelson-Hall, 1992.

Brian, Denis. *Pulitzer: A Life.* New York: John Wiley & Sons, 2001.

——. *Sing Sing: The Inside Story of a Notorious Prison.* Amherst, NY: Prometheus Books, 2005.

Brown, Craig. *Murder in the Adirondacks: An American Tragedy Revisited.* Utica, NY: North Country Books, 1986.

Burrell, Brian. *Postcards from the Brain Museum: The Improbable Search for Meaning in the Matter of Famous Minds.* New York: Broadway Books, 2004.

Carey, Arthur A. *Memoirs of a Murder Man.* Garden City, NY: Doubleday, Doran and Co., 1930.

Chauncey, George. *Gay New York: Gender, Urban Culture, and the Making of the Gay Male World, 1890–1950.* New York: Basic Books, 1994.

Christianson, Scott. *Condemned: Inside the Sing Sing Death House.* New York: New York University Press, 2000.

Considine, Bob, and Fred G. Jarvis. *The First Hundred Years: A Portrait of the NYAC.* London: The Macmillan Co., 1969.

Corley, Florence Fleming. *Confederate City: Augusta, Georgia, 1860–1865.* Columbia, SC: University of South Carolina Press, 1960.

Crichton, Judy. *America 1900: The Turning Point.* New York: Henry Holt and Co., 1998.

de Vars, Michael. *In Re Molineux versus a Current Cagliostro.* Providence, RI: Arthur W. Brown, 1901.

Donovan, Robert J. "The Man Who Didn't Shake Hands," *New Yorker,* Vol. 29 (November 28, 1953), pp. 122–28.

Dreiser, Theodore. *The "Rake," Papers on Language & Literature*, 27 (spring 1991), 145–73.

——. *Sister Carrie*. Ed. Donald Pizer. New York: W.W. Norton, 1970.

Dunlop, M. H. *Gilded City: Scandal and Sensation in Turn-of-the-Century New York*. Newark: William Morrow, 2000.

Essig, Mark Regan. *Science and Sensation: Poison Murder and Forensic Medicine in Nineteenth-Century America*. Unpublished Ph.D. dissertation. Cornell University, January 2000.

Everett, Marshall. *Complete Life of William McKinley and Story of His Assassination*. 1901.

Forrest, Davis. "12 Trials that Gripped New York: How Gallant Old General Molineux Led a Lost Cause and Won." *New York Telegram*, January 13, 1931, p. 16.

Gabler, Neal. *Life: The Movie: How Entertainment Conquered Reality*. New York: Random House, 1998.

Geis, Gilbert, and Leigh B. Bienen. *Crimes of the Century: From Leopold and Loeb to O. J. Simpson*. Boston: Northeastern University Press, 1998.

Goldman, Mark. *High Hopes: The Rise and Decline of Buffalo, New York*. Albany: State University of New York Press, 1983.

Haller, John S., and Robin M. Haller. *The Physician and Sexuality in Victorian America*. New York: Norton, 1977.

Homberger, Eric. *Mrs. Astor's New York: Money and Social Power in a Gilded Age*. New Haven and London: Yale University Press, 2002.

Howard, H. E. *The Battle of Cedar Creek: Showdown in the Shenandoah October 1–30, 1864*. Lynchburg, VA: H. E. Howard, 1992.

Jones, Ann. *Women Who Kill*. New York: Fawcett, 1980.

Juergens, George. *Joseph Pulitzer and the New York World*. Princeton: Princeton University Press, 1966.

Klaus, Samuel, ed. *The Molineux Case*. New York: Alfred A. Knopf, 1929.

Kobre, Sidney. *The Yellow Press and Gilded Age Journalism*. Tallahassee: Florida State University, 1964.

Kurland, Michael. *How to Try a Murder: The Handbook for Armchair Lawyers*. Edison, New Jersey: Castle Books, 2002.

Lane, Roger. *Murder in America*. Columbus, Ohio: Ohio State University Press, 1997.

Lawes, Lewis E. *Life and Death in Sing Sing*. Garden City, NY: Doubleday, Doran & Co., 1928.

LeBrun, George (as told to Edward D. Radin). *It's Time to Tell*. New York: William Morrow, 1962.

Leech, Margaret. *In the Days of McKinley*. New York: Harper & Brothers, 1959.

Liddy, G. Gordon. *Will*. New York: St. Martin's Press, 1980.

Lingeman, Richard. *Theodore Dreiser: At the Gates of the City, 1871–1907*. New York: G. P. Putnam, 1986.

Livingston, E. A. *President Lincoln's Third Largest City: Brooklyn and the Civil War*. Brooklyn, NY: Budd Press, 1994.

Matthews, Brander. *His Father's Son: A Novel of New York City*. New York: Harper & Brothers, 1896.

Menand, Louis. "She Had to Have It," *The New Yorker* (April 23 and 30, 2001), pp. 62–70.

Merck's 1899 Manual of the Materia Medica, Together with a Summary of Therapeutic Indications and a Classification of Medicaments: A Ready-Reference Pocket Book for the Practicing Physician. New York: Merck & Co., 1899.

Merz, Charles. "Bigger and Better Murders," *Harper's Monthly Magazine*, Vol. 155 (August 1927), pp. 338–43.

Molineux, Roland. *The Man Inside.* New York: Samuel French, 1913.

——. *The Vice Admiral of the Blue.* Toronto: The Copp, Clark Co., 1903.

Molyneux, Nellie Zada Rice. *History, genealogical and biographical, of the Molyneux families.* Syracuse, NY: C. W. Bardeen, 1904.

Morris, Lloyd. *Incredible New York: High Life and Low Life of the Last Hundred Years.* New York: Random House, 1951.

Nash, Jay Robert. *Murder, America: Homicide in the United States from the Revolution to the Present.* London: Harrap, 1980.

Oppel, Frank. *Tales of Gaslight New York.* Edison, NJ: Castle Books, 1985.

O'Shea, Joseph A. "The Molineux Rule in New York: Evidence of Uncharged Crimes and Misconduct During the People's Case in Chief," 1990.

Pancoast, S. *Pancoast's Tokology and Ladies Medical Guide: A Complete Instructor in All the Delicate and Wonderful Matters Pertaining to Women, Fully Explaining the Nature and Mystery of the Reproductive Organs of Both Sexes and Love, Courtship, and Marriage.* Chicago: Thomas & Thomas, 1901.

Pearson, Edmund. *Murder at Smutty Nose and Other Murders.* Garden City, NY: Doubleday, Page & Co., 1926.

Pejsa, Jane. *The Molineux Affair.* Minneapolis: Kenwood, 1983.

The People of the State of New York, Respondents, against Roland B. Molineux, Appellant. Case on Appeal from the Court of General Sessions of the Peace, in and for the County of New York. Court of Appeals of the State of New York. New York, 1901.

Plank, Kathryn M. "Introduction to *The 'Rake.'*" *Papers on Language & Literature*, 27 (spring 1991), 140–44.

Procter, Ben. *William Randolph Hearst: The Early Years, 1863–1910.* New York: Oxford University Press, 1998.

Raphael, Morris. *The Battle in the Bayou Country.* Detroit: Harlo Press, 1976.

Reed, Thomas J. "How the Uncharged Misconduct Rule was Born," 2003.

Robinson, Henry Morton. *Science Catches the Criminal.* New York: Blue Ribbon Books, 1935.

Roehrenback, William J. *The Regiment that Saved the Capital.* New York: Thomas Yoselhoff, 1961.

Sante, Luc. *Low Life: The Lures and Snares of Old New York.* New York: Vintage, 1992.

Schechter, Marvin. "Molineux Unleashed: The New Mayhem," 1998.

Scott, Blanche Molineux. *The Molineux Affair.* Unpublished ms. Copyright 1978, Jane H. Pejsa.

Smith, Edward H. *Famous Poison Mysteries.* New York: The Dial Press, 1927.

Snyder, Robert W. *The Voice of the City: Vaudeville and Popular Culture in New York.* New York: Oxford University Press, 1989.

Stevens, John D. *Sensationalism and the New York Press.* New York: Columbia University Press, 1991.

Sutherland, Sidney. "The Mystery of the Poison Christmas Gift." *Liberty,* March 9, 1929, pp. 44–52.

Swanberg, W. A. *Citizen Hearst.* New York: Scribner's, 1961.

Thomas, Lately. *Delmonico's: A Century of Splendor.* Boston: Houghton Mifflin, 1967.

Thorwald, Jürgen. *The Century of the Detective.* New York: Harcourt, Brace & World, 1964.

Tiemann, William F. *The 159th Regiment Infantry, New York State Volunteers in the War of the Rebellion, 1862–1865.* Brooklyn, NY: William F. Tiemann, 1891.

Timberlake, Craig. *The Bishop of Broadway: The Life & Work of David Belasco.* New York: Library Publishers, 1954.

Train, Arthur. *Criminal Justice in America.* New York: Scribner, 1926.

Tucher, Andie. *Froth & Scum: Truth, Beauty, Goodness, and the Ax Murder in America's First Mass Medium.* Chapel Hill: University of North Carolina Press, 1994.

Tully, Andrew. *Era of Elegance.* New York: Funk & Wagnalls Co., 1947.

Tyler, Randall Irving. *The Blind Goddess: Being a Tale of To-day, Showing Some of the Undercurrents of a Big City.* New York: Stuyvesant Publishing Company, 1899.

Ward, Geoffrey C., with Ric Burns and Ken Burns. *The Civil War: An Illustrated History.* New York: Alfred A. Knopf, 1992.

Wert, Jeffry D. *From Winchester to Cedar Creek: The Shenandoah Campaign of 1864.* Carlisle, PA: South Mountain Press, 1987.

Willis, J., and R. Wettan. "Social Stratification in New York City Athletic Clubs, 1865–1915." *Journal of Sports History,* 24 (spring 1997), pp. 45–63.

Winter, William. *The Life of David Belasco.* New York: Moffat, Yard and Co., 1918.

Younger, Irving, Michael Goldsmith, David A. Sonenshein. *Principles of Evidence.* Third Edition. Cincinnati: Anderson Publishing Co., 1997.

ACKNOWLEDGMENTS

As the dedication to this book suggests, I owe my greatest debt of gratitude to Will Molineux, Roland's grand-nephew, who gave me complete access to his trove of family documents and—even better—quickly became a valued friend. I am also grateful to Ross Molineux, who first put me in touch with Will.

Among those who offered various kinds of assistance during the research and writing of the book, I wish to thank Eve Berliner, Clare Eby, Mark Essig, Tom Gilson, Linda Goetz Holmes, G. Gordon Liddy, Jane Pejsa, Richard Pope, Thomas J. Reed, Marvin Schechter, Nancy M. Shawcross, Marie Spearman, and—at the Paul Klapper Library of Queens College—Marianne Conti Stein and Evelyn Silverman.

I owe more than I can say to my editor and friend, Linda Marrow. My agent, Loretta Barrett, has been there for me every step of the way. Dana Isaacson has offered invaluable advice, and Dan Mallory unstinting assistance.

Finally, I wish to convey boundless love to my research assistant. From her research assistant.

INDEX

Note: RBM refers to Roland Burnham Molineux

PHOTO: © WHITNEY WARD

Harold Schechter is a professor of American literature and culture at Queens College, the City University of New York. He is widely celebrated for both fiction and true-crime writing, including *The Serial Killer Files.* He lives in Brooklyn and Mattituck, Long Island, with his wife, the poet Kimiko Hahn.